The
Tejano
Community,
1836–1900

THE TEJANO COMMUNITY, 1836–1900

by
Arnoldo De León

with a contribution by Kenneth L. Stewart

University of New Mexico Press : Albuquerque

Library of Congress Cataloging in Publication Data

De León, Arnoldo, 1945–
  The Tejano community, 1836–1900.

  Bibliography: p.
  Includes index.
    1. Mexican Americans—Texas—Social life
and customs. 2. Mexican American—Texas—
Social conditions. 3. Texas—Social life and
customs. 4. Texas—Social conditions.
I. Title.
F395.M5D4   976.4′0046872   81–52053
ISBN 0–8263–0586–5   AACR2

Partial funding for the composition of this book
was provided by the Mellon Foundation
through a grant to the
American Association of University Presses.

To
BARRY A. CROUCH

Contents

Illustrations

Tables

ix

Preface

Pursued in this study are a number of goals. First, as in the recent literature on Afro-American history, which attempts to view slaves not as the object but the subject of historical inquiry, answers are sought to a fundamental question: what did Mexican Americans in Texas do for themselves, and how did they do it in the post-1836 Anglo American world that relegated them to dependency? Second, an attempt is made to define *Tejano culture*. What characterized the culture of Tejanos after Texas came under white domination? Was it a facsimile of Mexican culture? Or, did it change as it interacted with Anglo American culture? What were the results? This endeavor at definition has been stimulated by the contemporary debate among social scientists over what Mexican American culture is.[1] Also provided in the book are insights into the world Tejanos made for themselves in the era before Texas moved from an agrarian epoch into an urban and industrial one. Necessarily, then, this is the story of Tejanos living in agrarian Texas in the decades before manufacturing, urbanization, and other modernizing forces changed the state in the early twentieth century.

In researching and writing this book, I did not attempt to look into patterns of land dispossession, to study Tejano figures of the period, to interpret the literature of the Tejanos, to focus on the concept of social banditry, to subject a particular community in South Texas to historical investigation, to determine migration patterns, to

relate the history of labor movements, or to explain the decline of
the Tejanos. Instead, I have described and analyzed the lives of
ordinary people to tell how they lived amidst poverty and dependency and how they managed to lead a normal life under those
conditions. An important theme throughout the study is attention
to those aspects of their autonomy that kept them from becoming
totally victimized by external forces. Tejanos became active participants in the social process of forging a cultural groundwork that
permitted them to live in an Anglo American world that stigma-
tized them as conquered, second-class, and inferior.

I explain not what whites did to Tejanos but how Tejanos took
environmental, social, economic, and political circumstances about
them and developed a bicultural identity that equipped them to
resist oppression. In his suggestive article "Deficit, Difference and
Bicultural Models of Afro-American Behavior," Charles A. Valentine
maintains that the idea of biculturation explains how people "learn
and practice both mainstream culture and ethnic culture at the
same time." Indians in reservations, Negroes in ghettoes, and other
subgroups, he notes, are simultaneously enculturated and socialized into two different ways of life—their own subgroup lifestyle
and mainstream Euro-American culture.[2] The model has appropriate relevance to the Tejano experience, for Mexican Americans
have historically drawn from Mexican culture as well as derived
patterns of behavior from Anglo American culture. The result has
been the dual identity suggested in the term Mexican American
and in the more contemporary notion implied in the self-designated
label *Chicano*.

The Texas Revolution of 1836 marked the end of Mexican rule in
Texas and the beginning of the imposition of an Anglo American
milieu upon the indigenous Hispanic population. Mexican culture
underwent a rapid evolution after 1836. No longer could the native
Tejanos identify with a single language, with the old communal
life, with the old ways of politics and economics. The new historical
reality demanded that they adjust their manner of living to stay
attuned, that they acquaint themselves with the dominant culture
and come to grips with it. An unchanging allegiance to Mexican
culture meant disaster because it precluded the participation so
essential to gaining a role in the system that had supplanted the old
one. Only by a process of development, adaptation, adoption, socialization, and biculturation could Tejanos ready themselves to

function in the different setting. Simultaneously, they remained
ethnically Mexican as traditions, in-group relationships, and immigration from Mexico constantly reinforced their primary environment.

Within the society imported from east of Sabine, Tejanos took
root and devised vital cultural reponses to the emerging order.
They adjusted—some reluctantly, some gladly, some necessarily.
Obviously, they did not start speaking English at once, or stop
eating *tortillas* and *frijoles*, or turn to American heroes to emulate,
or begin aping Anglo Saxon familial ties, or embrace other tenets
of the American ethos. In the course of time, however, Anglo
American institutions could not help but enculturate them into
mainstream concepts, values, judgments, and patterns of behavior. As early as 1828, José María Sánchez, touring Texas in behalf of
the Mexican government, observed that Tejanos had "accustomed
[themselves] to the continued trade with the North Americans
[and had] adopted their customs and habits. . . ."[3] Certainly, contact and interaction with Anglo politicians, employers, religious
figures, educators, and policemen, as well as with Anglo American
traditions, familiarized Mexicans with certain language codes, frontier survival mechanisms different from those they themselves utilized, with agricultural methods, home construction, and the like.
Anglo meals found their way to the table, the Anglo presence was
apparent in their folk tales and legends, nationalism revolved par-
tially around patriotic holidays such as the Fourth of July and
Washington's Birthday, and American games like baseball became
a part of their entertainment repertoire. As Anglo American civilization pushed into those areas in southern and western Texas where
Tejanos predominated, members of those communities also went
through a process of *biculturation*—that is, a transformation in
which a matured Mexican culture evolved into one that was simultaneously both American and Mexican.

But Tejanos socialized themselves to the setting on their own
terms. While racism and oppression made the great majority of
them politically powerless and financially poor, neither impinged
upon the Tejanos' cultural world. If dependency relegated them to
barrios and *rancherías*, it did not encroach upon the social distance and psychic prowess that Tejanos relied upon to determine
the degree of cultural adaptation they felt appropriate; or, put
another way, the extent to which they would accept the essential

while rejecting the undesirable. This autonomy permitted Mexican cultural principles, assumptions, and understandings to act as determinants in the process by which both native and recent arrivals forged a life style that worked in both a strange American world and the more familiar Mexican atmosphere.

Even as they participated in American institutions, Tejanos continued their own cultural patterns, making bearable their life as poor and marginal people. They retained Mexican food habits not just because external forces limited them to austerity but because items like *frijoles, tortillas, menudo, chiles, tamales,* and *nopalitos* were delectable and familiar. They continued living in *jacales* and adobe houses because these provided inexpensive means of shelter. They turned to the botanical world of *hierbitas*, not solely because they lacked professional medical attention but because they perceived that curative herbs alleviated their illnesses. They clung tenaciously to the Spanish language, not only because it reinforced their individuality and affirmed their membership in the Spanish-language community, but because it acted as a cultural force bringing together those sharing similar experiences and sustained the confidence and drive of a community victimized by both circumstance and design. They adhered to Catholicism while forging their own perspective of that religion and practiced survival techniques otherwise discouraged by institutional Catholicism. They celebrated Mexican secular and religious holidays not only out of patriotism and tradition, but because recreational forms mitigated between adversity and prosperity. They organized benevolent associations like the Sociedad Mutualista Mexicana, Sociedad Ignacio Allende, Sociedad Benito Juárez, Sociedad Mexico-Texana and others (whose constitutions were in both Spanish and English) because they acted as agents that understood the Tejano experience and rendered aid to members and *barrio* residents in times of crises. They depended on Spanish-language newspapers like the Brownsville *El Demócrata,* Corpus Christi *La Libertad,* San Diego *El Eco Liberal,* Rio Grande City *La Voz del Pueblo,* and others to inform them on a variety of topics, including matters of local interest plus current events in Mexico.

It was the process of social change, which over time, came to determine the uniqueness of Tejano ethnic culture. Left alone, that culture stood by itself—it had all the essentials for self-sustenance. As Mexicans, Tejanos understood one another, sensed the commonality of their experience, identified with "lo Mexicano," and emphasized that Mexicanness as part of their cultural identity. They interacted as Mexicans with one another: assuming leadership roles to defend the community in times of trouble, serving in municipal roles in Mexican *barrios*, laboring together and referring to co-workers according to Spanish-language job names (*mayordomo* or *caporal*, for example on the sheep range), exchanging gifts like *rebozos* and *sombreros*, and brandishing a tone of cultural resistance during *fiestas patrias* celebrations, to name only a few examples of ingroup interplay.

At the same time, allegiance to Mexican culture deterred them from economic, social, and political positions otherwise guaranteed by law. It prohibited them from sharing or taking control of those broader institutions that determined their lives. Tejanos could have perhaps gained equality by renouncing the Spanish language, their self-identification, and subgroup behavorial patterns—although the banes of ethnocentrism and racism remained to be overcome—but most refused that alternative and opted to extract their means of livelihood by retaining their *Mexicanness*. Obviously, though, some saw gains in becoming like Anglos and foresook their cultural heritage. But most acquainted themselves with mainstream institutions and as Tejanos sought to overcome those barriers imposed upon them by the guardians of white supremacy.

To be sure, no set of definite attributes can be given to the Tejano community—it was too heterogeneous for that. Biculturation and degrees of it had much to do with locality, the economy of a region, time of residence in the state, family upbringing, social rank, education, as well as other factors, and Tejanos formed various world views vis-à-vis these factors. What some members considered correct so far as political viewpoints, social behavior, religion, and entertainment, for example, was unacceptable to others. Multifaceted currents of thought and action prevailed among different strains of social classes. In short, the Tejano community was what other communities throughout history have been—diverse and ever-changing. It was not a monolithic and passive, apolitical group as prevailing views of social scientists hold.

The relatively small upper class, for instance, included those who were staunch preservers of a "civilized" Hispanic way. In some cases, they dispatched their children to schools better than those that ordinary Tejanos attended, sought to marry Anglos because they believed that marriage ties would elevate their social status (or at least, not lower it), dressed in a way they thought benefited their rank, held separate dances, lived in neighborhoods away from the barrio, and refused to mix with their less fortunate kinsmen. The upper class also included a second element of families who wished alliances with Anglo society in hopes of bettering themselves, as was the case among some in the ante-bellum years that defended slavery as a way to economic progress. It also consisted of those who sided with Anglo politicians to preserve their achievements and others who identified more with United States institutions than Mexican ones. At the same time, there were others in a third group in this class, who despite their claims to "difference" with *la raza*, did not totally repudiate their heritage or separate themselves from the lower class of Tejanos. They came to the defense of that Tejano community to protest indignities, took a stand against white supremacy, organized mutualista societies, and attended to the needs of their own people as doctors, lawyers, or teachers.

Frequently, members of this upper stratum would shift about to play many roles. The case of José Antonio Navarro is instructive. He succeeded in helping to pass a contract law through the legislature of Coahuila y Tejas in 1828 that recognized Negro slavery, signed the Declaration of Independence against Mexico in 1836, enrolled his son Angel at Harvard University in the 1840s, sent his boys to fight for the Confederacy, and emerged as a leading white supremacist in the San Antonio area during Reconstruction. This same man defended the cause of la raza on numerous occasions after the Texas Revolution, insured (through an interpreter) at the state constitutional convention in 1845 that Tejanos would receive the franchise, and became a vociferous opponent of the Know Nothing party in the 1850s. He was neither the monolithic "all-American" or "Uncle Tom" that historians of the right and left have portrayed him to be. Instead, he was a complex figure who exemplified the dexterity of many members of the Tejano community who could assume various roles depending on personal motives or whatever circumstances compelled them into a called-for behavior.

At the bottom of the social ladder, the poorer Tejanos did not have the opportunity to discriminate against someone beneath them or form marriage or business ties with Anglos as members of the upper class did. While they were the ones who practiced Spanish-

Mexican work rhythms on the range, went to *fandangos* and *bailes*, formed the rank and file of political factions or parties, sold their goods on city sidewalks, maintained a regenerative folklore tradition, and, in other ways remained the most loyal to their Mexican past, not all fit into a convenient stereotype. They themselves sided with opposite political parties, worked in various occupations, adhered to different religious denominations, entertained themselves in diverse ways, and manifested diverging degrees of biculturation. Still, it was this element that made up the backbone of the Tejano communty.

Expectedly, interaction within and between cultures produced both friction and harmony within the community. Thus association among the several social classes was as diverse as the makeup of the group. At times, it was agreeable; at others, strained. In point of fact, it was like other communities universally, where complex relations are the norm and not the exception.

Down through the years, this heterogeneous community succeeded in doing the best it could for itself despite white society's determination to render Tejanos politically powerless, maintain them as part of an exploitable work pool, and deprive them of social equality. By familiarizing themselves with political procedure, they took land grant cases to court, served in a number of governmental posts, and even extracted concessions from the Anglo American system through political bossism. Tejano entrepreneurs learned to stock American goods as Mexicano consumers incorporated the new items into their diets; and merchants learned the tastes of white customers and conformed their entrepreneurship to exploit those demands. In urban areas, Tejanos made their living as policemen and public servants or as water haulers, bakers, artisans, and at other undertakings that serviced both Anglo and Tejano communities. *Rancheros* meantime learned how to sell their stock in the American market. On the range, *vaqueros* applied Mexican techniques to cattle and sheep ranching and integrated themselves into the work force of the Anglo cattle kings of South and West Texas. On the social front, Tejanos repeatedly inveighed against injustice and invoked the principles of American democracy in seeking to right those wrongs. They knew that segregation, social subordination, and derogatory stereotyping all violated the spirit of the law and thus refused to accept such a fate as part of a natural order.

Despite racism, oppression, and exploitation, Tejanos maintained the psychic security to keep on going. It was this mental peace of mind that gave them the hope that the political system might be goaded into answering their needs. It was belief in themselves that allowed them to maintain control over their lives despite the demeaning and dehumanizing character of some of their employment. It was inner resolve that underlined the stability of the Tejano family and allowed Tejano men and women to sustain their efforts at wresting a living from the environment. It was self-assurance that allowed Tejanos to use religion to their advantage and not become its passive subjects. It was entertainment that gave them a necessary reprieve from the harshness of their existence. And it was the establishment of *mutualistas* and newspapers that rendered them the institutional mechanisms so crucial for maintaining their identity as bicultural people. For the vigor of the nineteenth century community was not solely its skill at fending for itself, or its ability to forge its own religious view, or its consummate prowess at putting food on the table by various means, or its capacity to find respite in entertainment, or its aptitude at creating institutional survival forms. Not any single one of these made the Tejano community a forceful, robust, and resilient one, but all.

I gratefully acknowledge the contribution a number of people made to the book. Kenneth L. Stewart, Department of Sociology, Angelo State University, worked closely with me to see that the preliminary findings from our ongoing study of Tejano demography were incorporated into the manuscript. The quantitative angle of the work reflects the fresh insight he is bringing to the study of Chicano history and the commendable grasp he has of the quantitative method. Saúl Sánchez, formerly professor of Modern Languages at Angelo State University and now at Laredo Junior College, collaborated with me in interpreting and writing the chapter on folklore.

Malcolm D. McLean, Professor of Spanish and History at the University of Texas at Arlington, took time off from his work on the Robertson Colony Papers to make editorial corrections. Dr. David J. Weber of Southern Methodist University provided many helpful suggestions on how to improve the thrust of my message. Mr. Joe Bill Lee and his staff at the Porter Henderson Library at Angelo University, especially Polly Crawford and Philip Holly, Acquisitions Librarian, rendered valuable service in getting me needed documents from around the country. My colleagues in the History Department at Angelo State Unviersity, including our secretary Jo White, gave me their wholehearted support, as they have done throughout my teaching career here.

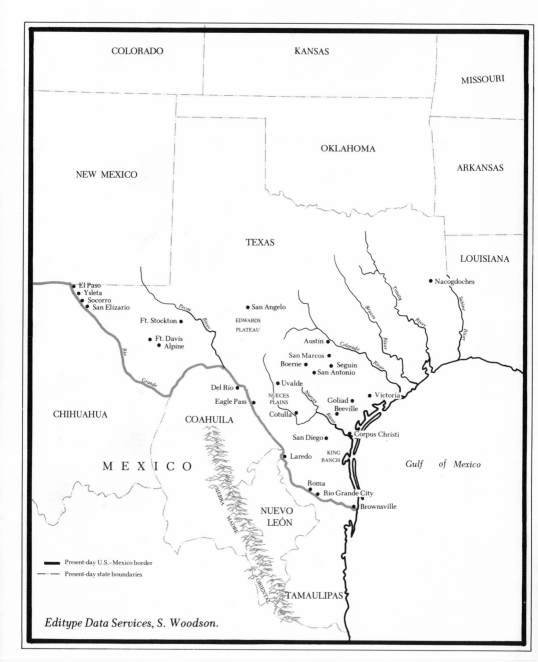

The Tejano Community

1

Spaniards, Mexicans
and Americans

While the Hispanic presence in Texas may be traced to 1519
when Alonso Alvarez de Pineda explored and mapped the coastline
between Florida and Vera Cruz, actual occupation of the territory
occurred in June 1716 when Captain Domingo Ramón arrived in
New Spain's northern province with several families, more than a
score of soldiers, and a dozen missionaries. They built forts and
established settlements that sustained missionary work among the
Indians. By the end of the year, the small but energetic group of
colonizers in East Texas had erected six missions, a *presidio*, and
founded modern Nacogdoches. Two years later, another expedition led by Martín de Alarcón established the Presidio San Antonio
de Béxar and the Mission San Antonio de Valero along the San
Antonio River, while Spanish settlers from the Canary Islands located on this site in 1731. In subsequent years, the Spaniards
established other garrisons, missions, and civilian population centers
—among them La Bahía (Goliad), founded in 1721 as Presidio La
Bahía del Espíritu Santo, which moved to its present place in 1749.
The colonizing efforts of José de Escandón in the 1740s and 1750s
resulted in a number of permanent communities along the Rio
Grande, among them Laredo.[1] In these several areas resided the
few eighteenth-century colonists whose presence established Spain's
claim to Texas and limited encroachment by outside powers.

What kind of people entered the province in these incipient
colonization projects? Many came from Coahuila and other north-

eastern states and tended to be either Spanish, *castas* (mixed-bloods), or Tlascalan Indians, the latter group a civilized tribe that had once lived under the Aztecs. A good majority of these founders, then, were the product of generations of *mestizaje,* that is, the interracial mixture of European Spaniards and Mexico's indigeneous Indians. Subsequent efforts to settle Texas with entire colonies transplanted from Mexico failed because too many feared venturing into an uncertain land where Lipan and Comanche marauders roamed freely. As a result, population growth in the province resulted from the castas and Mexican Indian soldiers in the presidios intermixing either with women in nearby communities or native Indians who had been Christianized in the Texas missions. From this practice, extra-legal settlements made up of families of soldiers or of settlers from Mexico sprung up around the missions and the presidios near Goliad, Nacogdoches, and San Antonio.[2] A heterogeneous society quickly emerged.[3]

For the most part, these founders, whose number fluctuated around three thousand during the final quarter of the eighteenth century,[4] have been anonymous souls in the history of Texas. Spanish borderland historians have focused on such things as the mission, the presidio, and the *rancho* as frontier institutions, or on explanations that account for the ultimate decline of Spain in Texas. Yet, a culture clearly thrived in the province from 1716 onward and continued to endure long after the ending of the Spanish stay.

How did these people—the original Tejanos—keep going when faced with epidemic diseases, the constant threat of Indian attacks, and the need to wrest a living from a hostile environment? First, the *pobladores* (populators) imported a matured Mexican culture. Both the Spanish and Indian ancestors laid claim to high civilizations. Indeed, the Tlascalans that came to Texas from Mexico differed radically from other nomadic and primitive tribes in both New Spain and Texas. Socially and culturally, the mixed-bloods descended from stock equipped for survival in a hostile setting.

Also, the pobladores and their progeny adapted themselves to the rigors of the frontier. Removed from New Spain proper by great distance and living in a rural environment with a semiarid climate and sparse vegetation, they relied on survival techniques used in Mexico or invented new ways of getting along in the Texas terrain. Natural materials played a crucial part in the making of their houses. Mud mixed with straw, for instance, did well for *adobes*. The *jacal*, in which the walls were slender mesquite posts placed continuously in vertical rows, was a more prosaic structure. Thatched coverings served for roofs. Impervious to the weather, the jacales acted as a form of temporary housing that worked well even if many did, in fact, reflect their makeshift nature. The *villa* of San Antonio and the *pueblos* of Goliad and Nacogdoches featured both the adobe buildings and latter type of improvised housing. For food, Tejanos turned to the *rancho*, an institution which provided them with a plentiful supply of beef, while at the same time requiring a minimal labor force, and permitted them the advantage of moving the cattle quickly in times of danger.[5] The traditional mainstays of corn, *tortillas*, and *frijoles*, as well as wild game, supplemented the beef. For clothes they used buffalo hides when cotton material was not available. Their drinking water and irrigation was drawn from dams, *acequias*, and aqueducts patterned after those in both Spain and Mexico.[6] By using these techniques, Tejanos found the methods to adjust and survive on an unfriendly frontier.

Furthermore, society revolved around institutions that symbolized the old and the familiar. The mission, presidio, and rancho acted as centers of socialization as Tejanos came to grips with the frontier reality and established their roots. Families grouping themselves around the missions or huddling themselves about the presidios identified with a common way of life that permitted them to ward off the very forces that ultimately undermined Spain's political existence in Texas. Cultural patterns persisted then, as the Tejanos exercised common familial structures, housing traditions, food habits, religious attachments, special holy days, music, language, and social distinctions.

Also, the settlers had relative freedom to define and distill their own way of life in Texas. Even as the Spanish crown attempted to regulate their every action, castas and mestizos still enjoyed enough relative autonomy to follow the oft-used reaction of *"obedezco pero no cumplo"* (I obey but do not comply). After all, the king, however much he wanted his subjects to be like "Spaniards," could not dictate necessary responses essential for frontier survival. In defiance of moral values imposed by missionary society, people practiced entertainment forms that provided relief from the harshness of frontier living. Spanish Texans held *fandangos* (dances) in their residences where revelers engaged in drinking and dancing, actions which violated conduct deemed proper by representatives of the crown. Perceived by authorities as gatherings of shady characters, the occasions were means by which merrymakers made life meaningful and bearable. Although government officials imposed heavy fines for horse races, inasmuch as the games often took place during religious holidays or because the celebrants committed disgraces or violated good etiquette during the contests, the settlers still continued to hold them. And, while soldiers could not marry without permission from presidial officers, many engaged in miscegenation with Indian women in a setting where militiamen outnumbered the Mexican female population.[7]

The early Tejanos created for themselves a way of life that reflected concessions to the frontier. In some ways, Spanish-Mexicans changed in the eighteenth century, but essentially they carried on former practices that proved effective in the northern environment despite the distance from the mother culture. When the Spanish era ended in 1821, the year of Mexican Independence, the old and the familiar endured unperturbed: things changed at the top, but the only difference at the bottom was that Spanish-Tejanos were now Mexican-Tejanos.

The Spanish-Mexican population, excluding soldiers, numbered approximately 2,240 in 1821 and increased to over 4,000 by 1836.[8] San Antonio, Goliad, and Nacogdoches (also Victoria, founded in 1824) remained the main Hispanic settlements, and society continued divided into two classes—the *ricos* and the *pobres*. The former descended from the Canary Islanders of the 1730s or from Spanish families that held government positions, while the latter derived from the mixed-blood *pobladores* and performed common labor. Frontierlike conditions persisted—fear of Indian attacks lingered, manufacturing of essential articles like blankets, shoes, and hats were lacking, and disease was ever-present.[9] In the same period, Mexican Texas begin taking on Anglo features as white men from the United States commenced arriving by the hundreds.

Events in Mexico between 1821 and 1836 touched the lives of the Tejanos only peripherally. The substance and structure of local government remained the same after 1821. Political vicissitudes in Mexico City did little to alter those affairs, and the transition to the state government of Coahuila y Tejas did not disrupt the daily lives of Tejanos. They enjoyed a salutary rule over themselves and exercised some influence on issues at the state level.[10]

No dramatic historical modifications disturbed the cultural structure of the Mexican-Tejano community. Traditions and institutions of the colonial era continued: men still interacted with *alcaldes* and *ayuntamientos*, still measured their poverty or affluence in *pesos*, and even thought in terms of *gente de razón* or *gente sin razón*. Towns retained standard forms. *Plazas* occupied the center with streets crossing at right angles north to south and east to west. East sides of plazas were reserved for church buildings such as the cathedral, the chapel, or the chancery. Government and public edifices, among them the state house, the custom house, or the governor's palace, occupied the west side. Each town, moreover, had its own *ejido* or commons, its own *tierra de pasto* or common pasture, and its own *propios*, or rental lands for municipal revenue. Life for the common folks, who lived generally in jacales, centered around the *barrios* and *vecindarios* (neighboring populace). At this level, a resident *comisario* (or judge of the barrio) saw to the social welfare and administrative well-being of their respective neighborhoods.[11]

In the countryside, the *rancherías* reflected the cultural patterns of town life, for indeed, many of the owners were the wealthier citizens of the urban communities. Ranches in the area between Béxar and Goliad, which had been almost deserted after Indian attacks in the 1810s, experienced a resurrection. By the mid-1820s they dotted the entire stretch on both sides of the San Antonio River and its tributaries. A few of the ranch families "lived in the grandee style with many servants and retainers."[12]

The work force was poorer day laborers. With the United States now a potential market, ranch hands rode into the countryside, selected cattle from the huge herds, and drove the animals into makeshift *corrales*. They then separated, counted, branded or marked the cattle and prepared them for the *correduría* (drive) up the Camino Real from Béxar or Goliad to Nacogdoches. As many as 20,000 cattle (among them those of rancheros and traders) left Texas annually for the United States via this route.[13] The entire operation borrowed from the ranch techniques perfected by mestizo ancestors in the days when the rancho functioned as a frontier institution.

The mestizos also displayed their expertise in the handling of horses. An Anglo observer noted in the 1820s that

almost every stock raiser, for the purpose of raising young jacks the better, takes colts from their dams and puts young jacks to suckle in their place; these are called proof jacks. The colts are left to live as they can, and serve for the children to practice on in throwing the rope, riding, etc., at which they become so expert as to rope almost every [kind of] animals, bears, deer, etc.

In the 1820s and 1830s, Anglo American immigrants immediately recognized the mestizos as expert in the management of horse stock and "not surpassed perhaps by any other people in the Globe."[14] Whites proclaimed them as "universally acknowledged to be the best hands that can be procured for the management of cattle, horses, and other livestock."[15] Even at play, *vaqueros* displayed their remarkable horsemanship. After *rodeos* (roundups), they often engaged in days of contests of skill, which they called the *días de toros* (days of the bulls). Games included racing, shows of ropemanship, as well as the *carrera de gallo,* a contest in which *vaqueros* raced at full speed on their mounts and reached down to grasp the head of a rooster buried to its neck in the ground. Another event, the *coleada,* called for the mounted *vaquero* to catch up with a running bull, grasp its tail, and by an expert maneuver, throw the beast off balance.[16]

Only a limited number pursued nonagricultural work. Censuses of the period show only a small corps of artisans who earned their living as tailors, carpenters, blacksmiths, or masons. Many Tejanos engaged in the transportation of goods by using oxen to pull *carretas* (carts). The skill they displayed in training oxen or wild range bulls for their trade enabled them to dominate the carting industry until the 1850s.[17]

Entertainment resembled that of previous years. Municipalities, reflecting the continuity of old communal traditions, took the lead in the preparations for social functions. Traditionally, *vecindarios* came together and appointed quasi-official committees to take charge of the planned affairs. Composed of local officeholders, professionals, and ordinary citizens, these bodies collected funds, made the essential arrangements, and conducted the operations of the *funcíon.* The *Junta Patriótica* (Patriotic Committee), for example, involved itself in the official celebration of such events as Constitution Day, the Feast of Corpus Cristi, Christmas, Good Thursday and Friday, the Feast of San Felipe de Jesús, the Feast of the Virgen de Guadalupe, and the newer holiday of *Diez y Seis de Septiembre* (Sixteenth of September), the day of the winning of independence. It had been officially declared a national holiday by 1825. In Béxar that year, the festivities involved three days of revelry. The commemoration started on September 15 with a torchlight parade, a cannonade, and the ringing of the church bells. A solemn Te Deum mass, a day parade, speeches, and the official reenactment of the *grito* begin the next day. Prisoners were set at liberty, the military held a parade, and the young women were officially welcomed to the *gran baile*. The last day ended the festivities with citizens dressed in mourning to attend a "mass for the departed."[18] In subsequent years during the Mexican period, Bexareños celebrated the *Diez y Seis* with equal enthusiasm of feeling: meandering about the plaza, partaking of wine, liquor, and delicacies, and dancing the *fandango*.[19]

Béxar was not the only municipality to commemorate this national holiday. In 1832, La Bahía put on a dramatic performance that featured local people representing the opposing forces of the War for Independence. A gaily decorated carriage carried a little Indian girl (the protagonist) outfitted in all the splendor of Indian royalty. Twelve Spanish ladies (the antagonists), dressed in silks and costly laces and jewels, walked on either side holding up long lines of white ribbons fastened to the carriage. Officers of high rank pushed the carriage forward as soldiers marched in front.[20]

Fandangos held at dancing and gaming halls or in the plaza attracted a fair portion of the population. According to ritual, young women sat on benches on either side of the dance room, waited for the music to start, and then made their selection from the line of prospective men dancers. At the end of each tune, gentlemen led their partners to a table in a corner of the room for delicacies that included pastries and coffee. Each *señorita* chose some baked sweet, but instead of eating it, tied it into a piece of cloth brought for the purpose. Every dance augmented her supply of delicacies so that by evening's end she accumulated a goodly amount of provisions. Not infrequently by observing this tradition she supplied her family's rations for the following day.[21]

Other entertainment forms during the Mexican period included billiards, ball games, cockfights, and raffles. As was the case during the Spanish era, gambling pervaded the occasions so that *ayunta-mientos* resorted to outlawing dice and card games in an effort to prevent the vice.[22]

As for religion, Tejanos practiced a nominal frontier Catholicism. The Catholic Church had all but abandoned its work in Mexico's far northern frontier during this period. In Texas, the responsibility for administering the sacraments rested on two priests whose reputation, unfortunately, bordered on the disgraceful. The Catholic presence of old was an anachronism, and instruction from the top had ended in inaction.

Tejanos for the most part carried on the religion of their Mexican forefathers who, over several generations, had fashioned a religion that combined tenets of institutional Catholicism with indigenous rites. When white Texans in that period described Mexicans as religiously decadent, their observations revealed much more than racist mentality; the characterizations do suggest something about how Tejanos defined religion. According to J. C. Clopper in San Antonio in the late 1820s, the religion of Bexareños generally consisted of repeating "Our Fathers," "Ave Marías," "Credos," and other prayers, for few understood religion "as a gracious affection of the heart and soul [but grasped it] as mere requisition of personal mortification in form of penances" and the like.[23] While a Mexican professed Catholicism and carried the crucifix, the rosary, and other religious symbols, wrote another observer about residents of San Antonio in the 1830s, "religion with him is more a habit than a principle of feelings."[24] What the masses of Mexicans did was to retain the connection with Catholicism while placing barriers between themselves and the rituals of that religion that otherwise burdened them and exacerbated their life as poor people. To have complied with doctrine that called upon them to be humble and reminded them that a greater reward awaited them in the afterlife meant resigning themselves to conditions already insufferable.

Tejanos manifested attachments to Catholicism in many ways. Religious holidays seldom passed unobserved as Juntas Patrióticas took the initiative in acknowledging them. When Béxar celebrated *La Semana Santa* in the 1830s, the people rose at dawn on Palm Sunday and attended church services to recall Jesus' entry into Jerusalem. On Wednesday parishioners prepared themselves for the Eucharist by confessing, and on Thursday they received communion during solemn High Mass. In the afternoon they brought sweetened bread for blessing in remembrance of the Last Supper and witnessed *El Mandado* (The Orders), a ceremony in which twelve men dressed as Apostles sat at a long table as the priest, assisted by acolytes, washed their feet. In the evening the faithful returned for hours of vigil as they prayed and sang. Early on Good Friday, the congregation gathered for the ceremony of the Adoration of the Cross in which the crucifix was unveiled to be kissed by the priest and people. Two men then took the image of Jesus from the cross and led a procession around the church and square, the body of Christ was placed on an improvised bed inside the church, as the aggregate then considered Mary's great sorrow. On the final day, the priest blessed a fire, to be kept aflame for the next year, said mass, and removed the purple covering from the altar and images. Then the assembly received holy water to ward off danger and relieve sickness during the year.[25]

Like other peoples in other places and other times, Tejanos possessed a creative and regenerative folk tradition. Folklore provided an essential world view as Tejanos questioned their status as poor people and searched for answers to explain things that seemed incomprehensible. It also served as a psychological link that identified them with their environment, provided community solidarity, and gave them a dignified view of themselves and their life style.

Thus, legends of diligent *padres* (priests) performing miracles for the unfortunate and downtrodden filled their folklore. Among the most popular figures was Father Antonio Margil de Jesús, a dedicated priest who had accompanied Domingo Ramón to Texas in 1716 and had achieved many miracles, from delivering his missionary parties from thirst and danger on a number of occasions[26] to changing the "Margil Vine" from an unattractive plant into the beautiful vine that henceforth grew around San Antonio at Christmas time.[27] Other *padres* wielded similar powers, imploring the Virgin to help protect Indian neophytes from attacking hostile Indians or other menaces.[28]

Tejanos also employed folklore to express intimate feelings about courtships, relations between relatives, and often about love. Fidelity and faith disclosed itself in the legend concerning Don Ángel De León and his beloved Teresa ("a beautiful and high born maiden of old Castile"). Don Ángel had left Spain to serve God and King in Texas. Both yearned for one another, but then Don Ángel fell victim to an Indian arrow. The news traumatized Teresa until one day she learned that bells were being cast for Mission San José where Don Angel lay buried in consecrated ground. She hurried to the ceremony and as the molten mass filled the mold, she took the ring Don Angel had given her as a pledge of his fidelity and the golden cross he had hung around her neck and dropped them both into the crucible. According to the legend, on the day the bells rang near Don Angel's grave, she died in Castile, confident that the tolling of the bells had assured him that she remained faithful to the end.[29] Similar stories expressing the same theme dealt with the moulding of the bells of the mission San Juan.[30]

The Anglo-Texan victory over the Mexican army in 1836 and the resulting independence from Mexico marked a major institutional change for Tejanos. The revolution introduced new ways of doing things, a new language and a new socioeconomic and political order. Rapidly, Tejanos became virtually foreigners in their native land. The future seemed to augur travail.

Their fate did not rest solely on irrational tempers inflamed by the emotion of the war, for offenses against Tejanos continued long after memories of the Alamo and Goliad abated. In actuality, such transgressions sprang from deeply rooted Anglo American attitudes. American responses to the native Tejanos were shaped by feelings against Catholics and Spaniards and antipathy to Indians and Negroes. Anti-Catholic sentiment and hispanophobia had its origin in tracts in England in the mid-sixteenth century when propagandists, dissatisfied with the Roman Church, denounced the mass as blasphemous, the clergy for encouraging superstition, and the Pope for being anti-Christ. Since Spain was the most powerful of Catholic nations and the self-proclaimed champion of Catholicism, Englishmen easily merged their anti-Catholic and nascent Hispanic hatred. Political rivalry between England and Spain only exacerbated attitudes and soon the alleged atrocities inflicted by Spain against the New World natives begot a so-called Black Legend. Such prejudices arrived intact in North America where subsequent literary diatribes expanded upon them. Military conflict along the Georgia-Florida frontier and diplomatic animosity following the American Revolution abetted those feelings. Anglo-American immigrants to Texas carried those attitudes across the Sabine River.

Also, information related to the character and culture of the

without an exception gamblers and smugglers, making their living in that way."[42] And Alexander McCrae, touring Texas in 1835 under the auspices of the Wilmington Emigrating Society, revealed in unconcealed astonishment: "I for the first time saw females betting at a public game table. I do not suppose they were of respectable standing in society, from the company they kept; but I am told that it is not at all uncommon for Mexican ladies to be seen gaming in public."[43]

The morality of Tejanos likewise appalled Anglos. "There is an immeasurable superiority in the moral qualities of our people," reported a Mr. H. H. Breckenridge in 1835.[44] The *fandango*, so much a cultural facet of Tejano society, similarly evoked stunning responses from the Anglos. For example, George W. Smyth, arriving in Nacogdoches from Tennessee in 1830, was shocked to see *fandangos* "in which the priest and all participated, so contrary to all my pre-conceived notions of propriety." Many identified the dance with a decadent civilization.[45]

In the fifteen years before the Texas Revolution, the attitudes whites held toward Mexicans influenced their response to living under Mexican rule. Whites, who outnumbered the native Tejanos by ten to one in 1836, were not about to countenance being ruled indefinately by a people who in their view resembled Negroes and Indians, were inclined toward lethargy and indolence, and who spent their days gambling and doing lascivious dances. And, while the Revolution erased that possibility, it did not set aside already hardened feelings against both the Mexicans of Mexico and those of Texas.

Such attitudes,[46] combined with political and economic competition, governed the post-1836 relations between Anglos and Tejanos. From 1836 to 1846, the period between the Texas Revolution and the Mexican War, interaction between the two peoples restricted itself to the areas north of the Nueces River and east of San Antonio, but primarily to the old Tejano settlements of Goliad, Victoria, and Béxar. It was there that Tejanos held a firm grasp of the land base, dominated certain occupations such as that of ranch hands and *arrieros* (cartmen), retained an influence over politics, especially in San Antonio, and made up a substantial element in the society. It was in that region where Anglos were in closest proximity with Tejanos and where rivalry for supremacy first occurred.

In the aftermath of the revolution, Tejanos became the targets of attacks upon their holdings and their honor. Hundreds of Bexareños fled to the ranchos and finally to Coahuila. Those around Nacogdoches sought refuge in Louisiana. Families in the Goliad area sped to Tamaulipas, Nuevo León, and Louisiana. Throughout the new republic, many lost their lands through a number of subterfuges, including fictitious law suits, sheriff's sales, and dubious transfers of titles.[47]

Those that remained or returned after a short absence incurred further depredations from individual Anglos acting outside the law. John Browne, an officer in the regular army of Texas, visiting Victoria in 1839

found it filled with a set of men who [had] given themselves the title of a *band of Brothers*[.] I soon found that what they said was law[.] [T]hey are all in the cow stealing business and are scattered all over this frontier[.] I have been told that they drove off from Carlos Rancho a Caballarda belonging to Alderetta [José Miguel Aldrete] and [Juan N.] Seguín[,] that the owners know well where their property is but dare not to proceed to recover it.[48]

Harassment and persecution appeared as daily occurrences. In Béxar in the early 1840s, citizens complained that a criminal Anglo element treated them worse than brutes simply because "they were Mexicans."[49] Squatters moved into vacant property previously belonging to Tejanos.[50] In 1842, the precarious situation deteriorated further following the capture of San Antonio by two well-organized expeditions from Mexico in the spring and fall. The second raid enraged the white population and prompted some to consider banishing Tejanos from the Republic. One editoralist proposed:

there is no faith to be put in them; and until the war is ended, they should be compelled, every one of them, to retire either east or west from the frontier; or if they choose to remain, be subjected to the rigorous treatment due to enemies.[51]

Others formed into vigilante groups and took the law into their own hands. Angry citizens from Victoria, for instance, visited nearby Carlos' Rancho and compelled the fifty or so Mexican families who had settled there to leave the country.[52] In Béxar itself, volunteer soldiers acted very badly, having ventured to force the Mexican families from their homes, [causing them] to droop about in the woods and seek shelter wherever they could find it. Moreover to gratify their beastly lusts [they have] compelled the women and Girls to yield to their hellish desires, which their victims did under the fear of punishment and death.[53]

The rest of the decade did not improve things for the old Tejanos. The Mexican War served only to reinforce ill feelings toward these "sons of the enemy." Yet hostility did not result in a complete exodus. Fifteen hundred of the original Tejanos remained in the old Béxar-Goliad region during the period. By 1850, moreover, 600 Mexican born heads-of-households had entered the region since the revolution, while several hundreds of the émigrés had returned from their refuge to Nacogdoches, Victoria, and "New La Bahía."[54]

New clashes emerged, though, ostensibly over the issue of slavery but based in economic rivalries. Whereas Anglos viewed slavery as essential to economic development in the state, Tejanos understood it as oppression and for years had extended aid to slaves and helped them escape to Mexico. But by 1854, whites had reached the limits of tolerance. The town of Seguín drafted resolutions prohibiting Mexican peons from entering the country and forbidding Mexicans to associate with blacks. In October, delegates from different counties convened in Gonzales and implemented stringent measures to stop the Mexican menace. In Austin, where a citizens' committee accused Mexican residents of horse theft and exiled twenty families from their homes in the spring of 1853, similar resolutions were passed.[55]

Quickly thereafter, a "Cart War" broke out in 1857. While Anglos had wrested much of the economic foundation of the Central Texas region from Mexicanos by the 1850s, skilled arrieros continued monopolizing the freight business between San Antonio in the interior and the coast. White teamsters had sought strenuously to infiltrate the commerce, valued into the millions of dollars, but they had failed to undercut the lower rates charged by Tejano cartmen. During the summer, in the general area between San Antonio and the gulf, and Goliad in particular, they initiated an organized campaign of lawlessness, wanton injury, harassment, assassination, waylaying of carts, and pillaging and confiscating of valuable cargoes. The affair ultimately ended through a combination of pressure from the Mexican government, the American sec-

r   mpanies organizing to bring about
o   n had perished in the episode.[56]
                                       the old Tejanos of Central Texas
w   n Anglo and European immigrant
p   along the Indianola-San Antonio
rc   ivelihood as carters, packers, and
di   they lived in all Mexican commu-
ni.... like New La Bahía" and Alamita, or apart in a particular
section of a town, as in the case of San Antonio where they occupied the south and southwest sections of the city along the river
and the Laredo road. There, they now lived as a group overwhelmed
by a combination of Anglo, German, and Negro population.[57] These
early demographic patterns in Central Texas remained generally
stable for the remainder of the century.

In the area between the Nueces River and the Rio Grande, the
rivalry that appeared in Central Texas did not surface in the years
immediately after the Texas Revolution for only a few Anglos penetrated the region which technically belonged to the northern Mexican state of Tamaulipas. Thus, while proximity between Anglos
and Tejanos in Central Texas had resulted in competition for economic and political primacy, the separateness of these Tamaulipecos
spared them similar troubles. Direct competition for livelihood did
not occur until later.

The Tamaulipecos owed their origin to the settlements founded
by José de Escandón in the 1740s. Before the 1820s, most of the
original colonists lived in Laredo (population approximately 1,418
in 1819) and the towns of Camargo, Reynosa, Dolores, and Mier
located on the west bank of the Rio Grande. By the mid-1820s,
however, population spread northward into the present Texas counties of Willacy, Kennedy, Brooks, Jim Hogg, Duval, Jim Wells,
Kleberg, and Nueces. Approximately 350 rancherías existed in this
region by 1835, among them San Diego, San Juan, Palo Blanco,
Agua Dulce, El Sauz, Los Olmos, San Luis, Pansacol, Zapata, San
Ignacio, and Los Saenz.[58] It was into this area that some of the old
Tejanos of the Béxar-Goliad area had fled in their attempts to
escape the ire of Anglos in 1836.

Despite Tamaulipas' claim to the region, these Tamaulipecos
became Tejanos when the Republic of Texas claimed the Rio Grande
as its southern boundary. While diplomatically they did not become subjects of the United States until the Mexican War resolved

the question of the disputed territory between the Nueces and the Rio Grande, they nevertheless became citizens of Texas by settling lands under the new headright program of the Republic.[59] Despite their incorporation into Anglo-Texas, the area in general remained culturally Mexican during this period as only a few Americans ventured into the region. The 1850 census enumerated 1,665 Hispanic heads of households in the Rio Grande Valley with families averaging five persons including parents.[60]

The ending of the Mexican War in 1848 effected an arrangement comparable to the one in the interior of the state, except that in south Texas the Tejano population remained an overwhelming majority. The birth of Anglo communities like Brownsville, Rio Grande City, Eagle Pass, Roma, and Nuecestown, plus the building of army establishments like Fort Brown, Ringgold Barracks, Fort McIntosh, Fort Inge, Fort Merill, Fort Ewell, and Fort Clark signaled the arrival of white men.[61] The transformation brought with it war veterans and unscrupulous swindlers looking for the most opportune ways of acquiring land and fortune. In the Nueces County area, where all the land belonged to Mexicans at the time of the Texas Revolution, Anglos and Americanized Europeans had wrested it from Tejanos by the time of the Civil War.[62] In the Lower Valley, land grabbers used their acquaintance with the legal system and their association with friends in high places to rob old Mexican grantees. Charles Stillman, for example, used both threat and influence to acquire the valuable *Espiritu Santo* grant that belonged to the descendants of Francisco Cavazos.[63] By intermarrying with native Mexican women of the upper class, by developing ties with influential families, and employing political chicanery, the newcomers swiftly gained domination of the real estate and government of South Texas. They now executed the laws to their advantage.

The war also opened an era of disorder as border ruffians of both races preyed upon the property of settlers in the region, most of whom were Tejanos.[64] Anglo American desperadoes treated the Mexicans with open disdain and called them "greasers." Others, like King Fisher, dealt with them as if they did not count and took advantage of the presence of American authorities to harry them. Resentment against the Anglos finally reached its extreme when on July 13, 1859, an encounter between a local rancher named Juan "Cheno" Cortina and the Brownsville city marshal left the lawman

injured; the incident enraged the Anglo population in the city. For
a while the initiative passed to Cortina and his followers as they lay
seige to Brownsville and threatened "death to the *gringos.*" For
too long, Cheno proclaimed, whites had been despoiling Tejanos of
their land and prosecuting and robbing them "for no other crime
. . . than that of being of Mexican origin." His primary purpose, he
affirmed, was to seek redress for those wrongs, hopefully from
governor-elect Sam Houston. But by the time Texas Rangers and
federal troops extinguished the "insurrection" in early 1860, the
episode had left a number of people dead, much property destroyed,
and ugly tensions between the two races.[65]

By then, South Texas was divided into two zones—one Anglo,
the other Tejano—but bicultural features were appearing as well.
The region consisted of a line of new Anglo towns extending from
Corpus Christi, to San Patricio, to Beeville, to Pleasanton, down to
Uvalde. But a hundred miles of chaparral still separated the Nue-
ces country from the settlements along the Rio Grande where
Tejanos enjoyed numerical predominance[66]. Despite the fact that
Anglos controlled the major institutions, Mexican culture saturated
the border area, if not the hinterland of the chaparral. Indeed,
many of the Anglo and European ranchers and merchants became
Hispanicized white men.

During the decade and a half following the Cortina episode,
Texas did not change much. Instead, people fought the Civil War,
and the politics of Reconstruction turned their attention away from
the more pressing problems of growth. In Central Texas, despite
the influx of Mexican nationals into the area, the Mexican American population never quite matched the immigration trends from
the American South and European countries.[67]

Anglos continued victimizing Tejanos. Around San Marcos, noted
a San Antonio newspaper in 1870, the trees were "bearing a new
kind of fruit," that is, Mexican cattle thieves hung by so-called
vigilance committees organized for self-protection against the rustlers infesting that section.[68] In Boerne, where suspicion touched
Mexicanos for recent murders and depredations in 1868, a party of
volunteers from neighboring counties gathered to punish the unknown perpetrators of a wholesale murder that occurred five miles
east of town. Upon finding weapons that seemed to fix the crime on
the Mexicans, the vigilantes indiscriminately began executing them,
slaying seven Mexicans.[69] In Goliad County, a mob lynched Juan

Moya and his two sons in 1874 for allegedly killing a white family. Some days later peace officers captured the real killers, but those who had murdered the Moyas escaped prosecution.[70] These violent attacks were but an extreme form of the racism that frequently surfaced in everyday affairs.

Tejanos in South Texas faced equally violent times. Despite their numerical superiority (constantly augmented by Mexican immigration), the major institutions remained fundamentally in the hands of whites who seemed helpless in checking a veritable war of races between cattle thieves from Mexico and a motley array of Anglo ranchmen, rustlers, and cowboys encountering each other over "unbranded" mavericks. For crimes committed against them, white ranchers and citizens invariably sought vengeance by launching vendettas against local Tejanos. According to Texas Adjutant General William Steele, "a considerable element in the country bordering on the Nueces and west thought the killing of a Mexican no crime."[71] Senator Joseph E. Dwyer similarly reported that terrible outrages were being committed upon citizens of Mexican origin. In Bee County, he continued, whites brutally murdered a Mexican who refused to go play the fiddle for them.[72] Thomas F. Wilson, United States consul at Matamoros, likewise testified that white authorities disregarded aggressions upon Mexicanos and that no one made a great fuss over the hanging or killing of a Mexican in the neighborhood of Brownsville or along the frontier.[73] In 1875, the San Antonio *Express*, in a political diatribe against Governor Richard Coke, remarked that along the border regions "Mexicans were no longer safe upon the highways, or outside of the towns; that they will be shot down as if they were savages," and that a number had already been murdered in cold blood "just because they were Mexicans."[74] There is no telling how many Mexicanos fell victim to the reprisals.

The event symbolizing these border skirmishes at their nadir occurred in March 1875 when Mexican nationals "raided" Corpus Christi. They stole horses, appropriated the valuables of several customers shopping at a store they robbed, killed a Mexican American who refused to join their party, set fire to a business causing thousands of dollars in damage, and killed a member of the posse pursuing them as they retreated to the border. Whites retaliated with a vengeance: large parties of mounted and well-armed men, pretending to be acting in the cause of law and order, rode about the country committing brutal outrages, murdering peaceable Mexican farmers and stockmen.[75] Indignant bands headed toward Encinal County, about mid-way between the Nueces and Rio Grande, to a place named La Parra, directing their hostility toward Mexican squatters who were reported to have stolen hides buried or concealed on their premises. There, the attackers burned down the jacales and killed a number of men.[76]

These border troubles subsided by the late 1870s as Porfirio Díaz's *rurales* suppressed bandits from Mexico and American troops succeeded in preventing American cattle thieves from penetrating into Mexican territory. The easing of tensions coincided with economic changes taking place throughout the state. Texas entered an incipient phase of modern industrialization as railroads now seemed to connect most points in the state, bringing with them progress and prosperity. Béxar County suddenly emerged among the leaders in manufacturing, and San Antonio as the largest city in the state. South Texas now gradually shifted from subsistence agriculture to commercial farming, concentrating on the production of cotton. Immigration from Mexico continued; the 1880 census enumerating about 43,000 Tejanos. And for the first time, Anglos began penetrating West Texas en masse as the range cattle industry thrust westward and the sheep and goat industry found a home. Railroads followed, attracting farmers in their wake. Towns now made their appearance in an area where Mexicanos had lived somewhat apart from the Anglo masses for nearly a quarter century after the Mexican war.

In that western region, the Hispanic presence traced its beginnings to Spanish activity in the 1680s. In the nineteenth century, Tejano residents lived in the small communities of Socorro, Ysleta, San Elizario, and El Paso. Anglos had moved into this El Paso Valley in the 1850s, but their numbers did not disturb the Hispanic ambience there, indeed many assimilated themselves into Hispanic society and became Mexicanized gringos. West Texas settlements like Fort Davis, Fort Stockton, Alpine, and San Angelo grew out of the American westward movement following the Civil War. Mexicans came into those communities shortly thereafter searching for work as shepherds, vaqueros, and farm hands.

Racial friction and economic rivalry in West Texas resulted in the same pattern of violence found elsewhere in the state. In the El Paso Valley, a handful of Anglos in the early 1860s began monopolizing the nearby Guadalupe Salt Lakes upon which Mexican livelihood depended. Animosity slowly mounted and reached a violent peak in October 1877 when the monopolizers closed the lakes to Tejanos and killed Don Luis Cardis, a Mexican sympathizer. For the next three months, the Mexicans sought out the Anglos with recrimination in mind. Suddenly, the world seemed turned upside down for the small Anglo community in the Valley (5,000 Tejanos, compared to less than 100 whites) as the Mexicans sought to avenge the death of Cardis and regain access to the salt lakes. Finally, help for the Anglos arrived in the form of a company of Ranger volunteers, who were adventurers and other lawless men. They committed wanton outrages, including riddling two Mexican prisoners with bullets "unnecessarily and unjustifiably," slaughtering a Mexican and wounding his wife on the pretext that the Mexican had shot at them from inside his house, and committing rapes or attempting them. This was the infamous "Salt War."[77]

Similar violence typified the newer Anglo communities of West Texas. In the little town of Murphyville (modern Alpine), racial tensions had been increasing as each race talked of running the other out of town. When in mid-April 1886, a number of Mexicans reportedly raided the Cattle Exchange Saloon, gunning down a number of white patrons, armed Anglos swiftly responded, killing some of the Mexicans and driving the rest from town.[78] In the San Angelo area, where local Anglos considered Mexicanos a "race of mongrels, chiefly Aztecs, with a sprinkling of Spanish and Negro," indignant whites, for unknown reasons, lynched Jesús Salceda in nearby Knickerbocker in February 1891.[79] Following a feud in Presidio County, white cowboys in the summer of 1897 considered exterminating the Mexican sheepherders.[80]

Tejanos in the two other sections controlled by Hispanics prior to 1836 saw little relief from racism and oppression in the last twenty years of the century. In Cotulla, masked men in 1895 took Florentino Suaste from the jailer, lynched him from a mesquite limb, and riddled his body with bullets.[81] In June 1896, whites near Senior, Texas, mutilated and burned Aureliano Castellón for paying romantic attention to a white woman.[82] Fiendish cases of lynching in Eagle Pass and Brownsville in that era attested to the same pattern of violence in South Texas.[83] Troubles plagued the Tejanos in other ways, as when in 1898 White Cappers in Hays, Wilson, Gonzales, and DeWitt counties called upon landlords to

run off Mexican renters and to discharge their Mexican hired hands.[84]
Or, more fantastically, when during the Spanish American War,
Anglos accused them of sympathizing with Spain and conspiring
with *guerrilleros* from Mexico to attack the United States.[85]

Manifestly, tragedy had befallen the Tejanos after 1836. They
had come to live in a world where just about everything from their
skin color to their cultural ways evoked perverse racial responses.
Anglos saw Tejanos as being the color of "niggers" or resembling
the Indians in physiognomy, as being a "race of mongrels" set apart
by their physical differences from white men. They imputed to
Mexicans a childlike mentality and regarded them as unambitious,
indolent and satisfied with grinding poverty. They thought Mexicanos
were concerned only with frolic and pleasure, and the pursuit of
gambling, dancing, and sleeping the *siesta*. To whites, Mexicanos
were a sexually degenerate people lacking any morality. And as if
this were not enough, they repeatedly questioned the Tejanos'
Americanism, wondering if these people, culturally distinct, could
have true American sentiments.

White men sought gallantly to keep Tejanos at a distance. To
allow them the opportunity for equality meant risking the chance
of having Mexicanos presiding over them. Hence, their every effort was directed at handicapping Mexicanos, to make sure that
they remained subordinate and economically and politically de-
fenseless. Among the mechanisms that maintained them in powerlessness was employing the Texas Rangers as a legal corps to keep
them in their place. Oppression is what the 165,000 Spanish-
surnamed Americans of Texas still knew in 1900.[86]

2

Politics and Tejanos

Although Tejanos lived in a markedly different world after 1836, things were not catastrophic. True, white intrusion had disturbed their old communities, but Tejanos experienced little demoralization. They retained their "Mexicanness," identified with old traditions and beliefs, and carried on Hispanic practices while rejecting certain Anglo American ones. Meantime, like other conquered people seeking to survive under adverse conditions, they appraised the new situation and developed ways and means that allowed them control over their lives. In taking that initiative, they avoided total manipulation by external forces and thwarted what could have been their relegation to the periphery of the historical mainstream.

On the political front, a number of factors acted to discourage and impede participation in the governmental process. Poverty, for one thing, deprived Tejanos of the vital assets so crucial for organizing or assembling a successful political movement. As working people, Mexican Americans found little time for the consuming chore of holding meetings and planning strategy. Much of the Tejano community was foreign born and, as noncitizens, Mexicanos had no right to the franchise unless having taken out intention papers for naturalization. A study of census returns for representative counties in South Texas (Cameron, Starr, and Webb Counties), in Central Texas (Béxar County), and West Texas (El Paso County) for 1850 and 1900 reveals that about 53 percent of the Hispanic males twenty-one years of age and older in 1850, and 66 percent in

1900 were not native born. (See the Appendix for a discussion of this survey.) Thus, over half of potential Mexican-American voters were probably disfranchised. Even with intention papers, the size of the Tejano voting pool would not have increased dramatically. The 1900 census (the first to provide information on citizenship status) shows that literate, American-born, plus naturalized or filed Mexican American males twenty-one and over made up only about 12.9 percent of all Mexican American males of that age and older. But country of origin did not make Tejanos completely helpless when compared to whites, for many Anglo Americans were also of foreign stock. In 1850 (1860 in the case of El Paso), foreign born Anglo males twenty-one and over made up about 47 percent of the Anglo males of voting age and older, while in 1900 the percentage of foreign born Anglo males twenty-one and over amounted to about 27 percent. However, Tejano illiteracy did prove a serious disability. Minimal education not only restricted their familiarity with state and national issues but inhibited their grasp of political operations. Their educational handicap gave the Anglo majority a vast edge for it left a minority of more literate and knowledgable Tejanos to work and speak in behalf of the Tejano community. As can be seen in the census schedules, Tejano males twenty-one years and over collectively outnumbered their Anglo counterparts in South, Central and West Texas by at least 1,420 in 1900 (see Table 1). However, in the same year, only about 2,248 (12.9 percent) of the Tejano males of voting age were literate and either American born, naturalized, or filed. About 14,005 (88.2 percent) of the Anglo males of voting age were literate, American born, naturalized, or filed (see Table 1). The Tejano community, therefore, was weakened even before whites employed external mechanisms that made Tejanos a powerless constituency.

Diverse tactics were employed to minimize Tejano involvement. Race relations were characterized by the refusal of Anglos to accept Mexicanos organizing along ethnic lines with intentions of electing an "all Mexican" ticket aiming for self-determination. Texas Rangers could be and on occasion were, swiftly dispatched to abort such a plan. Further, the news media could mobilize public opinion against any attempts at self-improvement; for example, newspapers branded the followers of Juan Cortina and Catarino Garza, the Tejano activist who pronounced against Mexican President Porfirio Díaz in 1891, as ignorant greasers and *pelados* easily led into misadventure and crime. Also, Anglos might have tolerated the Mexican vote when it could be controlled, but attempts at disfranchisement to insure white supremacy abounded. Talk of registry laws and poll taxes was common and eventually culminated in 1896 in the case of Ricardo Rodríguez in which two San Antonio attorneys argued before a federal court, albeit unsuccessfully, that Mexican Indians were ineligible to vote. Further, despite the presence of numerous Tejano political figures at the local level, the two state parties hardly recognized them as possible representatives of Tejano needs. Neither party sought to integrate those men into their structure. Instead, Anglo politicians saw the Mexican as one to be "voted" by them in the interest of maintaining white supremacy.[1] When not to that interest, they could advance pretexts to neutralize Mexicanos, as when Tom Green County democrats in San Angelo ousted a Tejano delegation from their convention because the Mexicans did not speak English.[2]

Still, Tejanos had always tried to assert themselves from within the existing political system. Within a matter of months following the revolution, Tejanos in the Hispanic settlements around the Central Texas areas attuned themselves to the mechanics of the new order and sought to join, or at last participate, in politics as much as possible. Instead of fleeing to Mexico or elsewhere in repudiation of the Texas Republic, they adjusted to it and showed an interest in the new political order. Notwithstanding the travail they faced, the Bexareños of San Antonio took advantage of their numerical supremacy in the first election after the battle of San Jacinto. They elected a city government comprising of Tejanos who in one way or another had served in some responsible capacities before 1836. The city council included Manuel Martínez, Gabriel Arreola, Francisco Bustillos, Rafael Herrera, Pedro Flores Morales, Francisco Antonio Ruiz, Ramón Treviño, and Francisco Granado. Eugenio Navarro won appointment as treasurer, Manuel Pérez as secretary, and Vicente de la Garza as collector; only the mayor was Anglo. Until the year of annexation, Spanish-surnamed aldermen played a part in municipal affairs while influential Tejano citizens like Erasmo Seguín and José Antonio Navarro filled county and city judicial posts.[3]

While it is true that various Tejanos pursued personal ambitions by seeking a privileged position in the revolutionary government, they also endeavored to avert their fellow Tejanos' total victimiza-

TABLE 1. Estimates of Mexican-American and Anglo-American Voting Populations in Central, South, and West Texas 1850 (1860) and 1900

	Béxar County	
	1850	1900
Estimated Number of Mexican-American Males of Voting Age (21 and over)	596	3,823
Estimated Number of Anglo-American Males of Voting Age (21 and over)	1,189	11,911
Estimated Number of American Born Mexican-American Males of Voting Age	340	1,667
Estimated Number of American Born Anglo-American Males of Voting Age	617	8,496
Estimated Number of Naturalized Mexican-Americans of Voting Age	—	666
Estimated Number of Naturalized Anglo-Americans of Voting Age	—	1,941
Estimated Number of Literate Mexican-American Males of Voting Age	140	1,338
Estimated Number of Literate Anglo-American males of Voting Age	1,168	11,256
Estimated Number of American Born and Literate Mexican American Males of Voting Age	105	—
Estimated Number of American Born and Literate Anglo American Males of Voting Age	603	—
Estimated Number of Literate, American Born, and Naturalized or Filed Mexican American Males of Voting Age	—	1,099
Estimated Number of Literate, American Born, and Naturalized or Filed Anglo American Males of Voting Age	—	10,437

[a]The 1850 census treated the entire "Lower Rio Grande Valley" as a single area for information collection. The 1900 census broke the area down by counties, of which Cameron, Starr, and Webb are represented in this table.

| Lower Rio Grande Valley[a] | | El Paso County | |
| (Cameron, Starr, Webb) | | | |
1850	1900	1860	1900
2,022	10,377	912	3,106
490	860	318	3,115
811	3,424	504	870
269	616	171	2,512
—	793	—	488
—	110	—	308
619	1,048	234	506
490	753	314	3,065
321	—	149	—
261	—	159	—
—	790	—	359
—	684	—	2,884

tion. Their efforts, for example produced a concession in 1837 from Congress that the city clerk in San Antonio ought to be bilingual. In 1839, Senator José Antonio Navarro pressed in vain to have the Congress provide his constituents with some assistance if they could not speak English, prove title to their lands, or afford law suits. Indeed the presence of prominent and acceptable men such as Navarro and Juan Seguín, son of Erasmo Seguín, was one of many factors that impelled Anglos to recognize the Tejanos' civil rights (however ambiguous the meaning of these privileges). At the state constitutional convention of 1845, Navarro as the Béxar County delegate almost singlehandedly prevented the possible constitutional disfranchisement of Mexican Americans.[4] His action was but one example of Tejanos successfully asserting themselves.

Tejanos also actively dissented from and resisted practices that Anglo society endorsed. In the 1840s and 1850s, for instance, Mexicanos took the audacious step of sabotaging chattel racial slavery by rescuing Negroes from bondage and transporting them to freedom over the sparsely settled, semidesert frontier between Central Texas and the Rio Grande. Although whites in the Travis, Béxar, and Goliad county areas by 1854 took strong measures to curtail the activity, Mexican American resistance to slavery, persisted until the eve of the Civil War.[5]

Despite being a minority in Béxar County, Tejanos were politically active in the period between 1850 and 1900. (See Table 2 for profile of the Hispanic and Anglo populations of Béxar, 1850 and 1900). In the 1850s, for instance, the hysteria of the decade absorbed the Bexareños on the side of the Democrats against the Know-Nothing party. They resisted the latter's antiimmigration, antinaturalization, and anti-Catholic stand. At a convention of Tejano democrats held in San Antonio on June 28, 1855, members adopted resolutions denouncing the intolerance of the Know-Nothings, and at a second convention in July, José Antonio Navarro excoriated the movement in scathing terms:

A new secret party has risen as the opprobrium of all liberty; it is called the Know-Nothing and its motto suggests that it does not know just and generous sentiments; that it does not know anything except how to plunge the fratricidal dagger into the breasts of would-be free Americans.

They proclaim equality of rights, offer asylum and liberty to all types of humans, but nevertheless proscribe the Catholics on account of their religious beliefs, and desire a wide range for their own.

Table 2. Comparative Characteristics of the Mexican-American and Anglo-American Populations of the Béxar County, 1850 and 1900

	1850	1900
Population of County	5,407	70,251
Percent Mexican-American Population	46.7%	21.5%
Percent Anglo-American Population	47.5%	65.3%
Estimated Number of Mexican-Americans	2,525	15,104
Estimated Number of Anglo-Americans	2,568	45,874
Percent Mexican-American Rural Residents	36.6%	29.4%
Percent Anglo-American Rural Residents	41.9%	20.0%
Percent Mexican-American City Residents	63.4%	70.6%
Percent Anglo-American City Residents	58.1%	80.0%
Estimated Number of Mexican-American Rural Residents	924	4,441
Estimated Number of Anglo-American Rural Residents	1,076	9,175
Estimated Number of Mexican-American City Residents	1,601	10,663
Estimated Number of Anglo-American City Residents	1,492	36,699

The Texas-Mexicans are Catholics and may be proud of the belief of their fathers; they will defend themselves against such infamous aggression.[6]

In the election of August 6, Béxar voters rejected the Party almost unanimously.[7] Interest the next year continued as Bexareños kept abreast of Democratic and Know-Nothing politics as carried on in a battle of sharp political exchanges between two newspapers—the *Ranchero* (Democrat) and the *Bejareño* (Know-Nothing).[8]

Reconstruction touched Tejanos in San Antonio as it engaged other Americans in the post-Civil War North and South. Much aware of *the* issue of Reconstruction, city political figures clashed over the same ideology that preoccupied postbellum America—white supremacy versus equality for the freedmen. Here, Bexereños divided to take different stands, for unlike the issue of the Know-Nothing Party in the 1850s, it did not directly affect them as an ethnic community. In fact, both sides had representatives who descended from the old families of the city, and each played upon the sentiments of their followers to support their respective cause. As was the case on other occasions, the heterogeneous Tejano community took an ideological position that manifested biculturation and adaptation instead of strict commitment to its Mexican heritage. Of course, Mexican American interest in questions touching directly upon the Tejano community as an ethnic entity were viewed and reacted to with greater awareness of their impact on daily life.

The conservative party, organized in August 1868 as "Los Bexareños Demócratas," included men like Rafael Quintana, A. M. Ruiz, Manuel Yturri, José Peñaloza, Juan Cárdenas, and J. Antonio G. Navarro and espoused unabashed white supremacy.[9] Sternly behind conservatism, members of the party waged a committed battle against Radical rule. In 1871, Don Narciso Leal, a Democrat (conservative), criticized the state's high taxes before a responsive Spanish-speaking taxpayers' meeting. In another rally the same month at Mission Espada, conservatives Antonio Menchaca, Juan Chaves, L. Garza, and J. M. Peñaloza spoke to a predominantly Tejano assemblage in Spanish and succeeded in having resolutions passed backing a conservative candidate for Congress. When the same group held a similar meeting at Luna's Ranch (close to San Antonio) on the anniversary of Mexican Independence, Menchaca compared the resistance movement of Father Miguel Hidalgo y Costilla to the need to overturn Radical rule in the state through all legitimate means including supporting conservative candidates for Congress.[10]

The Radicals, on the other hand, defended the issue of equality for the freedmen. The Mexican-Texan Club, organized in July 1868, included Epistacio Mondragón, Juan M. Chávez, Fermín Casiano, Juan E. Barrera, Agustín Gutiérrez, Antonio P. Rivas, and other radicals. Like the conservatives, they campaigned vigorously for their cause, propagating their ideas through their newspaper organ *El Mexicano de Texas*, speaking before Tejano audiences, and organizing clubs fashioned after their Mexican-Texan Club in surrounding areas.[11]

As Reconstruction politics subsided and the nation turned to other issues, so too did Bexareños involve themselves in these matters.[12] The election of 1872, for instance, attracted men like M. Delgado, Anavato Martínez, Antonio Menchaca, Manuel Serna, Antonio P. Rivas, and Antonio Pérez, who organized a Mexican campaign for presidential candidate Horace Greeley, and others like J. M. Chávez and Juan Barrera who organized a predominantly

Tejano Ulysses S. Grant and Henry Wilson Club.[13] On other fronts, Bexareños attended and made input at local party conventions, not infrequently serving in meaningful capacities. In a Republican county mass meeting in September 1872, delegates chosen for the county convention of Béxar County included J. M. Chávez, Juan Franco, F. Martínez, Felipe Flores, Clemente Bustillo, Louis Muñoz, and Dolores Salazar.[14] During the proceedings of the Béxar County Convention of December 1875, Juan Cárdenas, Antonio Menchaca, and Modesto Torres were chosen to attend the Galveston Democratic Convention, others were selected to represent the county in the senatorial convention to meet at Boerne, while still other Tejanos won election to posts such as the Executive Committee in the Béxar County Democratic Party.[15]

Other political activities included organizing rallies on issues relevant to the Tejano community or in behalf of party politics. In one case in January 1876, Juan Cárdenas, Antonio Menchaca, Lino Sánchez, Anavato Martínez, Juan Barerra, Modesto Torres, among others, called a meeting of Tejanos to argue in favor of an important question before the city—voting $300,000 to the San Antonio Construction Company to bring the railroad into town. The organizers argued in behalf of the proposition while Anglo guests pointed out that as a laboring people, Bexareños would find employment in the railroad at good wages and that home owners in the trans-San Pedro Creek area stood to profit from increased land values once people moved in.[16] On another occasion in October 1886, a huge gathering of prospective voters congregated at Garza's Crossing in the Medina River (near San Antonio) to enjoy food and music and listen to Juan Cárdenas and Anglo politicians deliver political oratory in both English and Spanish.[17]

Surely many of the politically active realized their inability to gain the concessions they sought, but at least some made attempts at self-determination. Thus, in September 1878, Bexareños belonging to the Democratic party, many of them notable political figures (among them José M. Peñaloza, John Barrera, Lino Sánchez, Juan Cárdenas, Manuel Serna, Antonio Bruni, Juan Rodríguez, Manuel Yturri, Modesto Torres, and Francisco Galán), bolted a Democratic convention, charging the leaders of the party with using them as tools to secure fat offices and ignoring them on the streets thereafter. The Mexicans repaired en masse to a point west of San Pedro Creek, claiming a right to be represented on the Democratic ticket and resolving not to support those refusing to recognize their rights. They threatened to hold out until the Democratic party alloted them their share on the ticket, and, if refused, determined to run a ticket of their selection even if it meant defeat.[18] In September 1888, Manuel López, León Marechal, Elihu García, and Espiridion Cruz attempted to form a club of their own countrymen designed to take an active part in an upcoming county and municipal elections and to get anything they could from the candidates. In January 1893, Manuel López (apparently the same person as mentioned above) called for a Workingmen's Mass Meeting to put up a third man for mayor, although seemingly without success.[19]

While these Tejano spokesmen generally were from financially secure older families, they still shared a common language and culture with residents of the city's West Side; consequently, they often came to the defense of those in the *barrio* and served as vital intermediaries between it and the Anglo power structure. Thus, they frequently took the lead in expressing disapproval of injustices. In August 1883, when the lessee of the San Pedro park announced that thereafter Mexicanos would not be allowed access to the dance platform in the public grounds, Mexicanos expressed open indignation. A protest meeting in the recorder's court room immediately after the announcement resulted in formation of a Committee on Resolutions chaired by Capt. Juan Cárdenas. According to the resolutions Cárdenas presented to a second rally, the lessee's motive in keeping Mexicanos off the grounds was to appease whites who had threatened to stop patronizing him should he persist in admitting Mexicanos to the dance floor. The Committee denounced him as an ignorant coward and recommended that the mayor and city council instruct the city attorney to bring suit to recover possession of the San Pedro park and see that the lessee be permanently removed. The resolutions asked additionally that the attorneys representing the Tejanos be authorized to assist the city attorney in prosecuting the suit.[20] The protestors ostensibly won their point, for they regained access to the platform.

A similar kind of indignation occurred in 1893 when a local doctor named Frank Fanning killed one Juan Salas. Subsequently the doctor gave testimony to the effect that Salas confronted him in a dark street, and, despite warnings, continued approaching him. In self-defense, he had killed the Mexican. But the Bexareños considered the circumstances suspicious and upon hearing of Fan-

ning's release on bond, congregated at Washington Square to de-
nounce him. Orators eulogized Salas as an honorable and decent
man quietly making his way home on a well-lighted street only to
be shot by the doctor. The young attorney Antonio D. Flores,
however, advised the crowd that justice for Salas ought to be left
up to the law and that a jury ought to decide the doctor's guilt or
innocence.[21]

In October 1896, Bexareños once more gathered, this time to
protest an attempt to disfranchise them made by two Anglo attorneys. According to the lawyers, a Mexican national—Ricardo
Rodríguez—seeking naturalization papers did not qualify for citizenship because he was Indian. Thus, neither did he qualify for the
vote. This technicality, they argued, similarly excluded other
Tejanos. At a place used as a cockpit, some 200 Bexareños met to
discuss this attempt to undercut their political rights. A. L. Montalbo,
the leading spirit in the movement, addressed the crowd in Spanish, admonishing those in attendance that the upcoming November election included issues that would gravely affect the civil
rights of Mexicanos. He urged his followers to mass behind the
Democratic Party as it was the only party that heretofore had
recognized Mexican American rights. The meeting ended with
everyone signing the address. The next year the courts decided
that, on the basis of precedent, Mexicanos held the right to vote.[22]

Over time, the political activism of Bexareños produced elec-
toral successes, despite the repeated efforts by white society to
render them powerless. In the 1840s after annexation, Tejano political incumbents lingered precariously, and in the 1850s, J. A.
Urutia, Rafael Herrera, M. López, G. Soto, José Rodríguez, J. M.
Chavez, J. M. Peñaloza, and members of the Navarro clan served
as city aldermen[23] with Angel Navarro gaining election to the legislature.[24] During the Civil War years, F. Cassiano and José Martínez
served in city government, J. A. G. Navarro and L. Castro were
the assessors in 1861 and 1862 respectively,[25] and Capt. A. Barrera
and Second Lt. J. M. Peñaloza were among those winning in the
1862 military election of the city precincts.[26] During Reconstruction, F. Cassiano, A. M. Ruiz, M. Yturri and J. M. Chavez were
aldermen, Antonio Menchaca was ditch commissioner, and R. Quintana was treasurer.[27] Among military appointees were Mariano
García of the Reconstruction Board of Registrars of Béxar County.[28] In 1872, José Flores was listed as alderman of the city and

Eugene Navarro as city clerk,[29] José Cassiano as city assessor in the late eighties,[30] while Alejo Pérez was ditch commissioner (West Side) and León Váldez carried out duties as city jailer in the 1890s.[31] Francisco N. Sánchez was public weigher, Antonio Bruni was market master, and Ignacio Cassiano was pound master between the mid-1880s and the early 1890s.[32] Other men in San Antonio performed their civic functions by serving on grand juries and as members of petit juries.[33]

Incumbency at the county level paralleled that at the city. Pedro Cevallos served as justice of the peace and Calixto Nuñez as assessor collector during Reconstruction.[34] In the 1870s, Luciano C. Navarro was county surveyor, Rafael Quintana was a justice of the peace, Manuel Sánchez was a precinct constable, and Erasmo J. Chávez was county collector for a brief period in that decade.[35] Early in the 1880s, José E. García served as county tax assessor. Among those who held down positions for a substantial part of the decade were Juan E. Barrera, the deputy county clerk, Manuel Yturri, the deputy district clerk, José Cassiano, the county collector, and Rafael Quintana and Juan Antonio Chávez who became county commissioners. Other justices of the peace were Martín Delgado and Francisco Cervantes. A number of other Mexicanos acted as constables in the various county precincts.[36] With the exception of José Cassiano, who continued as tax collector, the Tejano presence in county government ostensibly waned by the 1890s as the area became more and more of an Anglo region.

The many who served San Antonio and Béxar County after the war for independence did so as the Tejano population progressively diminished in face of a growing white population.[37] All the while, Tejano office holders represented only a small proportion of all incumbents; yet the fact that they succeeded in winning elections and appointments suggests that vigorous political action amid a hostile surrounding led to victory. That incumbency almost disappeared by the 1890s had more to do with demographic than with the so-called apoliticalism various social scientists have attributed to Mexican Americans. It became virtually impossible for Bexareños to prevail against the Anglo majority; they were unable to muster the required strength from the Mexicano community or to gain favor among a constant stream of white newcomers who knew little of old Hispanic San Antonio.

About the only other county in the surrounding area showing a political animation akin to Béxar was Wilson county to the east. There, M. M. Zaragosa was tax assessor in the early eighties, V. F. Caravajal was county clerk, and Manuel J. Ximénez was tax assessor toward the latter half of the nineties.[38] More local political activity there and in the other central Texas regions probably existed, but that awaits a more meticulous study by historians. The same applies to the forgotten Mexicanos of the Texas panhandle who in Oldham county in the early 1880s displayed their political interest in the personalities of Juan D. Ertego, who served as county treasurer, and Eliso Borrego, the tax assessor.[39]

In the Rio Grande region where communities traced their origins to the 1740s and 1750s and where Anglo Americans did not enter until the ending of the Mexican War, Tejanos also pursued political activity as a form of preserving their gains accumulated under Spain and Mexico. (See Table 3 for a profile of the Hispanic and Anglo populations of the Lower Rio Grande Valley in 1850 and 1900). The old families, especially, rapidly adjusted to the post-Mexican War setting and continued to play, along with the Anglo minority that dominated politics, a role in community affairs. In the first election held at Laredo in 1847 under the laws of Texas, for example, thirty-seven of the forty voters were Tejanos as were five of the seven candidates running for justice of the peace. José María García and Juan Salinas served as part of the first county commission in Starr County (1848); A. A. Salinas in Cameron County (1848); and Yndalecio Domínguez and Marciano Munguía in Hidalgo County (1852).[40] During Reconstruction, that section took an anti-Democratic stand while supporting the Radical Republican philosophy of the popular South Texas native, Edmund J. Davis. According to one embittered white man in 1868, Mexicans in Zapata County all supported Davis. "I will assure the General that no planter ever had on his plantation a more cunning scoundrel of a nigger," went on the griever, "than the generality of Mexicans will average in this county." Furthermore, he alleged, County Judge Lauriano Vidaurri, a Davis appointee, was completely incompetent and unqualified for office.[41] In the gubernatorial election of 1870, Brownsville Mexicans were reported flocking to apply for naturalization to support their old leader Davis, much to the chagrin of conservatives. According to one newspaper, the Ku Klux Klan

Table 3. Comparative Characteristics of the Mexican-American and Anglo-American Populations of the Lower Rio Grande Valley (Webb, Cameron, Starr) in 1850 and 1900[a]

	1850[b]	1900
Population of Counties	9,920	49,311
Percent Mexican-American Population	79.8%	92.4%
Percent Anglo-American Population	10.3%	6.1%
Estimated Number Mexican-Americans	7,916	45,573
Estimated Number Anglo-Americans	1,022	3,008
Percent Mexican-American Rural Residents	NA	70.9%
Percent Anglo-American Rural Residents	NA	31.0%
Percent Mexican-American City Residents	NA	29.1%
Percent Anglo-American City Residents	NA	69.0%
Estimated Number of Mexican-American Rural Residents	NA	32,304
Estimated Number of Anglo-American Rural Residents	NA	932
Estimated Number of Mexican-American City Residents	NA	13,259
Estimated Number of Anglo-American City Residents	NA	2,076

[a]This table compares information for what the 1850 census taker termed the "Lower Rio Grande Valley" with the information for Webb, Cameron, and Starr counties in the 1900 census returns.

[b]NA means *not applicable*. There were no urban centers in the Rio Grande Valley in 1850, thus comparisons between rural and city residents are meaningless.

planned to interfere in the naturalization and registration of voters, but the Loyal League, composed of 200 men of the Davis Brigade, stood in readiness to protect the Mexican voters should the fear prove true.[42]

In Laredo, where a Tejano majority has always been the case, the *guaraches* (Republicans) and *botas* (Democrats) vied with each other for political supremacy, and each year Tejanos in the city clashed enthusiastically for the right to serve. Naturally, Spanish surnamed mayors from both parties won regularly: Antonacio Vidaurri in 1877; Rosendo García in 1878; Julian García in 1879 and 1880; Darío Sánchez in 1883; and Porfirio Benavides in 1881, 1882, and 1884.[43] Other victories accrued to Tejanos in lesser capacities. In 1881, Juan García won election for alderman of Ward No. 2 and

Dave Gonzales for alderman of Ward No. 6, and in 1884, Eloy Arguindque for alderman of Ward No. 1 and Julian García and Arturo Sabires for aldermen of Ward No. 2.[44] City officers in the 1890s included R. Vidaurri, secretary of treasury, M. García, assessor and collector, and José María Ugarte, market manager.[45] Santos Benavides represented the area in the state legislature in the 1880s.[46]

At the county level in the 1880s, Justice J. M. Vela served in the Webb county court, José María Rodríguez was Webb county judge, Cayetano de la Garza was county surveyor, Rosendo García was tax assessor, L. R. Ortiz wàs county clerk, and Darío Sánchez was tax collector.[47] Slates of predominately Spanish surnamed candidates were common: in 1884 Tomás Villastrigo ran for inspector; V. Juárez for commissioner, and M. Juárez for justice.[48] Among officeholders in the 1890s were Judge Rodríguez, Juan V. Benevades (county attorney), David Sánchez (tax collector), A. R. García (county attorney), A, M. Bruni (county treasurer), and A. Quintanilla (tax assessor).[49] Other political figures in that era were Amador Sánchez, district clerk, and Augustín Salinas.[50]

It was this kind of feverish involvement in politics that produced the so-called Laredo City Election Riot of April 1886. Both political factions, the botas and guaraches (Anglos and Mexicans made up both), held regular weekly processions that year, making political speeches and shooting anvils and cannons while creating other sorts of excitement. The recent killing of bota member H. Douglas, a city alderman, had created a tense setting for election day. On April 7, 1886, the botas decided upon a mock funeral to celebrate their victory over the guaraches—the election had been the day before. The guaraches in turn appeared in armed groups on the streets to prevent the bota procession. Inevitably, gun fire rang out and a general fusillade ensued causing a number of deaths and injuries, many among Tejanos. The confrontation quickly subsided with the intervention of peace keeping forces.[51] Tejanos took politics seriously in Laredo—even to the point of dying.

That social distinction existed between the Tejano poor and the older families who occupied political office was less important than that the presence of the latter permitted the poor to live in an environment of familiarity. Spanish-surnamed people served as county clerks, as supervisors of elections in the several wards, as policemen,[52] and the familiar Spanish prevailed over English in court proceedings. According to a New York *Times* correspondent in 1880:

The city's court proceedings were conducted in the Spanish language and at the present time American citizens who cannot speak or understand a word of English, and who know nothing but Mexican, served on the juries of the county and city, an interpreter being used to translate the evidence, the charge of the judge, and all proceedings.[53]

The pervasiveness of this kind of Tejano ambient not only called upon the Anglo minority to adjust to the Tejano way, but exemplified the salutary environment where Mexicanos underwent the subtle process of adjusting to American political life in their own language.

As in the case of Laredo, Brownsville Tejano elites adapted to the post-Mexican War political system and joined whites in controlling affairs in the town and county. During Reconstruction, Mexicanos played their part in rallies and conventions, registered before the Cameron County Board of Registrars, and won appointment by the Reconstruction government to various civil offices.[54] Tejanos served as mayors, as was the case when Thomas Hinojosa was elected in 1883, others as county treasurer (Celedonio Garza in the eighties and nineties), county attorneys (Augustín Celaya in the 1890s), and political tickets often displayed Tejano candidates running for such positions as county treasurer, county tax assessor, and county hide and animal inspector.[55]

In Starr County, Mexicanos vied regularly for political office, often against Mexicanos from opposing parties or factions, so that incumbents not surprisingly featured Spanish-surnames—among them Augustín de la Peña, assessor, Santana Caro, inspector, and Juan Escobar and Ramón Gonzales, commissioners, in the mid-1880s.[56] In the 1890s, Cruz Tijerina, M. P. Juárez, Emilio Zarate and E. Valásquez served as county treasurers, Pedro López and C. P. Albares as county surveyors, Braulio Ramírez and Julian Ramírez as tax assessors, Rafael Martínez and J. C. Guerra as tax collectors, and C. Valle as county clerk.[57] Tejanos also took an interest in national politics. They participated in a Republican procession held in Rio Grande City in November 1880 for presidential candidate James Garfield and his running mate Chester Arthur.[58] They also were involved in the politics of grass-roots conventions—at times attending state conventions as when Manuel Guerra, a successful entrepreneur from Rio Grande City and a political boss in the county, attended one in 1896.[59]

The same adaptation to the political process and a like desire to penetrate the system displayed itself elsewhere. Citing the minutes of the commissioners' first meeting (as taken from the first book of record of Nueces County), the Corpus Christi *Weekly Caller* of March 15, 1885 reported that among seven officials chosen, José de Alba won selection as chief justice and Carlos de la Garza as commissioner in July 1845. As Corpus Christi grew in the 1880s, Mexicanos continued involving themselves visibly in the city's politics. During presidential races, they took part in local campaigns: in the election of 1884, the Mexican Democrats and a Mexican band participated in the torchlight procession held on election eve; and in 1888 Tejanos helped in organizing the Democratic club to support President Grover Cleveland.[60] In the late 1890s, Corpus Christi claimed both a Club Republicano México Texano and a Club Demócrata México Texano.[61] As in San Antonio, Tejanos in Corpus Christi served as bailiffs and members of court juries in the 1880s and often appeared as officers assigned to hold elections for public school trustees in the several Nueces County districts.[62]

In Duval County, participation in politics was through the activities of the guaraches and botas. Through the two *partidos* (political parties), which included Anglo American politicians as well, Mexican Americans attended grass-roots political conventions, thus determining the direction of county government. By injecting their voices into precinct and county conventions, they helped determine the selection of delegates to congressional, senatorial, and representative district conventions as well as state conventions, selecting, for example, Camelio Ramírez as delegate to the state convention in 1886. Through this involvement, both parties elected members to various city or county posts. Voters, similarly interested in politics, demanded that Anglo members of the *partidos* address them in Spanish. In 1888, an Anglo politician reportedly drew applause from his Spanish-speaking audience by advocating the tariff protection of wool, arguing that Duval county was a wool and stock community.

Keenly interested in politics, Duval politicians involved themselves ambitiously in county politics. The year 1888 seemed to have been a particularly intense one as the botas announced a slate for county positions that included Julián Palacios for county judge, Abalino C. Tovar for assessor of taxes, Juan Pinz for treasurer, and Vidal García for inspector of hides and animals. Both partidos seized upon the *Diez y Seis de Septiembre* festivities at San Diego for electioneering, and the following month the guaraches imported Francisco S. Mendosa from Brownsville for some political oratory. Immediately preceding the election, the guaraches staged a grand rally before some two thousand people holding torches, banners, transparencies with mottoes and emblems, and American and Mexican flags. A band led the crowds along a line of march illuminated by Chinese lanterns to an area where Mexican American politicians addressed them.

Besides its intensity, the campaign caused the death of Anastacio Gómez in San Diego following an incident in which Francisco de Gonzales, editor of the newspaper *El Clarín*, had harassed Gómez' boy as the youngster, following a spring wagon carrying *bota* musicians, filed past the newspaper office. Gonzales reportedly pushed and punched some of the juveniles as he shouted "Qué Viva el Guarache!" The next day the elder Anastacio sought out Gonzales in a barber shop where the *guarache* had gone for a shave. Harsh words followed as Gómez challenged Gonzales to a fist fight ouside Encarnación Yzaguirre's barber shop. As both approached the door, Gonzales produced a gun and turned upon Gómez, apparently in an effort to ward off his challenger. Surprised, Gómez attempted to take the gun from Gonzales but received a mortal wound in the scuffle. Deputy Sheriff Lino Cuéllar, coming upon the scene, disarmed Gonzales, arrested him and escorted him to jail.

Peña in the southwestern part of Duval county, showed the same enthusiasm for politics and, there, the botas and guaraches also competed for county offices with equal vigor. In 1888, for example, bota candidates came from San Diego—"snake pizen," music and all—to lure voters into their ranks, and Dr. Andrew R. Valls of Benavides warned the Mexicans that Anglos were not giving them justice. When the guaraches arrived later, they gave a *baile* while several of their candidates made speeches, one of them telling Mexicanos to adopt English and educate their children so they could take part in government.

Given the racial views whites held toward Mexicanos in the nineteenth century, Mexican American cultural dominance in Duval

County, and the apprehension of whites over being outnumbered in practically all areas of the county, it was inevitable that racial feelings found their way into politics. According to reports from a newspaper correspondent, Mexican Americans in San Diego held a political meeting in July 1888 to organize for the approaching November election, their object, as the journalist understood it, to put "a full Mexican ticket out for all county offices of Duval in November." According to one source, representatives from Starr County participated in the proceedings where the convention selected delegates to meet in Concepción for the nomination of candidates. When the convention finally met, though, expectations failed to develop, because the ticket included both Anglo and Mexican American candidates. But fears of complete Mexican American domination lingered as another white newspaperman interpreted the election as a "war of races" between Americans and Mexicanos, and of violent opposition between them. "Unless Duval can secure the immigration of American citizens between now and the next election the chances are that the Mexicans will nominate and elect their candidates beyond any question," warned the correspondent. The feelings of hostility seemingly colored other elections, for in February 1892, someone signing himself "White Man" reported that the "White Men's Party" had emerged in response to racial agitation by Mexican Americans. Who was it, he asked, who had introduced the cry of Mexicans versus Americans in Duval county politics and injected "Raza for Carerra" to inflame the Mexicans against the Americans. The "White Men's Party" campaigned, according to the Beeville *Picayune*, on white men's principles.

In Benavides, political activity included serious electioneering, but bailes and other cultural forms also found their way into the campaign to attract voters. The town shared its load in county politics and often hosted grass-roots conventions.

Involvement in county politics by Mexican Americans was accompanied by participation in both city and county government. In the nineteenth century, and after, Spanish surnames regularly appeared in the official vote. Political incumbents included Judge S. Cuellar in Benavides in the 1880s, county commissioner G. D. García, county judge F. G. Tovar, and county assessor Pedro Eznal in the early 1890s. Manuel Garza Díaz and Julián Palacios served as justices of the peace for their respective precincts in the 1880s and 1890s. Lino Cuellar and Nic Benavides served as deputy sheriffs for the county in that same period.[63] Toward the end of the decade, Pedro Eznal became county clerk, Julián Palacios the county treasurer, and Arturo D. García the assessor.[64]

In the other areas of South Texas, Tejano incumbents similarly gave a semblance of the familiar to Tejano common folk coming in contact with a political system institutionally unfriendly to them. In Zapata County, for example, Spanish-surnamed officials often ministered to their needs: Camilo G. Davila was clerk for the Zapata County district in 1860, Isidro Vela was serving as chief justice of Zapata County when Mexican Civil War *guerrilleros* killed him in 1863,[65] and in the 1880s, Eluterio de la Garza, José D. Uribe, and G. Treviño were the county assessors and M. M. Uribe was county treasurer. Others serving in that decade were Felix García and Valentín López as county clerks. In the following decade, L. C. Navarro and Yndalecio Uribe were the county surveyors, Erasmus Uribe was county clerk, B. M. Gutiérrez, G. Treviño, and Z. Domínguez were tax assessors, and José D. Uribe, E. Flores, and A. Marulanda were county treasurers. The county judge for almost the entire last two decades of the century was J. Antonio G. Navarro.[66] In neighboring Hidalgo County, M. C. Garza served as county treasurer and A. Salinas as county surveyor in the latter 1880s, while T. M. de la Vina was the county judge, José Cárdenas the county treasurer, Camilo Pérez the county surveyor, and T. E. Olivares the tax assessor in the latter nineties.[67] In 1887, José María Guerra served as justice of the peace in Encinal County.[68]

In other Texas border cities, a similar identification with political position prevailed. In the latter nineties, A. García served as Dimmit County tax assessor; T. San Miguel as Maverick County treasurer, and in Presidio County, D. Alarcón served as tax assessor and in other capacities throughout the decade.[69]

Similar circumstances prevailed in the El Paso Valley. Because whites did not arrive in great numbers in that part of the state until the 1880s, Mexicanos continued presiding over politics there until demographic changes supplanted them. (See Table 4 for a profile of the Hispanic and Anglo populations of El Paso County in 1860 and 1900). While in El Paso proper[70] Tejano political incumbency declined perceptibly afterwards,[71] the same things did not occur at valley communities, for although a minority in town, Mexicanos retained the numerical advantage in the county areas. Thus Tejanos, most of them old time politicians who had served since after the

Table 4. Comparative Characteristics of the Mexican-American and Anglo-American Populations of El Paso County 1860 and 1900

	1860[a]	1900
Population of the County	4,640	24,033
Percent Mexican-American Population	74.7%	55.5%
Percent Anglo-American Population	8.3%	38.1%
Estimated Number Mexican-Americans	3,466	13,338
Estimated Number Anglo-Americans	385	9,175
Percent Mexican-American Rural Residents	NA	50.3%
Percent Anglo-American Rural Residents	NA	16.2%
Percent Mexican-American City Residents	NA	49.7%
Percent Anglo-American City Residents	NA	83.8%
Estimated Number of Mexican-American Rural Residents	NA	6,709
Estimated Number of Anglo-American Rural Residents	NA	1,483
Estimated Number of Mexican-American City Residents	NA	6,629
Estimated Number of Anglo-American City Residents	NA	7,674

[a]NA means *not applicable*. Since there were no urban centers in El Paso County in 1860, comparison of rural and city residents is meaningless.

Mexican War, continued occupying political positions, albeit precariously. In the first post-Civil War election in 1866, Republian Mexicanos elected included J. J. Luján for county clerk, Máximo Aranda for district clerk, and José María Gonzales, Julián Arías, and Gregorio N. García for county judges, Máximo Aranda was deputy collector, and Demetrio Urtiaga and Porfirio García served as justices of the peace.[72] In the 1880s, Tejanos wrested enough concessions from the Democratic Ring that now controlled county and city politics to continue occupying posts in the county commissioners' court—among them José María Gonzales, Juan Armendariz, Benigno Alderete, and G. N. García (replaced in October, 1888, by Jesús Montes when García accepted the position as customs inspector at San Elizario)—while José Baca was county judge in the early decade and men like Manuel E. Flores, J. A. Escajeda, and Octaviano A. Larrazolo—who later in his career served as governor and U.S. senator from New Mexico—served as district clerks, and

A. Guerra as county assessor.[73] Listed in the official directory of
1883 were justices of the peace José A. Apodaca (Precinct No. 1,
P. Rivera, constable), Demetrio Urtiga (Precinct No. 3, C. Marquez,
constable), Manuel E. Flores, president of the board of school
examiners, as well as Octaviano Larrazolo likewise a member of
the school examiners' board.[74] During county elections, others
acted as presiding officers at Socorro, San Elizario, Ysleta, and
Cuadrilla.[75]

More or less the same persisted until the 1890s. Larrazola was
elected as district attorney, José Escajeda as district clerk, the
county commissioners' court continued to include men like Juan
Armendariz and Jesús Montes, and other Tejanos retained super-
vision over precincts on election day.[76] The list of others seeking
office was lengthy and under the banner of both Republicans and
Democrats. Running in 1894 were M. E. Flores (Republican) against
J. A. Escajeda (Democrat) for district clerk and Seferiano Durán
(Republican) against José Apodaca (Democrat) for hides and animal
inspector in El Paso County.[77] In November 1898, the Democratic
ticket included Ike Alderete for district clerk, Juan Armendariz (of
Precinct No. 3) for county commissioner, P. Rivera (of Precinct
No. 3) for justice of the peace, and Franco Muñoz (Precinct No. 2)
and Miguel Padilla (of Precinct No. 3) for constables.[78] In January
1899, the commissioners' court appointed Jesús Montes road commissioner for Precinct No. 3 (Socorro).[79] Most of these political
figures participated in various county conventions, both Republican and Democratic.

In the smaller villages in the county where Tejanos remained in
the majority (Ysleta and San Elizario particularly), Tejano supremacy lingered.[80] In the 1860s and 1870s, leading figures at San
Elizario included Clemente Pérez, J. M. Luján, Telésforo Montes,
Máximo Andrade, and Gregorio García. Some of these men were
among those attending a San Elizario Democratic meeting in 1872
held to choose a delegate to represent El Paso County at a Gonzales, Texas, convention which in turn would nominate a candidate
for the Fourth Congressional District.[81] In the 1880s and 1890s,
Tejano figures still tended to dominate political positions.[82]

At Ysleta, politicial figures included Martín and Benigno Alderete,
Pablo Romero, José M. Gonzales, and José A. Apadoca.[83] In the
1890s town politics involved a lively rivalry between factions dominated by Tejanos (although whites also participated). In the mu-

nicipal election of April 1, 1890, the two tickets, one a Republican, the other a "People's Party" (Democrat), contested the vote: the Democrats claimed victory by a fifteen-vote majority, and the Republicans charged the opposition with voting fifty-seven Mexican nationals illegally. The dispute centered around the candidates for mayor, Republican I. G. Gaal, the incumbent, and Benigno Alderete, the Democratic challenger (People's Party). Ultimately, the Alderete faction forcefully removed Gaal through a rump council, only to see Gaal regain control of the original council. But, when the El Paso courts finally passed judgment on the election results, Alderete took control as the rightful claimant. [84]

While belonging to the Valley's elite Tejano element, like others elsewhere, these men often voiced the needs of less fortunate Tejanos. Thus Víctor L. Ochoa in April 1891, spoke before an assemblage of 300 Mexicanos at Little Plaza in El Paso and called upon them to organize for self-protection. He urged his listeners to stand together and demand the following from the city: not let its public work out to contractors but elect a superintendent of public works and let him employ labor from among resident citizens of El Paso (and not to engage cheap labor from the other side of the river as contractors did); fix a schedule of salaries to be paid for such labor; and pay the same salary to Mexican policemen and other Mexican employees of the city that it paid to whites performing the same kind of work. [85]

Tejano politicians from privileged backgrounds participated in the political system with assistance from the lower classes and in turn represented the interests of their supporters. What they could carry out, however, depended on the limitations allowed by white society. A political system seeking to render Mexicanos powerless and to keep them in their place through outright repression, disfranchisement, exclusion from political parties, gerrymandering, cooptation, and the mobilization of bias, hardly tolerated revolutionary politics of an all Tejano government (unless its Americanism was unquestionable). The Tejano politician running on a strident pro-*raza* platform could hardly look forward to a long-term incumbency in that era.

Given a situation in which the system at large sought to suffocate their intentions, it was almost inevitable that some would turn toward unconventional means in their efforts to wrench concessions from that system. As a vehicle that offered them certain rewards in return for their vote, political bossism (individual and machine) seemed to provide that alternative when necessary. But, if one is to believe the accounts of opponents and have-nots, bossism involved such stratagems as taking out intention papers for noncitizens, herding these newly eligible balloters along with Tejano voters into deserted halls, supplying them with whiskey and rations, and marching them to the polls and coercing them to vote in a particular way. According to these reports, Tejano "cross-mark patriots" voted blindly without knowledge of the ballot, the law, or the system of government.[86]

Such tales contain certain truths but some members of the Mexican community deplored the practices. For one thing, Mexicanos echoed the Gilded Age Populist demand for reform through, for example, the introduction of the Australian ballot. In late 1891, Mexicans from Starr County—where, according to one paper, "the Aztec voter is only a tool in the hands of the corrupt politician"— were among those clamoring for the secret ballot. Since the Australian ballot system had been defeated in the 1891 session of the legislature and the constitutional amendment recently adopted for the registration of voters in cities of 10,000 or more population did not apply to any portion of the border sections, citizens of Rio Grande City (Starr County) were most vociferous. In a set of published resolutions, they urged the governor to include their recommendation for the adoption of the Australian ballot or recommend some other system of ballot reform at the extra session of the legislature for March or April 1892.[87] In Duval County, a petition circulating among Mexican (as well as white) citizens, also condemned political bosses for corralling "lower class Mexicans" and driving them to the polls like sheep and voting them. They criticized bossism for utilizing what they called a population of Mexicans who were neither by language, tradition, nor customs in accord with the institutions of the country and who merely declared their intentions of becoming individual citizens of the nation for the purpose of voting and sitting on juries. These petitioners similarly called for amending the election laws so that henceforth only those who were *bona fide* citizens of the country would be permitted to vote or serve on juries, the mere declaration of intent by those ignorant of the laws, language, and customs not to be considered a sufficient qualification for exercising the prerogatives of citizenship.[88] And in a mass meeting in De Witt County held in November 1884,

Tejanos resolved unanimously that the Mexican vote was emphatically not for sale and condemned George M. Pridgen who had accused them of selling their vote.[89]

For another thing, if Tejanos voted "blindly" as alleged by the have-nots, why would they have voted for Tejano candidates if whites with the economic advantage could buy their vote every time? Why would they have organized in protest groups against injustices? Why would they have divided into political factions along particular ideologies, and how would they have known where to go to pay taxes, to register vital statistics, and so on? Contrary to accounts that critics of bossism recorded about "dumb" Mexicans, many Tejano voters knew enough of the system to realize that concessions could not be extracted through the same institutional channels that were intended to oppress them. Probably, techniques throughout the state resembled those used by El Paso Mexican American "bosses." There, Tejano *políticos* received public jobs and patronage in return for organizing and influencing their fellow Mexicans to vote in a particular way. The historian Mario T. García writes:

Mexican Americans [in El Paso] organized themselves in what amounted to pressure groups within the Ring in order to extract from it not only political appointments and public employment for Mexicans, but also ethnic protection for the Mexican population of the city and county. In addition, the development of a sub-rosa machine by the Mexican Americans warned the Ring that the Mexican vote could be turned against them in favor of reform Democrats or the Republicans.[90]

And in San Antonio it was the Tejanos serving in various bureaucratic capacities who often took the lead in issues related to the barrio. Why they did so, when it may have imperiled their position, is open to conjecture. It may have been for personal reasons, or because, when Anglos spoke of Mexicans in racist terms, they also felt the sting of those remarks, or even because they realized, perhaps too late, that they were not getting from white society what they thought they rightfully deserved. Whatever the reason, they cannot be stereotyped as timid fellows in complete collusion with white America.[91]

Bosses found the Tejano vote recalcitrant sometimes, which is why machines worked feverishly at election time to "buy" the Mexican vote. Men like Jim Wells of South Texas, for example, did not find Mexicanos ever-faithful, indeed, on every election he found himself spending more money than anticipated for the upcoming contest.[92] Bosses knew further that if a politician did not deliver he could find himself vying for the same vote on election day as his opponent would certainly offer the same thing to buy the Mexican vote.

Tejanos, then, used the political system in a rational attempt to make it responsive to their needs. They voted, attended political conventions, and served in several elected or appointed capacities at the city or county level according to their particular political views. Tejano *políticos* represented integrated constituencies (both white and Tejano), Mexican Americans only, and still others (like politicians elsewhere) served only for purposes of self-aggrandizement. Serving at the local level may have prevented Tejano politicians from making an impact on the government in Austin and making it responsive to Tejano needs, but white society placed too many hurdles before the Tejano politicians to allow them election to higher offices (although a few served in the state legislature during the century). Furthermore, considering the times and environment in which Tejanos persevered, election at the city and county level seemed more important. For it was there that ordinary people came in close contact with politics and therefore where the occasion called for politicians who spoke Spanish and understood Tejano cultural ways.

And, if many of these politicians descended from the "better class" who many times did not represent the interests of the poorer Mexicanos, many others did. Anyway, such has been the history of oppressed people. It is the intelligent and the better off among them, those who have learned the system that infiltrate it either as opportunists or reformers. If they extracted only minor concessions, it had more to do with the strength of the institutions maintaining Mexican Americans in subservience than their incapacity to perceive the means to prod the system to act in behalf of Mexicanos. Far more importantly, the pervasiveness of these political figures, in areas where Tejanos lived, allowed Mexicanos, who were recent arrivals in the state or were only slightly acquainted with politics, the necessary environment for going on when forces worked to keep them in a condition of general powerlessness.

Plainly, the interpretation that the traditional studies of Tejano politics have advanced is misleading.[93] Their argument that Tejanos were passive figures who sold their vote for a song (or beer or ice cream) is a shallow description of one-dimensional characters seemingly unable to think intelligently. The authors of these older histories subscribed to the now anachronistic premise that Mexican culture was a traditional one tied to regressive values. Their documentation was meager and hence they were unable to see the diversity of Tejanos politics as described herein. Moreover, those writers emphasized the politics of the twentieth century (those views themselves are in need of revision) to draw conclusions for the nineteenth.

From what can be seen from this study, many Tejanos thought and acted politically. The Tejanos may not have understood all the intricacies of the political process, but, they certainly grasped what American perquisites were about. They sought involvement for more than the election-eve treats. Would women and children who amassed with their menfolk to protest indignities do so for purposes of being rewarded with ice cream and beer? No, like other people elsewhere whether oppressed or not, they saw politics as a way of participating historically and moving forward—even if at times that advancement was horizontal rather than vertical. Instead of being the static, backward, and nonjoining type depicted by past histories, Tejanos were a people with many dimensions who sought betterment in ways similar to their white and black counterparts in nineteenth century Texas.

3

Obreros and the Rural Scene

The manner of making a living in rural Texas did not differ markedly from what it had been under Spain and Mexico. Economic life remained basically agricultural after the Texas Revolution of 1836. Even the state's switch from a ranching to a farming economy in the 1880s and to commercial farming in the waning years of the century remained within the sector of agriculture. Mexicanos, therefore, continued working at agrarian jobs. As is indicated by the federal censuses, Tejanos in mid-century were entrenched in a rural society (see Table 5) while Anglos, still in the process of migration to the state, dominated the towns. After the 1850s, however, management of the agrarian economy progressively fell into the hands of Anglo American capitalists intent on using the labor of Mexicanos. The early rural structure thus changed notably. While the proportion of Anglo rural labor involved in farming increased dramatically from 1850 to 1900, the opposite occurred for Tejanos. Between 1850 and 1900, the number of farmers in the rural Mexicano labor force fell from 32.6 percent to 14.8 percent. The greater part of the Tejano community was then restricted to the more menial tasks of ranch and field work (see Table 5). Yet, these changes did not demand a new type of rural worker; it only called for more laborers with skills like those Tejanos already had.

Mexicanos, thus, carried on old labor methods and techniques. In the ranches, particularly, patterns traceable to the sheep and cattle cultures of the Iberian peninsula continued. Since they made

Table 5. Most Frequently Held Jobs Among Rural Workers, 1850 (1860) and 1900[a]

	Mexican-Americans		Anglo-Americans	
	1850 (1860)	*1900*	*1850 (1860)*	*1900*
Farmer	189 (32.6%)	301 (14.8%)	2 (0.7%)	59 (28.1%)
Laborer	108 (18.6%)	1,011 (49.8%)	14 (5.1%)	34 (16.2%)
Servant	38 (6.6%)	110 (5.4%)	—	9 (4.3%)
Carpenter	37 (6.4%)	30 (1.5%)	18 (6.5%)	—
Tailor	29 (5.0%)	—	3 (1.1%)	—
Cartman	21 (3.6%)	—	—	—
Shoemaker	21 (3.6%)	—	2 (0.7%)	—
Herdsman	20 (3.5%)	—	2 (0.7%)	—
Seamstress	17 (2.9%)	23 (1.1%)	—	—
Clerk	—	—	18 (6.5%)	—
Stonemason	1 (0.2%)	—	2 (0.7%)	—
Merchant	1 (0.2%)	29 (1.4%)	24 (8.7%)	5 (2.4%)
Military (enlisted)	—	—	54 (19.5%)	10 (4.8%)
Ranger (working for military)	—	—	49 (17.7%)	—
Wagoner	6 (1.0%)	—	6 (2.2%)	—
Miner	—	86 (4.2%)	—	—
Vaquero	—	77 (3.8%)	—	5 (2.4%)
Sheepherder	—	63 (3.1%)	—	—
Laundress	—	27 (1.3%)	—	—
Teacher	—	—	—	10 (4.8%)
	488 (84.1%)	1,757 (86.4%)	194 (70.1%)	132 (63.0%)
	N=580	N=2,029	N=277	N=210

[a]The 1850 (1860) results given in this table are based on samples drawn from the census of the rural areas in Béxar County and the Lower Rio Grande Valley in 1850, and in El Paso County in 1860. The 1900 findings are based on samples drawn from the census of the rural areas of Béxar, El Paso, Cameron, Starr, and Webb counties in 1900.

up the core of the pastoral work force, Tejanos ran things according
to traditions generations old. In the course of many decades, they
imposed an indelible imprint on habits and rhythms and added a
coloration to the means of production that distinguished the border
sections from regions of the United States where Tejanos played no
part in their transformation into a capitalist success.

Very naturally, then, Tejanos turned to their ranching skills in
the decades after the Texas Revolution as they made the transition
into the new society. In a number of works, historians and students
of the western tradition have described at length this particular
Mexican deftness,[1] but less than a handful have focused on the
Texas *vaquero, pastor,* and farm worker. And those who do touch
upon the Tejanos' contribution depict them as colorful and quaint
personalities who were excellent as bronco busters and ranch hands
for white ranchers. Much is left unsaid about them as human beings
who knew the animals they handled by instinct, who dominated
the range and preserved their manhood by taking pride in what
they did best, who used their skills as a way of providing for their
families, and who could even look forward to climbing up the
economic ladder and become stockmen themselves.

Typical of the figures for whom romantic lore predominates
over historical description is the *mesteñeros* (mustangers). In truth,
the mesteñeros typified the Tejano obrero who had formed his
skills through trial and error, who had discarded the unworkable
along the way, who had the insight to improvise techniques that
rendered him the expected outcome, who had the organizational
qualities to inspire team play, and who looked upon his job as a task
to be done well and not haphazardly so long as it earned him his
livelihood. In the decades after the Texas Revolution, these mustangers routinely sallied into the western prairies after mustangs,
rendered them serviceable as saddle steeds within days, and sold
them to Anglos wanting horses.[2] Others continued the prerevolu-
tionary practice of driving herds annually to the United States for
good prices.[3] When an opportunity presented itself for marketing
the wild horses, as when Zachery Taylor's army of occupation passed
through the Nueces County area in 1846, Tejanos made it an occasion to drive good bargains for the mustangs.[4]

The mustang business continued until the 1870s, at which time
the number of wild horses thinned out from a combination of causes; mainly, though, because of the roundups, fencing, and attacks

by ranchers who saw them as nuisances that lured away their domesticated stock. Until that time, mesteñeros stalked the central and southern areas for the wild beasts, continuing old techniques of capture or improving upon them. Methods differed according to the circumstances, but a favorite plan called for constructing a *corral de aventura* (or pen to catch mustangs) in a clump of trees or brushes. Inserting mesquite posts deep into the ground, inclining them slightly inwardly, and tramping around them carefully, mesteñeros lashed the poles together at the top with strong rawhide thongs, creating a fence somewhat elastic but hard to break. From the entrance of the large circular pen they projected wings out into the prairie—the longer of these V-shaped wings extending more than half a mile, the shorter about half as long. The gate consisted of strong poles, to be closed at the opportune moment. Every effort was made to conceal man's handiwork, and the pens were situated and disguised so that the mustangs could not see the wings until they were between them. A product of improvisation, the entire trap consisted of nature's yields—mesquite, brush, treetops, rawhide, and other products.

After making these preparations, a *recibidor* (receiver) stationed himself at either wing. The *aventadores,* or starters of the *caballada,* located their prey and gave pursuit, hoping to chase the herd in the direction of the longer wing so that the *recibidor* there could turn the stampeding animals down the wing toward the gate. At this moment, the receiver from the opposite wing pointed in to keep the horses against the wing. Once the mustangs had been driven within the confines of the trap by the mesteñeros, the *encerrador* (the closer) hastily shut the gate, throwing a blanket over the poles to keep the horses away from it.

In times of drought, the mesteñeros awaited their prey at available waterholes. In such a case, they built *corrales de espiar* (or watch pens) near the watering spot with one wing reaching to the water and the other leading out so that the mustangs could be chased into the enclosure readily. Stationing themselves in strategic places nearby, they emerged stealthily from their hideouts to force the horses into the pen.

Or they could "walk the mustangs down." A lone man on horseback simply started following the band of mustangs. Although initially frightening them into flight, he followed on, until, after several days of the same running away and catching up, the walker came to be gradually accepted by the herd. Soon he could ride about the horses without disturbing them. Then, as he maneuvered the herd into or near the wings of a preestablished pen, confederates appeared to rush the mustangs into the corral.

But other means worked equally well. Good riders would take out after mustangs and run them down until within roping distance. Using a forty to sixty foot *reata* (rope) tied to the pommel of the saddle, the mesteñero held it in a coil in his left hand and the noose (about eight to twelve feet in circumference) in the right. Pursuing the mustang until sufficiently near, perhaps some thirty yards, he threw the noose around the mustang's neck and brought his horse to a sudden stop, thus immediately prostrating the victim.[5] Captured mares might be hocked, that is, rendered lame by cutting one of the leading tendons of the leg to prevent them from escaping. These horses made good broods when crossed with domestic stock, and in the 1830s some rancheros sold profitably from such large caballadas.[6]

Procedure, of course, did not restrict itself to any one of these methods, for topography and circumstances often demanded improvisation. On such occasions, rope loops were fastened to strong tree branches some sixty feet from the ground. By running the mustangs into the traps, the mesteñeros could catch them in the treacherous nooses. Because of the damage usually done to the animals, this generally proved rather ineffective.

A variety of taming schemes followed the catching. In the corral method, the mesteñeros threw a rope from the outside and dragged a horse through an opening in the fence made by removing some posts. To take the mustangs away, the mesteñeros could neck them to gentle horses or burros, fasten heavy wooden clogs around the front legs just above the hoof, or they could "side-line" them, that is, tie one end of a short rope around a front leg and the other end around a hind leg so as to handicap the wild mustangs and drive them away with gentle horses. When they had been taken two or three days distant from their accustomed range and their straps were removed by degrees, the mustangs became manageable and controllable and soon gentle enough to drive foot-loose.

The mesteñeros might also select the best mustangs (and release the rest) and by starving, preventing them from rest, and continually keeping them in motion, gradually gentle them and finally accustom them to submit to the saddle and bridle. "For this business," wrote a publicist in the 1830s, "I presume there is no nation in the world superior to the Spaniards of Texas."[7]

Or the *jinetes* (broncobusters) could simply take the horse, put a bridle on it, take it into the spacious soft prairie, mount it, flag it with the quirt, and let it plunge and rear until it tired and was subdued. After a few of these operations, horses were fit for use.[8]

In a society where those who dominated the economy saw Mexicans as an indispensible proletariat, however, Tejano mesteñeros and vaqueros became men of the range serving enterpreneurs on the make. Indeed, by the 1840s, Tejanos were driving large herds of cattle and caballadas of horses and mules to Houston for Anglo ranchers.[9] In later decades, whites hired them for Midwest cattle drives. Estimates indicate that one-third of all men going up the trail with herds in the last three decades of the nineteenth century were Mexicans or Negroes.[10]

Virtually all ranchers, both Texas-Mexicans and Anglos, employed Tejano hands when available. In the Pecos area, the Mule Shoe outfit had a number of Mexicans, including cross-eyed Brígido Sánchez, whose own brand was *B +S: B* for Brígido, *S* for Sánchez, and the *+* for cross-eyed. Others working for the same outfit included Pedro Serravio, Juan Serravio, Juan Postard, Camilo Terranzas, Juan Cana, and the cook Mateo. In the Pearsall, Cotulla, and Uvalde area, recalled cattleman Bob Lauderdale, a rancher named Cassin had a "fine bunch of Mexicans working for him, who were very devoted to him and always very loyal to me. Margarito Ortiz was the one I always made strawboss when I had to leave the home ranch; then there was his brother, Manuel, and Florencio Torres, Justo Torres, Margil Torres, Pancho Prado, Eduardo. de Clasados, and others."[11]

In that capacity as loyal hands these vaqueros won a role in western history as mentors of the Anglo cowboy. Texas ranching came to rely on a Mexican plan of stock management taken from these legendary cowmen. Applying time-tested skills vaqueros taught Anglo cowboys and ranchers about roping, branding, and handling cattle. C. C. Cox recalled the following about roundups at his ranch near Corpus Christi in the 1850s:

Once a week or oftener we would make a rodeo or round up of the cattle. The plan is to have one herding ground on the Ranche—the cattle soon learn to run together at that place when they see the vaceroes on the wing—and when those on the outskirts of the range are started, the movement becomes general, and no prettier or more interesting sight can be imagined than a rodeo in full progress—every cow catches the alarm and starts off at a brisk trot headed for the herding ground and by no circuitus route, but across hills and valleys—and converging as they proceed to this point of destination. The wildest and strongest always take the lead—but all have the same spirit to get there as soon as possible—the vacaroes follow behind to hurry up the stragglers— and when the round up is made—whatever may have been the purpose of the drive—whether to cut out and deliver Beef cattle, to brand calves—or merely to take out & *Doctor* such as have wounds from the blow flies—the cattle are cut out & taken to the pen and the herd dissolves itself and again scatters over the range—

With horses a different system prevails—Horse stock is kept in *Remudas* that is saddle Horses with one Bell mare—and mares and young stock are kept in Manadas—or lots of about twenty five mares—with a stallion to each Manada—the Horse becomes very much attached to his harum and will allow them to scatter in and when a number of these Menadas are thrown together for any purpose when turned loose it is wonderful to see these Horses separating and collecting their several households together— they know every animal of their ranch as well as the owner and are exceedingly vicious to a reluctant member of their family.[12]

Work rhythms among vaqueros often displayed as much sport as skill. W. S. Henry, an officer in Zachary Taylor's army, noted in Corpus Christi:

In roping mules to mark them, a Mexican goes into the herd, and dexterously throws the lasso over the one designated, and then all hands bend on and pull him out of the pen. Just as he goes out, a man at the gate, with consumate skill, throws a lasso, and catches the mule by one of his legs; and then commences the sport. The object now is to throw them to be branded. Sometimes it was done easily, but often times the mule kicked, jumped, and performed all sorts of girations.[13]

Such professionalism added another dimension to Texas ranching: namely, the *rodeo*, or, more correctly, the traditional games of ranching expertise associated with roundups. Range prowess very naturally spilled over into entertainment forms such as the *carrera de gallos* (running of the rooster) or *coleadura de toros* (bull tailing) and other games identifiable with rodeos. In South Texas at least, the skills of livestock management and rodeo performances became synonymous with the legendary Kineños—the vaqueros of the King Ranch whose reputation persisted unblemished into the twentieth century.

If *vaqueros* knew that other men profited from their talents and that the ranches of southern and western Texas prospered because of them, they also knew that such an arrangement did not make them any less manly. Not uncommonly the work force consisted of a *mayordomo* (foreman) and subordinates who spoke the same language, observed the same customs, and manifested similar ranch skills. If they were an exploited group of men, they also knew that formidable mechanisms worked to keep them there and that, despite their dependency, it was they who on the range presided as lords, and not the man in the big house. Feelings of superiority, manhood, and worth compensated for an otherwise second-class status, and did much to blunt the oppression of living in the Lone Star State.

Although Tejanos have continued to work the ranches of Texas, their heyday, like that of other cowboys, began its decline by the late nineteenth century as more and more pasture land was turned into crop acreage. By the 1920s, many of the old vaqueros in South Texas were turning to cotton picking.[14] But their role in nineteenth century ranching history had left its imprint on equipment, clothing, language, techniques, and even on themes of the songs to be sung.

The mark these vaqueros left, as Carey McWilliams shows in his seminal synthesis *North From Mexico*, was the persistence of a tradition that went back to Spain. Handed down from father to son over generations, that method allowed Mexicans not only a way of making a living but also gave them a role in the cattle economy that made them much more than the stoic personalities described by many American writers. Their excellence came from maintaining and perpetuating a practical and useable trade, and not from a racial suitability to range and manual work as contemporaries contended.

The same importance of heritage for excellence among vaqueros was also present in the sheep industry; there, too, Tejanos continued the work habits of their Iberian forefathers. In their conquest of New Spain, the Spaniards had brought with them their sheep breeding systems, their sheepraising social structure and patterns of labor division, their flock grazing techniques, and much more. Thus as the sheep industry came into its own in the Rio Grande Plain in the period following the Civil War, and as it spread into the western regions of the state in the last quarter of the century,

Mexicanos also came to play a part in the tending of sheep stock. Their abilities as shepherds reportedly matched their proverbial talents as vaqueros. "They are better suited to this business than any other race in existence," remarked John C. Reid, an itinerant on his way to the newly acquired Gadsden Purchase.[15] "I suppose all nationalities can herd sheep," wrote H. Bundy, a Pleasanton, Texas, sheepman in 1879, "but I have never found but one—the Mexican—that would fill the bill with me. The Designer must have had him in mind when he made the shepherd."[16] In the San Angelo area in the 1880s, where Mexicanos made up the agricultural work force, they earned similar accolades from white observers.[17]

Through a combination of necessity and dedication to purpose, Mexicano shepherds gave southern and western Texas a distinct atmosphere that set it apart from those areas where Anglos made up the primary sheep herding force. Although illiterate, these *pastores* (sheepherders) possessed the ultimate savvy about handling sheep. "It is natural for them," elaborated Bundy, "he can make a sheep herd like a company of well-trained soldiers, and to certain sounds and motions they will move this or that, the shepherd will do it with all ease; very often from one spot be able to herd them for hours without moving."[18] A lone shepherd could tend from 2,000 to 2,500 sheep on the plateau prairies of the San Angelo area[19] or, with two good dogs could drive an entire herd to the mountain pastures and back in the central Texas areas.[20] These and other tasks Tejano pastores carried out with dignity, pride, and spirit.

In most areas, duty required the pastores to accompany their flocks to grazing land and camp with them by night, sometimes for extended stretches of time. Outdoor life necessarily compelled preparations, and generally the experienced pastor equipped himself with certain essentials. From the hide of the dead cow, perhaps, he fashioned himself the necessary sling. Made primarily to skim rocks along the ground in front of the sheep to check their pace, the sling also served to scare off cattle in the line of march or to frighten away wolves threatening the flock. In the expert hand of pastores, the sling could fling rocks up to the size of a goose egg a tremendous distance. Instead of the sling, some pastores preferred a curved stick. About thirty inches long and rounded at the end, when thrown adroitly it could cut capers along the ground for some distance, and according to some sheepmen, produced better results than a sling in checking the sheep. Some pastores carried a water container, perhaps a canteen, and kept the cover damp to prevent the water from getting too warm. In a canvas satchel, they might carry a snack, or the midday meal when away from camp. Clothing, while revealing their impoverishment, at the same time displayed adaptation to the surroundings. Sandals made from cowhide, for example, were less costly than boots and in a job that required much walking, were a good substitute.

Grazing sheep on the range called for devising survival methods. Piles of brush or other debris could be turned into makeshift domiciles if the pastor did not bring his own tent; wool blankets often served as beds. To light their fires, pastores made use of punk or *mecha*. Three common articles kindled the campfire: either a piece of punk or cotton string; a piece of steel; and a piece of flint with hard edge, the harder the better. By holding the punk (or any piece of cotton fabric rolled up in the form of a continuous string) close to the edge of the flint, the pastor would quickly strike it with a piece of steel, perhaps the back of a knife blade. The blow caused sparks that ignited the cotton. It did not blaze but glowed red hot and could be extinguished only by smothering. Should the pastor exhaust his supply of tinder, he could turn to an old tree, scrape off its fungus (or the punk), and be ready to strike another fire. [21]

Flour, bacon, and beans found their way as mainstays into the pastores' provision. Breakfast might consist of bacon and cornbread, and the evening meal, the principal one after the return of the flock, consisted of brown, nutritious Mexican beans, which, cooked over the coals of the campfire of the previous night, were ready for serving by that afternoon. [22] An average monthly ration for pastores as recommended by H. Bundy, the Pleasanton sheepman, was

one bushel of corn meal, or thirty pounds of flour, or one-half bushel of meal and fifteen pounds of flour. Meats: Two muttons per month, or thirty pounds of bacon, or one mutton and fifteen pounds of bacon. Coffee: Four pounds per month. Sugar: Four pounds per month, and what salt is necessary. [23]

To be a pastor meant days of solitude, broken only perhaps by periodic night visits to neighboring camp grounds or ranches for indulgence in storytelling, music, cardplaying, and other amusements with other shepherds. [24] It also meant low wages and status: pay was less than twenty dollars a month (including two *cabritos*), and they were ranked at the bottom of the work force hierarchy. On large ranchos like the Callaghan, located in present-day Webb and La Salle counties, three other ranks presided over the *pastor*, all of them occupied, generally, by Tejanos. Vaqueros, their immediate supervisors, exercised a constant surveillance over three pastores whose flocks (approximately 2,000 per flock) ranged in the same neighborhood. The vaquero, who received higher pay than his subordinates, answered to the *caporal.* The mounted *caporal* supervised three vaqueros and thus directed the movements of about 18,000 sheep. Each month, the caporal turned in the accounts received from the vaquero to the highest authority, the *mayordomo* or the person in charge of handling the stock of the ranch. Usually a man of experience and skill in conducting the practical part of the sheep industry and one able to deal with the class of men employed to carry out his orders, the mayordomo was constantly on the range, going the rounds of the different camps, noting the condition of the sheep, suggesting changes of grazing grounds, attending to the hiring and firing, and receiving from the caporales their monthly accounts, which he turned in to the ranch superintendent or administrator. Under this so-called Mexican method, Tejano sheepmen kept ranches like the Callaghan and others (including some Tejano-owned) functioning smoothly and profitably.

Twice a year in the last quarter of the nineteenth century, teams of migrant shearers (often from Mexico) came together. Under the direction of a *capitán* who enforced obedience, maintained order, and entered into contracts with the owner as to the time, place, wages, provisions, and accommodations, these Mexican nationals crossed into the United States from the middle of April until June and from the middle of August until the end of September. The *tasinques* (shearers) headed for the South Texas counties or as far as Llano County.[25] "This makes over 400 shearers that have passed through Eagle Pass in the last week," reported an Eagle Pass correspondent in April, 1884, "bound for ranches on this side to work on the spring clip of wool."[26] Tejano pastores and other sheepmen joined in the *trasquila* (shearing). On shearing days, hands assembled inside large sheds (as long as 300 feet) of brush, reed, or palmetto roofs designed to give shelter to hundreds of sheep and crews of some twenty-five to forty men. The crewmen caught the sheep by a hind leg, dragged it toward benches four feet high by three feet in width, picked up the sheep, laid it on the platform, tied its feet with rawhide string, and commenced shearing. Skills and speed varied among the tasinques, some managing to clip only about ten a day but other more competent men could finish as many as thirty or forty. The bleating of sheep interspersed the snipping of shears, the joking of workers, and the warning of *golpe* as a shorn sheep left for the finished pen. A boy carrying a can of worm medicine, or one containing charcoal mixed with oil, worked diligently amid the operation. At the cry of *coalie* or *tecolero* he applied the medicine to a sheep accidentally cut. This repelled flies from the animals' wounds until the injuries healed.

In the meantime a man (perhaps the capitán himself) equipped with a book and pencil kept tally of the number of sheep tied down by the shearers. The *laneros* also kept busy gathering up the sheaths of wool, tying up each coat separately, carrying each in an apron (attached to their waist), and delivering it to the packers. The packers in turn received the fleece and placed it in large jute sacks suspended from tall wooden racks and kept open by stitching the top around rings. One man filled the sack, another packed the wool with his feet to get as much as 360 pounds into it, while others tied, weighed, marked, and readied them for market. Freighters, employing teams of sixteen or twenty horses, then conveyed the wool to its destination.

For each clipped fleece, the tasinques received a check from the desk to be counted and exchanged for money at the end of the day. The scrip, which served as legal tender in the camp, would be redeemed by the capitán according to the terms of the contract. If, for example, the capitán negotiated with the sheep owner at five cents a head, he paid the shearers something like three cents per sheep, using the rest for board, other help, or his own salary.

During this clipping season, the cook, himself a member of the crew, looked after the tasinques' appetite and they referred to him affectionately as *madre*. [27]

Like the vaquero, the pastor and tasinque in South Texas were no longer needed by the turn of the twentieth century as the Rio Grande Plain became devoid of sheep. The scene then shifted toward the Edwards Plateau, where San Angelo gradually earned a reputation as the "wool capital of the world." In that western region, Tejanos also made up the sheep-tending force, especially the shearing crews. Not surprisingly, the Concho Valley was the site of the only strike of sheep shearers, called in 1934 by Mexican American tasinques protesting low wages and poor working conditions.[28]

To Mexican Americans, work as vaqueros and sheep herders was a way of making a living at something they understood and did well, but for Anglo landowners it was a matter of utilizing an available labor source for converting the range lands to lucrative ventures. Many an entrepreneur perceived Mexicans as simply cheap laborers. Given the racial feelings that relegated Tejanos to second-class citizens, white men could not think of the masses of Mexicans as anything other than a people intended to do menial tasks. Later as Anglos saw Mexicans doing much of that kind of work (and doing a good job of it), they concluded that Tejanos were good primarily for toiling on ranches and in the fields. Such attitudes, coupled with the availability of Tejano labor in the southern and western regions, naturally impelled advertisers in the post-bellum period to proclaim the advantages of the Mexican work force in their midst. "This is a good point to procure Mexican labor," noted a Rio Grande correspondent in 1877, "good ranch hands with families may be had for eight or ten dollars per month with board, or they will find themselves and families for from twelve to fifteen dollars, per month with shelter."[29] The Corpus Christi *Weekly Caller* commented in 1885: "Soil and climate are suitable and cheap labor is at hand. Mexican farm labor can be utilized in the culture of cotton as well as during the picking season."[30]

In effect, such announcements exposed the system of occupational stratification that existed for Tejanos.[31] While in 1850 (1860) rural Tejanos were in fairly good standing, that deteriorated by 1900. During these years, Anglo American society spread appreciably into the rural scene, displacing Tejanos from the commanding role they held at the time of the signing of the Treaty of Guadalupe Hidalgo (1848). As is seen in Table 6, the percentage of laborers increased for both Mexicanos and Anglos; however, that increase reflected two different tendencies. For Tejanos it symbolized proletarianization while for Anglos it pointed to the demographic switch that occurred as they moved out from the urban areas in mid-century into the rural parts of Central, South, and West Texas. Nowhere is this more clearly reflected than in farm and ranch ownership where the precipitous decline of Tejano landholders was as considerable as the gain of their Anglo counterparts. The fact that the percentage of both Tejanos and Anglos in skilled labor,

Table 6. Rural Labor Force Composition, 1850 (1860) and 1900[a]

	Mexican-Americans		Anglo-Americans	
	1850 (1860)	1900	1850 (1860)	1900
Manual Laborers	34.3%	67.1%	8.7%	26.5%
Skilled Laborers	29.3%	12.0%	30.0%	10.8%
Merchants	0.7%	2.1%	13.3%	4.4%
Professionals	1.6%	1.5%	21.3%	11.2%
Ranch/Farm Owners	32.9%	15.8%	1.8%	31.4%
Other	1.2%	1.5%	24.9%	15.7%
	100%	100%	100%	100%
	(N=580)	(N=2,023)	(N=277)	(N=204)

[a]This table includes occupations listed in the censuses among the rural residents of Béxar County and the Lower Rio Grande Valley in 1850, of El Paso County in 1860, and of Béxar, El Paso, Cameron, Starr, and Webb counties in 1900.

Jobs were assigned to the above categories according to the consensus of a panel of four historians working independently of one another. Where consensus did not occur, jobs were assigned to the "other" category.

mercantile, and professional occupations did not grow between 1850 and 1900 may reflect the shift to commercial farming from ranching and sheepraising that took place during the latter decades of the century. As that transition took place, the polarity between farm and ranch owners and laborers became the dominating characteristic of the rural labor force (see Table 6). As presented in Table 7, these trends were especially characteristic of the fertile Rio Grande Valley area where Tejanos lived in large numbers.

Tejanos not equipped to work cattle and sheep, and unskilled Mexican nationals who came slowly but steadily from Mexico, then, turned to other forms of field employment. The emerging farms of the post-bellum period called for small armies of vegetable and cotton pickers. In their attempts to sustain themselves, their families, and their communities, Tejano farm hands thus worked for practically every farm from the border section up to the Central Texas lands. Following the general emancipation of slaves in 1865, Mexicanos commenced shuttling towards the rich bottom lands east of San Antonio to replace black labor, working for fifteen dollars a month and rations. In the 1870s, they worked alongside blacks in the Brazos area for the same wages, and the small Tejano

Table 7. Rural Labor Force Composition by Region, 1850 (1860) and 1900[a]

	Béxar County		Lower Rio Grande Valley		El Paso County	
	1850	*1900*	*1850*	*1900*	*1860*	*1900*
Mexican-American Manual Workers	3.6%	63.0%	—	67.0%	56.9%	74.3%
Anglo-American Manual Workers	6.5%	25.9%	1.1%	29.7%	23.8%	18.2%
Mexican-American Skilled Laborers	92.8%	—	47.5%	12.7%	13.5%	4.5%
Anglo-American Skilled Laborers	10.6%	1.9%	50.5%	23.0%	38.1%	13.6%
Mexican-American Merchants	—	—	1.0%	2.2%	0.6%	3.0%
Anglo-American Merchants	5.7%	2.8%	24.2%	5.4%	12.7%	9.1%
Mexican-American Professionals	3.6%	—	0.5%	1.5%	2.0%	3.0%
Anglo-American Professionals	39.8%	4.6%	7.7%	16.2%	4.8%	27.3%
Mexican-American Farm/Ranch Owners	—	37.0%	51.0%	15.0%	25.0%	15.2%
Anglo-American Farm/Ranch Owners	0.8%	44.4%	2.2%	12.2%	3.2%	31.8%
Mexican-Americans—Other	—	—	—	1.6%	2.0%	—
Anglo-Americans—Other	36.6%	20.4%	14.3%	13.5%	17.5%	—

[a]Percentages for 1900 in the Lower Rio Grande Valley are based on samples drawn from the census returns for Webb, Cameron, and Starr counties. Jobs were assigned to the above categories according to the consensus of a panel of four historians working independently of one another. Where consensus did not occur, jobs were assigned to the "other" category. The majority of skilled laborers in Béxar County in 1850 were cartmen.

population (approximately 100) in Travis County in that period made its living the same way.[32] On a Pecos area farm, Tejano hands in the late 1870s cultivated the fields for the white owner who took crops (corn and small white army beans) in return for the food he furnished them.[33] In the John McAllen Ranch of the Lower Rio Grande Valley, Mexican hands described as careful, industrious, quiet, and civil worked vegetables for fifty cents a day.[34]

As South Texas changed to cotton planting in the latter part of the century, Mexicanos became the mainstay of the cotton picking force, at times contracting as tenants on some of the ranches.[35] They worked the cotton fields of the lower border, of Duval County, of Eagle Pass, and the Corpus Christi area.[36] In Nueces County, they cultivated the cotton for seventy-five cents per day (boarding themselves) and picked it for seventy-five cents per hundred pounds, the farm owner furnishing only the sacks.[37]

Others searched out the crop and joined the migrant stream, pursuing a manner of livelihood unavailable before. In the 1890s, residents of San Antonio's Chihuahuita left their homes seasonally to pick cotton in the outlying areas.[38] *Piscadores* (cotton pickers) from as far away as Duval County travelled to Wharton County to do the picking and earn their living.[39] In October 1894, approximately 5,000 Mexicanos passed through Beeville from Mexican border towns on their way to the central and northern parts of the state where jobs in cotton fields already awaited them. "These Mexicans are hired on this side of the Rio Grande by agents of the larger farms, and are shipped in car load lots, with windows and doors locked, to their destination," reported the local paper. "After the cotton season the majority will work their way back to the border and into Mexico."[40]

The switch to commercial farming owed much to Mexican labor, for it was Tejanos who performed the back breaking task of clearing the lands of South Texas and shaping farms and ranches like the Miller Ranch near Corpus Christi.[41] Similarly, the Rancho Santa Gertrudis owed the removal of spreading mesquite tree tentacles to foot camps of transient Mexican workers seeking work during the hard times of drought and depression of the 1890s. Using their strong backs to swing axes, picks, and grubbing hoes, they chopped brush and grubbed roots, earning five dollars for every acre they cleared, fifty cents for each cord of wood they cut, and varying wages for such pieces as could be used for fence, corral, or gate posts. In addition, each worker received a weekly ration of seven pounds of flour, one pound of coffee, two pounds of beans, one pound of rice, one quart of molasses, and about a pound and a half of bacon.[42] Tejanos performed similar work in the Fort Davis and Fort Stockton areas during the same period.[43]

The number of Tejanos making their living in the agrarian sector leads to a question, were these ranch and farm hands Horatio Algers, or did they resemble their preindustrial Anglo and European counterparts who labored according to natural conditions and practiced routines of work and leisure incompatible with the so-called Puritan ethic? Many of those who came to form this labor force in the last decades of the century were recent arrivals from Mexico. Much research needs to be done to delineate time and work rhythms, but tentative suggestions may be advanced. On the one hand, Anglos imputed values of indolence to Mexicanos. In various settings and at different times Tejanos came to be regarded as an unambitious people uncaring about the morrow. Abbé Domenech, a missionary working in the Rio Grande Valley in the 1850s, wrote that the local rancheros labored little or not at all, that the mere shadow of work overpowered them, that their sole strenuous activity was leisure, and that they slept wherever they could under the mild temperate South Texas sky.[44] R. W. Johnson, an old general reminiscing about his Fort Duncan days near Eagle Pass in the same period, declared Mexicanos "the most indolent people in the world," people who celebrated continuous feast days, and subsumed themselves inordinately in the frolic and merriment of the festivities.[45] "Hungry-looking Mexicans" lounging upon monte-tables typified the night scene at Laredo in the 1880s, according to a San Antonio *Express* correspondent.[46] In Corpus Christi in the same decade, Mexicans could be prodded into working for a time, but they did not have the least fear of losing their occupation, noted a longtime native.[47] Despite abject poverty, Tejanos of El Paso in that same period took no note of time, said a New York journalist, yet remained happy and unworried.[48] And Bexareños, · observed an article in *Harper's New Monthly Magazine* (1890), lived "on a mere pittance, being well-contented as long as they have their cigarettes and coffee."[49]

Tejano rancheros themselves complained of their kinsmen's propensity for fun and frolic. In July 1891, for example, a ranchero signing his name "Cow Boy," wrote to a Spanish-language newspaper objecting to the constant ranch balls and fiestas in celebration of San Juan, San Pedro, and Santiago. This type of entertainment, he lamented, not only attracted the "lovers of Bacchus and Birjau" (the patron of sports) but demoralized the participants and led them toward a life of crime.[50]

While indolence may have seemed to characterize the behavior of preindustrial workers or may have been the manifestation of work patterns imported from the mother country, the profit record of South Texas in that period bespeaks of a hard-working people. The Laredo jurist José María Rodríguez, moved to come to the defense of a folk with whom he shared a common culture, wrote in his memoirs:

There is just one little matter that I would desire to say a few words about before I close this book, and that is to testify my admiration for the humble and hardworking Mexican laborers. I know of no class of men who are paid less for what they do than these poor men, and yet crime among them is almost unknown. It's true that once in a while they will have a little cutting scrape among themselves when they drink a little more than is good for them, but when it comes to real down-right honesty they can set a very good example to men who have had much better opportunities than they have.[51]

Conceivably, racists who insisted that the majority inclined to indolence and vice instead of industry, and admirers who commended Tejano *obreros*, registered the two extremes. Tejanos obviously held their own views toward labor. Texas, after all, remained an agrarian state until very late in the century, allowing Tejanos to apply preindustrial work habits. Living in a preindustrial state and periodically reinforced by unacculturated immigrants who came from a country not imbued with the Protestant ethic, Tejanos performed according to their own work patterns. In this view toward work they were similar to the immigrants from central and eastern Europe who formed the labor pool of northern factories. As a proletariat, Tejanos disregarded the clock and instead worked hard according to the need of the occasion, then eased their efforts during less demanding times. So did their white counterparts in other agrarian states, such as lumberjacks and railroad hands who worked hard and then took time off to enjoy the fruits of their labor. Retaining time-honored work habits, Tejanos incorporated traditions such as the afternoon *meriendas* (snacks) or the familiar *parrandas* (drinking binges) into their working styles. Displaying preindustrial work rhythms, they saw nothing sacrilegious in merriment in the work schedule.[52] At least that is what a group of Mexican laborers in the El Paso Valley demanded in 1898. A press account read:

Employers of Mexican labor have to employ queer means sometimes in order to keep their men satisfied. One of the most necessary things in dealing with Mexicans is to keep them amused. If you do not do this, the fellows will soon quit and go where they can have more pleasure mixed up with their pains. Floyd Payne has a ranch down the valley that is at present valuable principally for the wood that can be cut from it. His main difficulty is keeping Mexicans at work to supply the demand for wood.

Charley Peacock, who is in charge of the ranch, decided upon a *baile* to keep the help. Invitations were carefully written out in Spanish and delivered by special messenger. One man was given plenary powers to invite all the ladies in Guadalupe, a town of some 5,000 inhabitants across the river from the ranch. This man sent word Saturday that he would need two large wagons for the girls.

The house where the *baile* was held is an adobe about thirty-five feet long. In front is a covered porch having a smooth rammed earth floor. This porch is only nine feet wide so the boys widened it to eighteen feet and covered the addition with canvas. The dirt was leveled up and rammed down hard. Just before the dance commenced the whole space was sprinkled and then covered with a wagon of pure river sand. The gravel was swept off the floor and was left smooth and in fine condition for dancing.

When the girls began to arrive, they brought their ordinary clothes and carried their party clothes with them. As soon as they arrived they sent to the store for hairpins and vaseline. They went to the homes of the Mexican laborers and began to make ready for the ball. The preparation was a tedious job, especially to those who awaited the appearance of the ladies.

Wooden candlesticks were made and hung up on the wall of the house and on the pillars of the porch. Seats had been placed around the space.

At last, about 9:30, the ladies appeared, and the *baile* began in earnest. The men did not seem to be anxious to dance at first and the ladies seemed to have a hard time to get partners enough, but after a little the men got warmed up to the things and they stayed with it.

The music consisted of a violin, guitar, and cornet. They really made very good music. Besides the orchestral numbers there were four vocal selections, by both men and women.

The dancing was kept up until one o'clock. Then the refreshment room was thrown open and the company were fed in relays. Besides the regular Mexican dishes Mr. Payne had shipped down ten watermelons weighing something over 300 lbs., to help out. The refreshment room was then kept up until the end.

Representative of two important institutions in the lives of Tejanos are these illustrations of a family and a mission. The Morales family from Fort Concho Museum, San Angelo, Texas; Mission concepción de Acuña, San Antonio, Texas, from Eugene C. Barker Library, Texas History Center, University of Texas at Austin.

A water carrier in Brownsville, Texas, in about 1865. Eugene C. Barker Library, Texas History Center, University of Texas at Austin.

Burros with Load of Corn

Burros loaded with corn. Daughters of the Republic of Texas Library at the Alamo, San Antonio.

Tejano women washing clothes on the bank of the San Antonio River.
Daughters of the Republic of Texas Library at the Alamo, San Antonio.

A tejano hut. San Antonio Conservation Society, San Antonio.

71

Mexican *carretas* (carts) on Commerce Street in San Antonio. Eugene C. Barker Library, Texas History Center, University of Texas at Austin.

Facing page, top: Tejanos and others working as sheep shearers. The wool harvest each spring was a period of particularly hard work, most of it done by itinerant groups of Mexican shearers. Ragsdale Collection, Fort Concho Museum, San Angelo, Texas.

Facing page, bottom: Vegetable vendors on Military Plaza in San Antonio in 1883. The spanish governor's palace (left) and the "Bat Cave" building (background) were prominent in the plaza even in the nineteenth century. Jacquelyn Simmang King, Universal City, Texas.

74

"Corrida de la Sandía" painted by Theodore Gentilz has as its subject the "Watermelon Race" in San Antonio as part of the celebration of the Día de San Juan. Library of the Daughters of the Republic of Texas at the Alamo, San Antonio.

Facing page, top: The painting "Entierro de un Angel" by Theodore Gentilz depicts the funeral procession of an "angel," or a baptized infant, who having died sinless, went directly to heaven. Library of the Daughters of the Republic of Texas at the Alamo, San Antonio.

Facing page, bottom: The entire cast of "Los Pastores" with the devils (center) posing without their masks for a photograph taken by Capt. John G. Bourke in 1893. *Los Pastores,* M. R. Cole, Memoirs of the American Folklore Society, Vol. IX, Boxton, Massachusetts, 1907.

Col. Santos Benavides in 1864. St. Mary's University, Laredo Archives, San Antonio.

José Antonio Navarro. Eugene C. Barker Library, Texas History Center, University of Texas at Austin.

G. N. García, representative to the eleventh Texas legislature from El Paso. Eugene C. Barker Library, Texas History Center, University of Texas at Austin.

Juan N. Cortina in military uniform. Eugene C. Barker Library, Texas History Center, University of Texas at Austin.

The dancing continued after that with no intermission longer than five or ten minutes until long after sunrise. The candles flickered in the early dawn and went out, but the dancers still sailed on. After the sun was well up and the time had to be called for breakfast, according to the precedent set by Dewey at Manila, the merry revelers begged that they might be allowed to keep it up longer. If such marvelous endurance were applied in some more profitable direction it would be worth money.

The ladies' costumes were as a rule very elaborate. Many of the gowns were of silk. All the girls had their hair fixed very prettily and all wore many ornaments. Several of the older women took no part in the dancing but acted as chaperones.

It was a very orderly *baile*. No drinks of any kind were allowed, not even beer. The result of the *baile* seems to have been entirely satisfactory. But it established a precedent that may prove embarassing.[53]

Such was the link between work and culture and a work habit that combined a way of work with a way of life. And such work habits were not injurious to the economy; indeed, southern and western Texas equalled or surpassed in prosperity other Texas regions where workers toiled under the intoxication of the Protestant ethic.

That so many Tejanos earned their living as ranch and farm workers had more to do with the determination of white Texans to maintain a pool of menials than with a Mexican adherence to traditionalism. If Mexicanos had resigned themselves to their fate as hewers of wood or drawers of water, or even had accepted a racial order that left little space for Mexicanos at the top, then an entrepreneurial class among them would not have emerged; and if it had, would either have been a rarity or an exception. Yet, a respectable list of Tejanos surmounted the forces of exclusion to emerge as successful rancheros (see Table 7). For, despite systematic dispossession by Anglos following the Texas Revolution and the Mexican War, Mexican Americans either retained their holdings legally, or bought new lands that they converted into farms or cattle and sheep ranchos. The presence of this rancher class should make historians cautious about assessing nineteenth century Tejanos as unambitious people. The accomplishments of these rancheros point to the possibilities that might have been for all Tejanos had they enjoyed opportunities like those of Anglo common folk, many of whom went on to make promising lives for themselves and their families.

In the central and eastern Texas countryside, the old rancheros still endured (however precariously) in the years following the

Revolution of 1836. Near San Antonio was the ranch of Don Erasmo Seguín, with its ranch house easily recognized with its broad veranda and thick walls plastered white standing on a rise overlooking the river.[54] Below Goliad stood the Carlos Rancho—more of a community than a ranch. Belonging to Carlos de la Garza, it featured a double log house, a log store, commissary, jacales, and church.[55] At Rancho Flores, seventeen miles south of New Braunfels, long homes displayed the Mexican method of construction that made them almost impregnable to Indian attacks.[56] Similar features identified the ranchos of the wealthy Cantú family of San Antonio on Calaveras Creek and that of Ignacio (?) Castro, fifteen miles from San Antonio.[57] When Frederick Law Olmsted travelled through the central Texas area in the 1850s, he witnessed field hands working with improvised plows functioning much like a subsoil plow, ranchos large enough to require jacal like cabins for the laborers, and ranch owners either working alongside their hands, or others, exploiting bondsmen. On a ranch near the Calaveras he reported slaves working indiscriminately with hired Mexicans. According to hearsay, he elaborated, Mexican slaveholders treated their slaves cruelly but at the same time allowed them many perquisites which, while increasing their total income, made them discontented with their status.[58] These central Texas ranchos continued only so long as their owners kept in good standing with whites; for many, though, ownership quickly ended in expulsion, dispossession, and even murder in the years immediately following the revolt of 1836. Carlos Rancho, for example, was attacked by irate Anglos following Vásquez' raid on Texas, and the Tejanos there were expelled from their homes.

If the importance of the eastern and central Texas ranchos declined following the arrival of whites en masse, such was not the case in the area between the Nueces River and the Rio Grande. While large amounts of the most valued real estate in South Texas had passed into Anglo American hands by the time of the Civil War, Tejanos still retained titles to hundreds of acres. Small ranchos there identified the section as Tejano in culture and gave the region an aura of Tejanismo. That is, "lo mexicano" prevailed over "lo americano," manifested in the population predominance of Mexicans, in the use of the Spanish language and Mexican work patterns, in the persistence of Mexican social traditions, and in the influence, however subtle, that the northern states of Mexico had on the area. It was a place where Tejanos could move about as Mexicans instead of Americans, if they had to. Certainly, cultural change occurred, for Anglo hegemony over the foundations of the region's overall economy meant that Tejanos had to contend with Americanisms and that they could not at all times carry on as Mexicans.

But as a Tejano cultural zone, South Texas provided an important sense of belonging for Mexican American residents and the many ranchos (some of them actually small villages) testified to the cultural vitality that held its own against oppression. Named after their owners, after a saint in the calendar, or an incident related to its founding, these ranchos stretched all along the border.

Las Ánimas, El Fajito, Carricitos, Mulatos, La Jarita, San Juanito, Encantado, Rancho de Tipaguaje, Rancho San Juan of Don José Escamilla, Santa Rosa of Charles Stillman, and other ranches surrounded Brownsville in the 1860s.[59] While the fate of many of these ranchitos in the Lower Rio Grande Valley was to end in demise or transfer to whites, others continued as subsistence enterprises while still others became successful concerns. Don Macedonio Vela's Laguna Seca, for example, thrived in the latter part of the century. The little village consisted of nine substantial frame buildings, innumerable jacales, a general store, a shoemaker, two carpenters, a post office, and a number of families. Aided by his two sons, Ramón and J. M. Vela, Don Macedonio raised crops and livestock, often selling saddle horses in other areas of the state.[60] Simultaneously rancherías and hamlets like La Blanca (of John McAllen), Agua Negra, Rosario, San Francisco, Zacatal, Capote, Santa Cruz, Hidalgo, Santa Rita, Cotia, Como Se Llama, La Jara, Granjeno, Peñitas (composed of several very substantial and well-kept dwellings, two stores and a post office), and the Havana Ranch, a halfway station composed of several jacales, a *tendajito*, a school, and a Catholic church, were farther along the road to Rio Grande City.[61] In Starr County proper in the 1880s, Felipe Guerra claimed 25,000 acres of land worth $6,000 and 980 head of livestock valued at $4,390; Louis Martínez owned 38,318 acres appraised at $19,309, and 650 livestock worth $4,000; while 22,500 acres valued at $1,600 and 900 livestock worth $7,000 belonged to Sino Martínez.[62] Men like Juan García Barrera and José Ramírez Arce also owned modest ranchos around Rio Grande City while other ranches like Los Federales, La Gonzalina, Refugio, Las Potrancas, and La Grulla, further buttressed the Tejano presence in Starr County.[63]

In Zapata County (later Jim Hogg), Hipólito García's Randado Ranch stood out prominently as an example of a prosperous enterprise. It embraced 80,000 acres, had 25,000 head of cattle (which he sold to buyers as far away as the Indian territory), and in the 1880s, the little village of 300 had a store, a little mission, a tank, twenty or more adobe houses with thatched roofs, and its small graveyard. It featured a post office and a school that was the equal of any in the urban centers. School exams called for testing of language fluency in both English and Spanish. "The teacher," writing to the Corpus Christi *Weekly Caller* in January 1885, remarked that soon their county would not want for men capable of discharging their duties in either language. In a test conducted in 1885, examiners included the young merchants Don José M. Salinas and Mr. Ignacio de la Garza, a recent student at the college at Rolla, Missouri. On Saturdays, when vaqueros and pastores returned from the range, they regaled themselves at the weekly dance generally held on the bare clay of one of the huts. Once a month the priest arrived on horseback to celebrate mass in the adobe mission.[64] Among prominent traders at Randado were Ramón Guerra and his partner José M. Salinas, who managed to sell about fifteen to twenty thousand dollars worth of horses annually having imported them from Mexico.[65]

Similar ranchos made good in areas surrounding Laredo. Before the Mexican War, rancheros had looked to Mexican border settlements for trade, but after the conquest they turned to American markets also. In the 1870s, well-to-do rancheros who sold to white cattle drivers for midwestern markets included the following: Blas Gutiérrez, owner of the Barrocita Ranch; Juan Torres of the Bernal Ranch; Stanislado Flores of the Salamonena Ranch; Louis Martínez of the Palongarna Ranch; Ramón Guerra, Camilo Sáez, and Louis Ramírez, joint owners of the San Antonio Viejo Ranch. Also around the Laredo area, Jesús Peña owned the Las Animas Ranch; Pedro Flores the Alverica Ranch; Juan Manuel Flores the El Mesquite Ranch; Tenacio Jugario the Pata Ranch, and Martín Gonzales the Tiendas Ranch.[66] In the 1880s and 1890s, Darío Sánchez imported cattle, dogs, and poultry from Kentucky; Judge J. M. Rodrǵuez shipped cattle to Chicago; while Pedro and Resulgo Flores from the Alberca de Abajo Ranch prospered; as did Juan Ortiz, owner of

50,000 acres in Webb and adjoining counties.[67] Los Ojuelos in Encinal County (now Webb County) resembled Randado of neighboring Zapata County. The village proper contained a population of nearly 300, two stores operated by Lagaro Ochoa and J. M. García, and a school census of ninety-three. Don Dionisio Guerra, the patriarch of the village, maintained a strict policy as to who could reside in the village—he charged nothing for rent, but residents had to send their children to school.[68]

North to the Nueces River, other Tejano-owned ranchos added to the picture of a pervasive Tejanismo. In the 1850s, the rancho of Cecilio Balerio exemplified the potential of a Tejano ranch in a white society if permitted its own autonomy. A traveler noted:

at Cecilio Valerio's [sic] I saw about 400 head of horses, mares and mules. Some of the colts are good specimens of "half-breeds"—more particularly a powerful dark bay, American stallion with which he has crossed his Spanish mares, and produced large and likely colts. The success of this old Mexican shows what can be done by ordinary attention and perseverance on a stock farm in this favored country. A few years ago he had hardly a dollar. Running mustangs and trading them off to advantage, some distance from home, and from time to time reserving some likely animals to breed from, the old man is now very independent.[69]

In the 1880s, Juan Saens successfully raised watermelons and other crops at his ranch eight miles west of Corpus Christi; Crisanto Vela, owner of Las Latas, regularly sold his stock in various areas of the state; as did Cristóbal García of the Collins area; while Don Alvino Canales did well as a heavyweight ranchman. Other successful ranchos included that of Mateo de Hoyos, that of Florencio Mendoza in Petronila, and Rancho Santa Cruz of Ramón Salinas. In the Palito Blanco area (then in Nueces County), Tejanos like Gonzales and Canales owned large ranchos and in 1892 they shipped their cattle to the Indian Territory for grass and water.[70]

The Duval County ranchos in the later decades of the nineteenth century contributed to the feeling of Tejano cultural domination in South Texas, provided Tejano common folk with a sense of the familiar, and exemplified the prosperity that resulted when Tejanos controlled their own destiny. Around San Diego, the county seat, prospered ranchos like La Bebeda, Las Gorrilas of Don Domingo Rotge, the rancho of Don Francisco Ramírez,[71] and that of E. G. Pérez, one of the town's most prominent men. In the Benavides areas, Plácido Benavides and Daniel Gonzales were among the successful rancheros who traded their horse stock in East Texas. At Peña, ranchers like Antonio Vizcaya, Ysidro Vizcaya, Ramón Guerra, Alejo Pérez, and Antonio Gutiérrez all sold stock regularly in the San Antonio area, while D. and L. P. Peña sold beef to buyers from as far away as the Indian Territory, and Don Lazaro Peña took his own stock to Kansas City, Missouri. More successful ranchos included that of Mateo Sandejo, located six miles west of Mendietta, those of Santos Hinojosa and Ferman López, that of Simón Ramírez of Clovis, that of Juan Palacios of Concepción, and that of Jorge Alanis, a most successful rancher in the 1890s.[72]

In the trans-Pecos region additional successful ranchos could be found. The Gómez Cattle Company in the 1880s, for example, grazed cattle on the MF range (north side of the Davis Mountains), and in the 1910s, the great *alamos* and adobe buildings of Caezario Torres' old 7d Ranch in the Pecos area still stood as witness to the energy of its founder.[73]

Tejano rancheros did not restrict themselves solely to cattle, for owners raised sheep alongside their herds. Tejano stock raisers took their place among the successful sheepmen on the Rio Grande Plain. There, during the decades when the sheep industry reached its highpoint, they were as numerous as white sheepmen. In the Duval County area at about the same time, prosperous sheep owners included Rafael García, Santa Medina, Refrigia Vela de Guerra, Carlos Guerra, Porfirio Garza, San Juana Vela, María Antonio Jiménez, Victoria Guachola, Marcos Villareal, Macaria Muños, Pomposo Perales, Manuel Longorio, Squapito Sauez, Sisario Gadena, Enrique C. Alivarez.[74] Among the proprietors of large flocks were Manuel Vela, owner of some 12,000 sheep, Encarnación G. Pérez, owner of 10,000, and Cayetano Ríos, owner of another 10,000. In September 1880, Jacinto Guerra was among the largest merchants of San Diego, with about 100,000 pounds of wool in store.[75] In the Laredo area, prosperous sheepmen included Don Cayetano de la Garza, Cristobal and Porfirio Benavides, Nicholas Sánchez, owner of about 40,000 sheep, and Ambrose Rodríguez, owner of some 20,000 head on his own ranch.[76] Like cattlemen, these Tejano sheepmen added an aura of Tejanismo to the South Texas area that gave ordinary folk the sense that they were interacting with men who spoke their language, who shared cultural traditions, and who themselves were undergoing the subtle process of biculturation.

Tejano-owned farms sustained a way of life akin to that of ranchos specializing in stock and sheep raising. The poorer Tejano farmer-owners did their best with what circumstances allowed them, ordinarily relying on plows fashioned from logs, poles, and even tree branches. A sharp pointed piece served as the share, another as the handle. A long limb, rigged to this, passed between the oxen to the wooden yoke where strips of leather lashed it firmly to the middle. With this yoke fastened securely with rawhide to the horns of the oxen or cattle, Tejanos employed a wooden apparatus that contained no iron to turn the soil. A straight light stick with a pointed ten penny nail at the end of the hands of the plowman served as the goad to regulate the speed of the beasts. In this manner, Mexicanos tilled the productive lands of the El Paso and Rio Grande valleys with moderate results. [77]

When harvesting their crops, Tejanos used similarly crude but successful means. The farmers of the Big Bend area in the latter decades of the century, for example, improvised when it came to threshing wheat. According to John Ernest Gregg, the historian of Presidio County:

They would construct a hard surface adobe floor, and enclose this with a pole fence. The wheat, still in the straw, would be scattered over the floor about two feet deep, and then stock was driven into the enclosure. Then around and around over the grain the stock would be forced to travel and the grain would be threshed. The straw would then be thrown off the platform, and the grain gathered up for winnowing. This was accomplished by pouring the wheat out of vessels on to wagon sheets of tarpaulins. The process was repeated until all the chaff was winnowed from the grain. [78]

Their method of irrigation rivaled any other of that period. In San Elizario, Tejanos perfected a means reportedly unmatched by whites in 1883. [79] In the Big Bend, Mexican farmers used the "gravity ditch." The ingenuity showed by the farmers, wrote Gregg, was remarkable:

The mouth of the ditch was of necessity some distance up stream from the land to be irrigated. So the ditches were run along the higher benches of land than that on which the land to be irrigated lay. A small brush or rock dam was constructed so that it extended at an angle out into the river stream. This directed the water into the mouth of the ditch. While it is true that a rise in the river would wash out such a dam, it could be cheaply and easily replaced. These early gravity ditches were constructed without the aid of surveying instruments. A point would be selected from which to begin the construction of the ditch, and the water would be allowed to flow into the mouth of the ditch and the proper fall would be secured by digging in such a way that the water would continue to flow.[80]

But those farmers who could afford it quickly adopted agricultural innovations. In the Duval County areas, for example, Tejano farmers initiated the movement in cotton raising. Among the leaders in San Diego was Don Fabian Fabela, credited with having introduced it.[81] Rancher Encarnación G. Pérez of the city, also ranked among the prominent cotton farmers, operated his own gin, and erected a windmill in 1893 to water his garden.[82] Other Duval County rancheros delving into farming were cotton planters Plácido Benavides, Don Julián Palacios, Teodore and Alejo Pérez of Concepción, who relied on corn and garden truck,[83] and D. and Lázaro F. Peña, prominent rancheros of the Peña area who imported plows and other agricultural implements from Kansas City in the late 1880s to go into agriculture on a large scale.[84] According to a report published in the Corpus Christi *Weekly Caller* on May 2, 1891, some 3,000 acres in cotton and the same in corn were growing in commissioners' court precinct number two. The report included the names of the rancheros and planters plus the amount of acreage:

López	640 acres	2/3 in cotton
Los Indios	500 acres	2/3 in cotton
La Huerta	250 acres	2/3 in cotton
Juan Puig	170 acres	1/3 in cotton
Las Anacuas	150 acres	2/3 in cotton
Elario Benavides	250 acres	2/3 in cotton
Bassan's	200 acres	2/3 in cotton
Guajillo	600 acres	2/3 in cotton
José Ángel Barrera & Bros.	100 acres	3/4 in cotton
Benavides town	100 acres	2/3 in cotton
Santos Hinojosa	100 acres	2/3 in cotton
Piedras Pintas	500 acres	2/3 in cotton
José María Saens	250 acres	2/3 in cotton
Panchos Morales	80 acres	3/4 in cotton
Deodat Ruiz	80 acres	2/3 in cotton
Plácido Benavides[85]	60 acres	1/3 in cotton

In the Del Rio area, the Tejana-managed San Felipe farms prospered as a corn producing enterprise. According to one report, a man named Taylor and his Mexican wife moved several Mexican families into the "San Felipe farms" in 1867. By 1883, the bilingual Mrs. Rivers (the original Mrs. Taylor) had a place in the lower end of Del Rio, and through industry and hard work, ran the several corn mills prosperously.[86]

A study of Mexicanos in the agrarian sector, then, prompts a number of generalizations. The most evident one is that the mass of Tejano workers who composed approximately 70 percent of the rural labor force between 1850 and 1900 did not determine their own destiny. Though a hardworking people whose employment rate equalled that of rural Anglos by 1900,[87] Tejanos faced limited options for upward mobility, confined as they were to rural servitude. Compelled to work at a limited number of tasks, they found few choices in the form of newer jobs, a constraint that whites did not have to contend with. By 1900, there was an average of 29.4 Tejano workers for every job title held by Mexican Americans in the rural labor force, but there was an average of only 5.3 Anglo workers for every job title held among that group (see Table 8). This overrepresentation marked the salient oppression Tejanos faced when it came to economics. Despite this, their experience as a rural folk following the Revolution of 1836 suggests another reality. First, Tejanos adapted in both skilled and unskilled capacities as they sought to earn their livelihood after 1836. Second, not all were relegated to a proletarian status, for many penetrated ownership positions. A class of rancheros, descended from the native elite that dominated Mexican society before the Revolution and infused more

Table 8. Selected Characteristics of Rural Labor Forces in South, Central, and West Texas, 1850 (1860) and 1900[a]

	Mexican-Americans		Anglo-Americans	
	1850 (1860)	1900	1850 (1860)	1900
Estimated Percent of Labor Force	69.0%	77.4%	31.0%	22.6%
Estimated Percent of Ethnic Population Who were Employed	19.5%	30.1%	43.5%	32.9%
Estimated Number of Workers	2,400	13,080	1,080	3,813
Estimated Number of Workers per Job Title (identified in the census)	14.2	29.4	5.9	5.3

[a]This table is based on combined samples of rural workers in Béxar County and the Lower Rio Grande Valley in 1850, in El Paso County in 1860, and in Béxar, El Paso, Cameron, Starr, and Webb counties in 1900.

recently by a cadre of entrepreneurial-minded men, engaged in many a business operation, including out-of-state transactions, and comprised part of the heterogeneous Tejano community. Third, the presence of such a class dispels the notion of a Mexican culture universally hindered by values of fatalism, resignation, complacency, and traditionalism. The common workers displayed few signs of displeasure (regardless of whatever personal pain their lives wrought) with their condition as field hands through labor resistance, but it should be recalled that agricultural strikes in nineteenth century and even early twentieth century America were scarce in general.[88] Even if some Mexicanos retained older forms of rural work values, this traditionalism did not hinder adaptation and success orientation in an Anglo context. Finally, the Hispanic presence that permeated so much of southern and western Texas permitted common folk to interact in diverse situations with people of their own kind. That reality worked to ward off the pressures and anxieties that came with living in a hostile environment.

4

Obreros and the Urban Scene

Urban centers[1] were essentially Anglo focal points. From the beginning of Anglo rule, white men ventured into frontier areas founding towns close to their ranches, to military forts, and to hubs of commercial activity. They also came to predominate in older Spanish-Mexican pueblos like San Antonio and Laredo and, through guile and cunning, usurped the old political order and realigned business to their economic advantage. By mid-century they controlled the urban economies of Central and South Texas, and only El Paso County's remoteness postponed that hegemony until after the Civil War. They monopolized the more prestigious and lucrative occupations, namely the professions, the white-collar jobs, plus the skilled crafts, and left Tejanos to fend for themselves as laborers, servants, seamstresses, laundresses, and other forms of menial labor. The status of Tejano urban wage earners thus resembled closely that of their agrarian fellows (see Table 9).

Still, Tejanos manifested the same animation as could be found in the rural areas. To those opting for residence in the emerging cities, towns could be bases from which they might commute to jobs outside its limits or to vocations that took them to areas throughout the state; they could be a setting where life was earned through unskilled labor or through private enterprise; or they could be an entity to be served in bureaucratic capacities. In whatever endeavor, Tejanos adapted and pursued the means for individual and group advancement. In most cases, though, they succeeded in

Table 9. Most Frequently Held Jobs Among Mexican-American and Anglo-American Urban[a] Workers, 1850 and 1900

	Mexican-Americans		Anglo-Americans	
	1850	1900	1850	1900
Farmer	—	25 (1.8%)	—	20 (1.9%)
Laborer	—	439 (31.7%)	1 (0.4%)	51 (4.8%)
Servant	—	86 (6.2%)	3 (1.3%)	46 (4.3%)
Carpenter	2 (2.7%)	26 (1.9%)	15 (6.4%)	21 (2.0%)
Tailor	2 (2.7%)	—	4 (1.7%)	—
Cartman	43 (58.1%)	—	—	—
Shoemaker	2 (2.7%)	—	3 (1.3%)	—
Seamstress	—	34 (2.5%)	—	29 (2.7%)
Clerk	4 (5.4%)	22 (1.6%)	11 (4.7%)	58 (5.4%)
Stonemason	4 (5.4%)	—	7 (3.0%)	—
Merchant	—	35 (2.5%)	10 (4.3%)	35 (3.3%)
Military (enlisted)	—	—	80 (34.3%)	25 (2.3%)
Wagon Surveyor (working for military)	—	—	34 (14.6%)	—
Wagoner	—	—	11 (4.7%)	—
Laundress	—	102 (7.4%)	—	—
Drawnwork	—	43 (3.1%)	—	—
Cook	—	40 (2.9%)	—	23 (2.2%)
Railroad Worker	—	29 (2.1%)	—	103 (9.6%)
Salesman	—	24 (1.7%)	—	34 (3.2%)
Bookkeeper	—	—	—	23 (2.2%)
Teacher	—	—	—	40 (3.7%)
Lawyer	—	—	—	21 (2.0%)
Machinist	—	—	—	25 (2.3%)
Barkeeper	—	—	—	23 (2.2%)
	57 (77.0%)	905 (65.4%)	179 (76.7%)	556 (52.1%)
	N=74	N=1,385	N=233	N=1,069

[a]As represented in this table, *urban workers* were those reported in the census returns for San Antonio in 1850, and for Brownsville, El Paso City, Laredo, and San Antonio in 1900. Scholars who specialize in the study of urban history include a number of factors such as "loyalty to town" and abundant "freedoms of choice" in the definition of an urban area. Among other factors they consider are the compactness (that is, size and density) of population and the existence of a diversity of specialized functions. These are the two fundamental criteria used in designating urban locations for the purpose of this analysis. Specifically, areas of 6,000 or more population which had at least 3 percent of their total labor force in each of the manual, skilled, mercantile, and professional occupational categories were counted as urban locations.

extracting what was possible from a niggardly white society. Their diligence and resourcefulness belied the nineteenth century notion that considerd them a lazy people.

Among those residing in the urban areas and going out to earn a living were *arrieros* (mule and ox drivers), who in the middle of the nineteenth century worked with a pair of oxen and an improvised *carreta* (cart). With skills unmatched by white teamsters, they dominated the freighting business in the pre-Civil War years. "The Mexican appears to have almost no other business than that of carting goods," wrote Frederick Law Olmsted. "Almost the entire transportation of the country is carried on by them with oxen and two-wheeled carts."[2]

In large carts mounted on a single pair of wooden wheels, they carried goods from the Indianola and Matagorda Bay areas to the interior of the state. Constructed without a particle of metal, the carts resembled immense crates moving slowly and irregularly, but advancing surely as patient, plodding oxen pulled from a yoke fastened by thongs to their horns. The five to seven foot wheels of the *carretas* consisted of thick, broad cottonwood puncheons fastened together with wooden pins and thongs of rawhide. The axle was made from liveoak or pecan wood and rugged timber made the cratelike body. Under this arrangement, problems arising with the carts could be fixed by a reliance on nature. If the yoke or a wheel broke, they could cut down a tree and mend it; if a chain broke, they could kill an ox or mustang and fabricate a leather trace to replace it. Varieties of carretas could be made of framework for light service or built to carry heavy loads—such as those designed for cross-country freighting. Thick canvas sheets protected the load from sun and rain.[3]

In those types of vehicles, arrieros routinely moved clothes, hats, cook stoves, sewing machines, clocks, and other items.[4] Under contract with the federal government, they also carried corn and public property to the several federal posts in the western areas in the 1850s,[5] and continued servicing the several frontier forts built to guard against Indians in the postbellum period.[6] During the Civil War, Mexican teamsters worked alongside Confederates in transporting cotton from Louisiana and East Texas to Mexico as the South sought to prevent capture of the staple. By coupling wagons and putting cotton frames between the standards, arrieros could outfit the wagons to carry twelve to fourteen bales. To secure the load, teamsters bored holes into the frame. The cargo, when placed on top of these wooden pins, held firmly. By fastening a long pole, or poles, to the front axles, then taking the pole (or poles) over the top of the cotton and fastening them to the rear axles, they held down the top row of the bales. [7]

The expansion of the railroad and the appearance of the prairie schooner after the Civil War displaced the carretas (see Table 9), although men like the Gil brothers of Laredo carried on a substantial freighting business to towns like San Antonio and Corpus Christi with improved vehicles. [8] Many of the old arrieros, however, now shifted to the larger Mexican trains that transported goods along the Chihuahua trail, adapting easily to these more cumbersome freighting carriers. [9] But in their day, they had made an immense contribution to the state of Texas, and indeed, had shown that skill and commitment to purpose could wring out profits both from government and private contractors at a time when the general society looked upon Tejanos as un-American and not worthy of trust.

Urban dwellers also left their homes to have a hand in the railroad construction that followed the Civil War (see Table 9). In the 1870s, for example, Mexicanos from San Antonio worked alongside other laborers on the Central Railroad, earning fifteen dollars a month and rations. [10] In the 1880s, Tejanos were a majority of the work force laying track for the Texas and Mexican Railroad, [11] and they also labored on the railroads of El Paso in the 1890s, although as a smaller element. [12]

Those with few skills and who preferred work in the city proper engaged in a variety of low-grade occupations. Tejanos never enjoyed an economic advantage over Anglos except in San Antonio— and there only until the 1850s. As already discussed, they entered developing urban areas where Anglos themselves administered the economy. The only area where Tejanos had enjoyed anything resembling a monopoly was in old Béxar, where in 1850 Bexareños reigned over commerce as arrieros. That case, though distinctive, is instructive—there the number of men in the skilled crafts (mainly cartmen) fell from 95.9 percent to 20.3 percent between 1850 and 1900, while the percentage of Anglos in the same category displayed no substantial decline. The 1900 census returns make it apparent that by then Tejanos filled most menial laboring needs in the cities (see Table 10). In the Fort Davis area, for example, local residents worked as laborers, gardners, adobe makers, and teamsters in the 1860s.[13] Many served as domestics and servants. At Fort McIntosh—and probably at the rest of the government installations along the border—Tejanos hired out to officers at the post;[14] in Corpus Christi toward the end of the century, they worked almost exclusively as the servant corps on neighboring ranches.[15] Nascent industry offered few opportunities. In the 1880s, villagers around the San Juan Mission (San Antonio) worked as operatives at a local wool scouring mill, processing about four tons of wool a day and readying it for shipment.[16]

Other Tejanos either improvised ways of making a living or, perceiving a money-rendering venture, exploited it. Not infrequently, they ministered to their communities by supplying needed services that developing towns were ill-equipped to provide. In San Antonio in the 1850s, for instance, some sold half a cord of mesquite wood at two dollars a load.[17] Others hauled water from nearby streams or rivers and sold it to townspeople. In the border-areas at mid-century, *barrileros* transported water from the Rio Grande in casks having two axles attached to the barrel's ends. By fitting a cord to these axles, barrileros rolled the casks without much fatigue or inconvenience.[18] Or they could attach a spindle or

Table 10. Urban Labor Force Composition, 1850 and 1900[a]

	Mexican-Americans		Anglo-Americans	
	1850	1900	1850	1900
Manual Laborers	1.4%	58.1%	6.5%	24.1%
Skilled Laborers	95.9%	20.3%	44.8%	37.6%
Merchants	—	7.5%	9.5%	17.9%
Professionals	—	5.1%	4.7%	15.2%
Ranch/Farm Owners	—	3.0%	—	2.3%
Other	2.7%	6.0%	34.5%	2.9%
	100%	100%	100%	100%
	(N=74)	(N=1,383)	N=(232)	(N=1,067)

[a]*Urban workers* here are defined as they were in Table 9.

   Jobs were assigned to the above categories according to the consensus of a panel of four historians working independently of one another. Where consensus did not occur, jobs were assigned to the "other" category.

staple to the center of a brace at the heads of these sixty gallon barrels and pull them by attaching the loop of the end of a rope to the spindles or staples. According to a Union soldier, "A Mexican water hauler will pull up a steep grade with as much ease his barrel of water as a jack would the same amount upon a dray." Water carts in the final decades of the century were barrels or small hogsheads mounted on wheels with a cloth hose attached and a burro pulling them. In mid-century, these "haulers of water" earned from two to four dollars a day according to the number of barrels they hauled, and in later decades buyers paid anywhere from a "picayune" to a "bit" a barrel.[19] Water haulers continued servicing barrios in similar ways well into the early years of the twentieth century.

The rapid growth that started in the towns of ante-bellum central Texas and continued there and in postbellum towns of southern and western Texas demanded skilled artisans, and about one-fifth of Tejano obreros (according to the 1900 census) so qualified. In most towns, Mexicanos made their living in such trades as stonemasonry, furniture repair, plumbing, silversmithing, tinsmithing, blacksmithing (Francisco Álvarez and Simón de la Peña among the most noticeable in San Antonio in the 1880s and 1890s),[20] and shoemaking (Manuel López, Nazario Luján, and Espiridion Cruz among those listed in the San Antonio directories of the final decades of the century).[21] Throughout the state, many maintained themselves and their families as construction workers, building homes and other edifices. The job of building the commandant's quarters at Fort Ringgold, for example, reportedly went to one Eusebio Cavazos.[22]

Much more study into the role these craftsmen played in the civilization of southern and western Texas remains to be done. What cultural part, for example, did Tejano artisans play in the economy of those areas? Did Mexican immigrants coming to Texas bring a particular expertise, say of the Aztec tradition? Could South Texas, where too few Anglos were available to attend to those jobs, have become an economic empire had there been no Tejano artisans? What was the legacy of these Tejanos? Were Mexicanos the ones who built the Spanish-styled homes of southern and western Texas; and did they add their own *Mexican* touch to them? White men obviously appreciated the Moorish roofing, the look of adobe, and the patio layouts and built their town and ranch homes in that pattern. Along those lines, what did blacksmiths, silversmiths, and other craftsmen contribute to that society? But much more importantly, what perception did Tejanos have of themselves knowing that their work was equal to if not better than Anglos? And what did they feel knowing they were carrying on their forefathers' skilled traditions, which withstood the test of time and ever changing architectural styles? Like the vaqueros on the range, they could not have regarded themselves as less than manly.

The existence of a large Mexican work force made for an atmosphere of familiarity akin to that in the rural areas where an Hispanic ambience allowed a Tejano community to function in a bicultural setting. In these urban areas, also, townspeople interacted with Spanish-speaking tradesmen who either worked for Anglo businessmen or had their own shops. Few Tejanos would have been bewildered in a setting where services could be delivered in common ways.

Urban dwellers likewise became vendors of consumable products. Those without the advantages to invest in more formidable undertakings customarily gathered in a specified spot in town to set up shop as *vendedores;* as cities grew, this area became known as the Mexican section. In emergent Rio Grande City in the 1850s, participants convened in open markets to sell vegetables, goat meat, sun-dried beef, cakes, and confectionery.[23] During the Civil War, Brownsville's market thrived at a local two-story brick building[24] and in the 1890s, at Market Plaza. There, vendors brought their home-made *dulces* (candy) and potfuls of *tamales* in the evenings. But some preferred locations other than the Plaza. Dulce vendors, especially, often brought little tables and stools and stationed themselves in a favorite spot on the street while others perambulated from one end of the city to the other, carrying their *dulces* on wooden trays. Both exposed for sale all manner of sweet things, including the favorite dulces made from *piloncillo* (Mexican sugar). Street vendors in that same period ventured into Fort Brown to push their articles.[25]

Likewise in Laredo in the 1880s, candymakers stood on street corners selling their sweet wares, among them *nueces dulces* and *queso de tuna*—the first a delightful compound of pecans, cinnamon, and sugar; the latter a sweetmeat made of the juice and pulp of the fruit of the prickly-pear cactus. A conserve of cocoa-nut and squares of pumpkin candies, crisp without and soft within, further enticed customers.[26] At night, also, Mexican men and women stationed themselves at the market plaza with eating tables to sell their cuisine.[27]

But it was San Antonio that epitomized the tradition of outdoor salesmanship in the final decades of the century. For what appeared to whites (both residents and travelers) as "quaint" was in actuality the way in which Bexareños, keenly attuned to the wishes of the white consumer, met a market need. It did not take Tejanos long to determine that the way they prepared their meals seduced the white visitor (or for that matter, any hungry person) and that there was a profit to be made from delectable Mexican food. Nor, perhaps, did it take them long to perceive that a profit could be made from peddling their so-called quaint products either as cheap commodities or as souvenirs. It was, after all, the thousands who came to San Antonio to see the quaint that made the city's market place unique. What evolved as commonplace in the city then (and reproduced elsewhere) showed how bicultural Mexican Americans could appeal to the vanities and weaknesses of whites in the ongoing Tejano struggle to subsist under imposing adversity.

In Laredito or Chihuahuita, the Mexican section of San Antonio, merchants spread little tables on sidewalks as passers-by purchased rolls, chocolate, and bits of pastry. Vendors sold candies, porcupineworks, bunches of magnolias, and great, ineffably sweet Cape jasmines from the coast, while Mexican women, veiled by their *rebozos*, displayed wicker cages full of mocking-birds, vivid cardinals with red crests, and lively little *canarios*. Vendedores offered skins of leopards and ocelots (dressed by Indian women with the brains of the beast until they were supple as silk); wonderful Mexican needlework (made on the drawn thread that rivalled the Old-world laces); and earthen pipkins or *jarritos* ornamented with *molinillos* (that is, wooden sticks, set in many rings, which, rolled upright between the palms, made the chocolate foam in the pipkin). And few transactions occurred that did not involve the customary *pilón*—the ritual of throwing an additional item into the bargain. The old and the young mingled as the fervor of daily enterprise was complemented by flies and other nuisances, concomitants of these sort of outdoor arrangements.[28]

Blazing fires, flickering lamps, illuminating lanterns, chattering sales persons, and laughing patrons all combined with peppery viands to transform another of San Antonio's singular market practices—the chili stands—into one of the most salient examples of Bexareño night life. At dusk, vendors commenced carting their paraphernalia into the fringes of the plaza and arranging small tables about a wood fire. Soon the area was busy. Huge vessels from which floated tempting aromas of Mexican viands rested over smouldering fires; dishes, pots, and pans filled the tables. Mexican men and women hovered about the food, dishing up *frijoles* and other savory concoctions. Young, tastefully-dressed *señoritas*, the so-called chili queens, served the customers heaping bowls of *chili con carne* and beans, which, with a generous supply of *tortillas*, sold for ten cents in the 1880s. Sometimes, young men appropriately and colorfully dressed in Mexican outfits, swaggered and strolled through the crowd singing and strumming the guitar, often winning the approval of the crowd, which showered them with coins. On other occasions, señoritas performed Mexican national dances like the hat dance. By late evening, the merchants started removing the paraphernalia to allow vegetables and forage vendors to occupy the plaza the next morning.[29]

But the selling of Mexican cuisine did not restrict itself to the plaza, for vendors in the barrio west of the San Pedro Creek learned to turn to their advantage American curiosity of their cookery. Many made their homes into makeshift eating places, furnishing them with long tables and wooden benches. There women furnished tortillas, coffee, and various palatable compounds enhanced with pepper. In the 1870s, whites flocked to the improvised kitchens of Laredito to partake of the food that only the quaint could deliver.[30]

The continuity of such salesmanship attested to the resiliency of entrepreneurial fashions that could be imposed on the American economy and not be demolished by an American way of life that disdained the "backward" ways imputed to Mexicanos. For the selling of wares and delicacies to a consuming public did not differ much from the way in which Tejano kinsmen sold in Mexico. But Tejanos adjusted that Mexican cultural form to fit the circumstances where buyers included not only Tejanos but Anglo Americans as well. They learned quickly the tastes of the Anglo consumer and conformed their entrepreneurship to exploit those demands. But the practice of outdoor salesmanship nevertheless stamped Texas cities having a substantial Tejano population with a cultural fashion identifiable, not with the Poles, the Germans, the Czechs, but the Mexicans. As such, it displayed the Tejano cultural link with the mother country. In this adaptation, the Tejanos were one of numerous immigrant groups that have retained cultural continuity in ethnic enclaves.

Not every Tejano businessman made his living as a street vendor, of course; a moderate number belonged to a property-owning class that managed establishments that produced comfortable returns. This small class of urban entrepreneurs, like their agrarian counterparts, either retained some semblance of their preconquest businesses or even expanded upon them following the Revolution, or, in the case of southern and western Texas, after the Mexican War. Newcomers invested money in their own establishments and got them going. Together, this class amounted to about 7.5 percent of the Mexican American urban labor force according to the 1900 census.

As a mercantile group that understood their Tejano clients, these men of means conducted their business in a fashion familiar to Tejano consumers and provided goods appropriate to buyers with a Mexican cultural base but undergoing changes in consumer tastes. If, because of their class, these Tejano businessmen did not identify with the manner of the poor, they were often part of a primary environment where Tejano culture underwent formation, definition, distillation, and evolution.

Proprietors included storeowners like Manuel Guerra in Roma, one of the wealthiest and most substantial merchants of the Texas frontier. He owned business establishments in Roma, Rio Grande City, and other border areas, and he sometimes journeyed as far as New York to purchase his goods.[31] In Laredo, A. M. Bruni and Brother and J. Armengel ranked among the more successful grocers. The most extensive and wealthy firm in the city was the house of J. Villegas and Brother (comprised of Joaquín Villegas and Quintín Villegas), importers and wholesale dealers in groceries, commission merchants, and manufacturers' agents. The firm imported large quantities of miscellaneous products, and its trade extended all over the state.[32] In Duval County, merchants like Avolina and Francisco Tovar of San Diego traveled to Galveston and New Orleans to buy their stock of goods, while others such as Toribio and Armando Guerra bought theirs in areas like San Antonio. Entrepreneurs like Antonio Rosales and José María García of San Diego and José Vaello of Benavides[33] prospered similarly. In the county areas of South Texas, F. P. and P. Guerra managed a store at

Rancho San Antonio Viejo (Starr County), Prajedis Guerrero at Naranjo Ranch, and Magdaleno Flores at Havana, Mauricio Gonzales at Palito Blanco, and S. Gutiérrez of Soledad Wells.[34] Regarding Tejano stores in Eagle Pass in the 1890s, an observer wrote:

Every store is a *tienda barata* (cheap store), and all have names as Tienda del Gallo (store of the cock), Tienda de los Mexicanos, and so forth. They are one-storied and flat-roofed the most modern ones built of brick, the others of adobe, which last forever; they have earthen floors or cemented ones, perhaps.[35]

In large cities like San Antonio, profit-oriented Tejanos ventured into a wide range of capitalist undertakings after the 1870s. Narciso Leal was a livestock and general commission merchant (including real estate)[36] as were the Morín brothers (José L. and Thomas H.).[37] Leonardo Garza was a land salesman with the Occidental Land Company.[38] Others in real estate were Pedro Rosales, Antonio P. Rivas, Juan Manuel Chávez, and Florencio S. Gonzales.[39] The Pereida brothers (José J., Gumesindo F., and Rafael M.), watchmakers and jewelers,[40] were among numerous successful entreprenuers listed in the city directories of the 1880s and 1890s alongside a cadre of grocers, butchers, and retail store merchants. Luciano Leal and Pablo Luján offered their services as detective investigators in the city in the 1890s.[41]

Sufficiently dexterous to succeed in other branches of the business sector, Mexican American merchants in Texas entered into every endeavor promising to render profits. Those wishing to whet one of the public's appetites went into the bakery, restaurant, or saloon business.[42] Some managed their own hotels,[43] their own portrait studios,[44] their own barber shops, their *boticas* (drugstores),[45] or their own print shops.[46] Others like Francisco Villasēnor of Corpus Christi in the 1880s, Fabian Fabela in San Diego at the same time, and Luis Esparza of San Antonio, put their crafts to use by servicing their respective communities as tailors.[47] The prosperity of men like Silverio de la Peña—who owned a two-story drugstore and residence at Rio Grande City valued at $10,000 in 1887[48]—while not typical of Tejano prosperity nevertheless was not uncommon.

Tejanos turned to business not only because it led to dividends, but because Texas' Jim Crow system almost compelled them to minister to their own communities. Dependent upon people with limited buying power, most eked out modest profits at best. As representatives of the same culture, however, they contributed immeasurably to the Tejano community by serving it on its own terms, by transacting business in Spanish, by providing goods appropriate to Tejano culture, and by giving consumers a dimension of familiarity when interacting with one aspect of the state's economy. Their importance lay not so much in profits, for their businesses probably yielded little, but in the fact that they acted as cultural buffers that aided in warding off oppression.

A small body of professionals also appeared concomitant with the expansion and growth of the urban areas where Tejanos resided. The increase in population throughout the state called for practicing professionals who could fill the needs of the growing number of Tejano inhabitants. Those who represented this class tended to be either Mexicans from Mexico or the progeny of old-line families who had been to Mexico or to American colleges like that in Rolla, Missouri, for their studies. Such Americanized Mexicans sensed that school attendance, whether in Mexico or the United States, paid off in success and profits. As a class, they could service Mexicanos, Americanos, or both.

The cadre of teachers that tended to the different communities included people of diverse background—some had less than a college education but others claimed excellent credentials. Professor Luis Puebla, for example, who directed the San Diego public school system in the late 1880s, was a Mexican immigrant educated at Georgetown College, Washington, D.C. Francisco Carrillo, who taught in neighboring Benavides at the same time, was born in Mexico City, had graduated from the military school in Chapultepec, and after fighting against Porfirio Díaz in Mexico, had sought refuge in American public schools.[49]

Spanish language newspaper editors such as José López Montalbo of *El Horizonte* and *El Disputado* of Laredo and Catarino Garza of *El Libre Pensador* (Eagle Pass) and *El Comercio Mexicano* (Palito Blanco) also had received instruction outside the state.[50] Alberto F. Martínez, editor of *El Cronista* in San Antonio in 1898, was a Spaniard who lost his teaching job in the city's public school system when he sided with his native Spain during the Spanish American War.[51]

Spanish-surnamed physicians were not uncommon to areas with large Hispanic populations. Dr. Carlos Castro, a Cuban, seems to

have worked in Brownsville's Mexican section in 1860,[52] as did
Vicente Cerda in 1880.[53] Dr. M. Martínez took care of some of
Cameron County's health needs in 1900.[54] Crisoforo Solis attended
to Mexicanos of Starr County in the same period.[55] In Laredo,
doctors included Manuel T. Leal, D. Montemayor, J.C.D.F. Váldez,
Martín García, F. Garza, and J. Váldez in 1900.[56] Spanish-born
Francisco Estapa was among those who received patients in Hidalgo County in the seventies.[57] Dr. Cresencio Ariola (a native-
born Texan) worked in Atascosa County in 1880,[58] Berveva Gonzales
in Maverick County in the same year,[59] Dr. Melencio A. Martínez
practiced in Corpus Christi in 1885,[60] and G. de la Fuente in
Duval County in 1900.[61] Pedro Batista, Manuel de la Garza, Plutarco
Ornelas, Pablo Rodríquez, Pablo Díaz, Lino Villareal, Hilario
Martínez, Abraham Díaz, A. de la Lama García, Miguel S. Villareal,
and Domingo Gonzales, all were involved in medicine in San Antonio at one time or another in the 1880s and 1890s.[62] El Paso in
the 1890s included distinguished physicians like Dr. Antonio de la
Campa, Dr. Juan Rechy who specialized in pulmonary diseases,
and dentist M. N. Samaniego.[63]

Professional men also included numerous druggists. Among them
in Cameron County were Ramón López in 1860,[64] Silvestre Varón
in 1870,[65] and Isidro Pérez in 1900.[66] Antonio Chapa and Eulogio
Sánchez practiced pharmacy in Laredo at the turn of the twentieth
century.[67] Other druggists in South Texas included Silverio de la
Peña in Corpus Christi (and in Rio Grande City) in the 1880s,[68]
Juan Herrera and Bruno Rios in Duval County in the latter nine-
teenth century,[69] and A. Contreras in Rio Grande City in 1900.[70]
Hilario Martínez, Francisco P. Flores, Francisco Z. Díaz, Peter D.
Estrade, Jr., and F. A. Chapa made their living in the same way in
San Antonio in the nineties.[71]

On the legal front were attorneys like Castillo Montero in Brownsville in 1870, Juan Benavides in Laredo in 1880,[72] Juan Z. Canales
and Justo Cárdenas in that same city in 1900,[73] and Antonio D.
Flores and Leonardo Garza, Jr., in San Antonio in the 1890s.[74] The
duties of notaries public were filled by Juan E. Barrera, J. F.
Cassiano, and J. E. García in San Antonio in the 1880s and 1890s as
well as other Tejanos throughout the state.[75]

Not all professionals claimed the latest American academic training. Many of those listed in the census as teachers, for example,
came from Mexico and probably taught in Spanish. A few were too

young to have completed formal instruction. Some of those who listed their occupation as doctors may have received less than a medical education and even may have been *curanderos* (folk healers) who, in translation, gave their vocation as doctor. The census, for example, recorded some druggists as being illiterate. These observations may also apply to other professionals.

Yet, these differences should not detract from the fact that such a professional class did include many who were very qualified people. Besides, even if some lacked a formal education, their presence in almost every area of the state shows that Tejano communities did what they could to help themselves. Mexicanos tried to elevate educational conditions in areas where the lack of college graduates might degenerate into ignorance; they turned to what was available to offset that ignorance. Persons with some training in the miracles of *hierbitas* (curative herbs), could likewise tend to problems of health. In this respect, these Tejano communities did not differ much from other frontier settlements in the United States where isolation compelled people to do something in their behalf, or slave communities before the Civil War, where conjurers healed the sick.

But not all Tejanos in the cities pursued manual labor, business endeavors, or professional careers as a way to make a living. Many served their community in government capacities—as sanitary inspectors, quarantine officers, or custom collectors in the border areas, for example. In filling these jobs, the Tejano experience was similar to that of blacks and immigrants, many of whom took city positions as their first step into the economic mainstream. Public works afforded them another avenue for subsistence. Manuel Longoria, for example, received remuneration from the Corpus Christi city council in the 1880s for working the city streets with dray and removing dead animals. Juárez Hernández had a similar job but was charged with removing loads of oyster shells, and in the 1880s Florentino García rendered service to the fire department, while Jesús Reyna and J. M. Flores received reimbursement from the commissioners' court for burying paupers. Others in Corpus Christi found lighting the city lamps a means of livelihood, and still others worked as overseers of road precincts. Among these men in the 1880s were Abrán Pérez, Manuel Váldez, Juan Hinojosa, José Váldez, Ramón Morano, Andrés Canales, M. M. Ballí, Luciano Bazán, Ysidro Garza, and Bartolo Peña.[76] In Duval County, Loretto

García worked as a road overseer in the 1890s, and Captain E. Peña worked the chain gang in cleaning the streets of San Diego.[77]

Many more were the positions that Tejanos occupied. In some towns, especially where they outnumbered whites, they made up part of the fire departments.[78] Some were mail carriers: among them Demetrio Silva who carried correspondence between San Patricio and Corpus Christi in the 1880s and J. M. Vela who did the same on a route from Delfina to Hidalgo in the 1890s.[79] Some even received federal appointments to the post office: Silverio de la Peña was postmaster in Rio Grande City in 1893,[80] Pedro Candelario worked as a distributing clerk in 1896 in the El Paso post office, while Pilar M. Maese, who entered the postal service in the 1880s, eventually became an assistant postmaster in El Paso.[81] Routinely, Tejanos served as census enumerators every ten years, especially in the counties of South Texas.

In the larger cities such as El Paso, city and county governments regularly paid Mexicanos for services rendered. In San Antonio in the late 1880s, where Alberto Cassiano was a clerk in the county collectors office and Francisco Galán was sanitary inspector for the west side, much the same situation existed.[82]

In a white man's state where citizens frequently relied on police powers to keep minorities in their place, many Tejanos held law enforcement positions. A few rose to high rank, generally in the border sections where Mexican Americans predominated. The Cameron County police force, for example, where Tejanos invariably made up the rank and file,[83] boasted of the popular Sheriff Santiago A. Brito in the 1880s and 1890s. Born and raised in Cameron County, according to reports, he won acclaim from both Anglos and Tejanos as the best sheriff the county ever had. Considered a man of judgment and common sense, one thoroughly dedicated to his job and brave to a fault, he earned a reputation as the "bandit's terror" during his tenure as sheriff. With deputies like Hipolito Tamayo, Hipolito Martínez, José María Esparza, Aldolfo Guerrero, and others, he hunted down outlaws, cattle thieves, enforced the peace, policed the area to prevent smuggling, protected the Tejano population of the Valley, and tracked down outlaw gangs, both white and Mexicano, who preyed upon Tejano owned *ranchos*. "Of his life and services on the frontier several volumes of thrilling interest could be written," wrote a newspaper correspondent in 1889. "The only trouble is that the press and public would be certain to say that they were exaggerated." He died in the line of duty, murdered by assassins. Making rounds with his deputies at 2:30 A.M., he had left a *baile* in Brownville's Plaza de los Gallos; gunmen crept up behind his carriage and fired shots into it, killing the sheriff instantly. The whole county mourned the tragedy. [84]

Neighboring counties similarly submitted to the protection of Tejano policemen. Men like sheriffs Eohemio García in 1860, David Gonzales and Darío Gonzales in the early 1880s, [85] and Darío Sánchez, in the latter part of the eighties and nineties, [86] carried out their duties in Webb County with no less consideration than any other peace officer in the state. The same could be said about L. B. Ortiz and his brother, deputy sheriff Santos Ortiz, Sánchez' successors, as well as sheriffs Porfirio Benavides, Jacobo Salazar, and L. R. Ortiz who served in the mid-1890s. [87] In Laredo itself, Don Higinio García served as city marshal in the early 1880s, and Eugene Iglesias served in the same office in the 1890s, assisted by deputy marshal Plutarco Ortiz. Policemen Luciano Muñoz, Jesús Sandoval, Julian García, Salome Méndez, José M. Moreno, Leonides Montemayor, Manuel Barrera, José B. Garza, Abelino Peña, Martín Villastrigo, and Porfirio Laurel, comprised only part of the integrated peace-keeping force of the 1880s and 1890s. Rosendo Guerra was United States marshal in 1893 and Dolores Cano in 1900. [88]

So long as Mexicanos retained a demographic majority in the border areas, Tejanos continued serving in every law enforcing capacity. José María Villareal and J. D. Uribe served as Zapata County sheriffs in the 1880s. [89] Spanish descended León Estapa was sheriff of Hidalgo County in the 1870s during Reconstruction and deputy sheriffs there in 1900 included Victoriano Reyna. [90] Among other border deputy sheriffs in the latter decades of the century were Marcos Ortega in Rio Grande City and Bonefacio Díaz in Eagle Pass. [91] In the extreme west Texas section of the state, Juan Armendariz and Benito Gonzales served as El Paso County sheriffs in the 1870s and 1880s, respectively. [92] Tejanos made up the rank and file of police forces in small villages of the county as well.

But population alone fails to explain the presence of Tejanos as lawmen, for they were present in other agencies in cities where whites either outnumbered them or tenaciously controlled politics. In Duval County, for instance, where Tejanos outnumbered Anglos but Anglos in turn controlled politics, Lino Cuellar won distinction as a deputy sheriff in the 1880s, as did Nic Benavides in the 1890s.[93] Both chased after Catarino Garza in 1891 and 1892. In the Nueces County of the 1880s and 1890s, where whites still vividly recalled the Corpus Christi Raid by Mexican bandits in 1875, Pablino Coy won the respect of county residents who lauded his exploits as deputy sheriff.[94] In Corpus Christi itself, Caferino Vidaurri was a deputy sheriff in 1888, Marciano Ramírez a city policeman in 1883, and Martín Hinojosa a mounted policeman in 1891.[95]

Much the same situation held for some of the Central Texas areas. In Wilson County, an area of Tejano ranchos and land grants before mid-century, Tejano resilience manifested itself in the hold they still retained in county law offices after the Civil War. In the 1870s a Mr. LaZerda was the county sheriff and Juan Flores served as one of his deputies.[96] Manuel J. Ximénes, a deputy sheriff in the late 1880s, became Wilson County sheriff in 1890, served until 1894, then resumed the office in 1899.[97]

Participation in San Antonio's peace-keeping body typified the example of the Tejano ability to retain some presence in the law enforcement corps despite Anglo prejudice. Numerical superiority in the city, possession of land, control of economics, politics, and the police passed into American hands by the 1840s. Only Tejano cultural influence remained. Yet, amid these circumstances, numerous Tejanos (vestiges of the older families, one suspects), occupied a number of peace-keeping offices after the 1840s. During Reconstruction, for instance, Pedro Cevallos served in the State Police.[98] While the office of Béxar County sheriff remained elusive to them, a number served as deputy sheriffs. Pedro Cevallos was among them in the 1850s, Ignacio García, Esteban Sandoval and Manuel Sánchez in the 1880s, and Antonio Herrera, Manuel Móntez, José Quintana, Domingo L. Díaz, and Geronimo Quintana in the 1890s.[99] In San Antonio itself, the city council elected Alejo Pérez as assistant marshal in January 1875, and Juan T. Cárdenas served as deputy city marshal in the 1870s and 1880s.[100] City policemen included J. M. Cadena, appointed in January 1872, Juan E. Barrera, who replaced him in July of the same year, Jacobo Coy and Francisco Galán, who served in the early 1880s,[101] Andrés Coy, F. Garza, and Alejo Pérez who were part of the police force throughout the decade,[102] and Rafael R. Martínez, who continued as both police officer and county jailer into the 1890s.[103] In the last decade of the nineteenth century, Celedonio Cadena, Alejo Móntez, Rumaldo Pérez, Ignacio Chávez, and Jacinto Gonzales were among the Tejano policemen in the city.[104] Not infrequently, these police officers served as a link between the Tejano community and the Anglo system of justice. As such they acted as mediators in a conflict of cultures and values in an effort to ameliorate Tejano oppression.

Few Bexareños in that period, however, attracted the attention that accrued to city policeman Jacobo Coy for his part in the killing of the notorious outlaws "King" Fisher and Ben Thompson. Thompson, a feared gunslinger, and Fisher, who once boasted of having killed thirty-seven men, "not counting Mexicans," had gone into the Vaudeville Variety Theatre (a gambling house) in San Antonio where Coy was a special officer, assigned to preserve the peace. About 10:30 P.M. on March 11, 1884 a squabble arose between Thompson and one of the owners (ill-feeling already existed between the two parties). At this point, Thompson pulled his gun and struck the owner in the mouth. Coy grabbed the barrel just as the gun fired. Fisher joined the struggle between Thompson and the big Mexicano. All three fell in a heap, Thompson's pistol roaring all the while. When things cleared, Fisher and Thompson lay dead on the floor. Coy picked himself up, only slightly injured. The coroner's jury found that both died from bullets fired from Jacobo Coy's pistol and that of the operator with whom the argument originally started. The killing was deemed justifiable homicide. Thompson and Fisher's apologizers, however, have questioned the coroner's verdict and still insist the two outlaws fell victims to unknown assailants.[105]

In the urban scene, then, old ways of working within the city continued, or new ones were devised, old crafts persisted or were learned, and old business techniques prevailed or were revised. Venturesome Tejanos looking beyond nonskilled tasks, adjusted to city life, and penetrated newer openings. In playing a part in every phase of a city's makeup, they, in turn, offered goods and services in common ways to other urban dwellers, or at least provided a dimension to the border towns, or the Mexican section of predominately Anglo towns, that softened what researchers now call cultural shock among those that might suffer from their contact with American institutions.

The numerous means by which Tejanos earned their living attested to their ability to wrest concession from a white society that kept them on the periphery of Anglo American life. Still, the accusations of indolence as reported in the agrarian sector extended to the cities. W. H. Watts, superintendent of the El Paso Water Company, claimed in 1896:

When a Mexican laborer wants to take a day off, he can be relied on to dig up a saint or some kind of anniversary to celebrate. On St. John's day all my Juans are out celebrating, and the Joses, Pedros, et al. get out of their work on St. James' and St. Peters' days. But a new anniversary was rung in on me this morning. One of my men was missing and I asked Louis Behr [sic?] what saint's day he was celebrating. Louis said the man was not celebrating any saint today, but was celebrating the anniversary of the burning of his house; that he was remaining home today to prevent fire from repeating the performance. Next they will be celebrating the anniversary of the death of some pet dog or burro.[106]

Such actions as Watts railed against may have been the manifestation of preindustrial work habits, but at the same time were not characteristic of Tejanos in every facet of urban life. *Obreros* quite naturally would have run off at every chance to pursue fun and frolic when faced with the choice of hard work at servant wages. And Anglo entrepreneurs themselves would have placed no confidence in Tejano laborers. To the contrary, they advertised the abundance of cheap Mexican labor as an advantage to industry in developing southern and western cities.[107]

Tejanos would be expected to occupy only the lower rungs of the economic ladder given the socioeconomic structure of late nineteenth century Texas. After all, *obreros*, who made up only about 40 percent of the urban labor force by 1900, hardly were in a position to manipulate the economy to their advantage. While they were as dedicated as any other worker in the state (about 30 percent of both Tejano and Anglo populations were employed by 1900), the urban economy still left them little space for rising above a proletarian condition. Like Tejano workers in the rural areas, they were clustered around a relatively limited number of jobs without the alternatives open to Anglos (see Table 11). Despite that, they frequently were on lists, published by newspapers periodically, of citizens who paid taxes on property worth over $10,000. While those included probably came from a landowning rather than an urban business elite, they still ranked among respected citizens in

Table 11. Selected Characteristics of Urban Labor Forces in South, Central, and West Texas, 1850 and 1900[a]

	Mexican-Americans		Anglo-Americans	
	1850	*1900*	*1850*	*1900*
Estimated percent of Labor Force	25.6%	39.4%	74.4%	60.6%
Estimated percent of Ethnic Population Who were Employed	17.3%	35.8%	54.1%	36.2%
Estimated Number of Workers	277	10,937	807	16,815
Estimated Number of Workers per Job Designation	4.6	11.6	5.8	6.4

[a]As represented in this table, *urban workers*, were those reported in the census returns for San Antonio in 1850, and for Brownsville, El Paso City, Laredo, and San Antonio in 1900. Scholars who specialize in the study of urban history include a number of factors such as "loyalty to town" and abundant "freedoms of choice" in the definition of urban areas. Among other factors they consider are the compactness (that is, size and density) of population and the existence of a diversity of specialized functions. These are the two fundamental criteria used in designating urban locations for the purpose of this analysis. Specifically, areas of 6,000 or more population which had at least 3 percent of their total labor force in each of the manual, skilled, mercantile, and professional occupational categories were counted as urban locations.

the community, and, judging from the pride that the newspapers took in publishing those lists as a reflection of that area's prosperity, they were looked upon as exemplary members of the community.[108] Those lists still appeared in the latter years of the century by which time, according to an older generation of social scientists and historians, the Tejano community consisted of nonachievers who had resigned themselves to a luckless fate long before.

Though Afro-Americans in the central areas, and Indians in the El Paso Valley, added to the ethnic variety of labor in nineteenth century Texas, Anglos and Mexicanos composed the greater mass of the work force. Of a little more than 4,000 Mexican and Anglo Americans working in Béxar and El Paso counties and the Lower Rio Grande Valley in 1850 (1860), Tejanos were about 56.2 percent and Anglos about 43.8 percent. Out of some 45,000 Mexican and Anglo Americans who made up the work force in the same areas in 1900, about 53.7 percent were Mexicanos as opposed to 46.3 percent whites (see Table 12). Sociologically, these two sectors of the labor force displayed certain cultural similarities but also distinct ethnic traits. According to the 1900 census, for example, the percentage of Tejano workers who headed households (and thus sup-

Table 12. Selected Characteristics of Mexican-American and Anglo-American Workers in Texas, 1850 (1860) and 1900[a]

	Mexican-Americans		Anglo-Americans	
	1850 (1860)	1900	1850 (1860)	1900
Estimated percent of Mexican and Anglo-American labor force	56.2%	53.7%	43.8%	46.3%
Estimated Percent of Ethnic Population	19.2%	32.2%	47.7%	35.4%
Estimated Number of Workers	2,677	23,830	1,887	20,546
Percent Workers Who were Heads of Households	61.3%	57.5%	28.1%	54.5%
Percent Child Workers (less than 19 years of age)	16.4%	16.1%	4.7%	9.6%
Percent Living in Single-Family Dwellings	46.8%	60.5%	16.9%	41.5%
Average Number of Children per Workers Household	2.7	3.6	0.7	2.7
Percent Living in Nuclear Families	62.8%	82.7%	16.7%	66.5%
Percent Living in Male-Headed Households	86.4%	84.7%	96.9%	80.8%
Average Age of Workers in Years	31.8	33.7	29.9	35.0
Percent Male	83.0%	83.4%	95.1%	81.0%
Percent Foreign Born	47.1%	61.2%	44.8%	24.3%
Percent Literate	25.1%	13.0%	86.6%	92.2%
Percent Married	—	47.9%	—	49.4%
Percent Home Owners	—	18.6%	—	20.0%

[a]This table combines the labor force of Béxar County and the Lower Rio Grande Valley in 1850 with the labor force of El Paso County in 1860. The 1900 estimates are based on the combined labor forces of Béxar, Webb, Starr, Cameron, and El Paso counties in 1900.

ported dependents through their labor) approximated the percentage of Anglos. The proportion of Mexicano and Anglo workers living in male-headed domiciles was also quite similar, and little distinction existed between the average age of the two working groups; although the Tejanos in mid-century were about two years older than the Anglos, they were two years younger in 1900. In the case of married workers, percentages again were quite equal between the two groups; there, however, the likenesses ended.

Tejano workers lived in single family dwellings more frequently than Anglos, and the nuclear family more commonly prevailed in the culture of the Mexicanos. In addition, the Tejano *obrero's* household included about one more child on the average than did the household of the Anglo worker by 1900. Thus, it appears that the average nineteenth century Mexican American worker took on the task of supporting more dependents in a more autonomous and self-contained family household setting than did the average Anglo American laborer. Moreover, the average Tejano worker probably confronted the task in the face of increasingly formidable barriers to adequate support of a family. For example, due to an influx of Mexican migration following the Civil War, the percentage of foreign born Tejano workers between 1850 and 1900 increased significantly. In contrast, the proportion of foreign born Anglo workers decreased conspicuously. Also, a gap separated the illiterate (in English) Tejano *obrero* from his literate counterpart. Native birth and literacy in English were personal traits making higher income producing jobs more accessible, but an increasing number of nineteenth century Tejano laborers faced the task of supporting their families with the absence of those advantages.

Both Mexicanos and Anglos depended upon child labor to supplement family income, but of the two groups a higher percentage of Tejanos under the age of nineteen years made up the labor pool (see Table 12). As might be expected, the occupational status of Mexican American children mirrored the position of the adult laboring population. At mid-century, many young Tejanos had joined their fathers as cartmen, carpenters, and herders. By the latter decades of the century, however, those occupations had either disappeared or decreased in terms of accessibility, and the representation of Mexican American youths in skilled laboring area abated. By 1900, approximately 43.4 percent of young Tejanos in Béxar, Cameron, El Paso, Starr and Webb counties were employed as common laborers. This compared to only about 19.1 percent among youthful Anglo workers in the same areas. On the other hand Anglo American child workers entered the emerging service occupations, such as clerical work, in greater numbers than their Tejano couterparts (see Table 13). Just as adult Tejano laborers were proletarianized at a more rapid pace than adult Anglo workers, so were the children of the Mexicanos.

Occupational status, income, and wealth are never perfectly correlated in specified populations, but a correspondence between them is often apparent and expected. Among the trends found in large-scale studies is that higher occupational status leads to greater income earning capacity, which generates an increased ability to

Table 13. Jobs Most Commonly Held by Mexican-American and Anglo-American Child Laborers (Less than 19 Years Old), 1850 (1860) and 1900[a]

	Mexican-Americans		Anglo-Americans	
	1850(1860)	1900	1850(1860)	1900
Cartman	24.5%	—	—	—
Clerk	1.9%	1.9%	1.6%	12.2%
Carpenter	15.1%	1.6%	—	—
Shoemaker	4.7%	0.5%	—	—
Tailor	9.4%	—	—	—
Servant	13.2%	11.9%	—	15.3%
Herder	15.1%	0.7%	3.3%	—
Seamstress	2.8%	0.9%	—	2.3%
Laborer	0.9%	43.4%	—	19.1%
Enlisted Military	—	—	24.6%	—
Wagon Surveyor for Military	—	—	55.7%	—
Sheepherder	—	5.5%	—	—
Vaquero	—	2.4%	—	0.8%
Railroad Worker	—	0.9%	—	2.3%
Drawnwork	—	4.7%	—	—
Miner	—	2.3%	—	—
Dairyman	—	—	—	2.3%
	87.6%	76.7%	85.2%	54.3%
	(N=106)	(N=579)	(N=61)	(N=131)

[a]This table presents only the most commonly held occupations among a sample of workers under 19 years old in Béxar County and the Lower Rio Grande Valley in 1850 and in El Paso County in 1860, and in Béxar, Cameron, El Paso, Starr, and Webb counties in 1900.

convert income into various forms of wealth. A similar pattern is suggested by the disparate labor trends between Mexican and Anglo Americans in the latter part of the nineteenth century; as a result, a growing inequality of wealth between the two segments of the Texas population can be reasonably inferred.

Unfortunately, limitations in data provided by census reports inhibit extensive documentation of such an inference. Aside from the inexactness resulting from erroneous recording of wealth holdings, the specific types of wealth-related information varied from one census count to another. The returns for 1850 and 1860 included estimates of the dollar value of a respondent's personal estate, but the 1900 reports left out such information. That exclusion precludes a direct comparison of personal wealth holdings across time. Nevertheless, some documentation of the inference that divergent labor trends between Mexicanos and whites led to inequalities in wealth is possible.

According to the 1850 (1860) census returns for Béxar and El Paso counties and the Lower Rio Grande Valley, almost three times as many Mexican Americans held personal wealth as Anglos. Based on sample data, an estimated 71.5 percent of all personal wealth holders in South, Central, and West Texas were Mexicanos, and 28.5 percent were Anglos. At the same time, however, only about 10.4 percent of the total Tejano population had managed to accrue any amount of personal riches, while about 14.5 percent of the overall Anglo population had. Thus, within fourteen years after the Texas Revolution, the Anglo American population seemingly enjoyed slightly greater opportunities to convert some portion of their income resources into personal wealth despite the fact that Tejanos of means outnumbered Anglos. Evidence pertaining to the distribution of wealth among Mexicanos and whites supports this observation further. As is seen in Table 14, a direct relationship existed between the ethnic characteristics of the Texas population and the magnitude of wealth holdings. Over half (53.7 percent) of the Tejanos who had managed to accrue wealth had done so only

Table 14. Distribution of Personal Estate Values Among Mexican-American and Anglo American Wealth Holders, 1850 (1860)[a]

	Mexican-Americans	Anglo-Americans
$1–100	53.7%	12.2%
$101–1000	30.2%	38.1%
$1,001 or More	16.1%	49.7%
	100%	100%
	(N=353)	(N=155)

[a]This table combines wealth holders in Béxar County and the Lower Rio Grande Valley in 1850 with those in El Paso County in 1860. Based on these sample findings, there were probably about 1,446 Tejanos and 576 Anglos in Béxar and El Paso counties and the Lower Rio Grande Valley who had accrued some personal wealth. Thus, it is estimated that 71.5 percent of the personal wealth holders were Mexicanos, and 28.5 percent were whites. At the same time, an estimated 10.4 percent of the total Mexican-American population and 14.5 percent of the total Anglo population appears to have accrued some personal wealth.

up to a value of $100, while nearly half (49.7 percent) of the Anglo wealth holders had accumulated personal estates valued over $1000. A proportionately greater number of Anglos, then, were able to generate personal riches of greater monetary value than the Mexicanos. Though the lack of information in the 1900 census regarding personal estates hampers efforts to document the continuation of these inequalities over the course of time, such disparities quite likely persisted. Indeed, a number of trends, such as the decline of Tejano farm and ranch owners and the corresponding increase of Anglo owners, suggest that inequaliities in wealth were not only perpetuated, but increased over the last half of the nineteenth century in Texas.

In summary, quantitative comparison of Mexican and Anglo American laboring trends shows that Mexicanos were increasingly concentrated at the lower end of the occupational sector during the last fifty years of the nineteenth century. The Tejanos accordingly fell victim to greater degrees of material deprivation and, relative to the Anglos of Texas, their impoverishment as an ethnic group accelerated. The trend corresponds closely to the situation in other parts of the American Southwest as depicted by recent scholars. Historians studying several California communities, for example, note that Mexican Americans ordinarily found themselves confined to the bottom of the occupational hierarchy over several generations. This they attribute to the existence of labor repression, dual wage systems, and the exploitative nature of occupational stratification within capitalist structures.[109]

Statistically oriented studies, however, do not tell the whole story. The fact that such works convey little in detail about historical patterns of culture is one of the major limitations of quantitative techniques. One might ask, what did it matter that Mexican Americans did not experience upward mobility at the rate of the white population? In a society of racist institutions, they had enough to do just surviving within an Hispanic subeconomy. The point is that they provided for themselves and ministered to their own in common and familiar terms, even shaping the dominant Anglo-controlled society in indelible ways. They kept some of their cultural traditions, and defined their own identity in a hostile world.

The achievements of the nineteenth century Mexicanos ought to be considered with the recognition that economic betterment was not all that common among the majority of American citizens,

regardless of ethnic characteristics.[110] Furthermore, advancement
ought not to be measured solely in terms of economic mobility.
The survival and persistence of an ethnic tradition took absolute
determination and fortitude on the part of the Tejanos of the nineteenth century. What ought to be appreciated is the singular capacity
of the Tejano community to preserve its integrity, to use every
means available to care for itself, to look to the future with a sense
of optimism, and to leave a heritage that still today offers a chal-
lenging opportunity for elaboration and enrichment.

5

Ordinary People

During the last half of the nineteenth century, most Tejanos lived in the southern and western parts of the state, continued being concentrated in the rural areas, and, in comparison to Anglos, still tended to be foreign born—about 42.5 percent of them in 1900 as opposed to only 15.9 percent of the Anglos in the same year (see Table 15). Most were ordinary people—*ordinary* in the sense that they could not be distinguished by their wealth, by their social status, or by their education. Good fortune did set off a few—the political elites, the professionals, the successful merchants—but most Tejanos were poor. As suggested by the census returns for 1850 and 1860, the personal wealth holdings among Tejanos ranged from a low of $56 per capita in Béxar County to a high of $199 per capita in the lower Rio Grande Valley. Comparatively, personal wealth holdings among whites probably ranged from about $298 to $753 per capita in the same areas during the period (see Table 16). As poor people, Mexican Americans lived in impoverished homes, ate foods valued for their sustaining qualities, looked to nature for assistance in the struggle against economic adversity, maintained a stable family life conducive to optimism, dressed as best they could considering their means, and spoke a language identifiable with the old and the traditional. In many ways, they did not differ from other ordinary Texans. But in many other ways they did—prejudice, exploitation, and violence lurked around them in a manner that did not touch whites. And like any other ordinary people, they pur-

Table 15. Estimates of the General Characteristics of the Mexican-American and Anglo-American Populations of South, Central, and West Texas, 1850 (1860) and 1900[a]

	Mexican-Americans		Anglo-Americans	
	1850 (1860)	1900	1850 (1860)	1900
Percent of Population	69.7%	51.5%	19.9%	40.4%
Number in Population	13,907	74,005	3,975	58,039
Percent Living in Rural Areas	88.5%	58.7%	62.5%	20.0%
Number Rural Residents	12,306	43,454	2,483	11,590
Percent Living in Urban Areas	11.5%	41.3%	37.5%	80.0%
Number Urban Residents	1,601	30,551	1,492	46,449
Percent Foreign Born Population	33.8%	42.5%	38.9%	15.9%
Percent Naturalized or Filed Foreign Born Population	—	57.3%	—	89.1%

[a]Characteristics for 1850 (1860) are based on combined sample data from Béxar County and the Lower Rio Grande Valley in 1850 with data from El Paso County in 1860. The 1900 estimates are based on combined data from Béxar, Webb, Cameron, Starr, and El Paso counties.

sued as best they could their rights to enjoy their life, their liberty, and their happiness.

Most Tejanos, being of modest means, lived in jacales or adobes.[1] Such structures, which were a continuation of eighteenth century mestizo survival instinct in the province, persisted into the 1890s and early twentieth century as Tejanos adapted to the environmental circumstances of southern and western Texas. Built for utility and protection, they pretended neither to beauty nor splendor; most, in fact, were crude and undecorated. Anglo observers described them as grotesque and primitive, but Mexicanos would hardly have looked upon them in the same fashion because clearly they served their function and purpose well. In Texas, this type of housing came to identify the Mexicano experience and set off the means of environmental adaptation from that of whites.

The natural, the discarded, and the available—in short the useful —provided the essential elements for construction of jacales. Like poor people in other places and other times, Mexicanos relied upon what material was available in nature or through happenstance. The framework or the walls came from local flora. These consisted of posts, generally from mesquite, cedar, and other trees

Table 16. Wealth and Wealth Holders (Personal Estate Values) of Mexican-Americans and Anglo-Americans by Region, 1850 (1860)[a]

	Mexican-Americans			Anglo-Americans		
	Béxar	LRGV[b]	El Paso	Béxar	LRGV	El Paso
Percent Ethnic Population Holding Wealth	4.1%	3.7%	28.7%	7.4%	21.0%	51.6%
Estimated Number of Wealth Holders	38	293	995	80	215	199
Average Dollar Value of Personal Wealth	$1,371	$5,367	$219	$4,010	$3,580	$1,268
Estimated Total Value of Personal Wealth	$52,108	$1,572,531	$217,905	$320,800	$769,700	$252,332
Estimated Personal Wealth Per Capita	$56	$199	$63	$298	$753	$655

[a]Data for El Paso County are based on the 1860 census returns.
[b]Lower Rio Grande Valley.

set up vertically, close together, and piled into the ground. Stabilized with raw hide, the interstices were then daubed with plaster made from substances indigenous to the area, generally mud or clay. In Eagle Pass in the 1890s, limestone and rock available locally filled the spaces, and a clay cement was made to plaster the walls in and out. In Laredo at the same time, some jacales had walls thatched and patched with old pieces of blankets and wagon sheets.[2]

For covering, builders depended on similar commodities, and roofs often displayed the same improvisation as the walls. Along river banks, as in San Antonio, dried reeds functioned as housetops,[3] while in other areas, cane thatched with tule, swamp flag, straw, or coarse grass was used.[4] As canned goods became available around Laredo in the latter decades of the century, Tejanos employed the discarded containers to mend holes in their roofs. Kerosene and tomato cans were flattened out and nailed upon the tops. "Some of these miserable dwellings were seen with roofs glittering in the sunshine and composed wholly of old tin cans of all kinds and sizes straightened out and fastened on. So it is that the greaser has found a use at last for these seemingly useless things," wrote Lee C. Harby, a reporter for *Harper's New Monthly Magazine.* Whatever the composition, they generally proved effective for their purposes. Straw roofs in Eagle Pass in the 1890s reportedly stood impervious to the elements and lasted in good repair for nearly thirty years. The particular grass employed, it was said, resisted fire and even when once ignited did not blaze but smouldered sullenly and could be extinguished with the bare hand.[5]

Simplicity characterized the rest of the jacales. Mud, pounded hard, or clay or earth beaten firm and made smooth with grease sufficed as flooring—at times depressed a few inches below the level of the street.[6] Blankets covered openings designed to serve as doors and shutters. These small structures, many times just one-room edifices measuring twelve foot by twelve foot, took a few days to build, cost little for material, kept out both heat and cold, and lasted many years.[7]

The interior reflected the same improvisation as the jacal proper. Ordinarily, factory made furniture was not found in jacales because the residents' poverty precluded it, and Mexican immigrants, poor themselves, rarely imported it. Instead, Tejanos created their household items out of whatever was available. Beds might be made from well-dried cowhides spread on the ground with straw piled upon them for comfort. During the day, *bona fide* beds occasionally served as a sofa or table and resumed their original function at night. The space designated as the kitchen area might contain a few chairs or crude benches, a board table, or, where the common necessary furniture did not exist, skins spread upon the earth floor served as a table. Kitchen wares included earthen utensils, kettles or iron pots, gourds for cooking, and invariably, a *mano* and *metate* for grinding the corn for *tortillas*. Bags, made either of woven grass or the useful *pita* of the country, stored the clothes and valuables of the inhabitants.[8]

Chimneys built in a crisscross of sticks put together in a birdtrap fashion, plastered within and without with a thick layer of mud or clay, served as an oven for indoor cooking.[9] But much of the food was prepared some twenty or thirty feet from the house in semidome structures of baked and blackened mud. The intense heat in these tightly closed furnaces resulted in deliciously baked bread or roasted meat.[10]

These Tejano domiciles, ranging from well-built constructions to wretched-looking hovels, radiated an aura of warmth and affirmed the home's role as a center of an active family life. Statues of saints customarily decorated the interior of the homes,[11] as did pictures of Mexican American heroes like Antonio Canales and Juan Cortina.[12] Children played about and domesticated animals roamed freely: donkeys, small goats, chickens, and dogs browsed around the premises.[13] Small gardens containing corn, peppers, onions, and other vegetables added to the picture.[14]

If the greater portion of the Tejano population lived in jacales, those residing in areas where timber was limited but mud abounded often inhabited adobes. Mexican Americans borrowed from an art perfected by Spaniards and Indians and employed it in those localities where already in use. San Antonio de Béxar, built in a period when timber was scarce, came to display buildings constructed of adobe or stone from local quarries. In the 1840s, travelers described the businesses and homes as simple one-story edifices washed blue and yellow and featuring flat roofs covered with dirt and gravel and including parapets three or four feet high for sniping in case of Indian attacks.[15] These structures were common well into the nineteenth century with their galleries (as the veranda and piazza and porch were called) and walls (originally designed to form a breastwork for the protection of defenders).[16] Still holding their form in the latter decades of the century, some displayed very good Moorish effects of projecting-stone and lattice-work.[17]

Adobe structures were more distinctive to the West Texas areas, although South Texas was not without them. In those western regions, Mexican Americans formed mud into bricks twelve to eighteen inches long and four inches thick, mixed chopped straw and gravel with it to improve the quality, and then left the blocks in the sun to bake. Stacked upon one another in a systematic fashion, they formed the walls, while grass and mud thickly laid over poles served as the roof.[18] The masonry kept the rooms cool in the summer and warm in the winter.[19] Those homes belonging to the more fortunate class often had walls two to three feet thick and, when plastered and whitewashed, presented a neat and comfortable appearance. Floors were of mud, concrete, or brick.[20] From the Fort Stockton area to the El Paso Valley, adobe homes occupied by Mexicanos identified farms and suburban estates in the latter half of the century.[21] In the city of El Paso itself, adobe huts still comprised the major kind of housing in the barrios in 1900.[22] With slight repairs, these products of improvisation endured for decades.

Jacales and adobes as domiciles identified a Tejano way of life in a way similar to that which associated tepees with Indians, sod-houses with the mid-western farmers, and the log cabin with south-eastern settlers. Tejanos borrowed from the Mexican frontier experience and applied it to particular regions when occasion demanded and circumstances permitted. As whites entered into areas where Tejanos predominated—that is, South Texas after the Mexican War and West Texas after the Civil War—they accepted construction methods similar to those of the Tejano or at least acknowledged the success of the Mexican model. Thus, the Santa Gertrudis Ranch at its inception resembled more a Mexican ranch than one fashioned after methods imported from east of the Sabine. Mexican hands working for Richard King in 1854 built the first jacales of wood and dirt with thatched roofs.[23] Even the federal military, when faced with the same environment, borrowed from the Mexican plan. Quarters in early Army posts often mirrored Mexican structures— the buildings occupied by the soldiers at Fort Duncan in the 1850s, for example, consisted of grass like many Tejano homes and were known as "thatched houses."[24] In the western areas of the state, adobe buildings appeared in emerging Anglo towns or on ranches because whites would turn to the technique most common to that region. Adobe stage-stands built along the Mexican pattern welded the San Antonio-El Paso link in the chain of mail in the 1850s. The *corral* or *patio*, twelve or fifteen feet high and two or three feet thick, was also constructed of adobe.[25] In the Fort Stockton area, the courthouse in the 1880s (later used as a Mexican school), was an adobe edifice as were the main building and the jail at Fort Davis in the same period.[26] Like so much of the Texas experience, by the time Anglos entered as settlers they found time-tested practices working successfully. Consequently, Tejanos acted upon white men instead of borrowing from a more innovative eastern American civilization.

In desperate or emergency cases when neither jacales or adobes could be built, Mexican Americans turned to other bounties of nature for assistance. In extreme cases, Mexicanos excavated several feet into bluffs and employed wit and ingenuity to improve caves. In Eagle Pass in the 1850s, for instance, a cross carpet of reeds thickly layered with grass and earth and resting on sturdy willow and sycamore poles was stretched across the top of the three sides to act as a roof. A plaster of mud slightly tempered with lime provided some whiteness and finish to the earth walls, and stratified sandstone quarried from the hills supplied a firm and durable floor. The front, latticed with reeds and cunningly veiled by the earth and herbage of the bank, made the caves impervious to the elements.[27]

However crude and inelegant looking they may have been, nineteenth century homes served as both excellent shelter, and as a vital cultural artifact in a country intolerant of the Tejano way of life. A family or community spirit in turn injected a sense of home into those impoverished shelters. After all, jacales, adobes, and other types served as the social arena where the most intimate relations took place, where families grew, where adults taught the young their proper roles and instructed them in acceptable norms, mores, and folkways of behavior. They served as the primary environment where personalities unfolded and where the singing, story-telling, and other traditions remained. Simultaneously, it was the place where those members of the family who interacted with white society as laborers or in other capacities passed on to the young those tenets borrowed from Anglo Americans as essential for surviving in a white man's country.

Jacales and adobes still remained as types of dwellings in 1900. How much change had occurred since their appearance in Texas in the 1710s and 1720s is difficult to discern. Obviously, the level of poverty for ordinary people had not changed much since the colonial period. Anglo sources reveal scant details about the improvements that might have occurred—they say little if anything about the switch to frame housing or to the use of kerosene lamps, glass windows, electricity, and other modern conveniences. It is possible that the absence of commentary by Anglo observers may have been because they saw nothing unusual about the use of such newer conveniences and thus saw no difference to report—their jaundiced eye usually focused on the contrast between themselves and Mexicanos. On the other hand, there may have been little change to report, for Texas society as a whole retained much of its past, even in 1900. T. R. Fehrenbach observes:

Texas entered the twentieth century with its basic society a full two generations, or about sixty years, behind the development of the American mainstream. Industry was in its infancy; among the people themselves the norms and patterns of the industrial society had no root. Texan speech was already becoming picturesque, because it retained earthy allusions forgotten by Northern city dwellers. The early nineteenth century American values were in no way eroded in Texas. There was no reason why they should have been. During a century of explosive conquest and settlement, the land changed very little, and the people not at all.[28]

In actuality, the housing of poor people in other parts of the world did not differ markedly from that of the Tejanos. The living conditions of new immigrants in the northern American cities during that same time are too well known to need mentioning here. Sodhouses still prevailed in the Midwest, and the homes of poor whites, both in Texas and the rest of the country, were a product of their poverty and had nothing to do with cultural values. In London, England, a sizeable portion of the laboring poor crowded into small rooms that lacked privacy, comfort, or common conveniences.[29] Tejanos lived in jacales and adobes because of their poverty and not because of an unchanging allegiance to primitivism.

That Tejanos sought better housing is evident from the experience of those who could afford accommodations where space, insects, and dirt might not be a problem. The same observers who called the adobe huts primitive praised the style and structure of the homes of the Tejano well-to-do that came from the same adobe mud.[30] Such homes, like the ranchos previously described, indicated the realm of possibility for Mexican Americans in a free society.

While food preferences and eating habits changed over time, Tejanos then and now never deserted the dishes they inherited from their Spanish-Indian progenitors. Their diet was similar to what poor people elsewhere have consumed, but the particular Indian ingredients Tejanos added gave their cuisine its distinctive Mexican flavor that distinguished it from other meals. These staples sustained them from one generation to the next and identified one other Mexicano way of life—a life style associated with *frijoles, tortillas, menudo, cabrito, tamales, chiles, nopalitos,* and so forth. If in adopting to the Texas scene Tejanos accepted so-called American food in the process of socialization, they on the other hand converted an entire white society to devouring Mexican food and within a matter of time had appended one more element to the Texas aura.

A few favorite staple foods nourished the Tejano community, and few Mexicans in any age have perished from dependence on them. When Juan Nepomuceno Almonte made his important survey of Texas in 1834, he reported that Mexicans generally relied on tortillas, beef, venison, chicken, eggs, cheese, milk, and the like.[31] More or less the same thing remained common for other generations of Tejanos. Bexareños, for example, relied on corn and beans supplemented with sharply peppered goat meat in mid-century[32] and, despite the community's change, they continued relying principally on hash made of dried beef rendered hot with red pepper. Along with this they ate onions and corn bread made into crackers.[33] The same austerity pervaded other areas. According to itinerants, Paseños seemed to depend solely on tortillas and red pepper in the 1850s.[34] Mexican rancheros in the San Patricio area relied chiefly upon tortillas and frijoles and, when their fare varied, it included *chiles* (red peppers), an egg or two, or *chile con carne* (red pepper with meat).[35] In Civil War Brownsville, daily meals consisted of bread and beef purchased at market each morning.[36]

Frijoles sustained Mexicanos as potatoes nurtured the Irish and porridge the Scots, wrote an observer. Stewed or fried in mutton fat and not too highly seasoned, frijoles were served for breakfast, dinner, and supper. Frying them in a quantity of lard with chile added variety.[37]

The old time Mexican shepherd of the open range days [wrote Roy Holt in an essay on the bean] put his frijoles in a bucket, added plenty of water, put in some pork (perhaps the rind), and then a tight lid with several holes in it on the bucket. Then he covered the bucket almost to the top with live coals and left the beans to simmer all night. At four o'clock he got up, put more coals around the bucket, and added some salt and, by the time he cooked his bread, the beans were ready for breakfast. For supper, perhaps the old herder had fried beans with chili pepper and onions to set off the taste.[38]

Tortillas ranked second only to frijoles as a mainstay and as an article identifying the Tejano way of life. The arduous and intricate process of preparing them required soaking the maize in water and lime to remove the hulls, grinding corn on the *metate*, and finally baking the cake on the *comal* (hot griddle). The metate, subjected to baking by fire to harden it, had two parts: first, the metate proper, a concave stone about one-half yard long by a foot wide and eight inches thick; and secondly, the *marco* (or *mano*), another rock resembling a rolling pin. After beating the corn with the *marco* on the *metate* and tossing, patting,, and flattening the dough (a procedure that took hours), the *tortillera* finally divided the result into small thin pieces and threw them on the comal. Tortillas contained no seasoning but the slight flavor of lime brought out the natural sweetness of corn.[39] No home was without the metate or comal, and no woman could have considered herself Mexicana without mastering the task of tortilla-making.

If Tejanos depended principally on frijoles, tortillas, and chiles, poverty and oppression did not restrict them solely to those staples; the frontier yielded a diverse assortment of foods. Considering the expanse of southern and western Texas and the relative autonomy of ranchos and *colonias*, Tejanos put food on the table by hunting, fishing, raising stock, and growing crops domestically. Astute at frontier survival, they devised resourceful means for hunting wild prey. Around Corpus Christi in the 1840s, Mexicanos used the stalking horse to get within rifle shot of deer grazing on the plains. Cautiously pushing the dried hide of the head, neck, and part of the body of a mustang before them, they advanced stealthily on their breast until close enough to consumate their purpose.[40] Javalinas, turkeys, quail, doves, rabbits, and duck also added to the variety.[41] In the 1880s, Tejanos daily lined the wharves of Corpus Christi Bay angling for red trout and other fish.[42]

Domesticated animals included pigs, goats, chickens, sheep, and cattle. Aside from the butter it rendered, milk could be clabbered with rennet from the cow or with the juice from the wild *santa pera* plant and made into a variety of cheeses including *panela, azadera,* and *queso molido* (used for *enchiladas*). Finished cheese was placed in a *zarso,* or cloth frame, and hung high on a tree so that nothing could touch it.[43]

Plants, both domestic and wild, satisfied nutritional needs of Tejanos. *Huertas,* or garden plots, seemed integral to both rural and urban Tejano households. Vegetable patches included corn, beans, peppers, onions, tomatoes, squash, pumpkin, melons, coriander, marjoram, parsley, anise, cumin, and other greens and spices.[44] The brown seeds of the *calabaza* (pumpkin), when dried, roasted, and then beaten to a powder in the *molcajete* (a stone mortar standing on a tripod), added a nutlike flavor to meat sauces and other dishes.[45] Native plants satisfied further necessities. *Verdolaga* (purslane), a heavy-leaved plant, was used like water cress. *Quelite* (pigweed) served as greens. Wild gherkins, which grew abundantly along creek beds, could be used either fresh or pickled.[46] Cacti, seemingly a useless plant, served Tejanos in multiple ways. The tender leaves of the prickly-pear cactus were minced and cooked with eggs; the leaves of the plant roasted, or, by peeling and cubing them, were made into *nopalitos; las tunas,* the fruits of these cacti, were consumed with delight when made into a firm, dark sweetmeat called *queso de tuna* (cheese of prickly pear).[47] The pitahaya plant produced delicious fruit and the *agarita* bush yielded great clusters of red berries which, when ripe, made delicious jelly. Trees furnished fruits while others like the *ebano* and *mesquite* supplied edible beans.[48] For intoxicants, Mexicanos called upon the *maguey,* a plant long-known in Mexico for its liquor yielding capacities. When Tejanos saw the long leaves of the *maguey* turning inward at the tips, they knew the time had come for it to bloom. They then dug out the center of the plant in the place where the stalk for the bloom was going to shoot up. Letting the sap or *aguamiel* accumulate in that basin, they took a cane tube and drew the *aguamiel* out into a goat- (or pig- or sheep-) skin bag. After fermenting the sap, Tejanos could enjoy the thick, milky-looking fluid known as *pulque*. Through still other processes, Tejanos derived two-ginlike beverages, *mescal* and *tequila* from maguey.[49]

Mexicanos made many types of food from the meats and vegetables they gathered to supplement tortillas and frijoles. The many culinary delights Tejanos concocted attested to the will of a people living in poverty to make their meals, however lean, as pleasurable as possible. Among their favorite dishes was a sort of stew made of beef or chicken (or any other sort of meat) mixed with pumpkin and a large quantity of red pepper.[50] Other native dishes included pots of chile and rabbit cooked in highly seasoned sauce.[51] *Tamal de cazuela* (corn and meat pot pie) and *chile guisado* (a kind of stew with green pepper sauce) were also part of their menu. *Puchero* (goat flesh or mutton) could be stewed with various vegetables, spices, and herbs to render a delicious meal.[52] *Cabrito* (kid) ranked second to no other delicacy.[53] And by making a hole in the ground, building a fire underneath it, lining the hole with stones, covering it up until hot and then placing the meat wrapped in a burlap sack to bake all night, Tejanos enjoyed a delicious well-browned *barbacoa* (now known as barbecue), which when served for breakfast with tortillas just off the gridle "ran the cabrito a close second as a favorite."[54]

Tamales certainly matched any other delicacy. Tejanos cooked them regularly but invariably on festive occasions. Preparation required mincing beef with pepper, wrapping dough around it, rolling the whole thing in corn shucks, and then steaming or frying them in boiling lard.[55] On occasion cooks varied the filling by adding currants and raisins or substituting chicken for beef.[56] However prepared, this Indian food was delectable and represented one of those products that whites eagerly endorsed as a Mexican contribution to the totality of the Lone Star State.

Eating habits remained unimpaired by proximity to whites because the autonomy and privacy of homes preserved the tradition of using the tortilla to convey food from plate to mouth, although Mexicanos may have resorted to more so-called acceptable ways in public settings. Tejanos had little use for tableware because Mexican food already provided a ready and consumable item to use in place of fork and spoon. By artfully taking a doubled piece of tortilla in the fingers, a person would heap food onto another and then carry food and tortilla to mouth. Beans and eggs could even be spread on tortillas when plates were unavailable, then folded and eaten.[57]

In using this mechanical ritual, nineteenth-century Tejanos probably saw nothing primitive or uncivilized about the art. Their descendants obviously have not thought so, nor have other Mexican Americans in other parts of the United States, for they have continued the method in the privacy of their homes. The same person who uses tortillas (in conjunction with a fork at times, perhaps) to eat in his primary environment, ordinarily resorts to fork and knife in the secondary Anglo-American setting. Seldom have Chicanos, poor or middle class, regarded the practice as a beastly custom, as nineteenth century Anglo obervers were prone to conclude.

The struggle for survival turned Tejanos' attention toward the botanical world. Universally, man has taken liberally from nature, but Mexican Americans employed and applied those products in ways that became identified as Mexicano. Nature gave them substances for medicinal purposes, items for use in improvisation such as the products that went into the making of jacales, and of course, edibles or consumable treats. Plants yielded commodities essential to the livelihood of a people living in poverty and colored part of a life style; but to the mind of racists in the nineteenth century, the ingenuity involved was overlooked and instead values of resignation and contentment were inputed.

Like their kindred in mother Mexico, Tejanos carefully cultivated *hierba buena, manzanilla, albahaca, ruda, estafiate, muicle,* camphor, rhubarb, and other medicinal herbs in gardens around their household. Tea brewed from the leaves and branches of the *cenizo* worked as cough medicine; *hierba amarilla* was good for sores; tea made from leaves of the *hierba aniz* settled nerves and that from the heirba buena helped heart ailments; ruda relieved ear aches; and the split leaf of the *sabila (zabila, zabida, aloe)* placed on a swollen part reduced inflamation. The syrup derived from the fruit of the *nacahuite* tree could be used for cough medicine.[58] The prongs of the Spanish Dagger came in handy in curing snakebites, for Tejanos believed that jabbing the points into the flesh around the wound let the blood out and permitted the poison from the daggers to counteract the venom of the serpent.[59]

Plants offered them still other uses. *Amole* (soap root)—the large fibrous roots of the *lechugilla*—possessed saponaceous properties and Mexicanos reputedly used it to bathe and to wash their clothing. The leaves could be used for making bagging and a rope called *istle*, while its fibers could be used for shoe thread. Similarly, the fibers of the maguey plant and Spanish Dagger could be used for rope.[60] Trees added to the repertoire: branches of the *chapote* were used to make baseball bats; the bark of the *huisache* provided dye for leather; and the fiber of the *pita* leaves made strong cords.[61]

In an immediate sense, nature sustained the physical well-being of those who relied on it. But to a much larger and more important degree, it was an important link to traditional ways. In this context, the flora eaten or taken as medicine nourished the culture of a Tejano community resolved to ward off destructive external forces.

To be sure, it is impossible to reconstruct the fabric of the Tejano family at this time. A precise picture of the nineteenth century family can emerge only after historians scrutinize church records and extant family papers, study vital statistics and movements of migrant families, and consider other variables. From that, they can compile a picture of kinships, of ideas Tejanos held about marital, familial, and kin obligations, and their views toward morality, pre-marital intercourse, child-rearing and socialization, and divorce. Tentative profiles, however, emerge from data drawn in a system-atic sampling of the federal census schedules. To begin with, the Tejano community was younger than its Anglo counterpart. The family itself resembled other Texas families in some respects, but departed from those features in others. On the one hand, Tejanos lived in households whose average size was not dramatically differ-ent from other Texas households, at least according to the 1900 census, which in comparison to the 1850 census, reflected the more settled nature of Anglo society. Moreover, no significant difference existed in the average years of marriage, again according to the 1900 census returns, the first to include data on that. On the other hand, the Tejano family displayed a more stable nature than the Anglo family. While extended families were slightly more com-mon to Mexican American culture, as is generally argued, single-family dwellings and nuclear family units were the rule by far, a feature more common to Tejanos than to Anglos. Also, Tejano male-headed households remained relatively constant over the period and were as prevalent as Anglo male-headed households by 1900. As may be expected of people from a lower socioeconomic standing, a higher fertility rate existed among Tejanos, thus more children were born. Considering their impoverishment, Mexican Americans suffered greater incidents of child mortality (see Table 17). Naturally, these characteristics varied according to regions, for historic forces unique to those environments produced diverging results (see Table 18).

Some contemporaries who saw the Tejano family firsthand spoke generously of it. "Their manner towards one another is engaging and that of children and parents most affectionate," noted Frederick Law Olmsted traveling in Texas in 1856. "This we always noticed in evening walks," he continued, "and in the groups about the doors, which were often singing in chorus—the attitudes expressive of confident affection."[62] Another observer found Tejanos "kindly in home life, particularly to the aged, and clannish to a

Table 17. Estimates of the Characteristics of the Mexican American and Anglo American Families of South, Central, and West Texas, 1850 (1860) and 1900[a]

	Mexican-Americans		Anglo-Americans	
	1850 (1860)	1900	1850 (1860)	1900
Average Age in Years	20.9	22.4	24.1	25.9
Average Size of Households	5.9	6.5	10.4	6.5
Average Years Married	—	14.5	—	14.0
Percent Living in Single-Family Dwellings	55.1%	64.4%	32.8%	48.9%
Percent Living in Nuclear Families	75.2%	87.1%	41.0%	77.8%
Percent Living in Male-Headed Households	85.5%	87.8%	94.0%	84.6%
Average Lifetime Fertility Among Childbearing Females	—	5.4	—	4.1
Average Number of Children per Household	3.3	4.2	1.7	3.3
Average Child Mortality per Childbearing Female	—	1.8	—	0.9

[a]1850 (1860) estimates combine sample data from Béxar County and the Lower Rio Grande Valley in 1850 with data from El Paso County in 1860. 1900 estimates are based on combined sample data from the 1900 census returns for Béxar, Webb, Cameron, Starr, and El Paso counties.

Table 18. Estimates of the General Characteristics of the Mexican-American and Anglo-American Populations of Texas by Region, 1850 (1860) and 1900[a]

	Béxar County		Lower Rio Grande Valley (Cameron, Starr, Webb)		El Paso County	
	1850	1900	1850	1900	1860	1900
Average Age of Mexican-Americans in Years	21.1	24.1	20.2	22.2	22.3	22.9
Average Age of Anglo-Americans in Years	23.6	25.6	24.5	26.0	27.7	26.3
Average Size of Mexican-American Households	5.7	6.9	6.1	6.7	5.4	5.6
Average Size of Anglo-American Households	11.6	6.7	5.5	5.4	12.9	6.9
Average Years Married (Mexican-Americans)	—	14.7	—	14.6	—	13.9
Average Years Married (Anglo-Americans)	—	15.3	—	14.0	—	12.1
Percent Mexican-Americans Living in Extended Families	44.0%	13.5%	2.4%	7.9%	28.3%	6.7%
Percent Anglo-Americans Living in Extended Families	30.2%	7.4%	3.9%	6.3%	4.3%	6.4%
Percent of Mexican-Americans Living in Single-Family Dwellings	—	55.4%	—	64.4%	—	67.8%
Percent of Anglo-Americans Living in Single-Family Dwellings	—	49.6%	—	55.9%	—	44.1%
Percent of Mexican-Americans Living in Nuclear Families	54.5%	81.6%	88.2%	87.4%	65.6%	87.4%
Percent of Anglo-Americans Living in Nuclear Families	35.6%	79.0%	65.7%	80.4%	22.6%	74.5%
Percent of Mexican-Americans Living in Male-Headed Households	82.1%	89.1%	84.6%	88.3%	86.4%	84.6%

	Béxar County		Lower Rio Grande Valley (Cameron, Starr, Webb)		El Paso County	
	1850	1900	1850	1900	1860	1900
Percent of Anglo-Americans Living in Male-Headed Households	87.5%	84.9%	89.2%	80.2%	100%	86.6%
Average Lifetime Fertility Among Childbearing Mexican-American Females	—	4.9	—	5.7	—	4.6
Average Lifetime Fertility Among Childbearing Anglo-American Females	—	4.4	—	4.1	—	3.5
Average Number of Mexican-American Children per Household	3.5	4.2	3.6	4.4	2.7	3.5
Average Number of Anglo American Children Per Household	1.9	3.6	1.8	3.0	0.4	3.0
Average Child Mortality per Childbearing Mexican-American Female	—	1.3	—	1.8	—	1.6
Average Child Mortality per Childbearing Anglo-American Female	—	1.0	—	0.9	—	0.8

[a]Characteristics of the population of El Paso County were derived from the 1860 census returns. The 1900 estimates for the Lower Rio Grande Valley are based on sample data from Webb, Cameron, and Starr counties.

degree, whole families of several generations occupying one hut."[63]
Family life was closely knit with members manifesting tender affection and dignity and reserve toward others in the household.[64]

While some observers spoke disparagingly of Mexican culture,
others were favorably impressed by the conspicious intimacy in the
Tejano family. One writer recorded:

Now it is a Mexican family transferring their altar—the Lares and Penates—
on a cart, the father leading it, the mother and grandmother totally ob-
scured by the things they lug along, an infinity of children round their
heels, dirty and ragged and with tangled hair, but with the blackest eyes
and whitest teeth, the ruddiest dark cheeks and most roguish smile ever
seen, and with the baby all but bare, strapped on a blanket on a mule's
back, sound asleep in the sun, as sweet a little morsel as the first baby
ever born in paradise. If it is a Mexican family in a cart encountered thus,
the mother is always on the front seat, while the father sits behind and
holds the baby.[65]

Tejano heads of families performed functions similar to those of
poor, preindustrial males, asserting their authority as the unit's
stabilizing influence. They acted as providers, as father figures, as
disciplinarians, as men who gave the vital sense of security in time
of travail and as examples of perseverence under stress. They worked
in almost every conceivable occupation permitted them by white
society, and with their wages they clothed and sheltered their
families. They did the hunting, the building of homes, and in a
number of other ways improvised to care for their loved ones. They
took charge of forms of entertainment to provide the community
with relief from its daily toil, organized *mutualistas* to render needed
services to a community living in poverty, defended the rights of
Mexicanos either morally or through resistance movements, and
extracted concessions from white society through a variety of survival mechanisms. At the same time they felt the brunt of racism
more so than their wives or children, for their manner of livelihood
brought them into intimate contact with Anglos. More than any
other figure, either prominent or obscure, the Tejano male provided an example to emulate in sustaining his family and community against adversity.

The role of Tejanas within the family and the community at large
resembled more or less that of the preindustrial woman. By and
large, Mexicanas practiced the pattern preindustrial experiences

prescribed for women: taking care of the family, doing the house-
work, and supplementing the family income by performing jobs
males relegated to them. If few Tejanas failed to win prominence,
their lack of accomplishments in no way reflected an alleged "backward Mexican culture." Instead, their condition stemmed from the
fact that an agrarian society did not permit Tejanas, themselves the
victims of families experiencing impoverishment and concomitant
difficulties, the elbow room to maneuver and rise to high stature.
In the traditional role that male-dominated society assigned them,
few women failed: they bore children and sustained generations
through adversity, and as wage earners they supplemented the
family income as vendedoras, as servants or chambermaids, and as
field laborers.[66]

As wives of poor men, they made the best of circumstances and,
like their male counterparts on their jobs, mixed their daily toil
with deliberateness. The chore of washing the family clothing, for
example, combined duty with diversion. Ordinarily, women resorted to the banks of brooks and rivers to do their wash. In the
extreme South Texas areas Tejanas customarily came together at
the Rio Grande and there scrubbed and chattered as the little
children splashed water in glee or lay in slumber on the ground.[67]
In San Antonio, where women traditionally washed their family
garments on the flat stones of the San Pedro Creek, they bent for
hours despite the toil on their physique. Still they managed to mix
fun with duty, washing themselves in the waters of the San Pedro
as they laundered.[68]

Tejanos spun and wove using only minimal facilities and essentials, but their patience and skill rivaled any other woman's.[69] In El
Paso, Mexicans took five or six months to make a good blanket by
hand, but according to one white observer in 1849, the products
were long lasting and superior to all other blankets in keeping out
the rain and wind.[70] Multi-colored blankets used in San Antonio in
the 1870s similarly served Tejanos well in the winter to resist the
weather. Designed with a hole in the middle through which the
wearer put his head, they covered almost the entire body and shed
water "like the back of a duck."[71] In late nineteenth century Hidalgo County, poor ranch women carded wool, spun it, wove the
cloth, made garments by hand, and used native dyes to beautify
them.[72]

In the 1890s, women of Brownsville earned a reputation for

excellence in the art of making "drawn work." Their doilies, made of coarse linen and worked with heavy thread furnished by the customer, were eagerly bought, and the price increased in that decade commensurate with demand. Orders came in from people throughout the country for single articles, such as tablecloths, centerpieces, carving mats, tray-cloths, bedspreads, and pillow shams— items that cost from ten dollars to one-hundred fifty dollars. [73]

In Hidalgo County at that time, where quilting parties amounted to social events, the woman making a quilt carded the wool, made a *forro* (lining), and stretched it on a frame. She then notified neighbors, relatives, and friends that all was ready for the *punteo* quilting (or quilting party). Beautiful quilts resulted from these combination work-social gatherings. [74]

The children shared in the responsibility for providing for the family. According to Nannie Emory Holding, a Methodist missionary working among Mexicanos of the Lower Rio Grande Valley in the 1880s:

There is a strong feeling of obligations resting upon Mexican girls to help 'papa' or 'mamma'. As I write several of our children come up before me as in the midst of life's battle, having the support of a large family bearing upon them. Invariably, to my question of why this or that may not be accomplished with the salary, the answer is, 'papa needs it,' or 'brother has no work, and mamma must have it.' I have very rarely known one of them to spend her salary in personal gratification. [75]

In agrarian Texas, the Tejano family unit resembled the preindustrial family that generally concerned itself with the means of survival and improvement of circumstances. Males took charge of their duties as providers and heads of families, women acted as mothers and supplementers of family sustenance, while children contributed their share to the family load. From this structure, adult members embarked to find themselves in straits similar to that of their parents, to forge their way into circumstances more auspicious than those they left behind, or in other cases, to take paths simply on the wrong side of life.

When white observers described Tejanos as fatalists, they were saying more about themselves and their feelings than about Tejanos. The struggle of lower class Mexicans, both in the United States and Mexico, has not been with themselves but with environmental elements and against class and racial constraints. Those coming from a household where values of passivity and resignation existed would have seen no point to political participation, to learning about the American constitution and its guarantees for all, to finding job opportunities in emerging cities, or taking business risks. If with the passing of time, few overcame their poverty, it was not simply because they lacked ambition or were present oriented, rather it was largely because white society clung to fixed patterns of racism and exploitation. The very fact that Tejanos made that stubborn society responsive to many of their needs belies both the past and modern assertion that families failed to encourage optimism and hope.[76]

Tejanos dressed commensurate with circumstance and occasion. Some wore what appeared to be rags, but others dressed quite respectably. Some donned loose (sometimes too loose) clothing that reflected the uninhibited while others covered their persons modestly in tighter clothing. Some sported buckskin, others cotton, and others both. Tejanos outfitted themselves appropriately for work and yet dressed tastefully for special events. Fashion reflected both the condition of impoverishment and their desire to dress appropriately for the proper moment. Mexicanos dressed themselves and their family with clothes that exemplified dignity when impoverishment deprived them of much of that.

Cotton material entered conspicuously into much of their attire. In the late 1840s, Paseño males generally dressed in white domestic muslin and wore pants tight around the thighs that widened near the hem. Shirts resembled American products but featured wider sleeves and did not open at the sides.[77] Over their large white cotton drawers, others wore pantaloons (opened at the outer side) which displayed rows of gilt buttons and other ornaments. A red silk sash was then wrapped around the waist. In cold weather a serape or blanket covered the entire person.[78]

Their work clothing was especially suitable for conditions on a ranch or farm. At the time when frontiersmen and farmers initially made their way across the Sabine River to populate Mexican Texas, the Tejanos were using boots and sombreros. And after the Revolution, it was not Tejanos who adopted the leather mocassins and "coon skin" caps of white men; rather it was Anglos who switched after they learned for themselves the advantages of wearing the boots and cowboy hats of the Mexicans. Indeed, Sam Houston

more than once showed up in Washington, D.C., during his tenure as Texas senator, wearing a serape and other articles of Mexican
dress. Like so much of what later became Texan, western wear was
in actuality the result of a cultural exchange that occurred generations ago when Anglos met Tejanos.[79]

Commonly, women wore loose cotton garments (like morning
dresses) of various colors, including the traditional black.[80] A *rebo-
zo*, a silk or cotton scarf about six or eight feet long and two or three
feet wide and valued anywhere from one to thirty dollars, covered
the head and shoulders.[81] Their appearance, depending upon diverse factors, ranged anywhere from the slovenly to the neat, even
the elegant.[82]

Like clothing, hatwear revealed circumstances and style for the
occasion. While some wore the traditional Mexican sombrero, the
poorer classes wore a variety of straw hats.[83]

Those of the better class dressed in keeping with their economic
standing. In the 1860s, men of the wealthy classes in Brownsville
wore pants with rows of jewels or pieces of silver coins down the
entire outside seam. Hats with brims of an enormous width displayed bands of various workmanship and featured different patterns, many of them embroidered with silver or bullion worth
several dollars. Highly priced shawls of every conceivable form,
style, color, and material accompanied the dress.[84] Much the same
could be said of upper class Bexareños in the 1840s, who usually
wore calico shirts and wide trousers with fancy colored sashes about
the waist. They sported broad-brimmed hats of reddish white, with
silver ornaments or colored beads adorning the band.[85] In the
1870s, one particular observer described Mexicans in San Antonio
as wearing broad-brimmed woolen hats of gray or blue with bands
coiled about them representing snakes. "The number of these snakes
is said to indicate the rank or estimation in which the wearer of that
hat is held," he said, "one snake indicating a gentleman, two snakes a
more advanced gentleman, and three snakes an exalted gentleman."[86]

And when, and in which way, did clothing fashions change?
Again, the question poses difficulties for historians. For one thing,
fashions have the habit of going and then returning to vogue. For
another, Tejanos retained much of their clothing traditions—
rebozos, sombreros, serapes, and the like which identified the
Tejano lifestyle in the twentieth century also. In the same way,

such things as boots and cowboy hats became entrenched as part of the Texas landscape and continued into the next century intact. Further, unlike the historians of the Afro-American experience, Mexican Americanists do not enjoy access to collections like those of the "Slave Narratives" collected by the Works Project Administration during the Depression of the 1930s. Anglo sources again reveal the quaint about Mexicanos, and observers simply did not take pen in hand to record the clothing Tejanos wore if it was like theirs. The paintings and sketches by the artist Frederic Remington, for example, generally depict not only fashions but Mexicanos in a stock manner that induces images of backwardness, lethargy, and inertness. One can only conclude, as with other aspects of Tejano culture (and indeed with the case of Anglo American dress), that Tejanos adopted a bicultural type of dress and continued receptive to change.

Language reinforced Tejano individuality and reaffirmed membership in the Spanish-speaking community. It acted as a cultural form bringing together those sharing the same experience and served to sustain community confidence and drive. Like that of other people's in other ages and other places, their language contained the essential ingredient of commonality that functioned to unify a dynamic community in flux.

Tejano speech patterns revealed the elaboration of a nonstandard rural language. The Tejanos by the time of Mexican independence had been removed from Mexico for generations and had taken to misspelling words and using colloquialisms. According to the historian Andrés A. Tijerina, the Tejanos of Mexican Texas used words which had fallen into disuse in Spain by the later 1500s. Their official correspondence included terms such as *ansi, asina, naiden, trujo, lamber, escuro, dijieron, vide, anque,* and *adrede.* Common vocabulary included words modified to suit the Texan uniqueness. *Mesta* became *mesteña; pelinegro,* meaning black haired or black sheep, was altered to the term of contempt *pelegrino* and applied to the colonization measures of Anglo Americans in the 1820s and 1830s.[87]

Several white observers noted the pattern. According to one, Tejanos employed a linguistic code "called 'Mexi', a kind of Spanish patois, differing widely from pure Castilian."[88] It bore "about the same relation to Spanish that the Canadian patois does to real

French or Pennsylvania Dutch does to German," reflected another.[89] Bexareños in that period spoke their Spanish so adulter-
ated and corrupted that "it grated like harsh thunder upon the
chaste ear of the polished Castilian," wrote still another.[90] But, no
matter how allegedly substandard it may have been to white observers, it was nevertheless a fully formed grammatical system
with no deficiencies as a communication network within the Tejano
community itself.[91]

Few to date have studied the pattern of nineteenth century
Tejano lexicon and those who have assumed that the Tejano vocabulary reflected the importation of Indian-Spanish idioms from Mexico. More plausibly, Tejanos as other Mexican Americans of the
time, molded their own variant and then expanded upon this ver-
sion, but not so far as to speak the so-called Tex-Mex of today. Most
nineteenth century Tejanos living in their own enclaves held not
much more than a rudimentary grasp of English, which they employed only when interacting in English-speaking settings. *Caló*
and *pachuquismos,* as linguists discovered, are twentieth century
developments, and the prosaic code-switching could not have
emerged until such a time as well. Molded by the circumstances of
living outside the linguistic mainstream for a number of centuries,
the language of nineteenth century Tejanos served primarily as a
means of communication for an illiterate lower class people, expressed a commonness of experience, and reinforced their identity
as Mexicanos in a state that daily placed emphasis on "talking
American."[92]

6

Religion and Life Experience

In his study "La Iglesia Católica y el Chicano de Sud Tejas, 1836–1911," the historian José Roberto Juárez characterizes the relations between the Catholic clergy and Tejanos of South Texas as being distant. By the time of the Texas Revolution, he notes, the Church had practically turned away from its charges. Clergymen working among the Tejanos in the subsequent decades tended to be non-Texans, frequently from Europe, did not speak Spanish, and misunderstood Mexican American culture. Over all, he concludes the institutional Church acted towards Mexicanos with indecision and indifference—the clergy often expressing unabashed feelings about wanting to work anywhere else except among what they termed the "Mexican greasers." Still, Juárez writes, Tejanos in that period continued attached to the Catholic faith familiar to them. It was, however, a Catholicism that did not have the intellectual content of its European counterpart simply because a native clergy did not exist in sufficient numbers to attend to the hundreds of ranches dispersed through the vast territory.[1] In general, Juárez' observations both about the clergy and Tejanos of South Texas apply to all of the state.

The Catholicism to which Tejanos subscribed, of course, adhered to the basic canons of·that religion. But long before the Texas Revolution and the interaction with insensitive priests in the state, the forefathers of the Tejanos had combined parts of Indian religion with that of Europeans and forged perfunctory beliefs that corres-

ponded to the New World environment. Indeed, the efforts by
Catholic missionaries to extinguish the Indian influence during
New Spain's colonial period often ended in compromise and the
application of Catholic tenets to Indian rites.[2] That was the religion
that the *pobladores* of colonial Texas had brought with them and
had practiced up to the Revolution of 1836.

Like other vital cultural traditions that continued after the Revolution, these old beliefs persisted practically undisturbed because
the non-Hispanic clergy paid Tejanos only slight attention. As before, but admittedly under different circumstances, their religion
met the needs of their existential condition. As in all cultures,
religion explained something about their misfortune, provided optimism for living under duress, and at the same time encouraged
the necessary mental state for enduring life's travails. Under Anglo
American domination, as under Spanish rule, common Tejano folk
managed to practice survival techniques otherwise discouraged by
institutional Catholicism. Put another way, this nominal view permitted them the attachment and disposition toward that religion
while simultaneously allowing them the psychic margin to circum-
vent the proscriptions of institutional Romanism. Those coming
from Mexico after 1836 brought with them a similar religion, thus
buttressing and inspiring an attitude consonant more with life experience than theology.[3]

Those who observed the Tejanos' frontier religion in the years
after 1836 said much the same of what other itinerants stated before the Revolution—that Mexicanos adhered to their religion while
not exactly able to define institutional Catholicism. Catholicism for
Mexicanos, noted a veteran of 1836, consisted "mainly of knowing
how to make the sign of the cross, together with unbounded reverence first, for the Virgin Mary, and secondly for the saints generally, and the priests."[4] Bernard Doyon, a church historian, cites sources
describing Tejanos in the Lower Rio Grande in the middle of the
century as displaying great faith in the Church despite their poverty and spiritual ignorance. They desired religion and boasted of a
readiness to die for it, the source noted, yet they hardly knew what
their religion was.[5] And Dominic Manucy, a Catholic priest assigned to South Texas in the 1870s, similarly related that couples in
that area often did not marry by the Church, violated other sacraments, lived in ignorance of the fundamental principles of their
religion, yet made sure that their children received baptism and

confirmation. Much of that, he said, was the fault of the Church, which, both in Mexico (whence Mexicans migrated) and in Texas, did not attend to them sufficiently.[6]

Catholicism as it was interpreted and practiced by impoverished Tejanos helped make their life tolerable. Overall, they resisted the passivity and resignation that the institutional Church sought to inculcate because these values clashed with their attempts to improve their conditions both morally and materially. Instead, Tejanos defined their religion in terms that made the resultant leniency lighten the burden of misfortune. Thus did an Episcopalian minister observe about Brownsville and Tejanos in the 1850s:

It was a city where there were not enough of those who showed any regard for Christianity to make its influence appreciable. Sunday was like any other day, except that it was more noisy and worst kept. Stores were open all day, the barrooms, the carousing, cursing, quarreling, and fighting were seen in every quarter of the town.

A deathbed repentence, writes the historian Doyon, often dissolved into thin air if the patient recovered:

To promise did not always mean to perform, and their elastic consciences felt no scruples. They would say innocently: 'To be baptised, to be married well, is not that enough? Mass, Easter, and the rest are good for pious people who like them'.

He writes in another context:

Living out of wedlock meant very little to the majority. 'We are all the same. . . . It has always been so . . . and who is going to take care of me and my children?' they would exclaim when reproached.[7]

Tejanos were often at odds with the institutional Church in their individual lives. They also took exception to priests who did not speak Spanish and who failed to take a social stand in behalf of their civil rights. When it came time to support the Church financially, they resisted it by holding back on donations or contributions to an institution they found irrelevant.[8]

Yet, Tejanos knew the limits of their remissness, for, after all, crucial elements of their religion sustained them through life as decisively as those cultural forms they practiced in defiance of basic precepts. They strictly observed certain Church traditions. As in the case of other aspects of life in Texas where Anglo society rendered them only minimal services, Tejanos put together means of helping themselves. In Nacogdoches in the late 1830s, Father John Timon, then on a visitation of the Republic, wrote that Mexican Texans attempted to keep up their Catholicism under the direction of a self-appointed layman who alternated between the bottle and his religious duties.[9] In 1872, Father Claude C. Jaillet, a French-educated priest stationed in San Diego, Texas, observed that Tejanos in the West Texas region around Fort Stockton and Fort Davis congregated regularly in one of the *jacales* and prayed the rosary without a clerical direction.[10]

Further, while Tejanos expressed dissatisfaction with the overall ministry, they respected the purpose of the priesthood. This regard manifested itself in the enthusiasm with which they greeted *padrecitos* (priests) who occasionally went out to their ranches in South Texas after the Civil War. They received the clergymen with great ceremony and welcomed them into their jacales to offer them poor meals of tortillas, frijoles, and coffee. As the laborers returned from the day's toil, families readied infants for baptism, rallied their children to receive catechism instruction, gathered at the largest hut to say the rosary and sing hymns, and unmarried couples living together prepared themselves for first confession, communion, and the sacrament of matrimony. The next morning, the hosts assisted the priests in converting one of the huts into an altar. They fashioned sheets into confessionals and ante-pendiums, scarves into valances, and shawls, embroidered with faded pictures, hung on walls behind the altar like tapestries. Women brought out their jewels and finery, decorated the altar with their *santitos* (images of saints), and turned the poor thatched cottages into makeshift sanctuaries. At dusk, rancheros came together in the improvised chapel to hear the instruction, say the rosary, and sing their hymns. In the 1890s, the padrecitos still rode about the scattered ranchos of agrarian South Texas and people still welcomed them in similar style.[11]

In the same spirit, Tejanos upheld the tradition of family altars within the home. Santitos in some corner of the house set apart the Tejano jacal or adobe in a fashion similar to the way that the molcajete and metate distinguished their kitchen from that of other ethnic groups. The private sanctuaries of the well-to-do sometimes displayed an ornateness that equalled their economic standing. That of Callisto Algeuin (Calisto Holguin?) in Socorro (El Paso Valley) in

1847, for example, included the Saviour nailed to the cross and the large inscription *INRI* above it, a life size image of the Virgin Mary, images of saints and household votive figures, and an infinite variety of symbolic roses and other flowers.[12] In the West Texas areas, noted Father Jaillet, almost all Mexicans had an image of the Virgen de Guadalupe in their homes.[13]

The sanctity of the *campo santo* (cemetery) similarly evoked the reverence of nineteenth century Tejanos. In San Antonio, the Cementerio de San Fernando, lying within the environs of "Little Mexico," revealed the special place of the dead among the living. Crowded together were the graves marked with white or black wooden crosses, with tin or wooden boxes with glass fronts that contained some souvenir of the departed, while decorating others were paper flowers tied on a bush near a grave, little figures dangling, or a tiny cross enclosed in a bottle. Largely the cemetery of the lower classes, their reverence for the sacred ground was expressed by placing the votive offerings on various graves. Some featured a baby's cradle placed above a tiny mound, or a broken toy, or an inscription reading *bebita mia* (my baby) on a cross.[14]

A number of other practices characterized Catholic ritual among Tejanos. In the years immediately following the Texas Revolution, women stopped to pray every morning before the statues of saints that decorated the Alamo's outer walls.[15] In the 1870s, when the great cathedral bell rang at noon, every Bexareño within hearing distance traditionally removed his hat and stood bareheaded until the tolling ceased.[16] Thus did this aspect of Tejano culture continue, while others, particularly those having to do with economic and political survival, changed.

The celebration of religious holidays further manifested the Tejanos' attachment to Catholic tradition. But saints' days to Tejanos meant much more than acknowledging the solemnity of the date, for generally the occasion involved festivities that rivaled other important secular days of importance. They honored the Catholic calendar that their Mexican parents before them had esteemed, and, like their ancestors, mixed both religion with frolic and in the process exploited to the fullest advantage two cultural forms that rendered them the necessary respite from the harshness of impoverished existence.

On January 17, Tejanos observed the blessing of the animals in honor of the feast of St. Anthony the Abbot, protector of animals.

The event, originating in the remote provinces of Spain, saw a procession of pets, from the canary to the family cow or horse, being gaily decorated and taken in a parade to the local parish church for the invocation or blessing that would provide them with strength to serve their masters.[17] *Candelaria* or Purification followed on February 2,[18] and April meant the grand celebration of *La Semana Santa* when Tejanos considered the betrayal, trial, death, burial, and resurrection of Christ.[19]

Festivities continued the same way during St. Anthony's Day on June 13, St. John's Day on June 24, and St. Paul's Day on June 29. While allowing Tejanos to pay their respects to the traditional religion, at the same time the dates permitted them to inject traditional games, amusements, and dances into these observances. Of all three, the San Juan celebration overshadowed the other two, and in fact, often overlapped into St. Paul's Day. In mid-century, Bexareños celebrated it to mark the opening of the fruit and vegetable season when apples, melons, sweet corn, and pumpkin were in market.[20] Generally, it was a day associated with water and earned the sobriquet of *El Día de Bañar.* Ritual required that all go to the nearest pond, river, or lake for an early morning dip and give the body some sort of ablution in obvious commemoration of Christ's baptism by John in the River Jordan. If no body of water was available, a plain tub, *acequia,* or ditch served the purpose. Two other customs prevailed. First, women wishing luxuriant hair dampened the ends of their tresses and placed them on the doorsill where a second party chopped them with a hatchet in a haircutting rite. Second, serenaders traditionally called upon those homes where a member of the family bore a name derived from John to honor them with the traditional folk song *Las Mañanitas.* The Juan or Juanita expressed gratification by inviting the players into their homes for whatever refreshments seemed proper before dawn.[21]

In most areas of Texas, the nineteenth century Tejano communities paid homage to these various saints' days with an early morning religious ceremony and followed that, later in the day, with dances, gambling, cockfighting, horseracing, and other amusements.[22] In some cities, American and Mexican flags decorated plazas and hundreds of folk milled about them amid gambling, music, and rounds of alcohol. They patronized tables laden with food and confections and continued into the night visiting tents illuminated by suspended lights.[23] Of all the traditional diversions that found their way into these religious occasions, none was more popular than the *carrera de gallos* (running for the rooster). The game called for fleet horses, agile and skillful riders, and a rooster. At a signal the horseman carrying the bird struck out at a gallop with a corps of contestants in pursuit seeking to wrest from him the ribbon and flower decorating the rooster. An intensely exciting and dangerous chase followed as every competitor sought to gain possession of the bird and carry it to an agreed goal for a prize. Riders rushed for the fowl held tauntingly aloft by one and scuffled for possession of the coveted object. The sport, usually fatal to the chicken, was equally perilous to the rider. Severe bruises and serious wounds often resulted. Two or three contestants frequently came together with a vicious shock and found themselves struggling on the ground with broken necks and limbs. The death of a contestant was not uncommon.

San Juan days by mid-century were occasions for the *coleadura de toros* (bull tailing). Bulls were herded into pens and readied for the start of the contest. To engage in the tailing, riders prepared themselves for the release of the bull and started after the animal as it bolted the corral. The *vaquero* attempted to catch him by the tail, quickly wrap it around the horn of his saddle or under his leg and, by spurring his horse past the brute, hurl him into a somersault. If he performed skillfully and well, the rider returned to his place near the corral to the sound of the triumphal music played by the band and the *vivas* (hoorays) of the onlookers, but unsuccessful ones often returned to the accompaniment of a death march and jeers and rough jokes.[24]

The religious calendar year continued with the festive celebration of Santiago (St. James') Day on July 25 and the *Día de Santa Anna* on July 26.[25] Tejanos generally celebrated Saint Peter's Day on August 2[26] and *el Día de la Santa Cruz* on September 14.[27]

All Saints' Day (November 1) and All Souls' Day (November 2) marked the November calendar. On All Saints' Day, Mexicanos worshipped and exalted patron saints and invoked their benign blessing and at times worked up lively processions that featured music and marchers carrying banners, flags, and images representing different Mexican saints.[28] Traditionally, the entire family assembled on All Souls' Day to spend the day at the cemetery. The relatives brought momentoes to the graves and arranged the various articles upon, or near, the resting place of the dead. They decorated the graves of their deceased loved ones with artificial as well as natural flowers, with pictures of the dead or images of various saints, with bottles and oyster shells arranged around the graves, or even costly brass bedsteads set over children's graves and canopied with rich lace curtains. Masses were celebrated for the repose of the souls of the departed on this day.[29]

No month matched December for its array of religious holidays and concomitant festivities. December 8 was observed as Immaculate Conception[30] but December 12, the *Día de Nuestra Señora de Guadalupe*, Mexico's patron saint, touched Tejanos particularly. San Antonio celebrated it in the 1840s with a spirited procession led by the local priest and twelve girls dressed in white carrying a platform bearing a richly and gorgeously dressed image of the Virgin and a lighted wax candle in their free hand. Enlivening the march, fiddlers played as the general population accompanying the cavalcade fired off guns and pistols and showed their devotion in various ways. The march proceeded through the squares and principal streets and stopped now and then as members knelt and recited an *Ave María* or *Padre Nuestro*. Finally, it arrived at San Fernando Cathedral on the Main Plaza. After a long ceremony, the celebrants dispersed; the better class, carrying the patronness, adjourned to one of their homes with them for an all-night dance.[31] When Juárez, Mexico, celebrated the Día de la Virgen de Guadalupe in 1884 with food, sports, cockfights, horseracing, and Indian dancing, Tejanos from El Paso flocked across the river to partake of the festivities.[32]

At Christmas time, *Los Pastores*, a Spanish medieval drama introduced into Texas by Catholic missionary priests, found its way onto stages in backyards, churches, or vacant rooms. From the middle of December to January 6, this reported creation of Lope de Vega, the master of the Spanish theatre, was reproduced by Tejano farmers and work hands who labored indefatigably for weeks on their costumes and parts. Passed from father to children by oral transmission, this miracle play revealed the Tejano attachment to religious tradition despite their estrangement from institutional Catholicism.

As staged in San Antonio (where it was most popular) in the latter part of the nineteenth century, *Los Pastores* opened with a shepherd choir that served as the chorus, interpreting the drama for the audience. Toy sheep and cattle, a wax angel hanging from above, an effigy of the Holy Mother, and a porcelain figure of the Christ child in a miniature cradle, all were present to set the stage for the action. Every sort of diminutive wax animal and other offerings enhanced the altar while candles and Chinese lanterns illuminated the religious scene.

As the chorus ended, a group of shepherds dressed in their ordinary clothing filed in to take seats on benches. Carrying an elaborately decorated shepherd's crook, they wore costumes of handsome beaded and embroidered sashes with beaded pouches designed to carry food. Angels singing the glad tidings of Christ's birth next appeared, as Lucifer, covered with paper spangles and attired in a gorgeous Chinese paper suit, a wire mask, dark stockings, and golden shoes, appeared seeking to dissuade the shepherds from following the Star of Bethlehem. Seeing Lucifer's failure, more devils wearing grotesque masks and strange costumes joined him on stage. Unmoved by the passionate arguments of the demons, the pastores deserted their flock to arrive at the manger where again they encountered the devils trying to persuade them not to worship. After another bitter exchange, the shepherds brought their offerings to the altar and rendered homage to Christ. The play, which at times lasted over three hours, concluded with a grand hallelujah chorus. The next night the action illustrated a subsequent chapter from the life of the Savior, and often several performances played in different parts of the city at the same time. Other towns staged the story also.[33]

Posadas, or Rests, also celebrated at Christmas, represented the nine days Mary and Joseph wandered in search of shelter in Bethlehem just before the birth of Jesus. According to nineteeth century tradition, a family stopped at selected houses to ask for posada or rest. Refused, they moved to a third house accompanied by the second family and the group increased at each posada. Refreshments were served at the last house as the assembled recited prayers before the manger or an improvised altar. The last posada, held on Christmas eve, became an all night vigil when the participants, after attending midnight mass, returned to celebrate till morning.[34]

The religious calendar ended with the *Día de Inocentes*, December 28. Celebrated in memory of the children who died under the edict of Herod in his search for the Christ Child, it customarily allowed folk to play tricks on friends in a manner similar to April

Day. As *inocentes* meant foolish (or gullible or sucker) as as innocent, the perpetrator cried *inocente* after each discomfiture of a particular victim.[35]

By combining amusement with traditional religious holidays, Tejanos used the occasion to pay heed to a system of belief that mitigated misfortune but also found still another way to define life according to their perspective. During festive times, they shifted their concerns from immediate conditions to the more rewarding sense of ethnic continuity, group identity, uniqueness, and solidarity. Like their brethren in Mexico, they looked upon these occasions as settings for enjoying and celebrating the good in life and not as times for lamenting life's problems.

Whether Tejanos celebrated their religious calendar with a great feast every year remains to be ascertained. Contemporary accounts do not establish such a pattern although they do indicate that such celebrations existed at the time immediately after the Texas Revolution—indeed that they were an extension of the colonial period. That such celebrations persisted into the 1890s is revealed in the observations of whites who regularly remarked (not always positively) about the "numerous fiestas" held by Tejanos and by the fact that books such as Harry Hansen's *Texas: A Guide to the Lone Star State*[36] listed some of the commemorations as still existing in the 1930s. Whatever may be said about their consistency from year to year, the fact remains that these fiestas played a part in the religious dimension of nineteenth century Tejano culture.

Besides holy days, other occasions lent themselves to religious observations and accompanying festivities. When Ysleta held a religious celebration in 1883 for Lady Carmen, the town's patron saint, the event turned into a great gala as eight priests honored her with prayer and mass. People dressed in their best came from miles around to see marching bands, witness fireworks displays, wander through the plaza, and enjoy themselves in a number of other ways in the two-day affair.[37] During church-related functions, Tejanos displayed much the same demeanor. In 1872, the upper class of Tejanos in San Antonio organized a "Grand Fair" to raise funds to finish the Cathedral of San Fernando de Béxar.[38] Concerts and other fund-raising projects for the benefit of the church organized by parishioners were common.[39]

Even funerals took on the aura of festivity. The death of a loved one at times featured more merrymaking than mourning, and some nineteenth century funerals, aside from their social function of bringing relatives and friends together, became spirited occasions. By celebrating the departure of the deceased in this way, Tejanos may have been carrying out Spanish-Indian Catholic tradition, but at the same time they were behaving in ways not uncommon to preindustrial people. Whether in England or in the South's slave community, poor folk have often gone to excess in their resolve to provide their loved ones with a proper interment. Thus when the child of Miguel Cortenoz [sic] died of measles at Nacogdoches in 1836, the father arranged for a traditional wake and funeral. According to William Fairfax Gray, a land agent for a New York company who recorded the event,

The child was laid out in a room opening on the street in full view. During the evening the neighbors began to assemble, a violin was obtained, and the musician played all his liveliest airs for their amusement. No grief was manifested by anyone but the bereaved mother, and the contrast between her wailing and the lively tones of the violin was horrid. About 12 o'clock at night the corpse was moved from the dwelling house to the *Monte house;* kept by the father, accompanied by the violin and all the company. There it was laid out in form, and the company *danced* to the violin all night. This morning tickets of invitation were issued to the citizens to attend the funeral. M. Cortenoz is popular with the American population for the part he lately took in some Indian affairs, and many of the Americans attended the funeral, which is an unusual mark of respect with them.

The poor, unconcious infant was sumptuously arrayed in costly apparel, a full dress, even to shoes, a nosegay in its clasped hands, and its head an other parts decorated with numerous artificial flowers and gaudy ribbons, which were made up and adjusted by the Mexican women, in public, while they chatted and laughed with as much glee as if it had been a country *quilting.* A silver crucifix dagger was placed in the bosom of the corpse, and it was carried to the grave by six young females in a recumbent and almost upright position. There was no priest but a *Sacristan* officiated and chaunted, the service. The procession was accompanied by a drum, fife and two violins, playing lively tunes. A crucifix was carried before the corpse; the persons in the procession were all uncovered. Some of them, twenty or thirty, carried spermaceti candles in their hands, all burning, and others of the Mexicans carried guns, which they fired off from time to time during the procession to the grave. Amidst all the preparation, merriment and noise, the wailing screaming, howling of the mother was heard from time to time, until the procession left the house; she remained behind. In the interior, I am told by Dr. Cameron, rockets are discharged during the procession, instead of the firing of guns. It is indeed considered by them an especial occasion for every demonstration of rejoicing, as they think the deceased has gone to Heaven. The mother alone permits the animal affections to predominate over her religious faith, and she seems to feel bound to make all possible demonstrations of outrageous grief. The following day, I am told, she goes about her business, or dances like other women, and shows no signs of mourning. Such are some of the inconsistencies and vagaries which poor human nature exhibits, under perverted religious influences, and deprived of proper mental and moral culture.[40]

Even during the course of biculturation, adaptation, and socialization in subsequent decades, the tradition lingered; when the practice ceased in its totality, if it did, remains obscure. In another case in the 1880s a local band consisting of a fiddle, a drum, a harp, and other instruments performed the ceremonies for a small pox victim. According to custom, they played two tunes at home where the corpse lay in repose—one a lively waltz and the other a sentimental piece—and two more pieces at the grave. According to an observer, it was an impressive ceremony in which those attending enjoyed themselves and considered it the nicest funeral of the season.[41]

In a child's funeral held at Laredo in the 1890s, the march to the graveyard displayed a similar mood. The priest led the procession in an open carriage. Next came the coach on which rested the corpse. On its box, a young man carried a coffin lid adorned with rose-colored cambric, and within, four young girls dressed as brides with wreaths and veils, supported upon their laps the little coffin, enveloped in rose-color and dressed with flowers. People followed the procession on foot. At the Catholic church, the girls, who looked neither grave nor sad, carried the coffin and placed it before the altar. After the burial service, they again bore the body to the carriage, resumed their place, and the procession headed for the cemetery for the burial of the little girl. "It seems strange indeed to those unacquainted with their ways, for it is almost like a merry-making, showing no sign of grief nor mourning," declared a journalist.[42]

In fact, though, nothing was strange about the ritual. Like their Catholic Mexican-Indian forefathers and their Mexican kinsmen in that century, Tejanos celebrated the death of a small child in the belief that the unstained soul of a baptized but unconfirmed child would go directly to heaven. Thus the death of an *angelito* (little angel) called for rejoicing. On the other hand, funeral services for adults might involve drinking and other forms of passing the time, but probably no hilarity.

Their religion, which eschewed some tenets of Roman Catholicism while accepting others, embraced a belief in the miraculous. By maintaining a faith in heavenly intercession, Tejanos found support for their feelings that God, perhaps through the manifestations of saints or the Virgin, regarded them as His people. Thus, when the Virgin reportedly appeared to a girl considered mentally deficient at El Sauz ranch (fifteen miles northeast of Rio Grande City) in 1898, it stirred much excitement among neighbors. Rumors circulated that those suffering maladies were flocking to the shrine and being cured by drinking tea made from nutmeg and rose leaves. When the girl proclaimed that the Virgin promised an appearance on the fifteenth (but did not say what month), a large number of Mexicanos prepared to make pilgrimage to see Santa María de Antoche (Antocha?) as the girl now claimed to be named. According to further reports, the Virgin appeared later in the month.[43]

Faith in *curanderos* (folk healers) was natural among people who could not depend upon white medical doctors and who, given the absence of such attention, had come to respect the remedies and talents of folk healers adept at tending to the ailing. The concept itself was based on beliefs common in rural Mexico since the days of the Spanish conquest in 1521. As in the case of other religious things, Spanish and Indian heritage had fused and produced a type of treatment based on popular beliefs and empirical experience. Rural and poverty-stricken folk then brought the concept to Texas both during Texas' colonial period and after. By accepting the powers of such a figure to render them relief through regenerative barks, *hierbas* (medicinal herbs), roots, and other products, the Tejano community helped itself. The medicine man was prominent in many a Tejano village and rancho.[44]

Considering the trust Tejanos placed upon one of their own for medical attention (and the poor have generally done the same), the fact that *curanderos* often succeeded in their task, and the fact that the *curanderos'* credibility surmounted suspicion, Tejanos turned with interest and enthusiasm whenever stories circulated about one's exceptional powers. In such a case in 1861, Mexicanos in western Texas and the Nueces and adjoining counties turned their attention to a particular *curandero* in northern Mexico and swarmed to the area around Mier and Guerrero to see the man rumor held to be the "God of Hosts." According to reports from the border, the "Saint," a sixty-five year old man referred to a *Tatita*, possessed powers to feed thousands of people with two or three tortillas, cure all diseases, restore sight to the blind, and in fact, perform all kinds of miracles. The vulgar looking and slovenly dressed curandero used *agua ardiente* (whiskey) and water as medicine and rubbed them on the affected parts of kneeling patients. Allegedly, he provided for his entourage of followers and devotees by buying beeves and dividing them among them and by giving them clothing with money acquired from unknown sources. Anglos, said the reporter, showed a similar interest in him and were flocking to the area.[45]

The arrival in El Paso of Teresa Urrea, La Niña de Cabora, created similar excitement among Paseños in the summer of 1896. Fleeing from assassins in Arizona who accused her of fomenting revolution in Mexico, she arrived in the city and set up makeshift headquarters to attend to the deaf, blind, halt, and afflicted. When young, she had suffered an attack of fever and while in a trance during her illness, had heard voices directing her toward a life dedicated to relieving the suffering of mankind on earth. She gained a reputation as a curandera and *sanadora* (curer) after that and continued to minister to the sick. While in El Paso, many sought her treatment. Newspaper accounts reported hundreds of people from the valley and mountains, as well as Mexico, arriving in the city and waiting in long lines to receive her attention. She tended to them by rubbing afflicted parts, annointing oil, giving simple herb medicines, and placing major emphasis on prayer. The essence of her religion was love of God and man, and, she did not charge for her services but accepted contributions. During her brief stay, she effected a number of cures among the infirm—both Mexican and Anglo. "While I try to persuade myself she is a fraud," confessed a correspondent for the New Orleans *Times-Democrat*, "I have to acknowledge that the cures are wonderful and I hear everyday or so of similar cures."[46]

No curandero in the nineteenth century or after matched the powers of Don Pedrito Jaramillo. Immigrating from Mexico in the early 1880s, he established himself in Los Olmos (Brooks County) where, as a curandero, he helped the sick through their faith in God's power to heal them. From there, he traveled on horseback to Corpus Christi, San Antonio, and Laredo, stopping at intermediate points to attend to the infirm. From miles around people came to Los Olmos on foot, horseback, wagons and buggies to be treated by Don Pedrito. In his twenty-five years in Los Olmos, he performed miraculous cures for literally thousands of sufferers. No curandero today receives the same honor and appreciation from Tejanos. He earned a place among the pantheon of saints whose statues distinguish altars in Tejano homes. Well into the twentieth century, people said masses for the repose of his soul, exhibited large pictures of him in their homes, and at least one firm supplying curative herbs used his picture and the trademark "Don Pedrito."[47]

Judging from newspaper accounts, which were more inclined to report what they perceived as the perverse in Mexicanos, folk doctors came in for their share of abuses. In 1860, for example, the Corpus Christi *Ranchero's* correspondent in Rio Grande City reported a case in which certain parties had accosted a woman they believed responsible for bewitching them. According to the story, Matías Ramírez, a wealthy landowner in the Roma, Texas, area had directed the kidnapping of Antonia Alanis, the accused witch, on the assumption that it was she who prevented his syphillitic son Ambrosio from recovering. The kidnappers had lassoed the old lady and dragged her before transporting her to Camargo, México, where Ambrosio lived. Across the river, the abductors severely beat her, stuck her body full of prickly pear thorns, and continued the sadism for the next two weeks. When Ambrosio failed to recover, the medicine man resorted to drastic measures, advising that she be set afire. The sick man had pigeon bones in his head, he thought, and only when the witch commenced burning would the bones protrude, allowing him to extract them. According to the correspondent, the remedy had been carried out and the woman roasted.[48]

Generally, curanderos practiced their traditional role of helping their patients recover through the use of popular remedies. As members of an improverished community, they could be counted upon in the absence of physicians to provide a crucial service to a community transmitting and adapting certain Mexican cultural patterns to Texas. As such the curandero was a product of a mythic belief of an ethnic group living in a condition of poverty and the offspring of a life experience that called for such a figure in its quest for survival.

Given the distance existing between Tejanos and the institutional Church, the minimal power that priests wielded over the people, and the Tejanos' nominal attachment to Catholicism, Protestant missionaries directed their missionary work to the state's Spanish-speaking citizens. Although it is practically impossible to determine the success of the Protestant proselytizers, Tejanos throughout the century attended their schools, participated in their services and helped in the construction of buildings. When the Reverend John McCullough established his Presbyterian school in San Antonio in the 1840s, he succeeded in recruiting a number of children among Catholic Bexareños.[49] So did the Presbyterian Yankee school teacher Melinda Rankin, who, in the 1850s, opened a small school in Brownsville for young girls who desired to learn English. Her Rio Grande Female Institute continued to expand in later years.[50] In the same area in early 1880, the Presbyterian Mission Church, U.S. South Assembly, reported having four day-schools with an attendance close to 100 and six Sunday schools with 160 children enrolled. It further claimed to have established three organized churches, with fourteen native ordained elders and deacons, a membership of 257 and a number of preaching stations along both sides of the Rio Grande.[51] In the 1880s, Presbyterian Tejano missionaries worked alongside white clergymen in bringing services to Mexicanos living on South Texas ranchos.[52]

Other Tejanos lent an ear to competing Protestant sects. In the 1870s, part of the Tejano population in the Medina neighborhood (San Antonio area) was being receptive to the Methodists and some joined them.[53] In San Antonio itself, Tejano residents regularly attended Protestant worship services in the postbellum period (the Methodists and Baptists seemed the strongest),[54] and in the Gonzales area, Mexican Americans listened to Reverend Arturo Castro preach in 1894.[55] In Corpus Christi, some attended the Mexican Mission Church in the 1870s and 1880s when Methodist services were conducted in Spanish.[56] The Reverend Santiago Tafolla, presiding elder in the San Diego district in the 1880s held bilingual services at the Mexican Methodist Church and reportedly preached to large congregations.[57] In Bandera, Mexicanos attended the newly finished Mexican Methodist Church in February 1886 and listened to Spanish-speaking clergymen deliver sermons in both languages.[58] In El Paso in the latter part of the century people also supported a Methodist Church,[59] while others attended St. John the Baptist Church in the early 1890s.[60] In the summer of 1893, the Reverend J. J. Mercado, A Mexican evangelist, preached in the city despite harassment from Catholics who sought to disturb his service.[61]

By taking those beliefs and practices from Catholicism that fit into their life as poor and oppressed folk, Tejanos continued syncretizing old religious world views. While seemingly backward and superstitious at times, their religion rejected the lessons of passivity and resignation historically inculcated into dependent classes by institutional Catholicism. They rejected the notions that they should be solemn and passive and be guilt-ridden because they violated some of its proscriptions. They did not feel less human or less Christian for their nominal views, nor did they regard themselves as reprobates. Instead, their religion, like that forged by other people to correspond to their peculiar conditions, gave them a vital insight into life, one which tempered externally imposed adversity. Like so many other facets of Tejano culture, that insight played a crucial role in perpetuating the conditions of normalcy in Tejano homes. It was what permitted them to go on searching for an improved economic, social, and political life.

For although economically, socially, and politically disadvantaged, Tejanos controlled their own primary environment. White society, however much it might attempt to control their economic and political lives, did not meddle to any great extent with their domestic life style. While attempts at cultural genocide by Anglo American institutions was part of their experience, Mexican Americans generally succeeded in repulsing those endeavors, as is evidenced by so many Mexican cultural forms that have survived. Mastery over themselves at home allowed them the power to perpetuate that religion's world view, just as it gave them the space to control other facets of their cultural milieu. Autonomy rendered them the sense of security and strength to control their own privacy and reaffirm their cultural uniqueness and difference from Anglo Americans. Thus religion was no small part of a cultural makeup that defined their identity as Tejanos.

In 1900, many of the state's Mexican Americans still lived in marriage without Church sanction, still remained niggardly as far as paying for funerals and marriages, but still acknowledged their

attachment to Catholicism. The Church, on the other hand, remained aloof, expressed anti-Mexican sentiments, and failed in
establishing a Mexican American clergy.[62] While the Church made
efforts to correct that relationship in the next century, Tejanos as
before took from it what they liked and rejected other things.
Many continued holding their own views on such issues as birth
control and extramarital sex, attended church irregularly, and as
before, continued as nominal Catholics.[63]

Folklore and Life Experience*

Historians searching for the role of folklore in the lives of Tejanos confront serious difficulties. Generally speaking, Mexicanos, like other poor and illiterate classes, did not record their lore; historians who seek access to this oral tradition have to rely upon what Mexicanos related to inquisitive whites. Although these compilations are reliable, what Mexicans relayed to these collectors must be scrutinized rigorously. It it possible, for instance, that Mexicanos did not trust the interviewers and told them only what they wanted them to hear. In addition, Tejanos may have been reluctant to relate tales that verged on the pornographic or those that revealed intimate feelings about race and other features of Mexican American culture that they believed whites could not comprehend. The tales, moreover, surely lost something in the cultural and linguistic translation. Anglo folklorists could not have captured the teller's intonation, stress, chants, and mimicking, all of which are common to Mexican American storytelling traditions.

Equally disturbing for the historian and folklorist is that these legends, myths, and other tales, collected in the twentieth century, forfeited the flavor of their nineteenth century milieu. Yet, grouped together from different sources and different times, they give a clearer indication of the part folklore played in the belief system and world view that characterized nineteenth century Mexican Americans.[1]

*Coauthor Saúl Sánchez.

In Texas, itinerants, historians, journalists, and other observers recorded the folklore of the state's Spanish-speaking community. But all historians owe a debt to the Texas Folklore Society for its indefatigable efforts in collecting Mexican American materials. Organized in 1909, issuing its first volume in 1916, and continuing until the present, the Society regularly published scores of items relating to Tejano life. Long uninterpreted or simply ignored, these and other collections reveal the views of a preindustrial folk as they came into contact with the predominantly agrarian society. They reveal not the behavior of a people living in the culture of poverty, but rather the culture of Tejanos who just happened to be poor. They identify the autonomous spirit of a community socialized, partly by choice, partly by force, as Mexican American.

Folklore provided an intrinsic survival tool for Tejanos; it identified them with the past and thus with an experience at once contiguous and familiar. It gave them a sense of history and thus the psychological affirmation necessary to endure in a setting that constantly reminded them that they came from practically nothing.

Because Tejano folklore was firmly planted in the Texas pre-Revolutionary War experience, it lent a profound sense of cultural continuity traceable to Mexico's colonial period. Legends about buried treasures, the naming of places, the origin of certain plants, miracles, and events involving the presence of Spaniards all related to Spanish themes, settings, characters, and the like.

No other aspects of folklore revealed the legacy of the Spanish experience as much as the legends about buried treasurers. Spanish *entradas* into Texas and searches by Spanish-Mexicans in later decades engendered a rich lore about mythical wealth and tales of hidden treasures. According to legends told by nineteenth century Tejanos, Spaniards had hidden fortunes in moments of crises (usually Indian attacks) only to be prevented by some happenstance from returning at a later date to retrieve them. Thus, precious treasures lay hidden in diverse areas of the state from El Paso to East Texas.[2] This folklore passed on to Anglo Americans who migrated to the state in later generations, became part of the fantasy of the new arrivals.

The Spanish past manifested itself in many other ways. Such folktales as that of "Pedro de Urdemalas" for example, revealed the presence of Spanish characters.[3] Border *corridos* (ballads) that appeared around the 1860s were a link to Spanish *romances*, although their subject matter and structure belonged to the New World,[4] while the *tragedia* (a ballad of tragedy) tended to resemble the epics of Medieval France and Spain (*La Chanson de Roland* and *El Cantar de Mío Cid*) in origin and theme.[5]

When Spanish domination ended for Tejanos in 1821, the post-Spanish experience threaded its way into folklore as had the colonial historical past. Thus an evolving and unfolding experience embraced tales of buried treasures left in Texas by Antonio López de Santa Anna or by *bandidos* and *rancheros*. For varied reasons associated with accidents, the law, or Indian attacks, Mexicans had left their goods at various points in McMullen County in hopes of returning some day.[6] Tejanos related these legends to whites who themselves continued the search for the elusive treasure in following generations.

Also, folklore exposed Tejanos as the bicultural people they became after the Texas Revolution. On the one hand, it displayed the interest that Mexican Americans still retained in affairs that occurred in the mother country. Through songs, for example, they eulogized Mexican heroes: with the *coplas* of *los franceses*,. Tejanos of the lower border hailed the exploits of Mexican president Benito Juárez in his struggle against the French imperialists of the 1860s.[7] Corridos praised the victory of Texas-born Ignacio Zaragoza over the French at Puebla on May 5, 1862,[8] and immortalized Catarino Garza for his revolution of 1891–92 against Mexican President Porfirio Díaz.[9] Social types, settings, traditions, and other elements similarly pointed to the Mexican cultural presence. On the other hand, as a folklore in flux, it displayed the Tejano's familiarity with the people who controlled Texas politics, economics, and society. Old legends about buried treasures, for one, showed a modification that included the presence of the *americanos*. In legends surrounding the battles of Palo Alto and Resaca de la Palma (May 8 and 9, 1846), the Mexican Army, pressed by Zachary Taylor's troops, lightened the retreat by burying its pay money and other valuables in the battlefield.[10] Other tales had Anglos, rather than Spaniards or Mexicans, burying treasure and then, because of unforeseen contingencies, never returning to retrieve it. Still others had the ghosts of white men guarding buried treasures, instead of the ghosts of Mexicans or Spaniards who had protected them before white men became part of the life experience of Tejanos.[11]

Similarly, corridos reflected the Tejano adaptation to the American setting and their evolving nature as a bicultural people. While the *corridos* about Ignacio Zaragoza celebrated the exploits of a Mexican national hero, it also celebrated the fame of a native Tejano (*general de la frontera*). And surely, Mexicanos would not have eulogized the exploits of Ulysses S. Grant in song (or even have been aware of him) had they retained immutable ties to Mexico and repudiated all interest in the United States. Because those two corridos were sung during the same period, they indicated the familiarity of the border people with the significance of the two men and the fact that the Tejano mind naturally identified with both.[12] Additionally, the corridos about the Catarino Garza revolution of 1891–92 displayed a Tejano familiarity with both Texan and Mexican events. *El Corrido de los Pronunciados* eulogized the attack of Garza upon Mexican territory, while the *Corrido de Capitán Jol* depicted Texas Ranger Captain Lee Hall as a coward and an ineffective fighter compared to the *pronunciados* that defeated him. This type of ethnocentrism attested to a way of life on the border colored by the interaction between Mexican Americans and white Texans.[13]

More aspects of folklore pointed to an experience of Tejanos well acquainted both with their past and their present. Folkloric themes indicated familiarity with time, featured settings, characters, and stylistic arrangements intimate to the narrator. Place names like Presidio, San Elizario, and San Antonio, ranchos belonging to well-to-do families, the Big Bend, and the *chaparral* country of South Texas, local flora like *el cenizo* and the *guadalupana* vine, all permeated the folklore and thus revealed the Tejano's closeness to his environment. Allusions to personalities like the widow Doña Fidencia Ortega of San Elizario, Bartolo Mendoza of El Paso County, the Cantú family of South Texas, to the peasant José Dias and to the rich Don Pedro Carrasco, similarly reflected the reality of their daily experience. Descriptive detail, symbolism, and other stylistic forms added specificity and a localized frame of reference, more plausible characters, strength of purpose, and a more meaningful and convincing portrait to that folklore.

The benevolence of a Christian God, common to folklore universally, was also shown in the religious dimension of their folk stories. In their case, He was an altruistic God seemingly an integral part of a world of disadvantaged people. A beneficient God took care of His people, intervened on their behalf in desperate moments, and fought off evil forces. He was a concerned God who intervened directly in order to give Tejanos relief from natural calamities. *Kineños* (residents of the King Ranch of South Texas), for example, related the story of a compassionate God bursting into tears that became the rain which brought relief to the drought-stricken countryside and His suffering people.[14]

Also, folklore revealed a protective God who intervened in times of great desperation. Time after time, He had come to the assistance of the legendary Father Antonio Margil de Jesús, the ubiquitous folkloric figure. Nineteenth century folklore credited Margil, accompanying the Domingo Ramón expedition in 1716, with working a miracle through the agency of prayer by turning an attacking "swarm of savages" near San Antonio into inoffensive deer. Then, as the expedition approached the city, Margil again rescued the thirsty party through another miracle that begot the San Antonio River.[15] That same year, he delivered another thirsty missionary party from its plight near Nacogdoches by a miracle that produced a living stream of cool water from a site that came to be called the Holy Springs of Father Margil.[16]

Folktales such as "El Cenizo" (which explained the creation of the cenizo shrub) and "La Guadalupana Vine" (which related how the *guadalupana* vine acquired its medicinal value) and the song "Nuestra Señora de los Dolores" (which recounted the powers of such a statue in Webb County) likewise revealed a faith, a moral uprightness, and a humility that testified to the privileged status and special relationship that Tejano vaqueros understood themselves to have with their Creator. In each, the miraculous intervention of the Divine warded off imminent catastrophe. In "El Cenizo," vaqueros arose on Ash (cenizo) Wednesday to rejoice over the desperately needed rain sent to them in response to their prayers. Likewise, the Virgen de Guadalupe had intervened directly to teach vaqueros that the guadalupana vine dipped in *mescal* had extraordinary medicinal values.[17] And "Nuestra Señora de los Dolores," an old statue of the Virgin Mary kept at La Becerra Ranch in Webb County, invariably responded to the pleas of drought-stricken *rancheros* in the latter half of the century. During dry spells they carried the unprepossessing image in solemn procession while mothers marched praying the rosary and chanting "Nuestra

Señora de los Dolores" (the song relating in ten assonantal *cuartetas* the affliction of the Virgin upon learning of the imminent crucifixion of the Lord). Legend had it that rain fell within days after the marchers arrived at the drought-stricken ranch.[18]

In each case, the Divine had intervened to bestow His blessings, not in behalf of one individual, but characteristically for the benefit of an entire community or group. In the legend of "La Guadalupana Vine" the Virgin intended the gift, in the form of the medicinal vine, for Mexicanos in general and the vaquero specifically. The wooden statue of the Virgin Mary ("of a dark color" and its paint "a kind of sticky-looking clay") to which Tejanos sang the verses of "Nuestra Señora de los Dolores," ostensibly represented God's people, the Mexicanos. In the legend of "El Cenizo," a considerate God delivered His blessings to *la gente* in the form of the rain.

A guardian God similarly defended His people from evil forces. In the legend of "The Devil's Grotto," a priest used the holy cross to overcome Satan and deliver the pagan people of Presidio, Texas, from the havoc wreaked upon them by the Devil. Converted to the Christian faith, the people thenceforth enjoyed good health, their crops grew abundantly, and they no longer feared Satan's evil designs.[19] Similarly, a legend concerning the old Mission de Nuestra Señora de la Purísima Concepción de Acuña supposed that the Virgin, responding to the prayers of a supplicating *padre* seeing his neophytes retreating into the safety of the Mission with Comanches close on their heels, had interceded at the gates and somehow held back the "wild tribes" at the very lintel as the neophytes rushed into the safety of the Mission just as the gates closed behind them.[20] In another legend, San Miguel, the patron saint of Socorro (in the El Paso Valley) came to the aid of the community when, during the Civil War, wild marauders from Major T. T. Teel's command commenced bombarding the old church at Socorro. San Miguel appeared in the tower waving a flaming sword and thus held them in check until the Major arrived from Ysleta to end the indiscriminate attack.[21]

Likewise, Tejanos carried on their traditional world view that explained the mysteries of nature and the universe. *Kineños*, for example, employed folk yarns to explain astronomical phenomena. They borrowed freely from Catholic theology and their experiences as vaqueros at the King Ranch in giving subjective renditions of the arrangements of the heavenly bodies.[22] For others, a similar world perception begot explanations of such things as the origin of the Earth's inhabitants, their place in the world order, their functions, and so on. Explanatory stories about birds especially followed such a scheme. Through folktales, Tejanos explained the mysteries in the *aves* (birds): the *paisano* (roadrunner) ran among the chaparral in order to hide his shame and disgrace after being punished for his vanity and arrogance; the owl called "Cú, Cú, Cú, Cú, Cú," as he searched for the Pájaro Cú who had become arrogant after receiving a coat of feathers from other birds that had clothed his naked body (the owl had posted bond that the Pájaro Cú would remain humble after receiving the coat); the male cardinal was beautiful while the female was a wonderful singer because the spirit of the plains could give only one gift to each; and, the song of the dove was a sob because she never saw the Christ Child when all the other creatures of the world came to worship Him (the dove was so humble and unassuming that no one thought of telling her the wonderful news). Similarly, *la cigarra* (locust or *cicada*) achieved its ugly form when his wife called upon the eagle, the monarch of all birds, to check the *cigarra's* roaming ways. The *cigarra's* eyes thus became popped and round and his colored wings turned an ashy gray (his wife, then wanting to be happy with the ugly creature, asked the eagle to make her like her husband).[23]

Hence, by borrowing from their theology and everyday experiences and then combining that with their worldly wisdom, Tejanos rendered seemingly rational explanations of phenomena with which they had daily contact. Structured around such a prosaic framework, the explanations achieved credibility. Folklore provided a vehicle through which rational explanations untangled the supernatural, be it prairie lights, ghosts and spirits, mysterious lakes, physical ailments, or psychological states of mind. Thus, in explaining *la luz del llano*, that mysterious red light that appears at night on the prairie, which scientists believe is caused by peculiar atmospheric conditions, Kineño folklore held that it originated out of a covenant between an old woman and an old wizard. In exchange for food for her starving girls, the woman had agreed to surrender them to the wizard four years later. When the wizard took them the mother was so disconsolate that she set out searching for them, risking the wizard's warning that she not hunt for them on the penalty of immolation. Finally caught and burned alive, the old woman nevertheless kept up the search. Hence, *la luz del llano* was a bundle of fire held together by the spirit of the old woman who still traversed the llanos seeking her lost daughters.[24] Unexplainable lights at night often were believed to indicate precious metals underground. Thus, legend held that the lights about Fort Ramírez (on Ramireño Creek in Nueces County) pointed to the money Ramírez had buried before Indians killed him in the early part of the century.[25] Strange and unexplainable events such as those occurring at Rancho El Blanco, an old Spanish ranch in what is now Jim Hogg County, could be explained similarly—for ghosts and spirits in different forms haunted buried treasures.[26] The appearance of a wraith at San Pedro's sparkling springs in San Antonio also signified the spirit of the tragic Francisco Rodríguez family that guarded the family's hidden treasure. Anyone daring to search for it confronted the specter of Don Francisco or his son or daughter, or the daughter's lover, who had, during Texas' colonial period, been part of a tragic scenario that had led to the treasure's burial.[27] Likewise the feared presence at Espantosa (part of a multiplicity of pools—*tinajas*—and small lakes situated for many miles up and down the west side of the Nueces River and fifteen to twenty miles back) of huge alligators with a horn on their noses, was a result of God's wrath upon Mexican robbers who had once upon a time enticed the most beautiful señoritas to the lake's banks and kidnapped them. In his terrible vengence, God created the reptiles to prey on the children, the women, and the bandits. But after exterminating the band, the monsters still craved for human flesh and, hence, Tejanos in the 1870s still dreaded the Espantosa.[28]

Tejanos also used folk tales as a means of explaining physical or psychological ailments. Such was the case concerning the robust young Eutiquio Holguín of nineteenth century San Elizario who suffered from a strange malady that rendered him paralytic. After all remedies failed, it became obvious he was the victim of the local witch of Cenecú. Traumatized nightly by the *bruja* (witch), Eutiquio finally managed to grab her hand and struggle with her one night. He gradually recovered after that and, when fully recuperated, paid a visit to the *bruja*. Finding all her *monos* (figurines), he threw them into the fire, and with that the witch of Cenecú lost her powers.[29]

And not illogically, a particularly distressing psychological state of mind caused by shock or tragedy found convenient explanation through folklore, as in the case of Elisa Váldez of San Antonio in

1888. A widow, she reluctantly consented to marry a second time. Still harboring feelings of guilt about infidelity to her dead husband, she had wandered away from the wedding festivity to be alone. Then she heard the musicians sing:

Toma el arpa con que canto Las hazañas de los reyes y de amor las dulces leyes De tu imperio seductor

At that moment she felt something pulling on her dress and, turning around, she saw a turkey. Frightened, the conviction forced itself upon her that the turkey was her dead husband coming to upbraid her for her forgetfulness and faithlessness to his memory. She knew then that her marriage could not be consummated, and, indeed, all Eliza did after that was wander around Mission Espada tending to her goat and her pet, the large turkey over which she sang Mexican love songs.[30]

The strength, the durability, and the phenomenal endurance of the mortar of which the Mission de Nuestra Señora de la Purísima Concepción de Acuña in San Antonio consisted, also found its explanation in folklore. It was as strong as brass and had resisted the effects of time because, according to legend, the priest had explained to the Indian workers that as the mission and church were to be erected in honor of the Virgin who was without sin, the mortar was to be mixed each day with fresh pure milk as a tribute to her purity.[31] So also could the beneficent properties of particular plants that rendered Tejanos so much curative services be explained.[32]

Stylized romantic tales and legends, ballads and *canciones* (songs), fables, and other folkloric stories focused on the notions Tejanos held about disenchantment with the opposite sex, filial responsibility, friendships, and other special relationships. The theme of love—especially between sweethearts—persisted in such tragic romances as the one involving María Morales and Alfonso Salinas. Legend held that María had defied her betrothal to a man of her father's choice by marrying Alfonso secretly. But as the newly wedded pair rowed along the San Antonio River, a deep whirlpool caught and swallowed them. So profound was their love that, when their lifeless bodies were found, they were clasped inseparably in each other's arms and had to be buried in the same casket.[33] Similarly, nineteenth century vaqueros and *campesinos* (farm workers) expressed their feelings of endearment toward special ladies in such canciones as "Adelita" and "La Trigueña."[34]

Folklore also employed elements of the supernatural to show the power of love over evil. In the tale of "Blanca Flor," the gambler Juan had given his soul to the Devil in exchange for five years of good luck. At the end of the period, Juan went to the Devil's retreat at the Hacienda of Qui-quiri-qui to fulfill his commands. While there he fell in love with the Devil's beautiful daughter, Blanca Flor, and through her help escaped his commitment to the Devil. Upon marrying Blanca Flor, the legend held, he renounced his former evil ways and both lived happily ever after. Love had redeemed the former gambler.[35]

Tejanos expressed the intimacy of filial relationships through folklore as well. In the tale of "La Luz de Llano," the mother's love for her daughters had been so eternal that the spirit of the old woman in the form of "la luz del llano" still searched for her lost daughters.[36] In contrast, the wrath of God visited the childbeater or unprincipled parent who abused little *inocentes* (innocents). In the "Devil on the Border," Tejanos related the story of a child-beating father who took his newborn baby from his wife to starve it. She cursed the brute: "May the Devil get you." About midnight a terrific whirlwind enveloped the rancho; the smell of sulfur became suffocating, and a dust of ashes choked the people. At daylight, the people hurried toward the place where the father had taken the baby. There they found the dead child, a white dove hovering over its little corpse. All that remained of the father was a heap of greenish yellow sulfur.[37]

Filial responsibility necessarily included socializing the young, and nineteenth-century Tejano folklore contained abundant tales on morals, lessons, and good examples to be imitated by the young. Advice, counsel, and admonitions played prominent roles in these stories. Among the many tales told to impatient children was the story of King Solomon, the wise man who had discovered the secret of returning from death. Telling his most faithful servant that he would die on a certain day, he instructed him further on how to wrap his body, how to dig it up after three weeks, and how to unwrap it so that it would be resurrected. The servant was to tell no one. But people soon started wondering about Solomon's disappearance and threatened the servant with death. Realizing that if he talked, Solomon would never return but that, if he did not, both he and Solomon would be dead forever, the servant revealed the story. "They had not been patient with time, and just for that the secret of returning alive from death was lost forever."

Another didactic story concerned a little boy with three bad habits: aimlessness, asking about people's affairs, and not controlling his temper. One day while running away from home he encountered an old man who gave him three pieces of advice for his last three *pesos:* don't leave a highway for a trail; don't ask about things that don't concern you; and don't lose your temper. Leaving empty handed and feeling swindled, the boy soon encountered three crises to which the *viejito's* (old man) advice applied. By following it, he came into a thriving business and a lovely wife as rewards.

Other tales, such as "Baldheads," were intended to warn the young of certain deceptive types. A country boy had entrusted his money to a bald-headed man who owned a *Casa de Encargos,* which the boy thought to be a bank. Returning a few hours later, he was told that he had deposited nothing. To recover the money, his father designed a plan. He took a bag full of buttons and washers to the *Casa de Encargos* and as he arranged for its deposit, the son entered asking for his money. The clerk, fearing to lose the larger sum the old man possessed, returned the boy's cash. The father then revealed the plot and, turning to his son, advised him: "Keep an eye on bald-heads."[38]

And a tale of the Alamo sought to inculcate children with the value of courtesy by alerting them that someday they might meet the *"padre."* According to this legend, the *padre* rewarded courtesy with gifts.[39]

As a cultural form, folklore defined the Tejano sense of values, ideals, and collective behavior. Those folktales that articulated the theme of retributive justice, for example, contained a repugnant, sometimes grotesque manifestation of supernatural evil that dramatized the consequences of unacceptable behavior. In the legend of "The Devil's Grotto," Satan arrived to bring all manner of distress to the unconverted people of the Presidio, Texas, area and left them in peace only after they were converted.[40] In the legend of "La Casa de la Labor," Doña Fidencia Ortega of San Elizario refused the parish priest Father Pedro a little wine to celebrate the feast of San Isidro and saw her beautiful ranch burn down the next day; the smouldering remains gave "testimony of the wrath of God." Shortly afterward she was seen "riding to the *laguna* on a bull that snorted fire" and plunged into the water never to be seen again.[41] More terrestrial though no less gruesome as symbols of punishment for bad behavior were "two slender hands" that drove Don Miguel mad for killing his lover's fiancé in the tale of "The Little White Dog."[42] Similarly, in the tale "A Boom in Guarache Leather," a set of mean-looking bandits met their punishment at the hands of the destitute José Días, who, sharing their camp overnight, innocently placed an ugly devil's mask over his face as protection from the bitter night's cold. Waking to find what they thought to be the very devil, the malefactors fled the campsite, scrambling over a cliff to their deaths.[43]

Stories that dramatized the favorable outcome of retributive justice, as adduced by the rewards granted the obedient in recompense for their desirable behavorial traits, were as common. In "A Hanged Man Sends Rain," Bartolo Mendoza, a convict destined for execution on a day that "seemed to grow hotter with each moment that passed," repented of his crime before God and thus summoned Providence to send relief to drought-stricken San Elizario. Upon expiring on the gallows, he sent rain from Heaven.[44] In a legend of the Big Bend country told by Natividad Luján in the early 1880s, his uncle Santiago had been killed by Indians sometime around mid-century and became "among the blessed who died for the Faith among the heathens" and his soul had journeyed to purgatory, there to be rescued by prayers said by his faithful descendants.[45]

Folktales featuring the compensation of those who lived acceptably and the punishment of those who lived unacceptably were as frequent. Juan Verdadero was one person whose exemplary behavior resulted in his being handsomely rewarded. According to the story, Juan never lied. But he became an innocent pawn between his *patrón* (boss) and a neighboring landowner who bet his farm that "any man under the urge of necessity will lie." Certain that Juan could be induced into a falsehood, the neighbor sent his daughter to Juan with an offer to exchange her valuable ring for the heart of the prize bull Juan herded. After an excrutiatingly difficult decision, Juan killed the bull for the ring. As he approached the ranch house, his *patrón* queried:

"Juan Verdadero, how is the herd?" "Some fat, some poor, upon my word." "And the white and greenish-colored bull?" "Dead, señor, dead," replied Juan.

Juan had not lied, so his *patrón* made him the administrator of the new estate that the neighbor surrendered.[46] But the case of Doña Carolina who lived in the mid-century El Paso Valley was different. She was haughty and arrogant until she suffered a harrowing experience while searching for her absent husband. After the ordeal, she was no longer the supercilious woman of former days, and eveyone noticed her new behavior.[47] *Desobedientes* (disobedients), *malcriados* (ill-bred persons), *sinvergüenzas* (no 'counts) and other nonconformists received the severest castigations. Tejanos had little tolerance for culprits who abused their children[48] or their spouses. One wife-beater was Don Paniqua, a magically powerful person everyone feared. One day his wife gave birth to a devil-baby who prophesied various horrors, both for the world and Don Paniqua. The raging Don Paniqua took the baby into the thicket and returned without it. No one knew what happened, but, when Don Paniqua died, the Kineños said, he became the foreman of the *infierno's* (hell) *corrida*. Other evil men, the Kineños maintained, went to work in Don Paniqua's outfit.[49]

Brief and pithy animal tales that took the form of fables focused on deviant and unacceptable behavior. For being too proud, the mockingbird had suffered the loss of part of his beautiful feathers; for being audacious in addressing his superiors as cousins, the *paisano* had been condemned to forget to fly and to feed on unclean things; for growing overbearing and cruel toward his ugly and less gifted wife, the male cardinal suffered the loss of his wife's respect; and, for being a spirited adventurer who ignored his mate, the *cicada* incurred its repugnant appearance.[50]

Like fables, corridos pointed to the Tejano value system. Lyrics often extolled the deeds of such great men as Ignacio Zaragoza, Ulysses Grant, and Catarino Garza, heroes who Tejanos looked upon as the personification of courage, liberty, and justice. The corridos not only exalted the adventures of those who challenged the powerful through defiance or confrontation, but they expressed delight in seeing the antagonist demeaned or denigrated—especially if he represented injustice and oppression.[51]

Folktales also expressed a reality in which Tejanos could poke fun at the world, at its inhabitants, and at themselves. They ridiculed the Devil in a tale involving Pedro de Urdemañas (or Urdemalas), a well-traveled and much-experienced *caballero* who arrived in hell to regale the Devil with the wonders of Texas. Hastening to see the marvels of Texas first hand, the Devil arrived in the state only to face a series of calamities with chili peppers, prickly pears, and an unruly cow. Returning swiftly to hell, he expelled Urdemanas who happily returned to Texas to pursue the life style of his former days.[52]

Also popular was the tale of Chano Calanche, who, for a bottle of wine, agreed to help some bandits rid themselves of a priest's body. Tricked by the killers into thinking that he had not buried the corpse—each time he returned to claim the bottle, he found the body of the *padrecito*, not knowing that the bandits had actually killed three priests—the drunken Chano finally decided to dispose of it once and for all. Lighting fire to the corpse, he stayed with it until he fell asleep. He awoke, however to find the padrecito at his campfire; it was actually a traveling priest that happened to stop to warm his morning meal. After the incident, the story held, Chano never claimed the wine and it was said that the prize occupied a place of esteem in the *cantina* (bar) for years after that and was never put up for sale.[53]

In a tale with a more universal theme, Tejano common folks mocked female curiosity. "My wife is not inquisitive," retorted a husband to his friend's suggestion that "all women are curious." But, when his partner took a box to the first man's wife with instructions to keep it sealed, the wife could not resist her curiosity. Upon opening the box, she unwittingly allowed the bird inside to fly away, thereby ridiculing the husband and her own ineptness at keeping secrets.[54]

And they could demean themselves, as in the song of "Coplas del Payo," which portrayed in a jesting manner the general misfortune of their lives. In this story, an overseer encouraged a forlorn lover—an ordinary worker like the narrator—to jump over a cliff.[55]

As poor and disadvantaged people, Tejanos employed folklore as a means of expressing wish fulfillment, wishful fantasizing, and ambitiousness. Such tales generally expressed expectations of winning against misfortune. One of those tales involved a poor, elderly couple who owned a miraculous dog capable of acting as a beast of burden, a hunter, and a racer. One day, a stranger arrived in a nearby town with a very swift horse that made short work of the local opposition. With a chance to make $10,000, the poor man matched his dog against the visiting steed. The dog won easily—in fact did not stop at the finish line but ran all the way to the moon—and the poor, elderly couple had gained their ambition to be wealthy.[56] Another tale involved a *conducta* (convoy) of weary, hungry men preparing to cook their meager meal at the end of the day. At that point Agapito Cercas spoke up: "Don't bother to cook anything. This very day a hog was slaughtered at my home. Just wait and I will bring you *carne adobada, chile con asadura,* and *tortillas calientes.*" He withdrew from the group, and, according to a witness, took off his clothes and disappeared. In a while, he called for his clothes and reappeared with the food he had promised. Some of the men started eating the appetizing meal they wished for, but others refused it suspecting the work of the supernatural.[57]

As an ambitious people not fatalistically resigned to their lot, Tejanos used folklore to constantly question their social condition. They displayed confidence in themselves and showed that they regarded themselves to be as good as the next man and that, if granted more favorable circumstances, they could overcome their problems. Further revealed was the high regard Tejanos had of themselves: that they were good enough to outwit more formidable antagonists, whether it be a wily coyote, a rich *compadre*, or a more fortunate neighbor.

This displayed itself conspicuously in several of the trickster tales. As a genre, these tales include the antagonistic forces of the weak (the underdog) and the strong (the oppressor) with a scenario in which the weak used their wit to overcome the powerful. Such was the case of the innocent man outsmarted by a wily coyote who had rescued him from a snake; the man had originally rescued the snake from a trap whereupon the snake had turned on him because "to repay good with evil" was *la costumbre*—the custom. Beholden to the coyote, the man compensated the animal "with good" (contrary to custom). The man soon learned that he had been too generous, for the coyote kept increasing the payment. Tricking the coyote, he finally unleashed his dog upon the opportunist. "It isn't right to repay good with evil," called the outwitted coyote. "Perhaps," answered the man, "'*pero es la costumbre.*' "

Commonly, the antagonist was a compadre, for Tejanos spoke in terms of their own culture and social conditions as ordinary people. One tale involved two compadres—one rich and the other poor, and the former arrogant and snobbish toward the latter. One day the poor man was so desperate for survival that he schemed to extract money from his more affluent compadre. But his rich compadre grew so angry at his tricks that he finally sought to drown his nemesis by putting him in a bag and dumping him in the sea. But the poor compadre slyly escaped the bag and surfaced to report that he had recovered the rich man's lost pearls at the bottom of the water. Eager to retrieve more jewels, the rich compadre persuaded the poor man to tie him in a sack and dump him in the ocean—all his worldly goods would be put in trust to the poor man for the favor. The poor man did as his compadre wished and became wealthy and was held in great esteem by the people of the town for his innocent little pranks.

In a similar tale, a poor man sought to get even with a rich compadre who looked condescendingly upon him because of his poverty. He succeeded in convincing the rich man of the powers of a newly purchased cap. All that was necessary to obtain items at the store was to say *"Debo de gorra"* (put it on the cap, cuff). "What a marvelous cap," said the rich man, "Sell it to me for $30,000." Feigning reluctance, the poor man surrendered it. But when the rich man attempted to buy an expensive diamond necklace with it, he found himself in jail for failing to pay. The poor man went on to live a life of luxury, while the rich fellow wound up in the mad house.

A tale indicating the awareness Tejanos felt concerning social distance involved Don Pedro Carrasco, the owner of many cattle, and José Días, the owner of a single but fat and very productive cow. Jealous of José, Don Pedro tricked José into killing his only cow, telling him of the high price *guarache* leather was bringing in the neighboring town of Aldama. Disappointed at being tricked into killing his only cow (the price of leather at Aldama was rock bottom), José was making his way slowly homeward when he came upon some money left by bandits. Taking his new found wealth, he arrived home to show the people the money which, he said, he had made off his cow. Don Pedro, thinking that the price of *guarache* leather was indeed high, killed his herd, only to find himself tricked by his sly compadre. Now José and his family became wealthy and gave money to the *santitos* (saints) and the poor.[58] Such trickster tales allowed Tejanos to engage the enemy and triumph over him. It also permitted them the psychic relief from oppressive conditions.

Nineteenth-century Texas folklore revealed an aspiring, scheming, dreaming, and changing people concerned with a multiplicity of things affecting them both as human beings and as an oppressed people. Like dependent classes elsewhere, Tejanos employed folklore to question their existence, to explain it, and to satisfy the mind as to the universe about them; but folklore was not limited to that. It also functioned as entertainment, as a way of eulogizing heroes and expressing discontent with "no 'counts," a means of expressing kinship, a vehicle for inculcating values and behavior patterns, a mode of teaching the lessons of acceptable ideals both to adults and the young, an art of poking fun at themselves, a manner of engaging in wishful fantisizing, and, much more importantly, a technique for passing on survival skills through fictionalized accounts where the weak could indeed triumph over powerful forces. Folklore, encompassing all these functions, acted not only to give identity and solidarity to a community that shared a similar experience, but it also provided them with a covert and subconscious form of resistance to oppression.[59]

Folklore, of course, is a universal cultural feature among all classes, and it was present long before Tejanos met Anglos in the 1820s. It persisted as a vital force of the Tejano nineteenth century experience, and it continued long after 1900. Indeed, it was in the first four or five decades of the twentieth century that the aforementioned Texas Folklore Society collected most of its materials. Primarily the tales and legends of Tejanos from the rural areas, that folklore, while manifesting the changes of the twentieth century, reflected themes, settings, and stylistic forms similar to the folklore of nineteenth century agrarian Texas. It continued being a part of the intimate side of the Texas Mexican experience—like that of raising families, worshipping in particular ways, and maintaining a language. That folklore thrived meant it was part of an expressive culture defined from within but that also took and rejected from outside standards, observances, and patterns as it saw fit.

Entertainment

In the relative autonomy of *barrios* and *ranchos*, Tejanos held gatherings, dances, and *fiestas*. These and other entertainments kept up tradition as well as turned attention away from the adversity Tejanos faced as a poor and oppressed people. Such festivities were a type of play that gave them respite from the rigors of work and other exhausting activities, but besides their gaiety these occasions fit their views, as a preindustrial people, that they ought to take time off from their work to celebrate and enjoy the shared experiences that made their lives meaningful. These festivities made for a state of emotional and psychological well being because the gatherings provided a resting time that in turn reinvigorated their efforts to keep on going and trying to improve matters for themselves and their families.

Among their popular entertainments until the middle decades of the century was the *fandango*. Originally the name of a dance of Spanish derivation, since the colonial period it had come to describe a certain kind of diversion—usually a festive gathering colored by gay strains of music, sinuous dancing, drinking, gambling, eating, and an overall commotion that gave the occasion an aura of both good and evil. As was done before the Texas Revolution, Tejanos held it in the streets, in makeshift dance halls, or fandango houses, at all times of the year, oftentimes daily and to it were attracted revelers from all parts of the Tejano community. In San Antonio in this era, violins and guitars strummed different strains of music, playing the equivalent of "Turkey in the Straw," while couples swung around in the full enjoyment of the Mexican polka or the *bolero*. The old tradition of escorting the *señorita* to a table for delicacies continued. Gambling tables about which both Mexicans and Americans crowded playing the popular card game of *monte*, still gave the places a resemblance to gambling sites similar to counterparts in other localities and in other times. Liquor circulated and, as in other settings where gambling, dancing, and drinking encouraged bellicosity, tragedies often occurred. Affrays, often fatal, were not uncommon.[1]

A similar kind of stir was part of fandangos elsewhere in the state. *Picadillos, enchiladas, chiles rellenados, frijoles, chiles colorados, tamales, tortillas,* and other savory and palatable dishes were available to the revelers. Clarinets, fiddles, or violins provided music; señoritas danced gracefully; gambling, drinking, and horse racing occupied others. As other entertainment forms that stimulate passions, so did the *fandango* lead to jealousies and rivalries that frequently ended in violence.[2] At least those were the impressions of Anglo Americans who were, however, prone to exaggerate the allegedly un-American side of Tejanos.

As a cultural form, the *fandango* neared its demise in the 1860s and 1870s as whites came geographically closer to Mexicanos. City ordinances were passed that prohibited this entertainment, which was regarded as alien to white society.[3] The *fandangos* lingered nevertheless in an illegal and a less conspicuous manner throughout the rest of the century.[4]

Bailes, akin to the *fandango* but less inclined to rowdyism, attracted the entire community and served as a cultural get-together for families, friends, relatives, and lovers. Tejanos seemed to have worked especially hard in the rural areas to arrange these popular bailes. The organizers often had to smooth, sprinkle, and pack dirt floors with boards until hard as brick; then they placed rough, wooden benches in a square surrounding the dance floor, lit kerosene lanterns, and negotiated for a guitar, violin, or accordian.[5] At the Miller Ranch near Corpus Christi, where Mexicanos held a dance once a month in the latter part of the century, they either erected a platform or, when that was impossible, used the open ground swept hard and clean. Decorations of all kinds hung from pole to pole about the dancing area. Señoritas dressed themselves attractively in ruffled and well-starched dresses that had colored sashes of long ribbons; young men who were equally well attired vied for their attention. Meat given to the ranch hands by Miller or bought from him permitted the sale of tamales and other delicacies. Refreshments, candies, and assorted concoctions provided further variety.[6] More or less the same arrangements existed at bailes in other parts of the state, both rural and urban.

Members of the upper classes meanwhile regaled themselves with more formal affairs. Throughout the century the upper class in San Antonio maintained its social distance from less fortunate Bexareños and entertained itself with formal balls rather than less ceremonial bailes. In 1866, for example, the elite of the city's Mexican society attended the New Year's Grand Masquerade and Fancy Dress Ball at Dryden Hall.[7] On September 21, 1883, members of oldline families like the Ximénes, Cassiano, Flores, Yturri, and Leal, gathered at Turner Hall for the ball given by the Mexican Social Club. The reception committee consisted of the wives of J. F. Cassiano, Plutarco Ornelas, and José Cassiano, among other assistants. The Italian band played to a well-dressed crowd.[8] On another occasion, on February 23, 1884, when the Mexican Social Club held an inaugural ball at the Casino, 200 couples attended the event and danced to the music of the Eighth Cavalry brass band.[9] When the Mexican Social club celebrated its rebirth in January 1891, the list of Bexareños included about the same circle plus a number of Anglos integrated into the organization. Having been lately organized for social and literary purposes, it presented an inaugural ball and concert that featured a violin solo, a poem by R. G. Guerrero entitled "To My Country," a piano solo, and a duet, plus musical activity that included the *gran marcha*, and *valses, danzas, cuadrillas, lanceras, polkas, shotices*, and other pieces.[10] Similar celebrations continued throughout the remainder of the decade.[11]

Aside from the formal dances, members of the well-to-do in San Antonio and elsewhere involved themselves in the activities of various social clubs. The border cities that started coming into their own in the 1870s now offered a social life that corresponded to their growth. In Rio Grande City, for example, the self-described best element of the town made up the Casino Club—a social, literary, and nonpolitical organization in the 1880s that accepted Anglos as well. Other such societies in the city included La Unión, which worked to better conditions of less fortunate Mexican Americans; Los Mexicanos Tejanos; and the Filopolitas Society, which apparently permitted low-income members into its ranks.[12] In Eagle Pass, a literary club in the 1880s held dances regularly and presented periodic dramatic performances in which participants envinced much talent.[13] In Laredo, young Mexican men of social standing organized a club named Hidalgo-Washington in March 1887 designed to improve their condition. They planned a reading room in their hall.[14]

Fiestas, grand and not so magnificent, held in every area where Tejanos lived in numbers, assuaged the burden of daily life, testified to the tenacity of Mexican American culture, and gave a flavor of Mexicanism, regardless of the setting. Thus the Henry Kinney fiesta of 1851 in Corpus Christi publicized the area as he intended it, but also impressed the guests with the vigor of a Tejano culture that permeated the territory. The bright colors and fancy dresses, the beautiful *rebozos* and graceful *tápalos* of the Mexican señoritas and señoras, the broad brimmed, richly ornamented *sombreros* of their male companions and their silver-trimmed *pantaloneras* and *chivarras*, their gorgeous saddles and bridles, let newcomers know that some cultural modification on their part was in order if they desired to turn the area into a capitalist empire.[15] The aura Tejanos bestowed upon such fiestas set them apart in cultural orientation from similar festivals held by white society.

As exemplified by those in San Diego (Duval County) during the eighties and nineties, *fiestas* included games of chance like the wheel of fortune and *lotería;* acrobatics and trapeze performers; stands of *dulces*, cakes, and other delicacies; refreshments like chocolate, coffee, lemonade, soda water, and ice cream; merriment, which included dancing; and exhibitions for purposes of raising funds to improve and adorn the city's plaza.[16] Likewise, in other cities men pressed around roulette tables and those of *los colores* while women took their chances at *curveta*. Others meanwhile danced, partook of the delectable dishes available, played games, and in other ways enjoyed themselves.[17] It was from such fiestas, in fact, that the little town of La Feria in the Lower Rio Grande Valley received its name. According to an early settler of the area:

The name of La Feria is derived from the fairs that were accustomed to be held at the Colimal Ranch. From what I was told by some of the old Mexican settlers these fairs were held during the month of September and everybody attended. Indians as well as Mexicans attended and participated in all the games, trading horses, and selling of hides and horse hair, *horongos,* and such other trinkets which Indian squaws made including specially beaded mocassins.[18]

Frequently these South Texas ferias of the final decades of the nineteenth century lasted three or four weeks. Held in the fall after the harvest season, they attracted ranch families from miles around —usually to the regional villages with the largest plazas. For days, the throng entertained itself at the bailes, at the *retreta* (the promenade around the plaza), at games and sports, or at the improvised booths, bartering with farmers who had erected them for the sale or exchange of farm products.[19]

National holidays, both American and Mexican, brought together barrios and ranchos, friends and acquaintances, families and relatives. As people who felt secure celebrating the patriotic events of both countries, Tejanos hurried to watch grand parades or special programs appropriate to the occasion or to participate in its events. Often American holidays enticed them as much as Mexican holidays. In San Antonio, the Mexican Club traditionally joined the city's celebration of Washington's Birthday in the 1870s;[20] and in San Diego in 1886, at least the better class of Tejanos went all out for the anniversary. Spiritedly, they attired themselves in various cosmopolitan costumes:

Miss Refugia García Tovar appeared as a French peasant; Miss Monclovia as the alphabet; Miss Flavia García as a Mexican flag; Miss Rosa Tovar as a Pack of Cards; Don Narcisco Peña as a Bishop; Lola García as Transteverine Lady; José María Tovar as a "Nigger Dude"; Tomasita García as a Telegraph; Virginia García as a Lady of the Middles Ages; Miss Lupe García as one of the Fine Arts—Paintings; Mrs. Francisco G. Tovar—Jardiniere; and Loreto García as an officer.[21]

In Brownsville, the Social Club gave a Washington Birthday Hop at the Opera House in 1889 which Mexicans attended;[22] and when the Aoy school (the Mexican Preparatory School) in El Paso commemorated Washington's Birthday in 1899, students presented a special program before a large audience of both Tejanos and Anglos at Chopin Hall at which Misses María Maldonado and Aurora Plon made a great hit with recitations on Washington and Hidalgo.[23]

Other holidays came in for their share of involvement as more and more Anglos made their way into south and west Texas towns and brought with them the desire to commemorate those days. When Brownsville celebrated the centennial in 1876, the Mexican Brass Band, political factions, and some Mexican misses (of the upper class) representing the several American states, marched in the procession. In 1892, the Mexican American community of the city joined in celebrating Columbus Day,[24] while in Corpus Christi the same year, the Sociedad Mutualista Ygnacio Allende celebrated Columbus Day by joining the parade and holding a Mexican dance.[25] On Independence Day (July 4), Tejano communities involved themselves enthusiastically in the festivities either as part of processions or as part of the program. In the border regions (where dignitaries from sister cities often attended the ceremonies), orators eulogized the heroes of the two countries and the histories of both nations as bands added to the spirit of patriotism by playing both American and Mexican airs.[26] In El Paso, several Tejano organizations participated in the Labor Day celebration in September 1899.[27]

Despite their acceptance of certain tenets of American ethos, Tejanos hardly severed cultural ties with Mexico. Thus Mexican patriotic dates such as the *Diez y Seis de Septiembre* continued to be celebrated as they had been in the early 1820s and 1830s. In San Antonio proper, commemoration of that day persisted during the period of the Republic[28] and probably through the 1850s and 1860s, although the local press and other primary accounts do not say much about its celebration during the two decades. Much the same applies to the areas of South Texas and West Texas.

By the later 1860s and early 1870s, however, local newspapers began reporting the events yearly and seemed to have expanded their coverage during the last twenty years of the century. Whether it had more to do with an interest that the press began to take at that time or the fact that Tejanos broadened their effort to celebrate the *fiestas patrias* in more grandiose ways, is difficult to determine. It may have been, for instance, that a rise in immigration from Mexico after the Civil War brought an increased awareness of the meaning of Mexican patriotism that in turn nourished the Tejanos' Mexican cultural tradition. Whatever the case, the celebrations of the post-1865 period provide the best insight as to the meaning of nineteenth century fiestas patrias.

Border towns such as Brownsville, Laredo, Eagle Pass, and El Paso in some years celebrated fiestas patrias jointly with the sister cities across the border. But wherever celebrations occurred they generally followed a similar pattern. San Antonio celebrations of the post-Reconstruction period exemplified the typical commemoration so far as organization, ritual observation, and routine were concerned, but they tended to attract more people and be held at larger fair grounds than ones elsewhere.

By the final decades of the century, the three-day celebration in San Antonio rivaled any County Fair or barbecue outing whites held during the same periods. Promoted and prepared by the *Junta Patriótica* (a committee whose responsibility for planning special observances in the neighborhood went back to the colonial period) and benevolent societies, the commemoration started early in the evening on September fifteenth as Tejanos from the barrio west of San Pedro Creek and from ranchos and neighboring counties began arriving in wagons, on horseback, or in family carriages. Assembling traditionally in the Mexican quarter (Military Plaza was a favorite spot before 1890 and Washington or Paschal square after that), the marshals in charge prepared the lengthy entourage for the march about the area. Patriotic devotion pervaded the San Pedro district—buntings, flags, and flowers bedecked the houses, a stick nailed to the roof of every jacal sported a flag, and larger homes and stores displayed banners and gaily decorated fronts. Fireworks illuminated the scene.

Responding to the command of the grand marshal, the ponderous mass (sometimes close to a mile in length) initiated its march. Typically, the American and Mexican colors moved saliently in front. Mounted police followed with the grand marshal and aides close behind. With horns blaring, a Mexican, American, military, or firemen's band (at times all) marched next as carriages transporting distinguished guests and dignitaries, among them Plutarco Ornelas, the Mexican consul, and city and county officials followed. Decorated floats representing prominent figures in Mexican history then succeeded. In 1886, floats carrying characters in full costumes represented six historical scenes: Cortez weeping under the tree after his defeat on *La Noche Triste;* Guatemozín in pursuit of Cortez; the proclamation of independence at Dolores; the Declaration of Independence by Hidalgo; his execution; and, the triumphant entry of Augustín de Iturbide into Mexico City. A number of societies, including the Mutualista Benevolencia, Sociedad Unión, Sociedad Benito Juárez, Sociedad Hidalgo, Sociedad Zaragoza, Gran

Círculo de Obreros, and others composed the ensuing groups. The executive committee of the fiestas and other invited associations, the Italian society, for example, followed. Finally came carriages containing people of local eminence, with citizens on foot and a motley collection of hacks, carriages, wagons, carts, and nondescript vehicles with men, women, and children rounding out the cast. Other components occasionally added to this procession that numbered into the hundreds of marchers, included members of the Knights of Labor, the Belknap Rifles, the United States cavalry, and other local clubs. Anglo Americans cooperated conspicuously in these observations, and blacks frequently joined the festivities.

From the place of origin, the procession took a customary route, its destination being San Pedro Springs (although planners sometimes selected another location), where the fiestas took place. Before 1890 the procession generally departed from Military Plaza and marched down West Commerce Street into Laredo Street, thence across Dolorosa, back to Main Plaza, and out Main Avenue to San Pedro Springs. But, as the celebration got larger, the marchers commonly gathered in Washington Park and paraded north along San Sabá to Paschal Square, then to Commerce Street, and then east to Military Plaza, around it to Dolorosa, along Dolorosa to Main Plaza, thence to Soledad (but sometimes as far east as Alamo Plaza) toward Houston Street, west along Houston to Main Avenue, north along Main to San Pedro Avenue, then to the Springs.

Meantime a festive throng awaited the procession at the grounds. Having patronized the numerous concession stands and entertainment booths erected during the day, they greeted the peregrinators on their approach. The leading figures and dignitaries in the procession now broke ranks and made their way towards the speakers' stage that organizers had appropriately decorated with the red, white, and green, the national colors of Mexico, and the red, white, and blue of the United States. Bands played national airs while the promoters awaited the exact hour when Father Hidalgo had sounded his Cry of Dolores. At 11:00 P.M. some notable Bexareño officially inaugurated the fiestas by giving the cry of independence and reading the Mexican Declaration of Independence. The crowd responded with shouts of *"viva la independencia"* and *"viva México"* as a battery of the United States artillery fired a twenty-one gun salute in honor of the occasion. The singing of the Mexican national hymn, the coronation of señoritas in honor of the observance, the prinicpal address reviewing the events leading up to the war for independence and eulogizing its heroes and their achievements, patriotic orations in either Spanish or English, songs like *El Cinco de Mayo*, and other cheers elicited frequent bursts of patriotism and much applause. Once the ceremonies concluded, the Mexicans resumed their meandering through the grounds, continuing to enjoy themselves enthusiastically by visiting the concession booths, participating in social games, or going to a ball at the local hall that the societies invariably sponsored. Fireworks, Roman candles, torches, and Chinese lanterns embellished the scene.

Tejano cultural virility was everywhere evident. The decorations, ornamentations, and arrangements bestowed a decidedly Mexican appearance upon the grounds. For the next three evenings, continuing until the night of the seventeenth, *raza* accumulated in the thousands, manifesting a lively mood—laughing, talking, drinking, feasting—as all nationalities jostled with them. Bands played waltzes and polkas, couples danced upon an open air platform, flags hung from trees and banners waved over tents, lamps twinkled, *cancioneros* coined music, compadres and amigos discussed the virtues of the heroes of Mexican independence, *viejitos* told stories, bartenders tapped kegs of beer, promenaders flirted, lovers retreated to shady corners, children rode the roundabout, adventurers rowed about the lake, and the elderly watched the mirth and pleasure of the young. Dusky and fair faced señoritas and those of olive hue, clad in Mexican costumes or their neatest gowns and brightest colors, strolled the grounds as *muchachos* admired them. The smell of hot meals permeated the surroundings as restaurant booths, covered with cloth of the national colors of Mexico and the American stars and stripes, dished out chile con carne, tamales, tortillas, enchiladas, (all with chile colorado), carne asada, pan dulce, pecan candy, fruit, confections, and refreshments. Señoras prepared their dishes in plain view, *ollas* full of frijoles and chile con carne sat over a fire, and stacks of tortillas piled on tables waited to be heated. More speeches, patriotic songs, recitations upon the chivalrous deeds of the Mexicans, theatrical dramas and concerts appropriate to the theme at hand, acrobatic acts, and other events enlivened the festivities.

Close to midnight on the seventeenth a display of fireworks indicated the impending official termination of the celebration. The crowd repaired to an open area where fire wheels, "whistling jags," and "devil among the tailors" rockets criss-crossed high in mid air. Scores of balloons drifted upward amid the shower of sparks and colored lights. In 1892, chief of pyrotechnics Nato Villarreal and his aides touched off nearly two hundred dollars worth of fireworks. At the close of the discharge, Mexicanos resumed their enjoyment and continued dancing until the early hours of the eighteenth.[29]

Second only to the *Diez y Seis* among the fiestas patrias was the *Cinco de Mayo*, which commemorated the famous victory of General Ignacio Zaragoza over superior French forces at Puebla, México, on May 5, 1862. This celebration likewise rallied Tejanos behind their identity as a people retaining ties to the mother country. Denizens of San Antonio's west side attired themselves in festival dress, hoisted Mexican banners on the flag staffs of their homes, adorned stores and residences with Mexican colors, set up booths with lively ornamentations, and in other ways outfitted the barrio for the occasion. In 1896, Bexareños came together and gaily lighted Washington and Milam Squares to take in a concert, listen to speeches, and eat, drink, and be merry. Held under the auspices of the different Mexican societies, the program at Washington Square featured the music of Aurelio L. Solis' Mexican orchestra. It included addresses by Francisco N. Sánchez in behalf of the Sociedad Benevolencia Mexicana, Santos B. Ramírez for the Sociedad de la Unión, Miss Adela Barrera for the Sociedad Benito Juárez de Señoras y Señoritas, Juan C. Morales for the Sociedad Mutualista, Juan Ramón for the Sociedad Hidalgo, Silvino Rodríguez for the Sociedad Morelos, M. G. Dena for the Círculo de Obreros, and Manuel López for the Sociedad Ignacio Zaragoza. After its conclusion the audience repaired to the Mutualista Hall where the public danced on the first floor and the members of the societies on the second; their dance was by invitation only.[30] The *Cinco de Mayo* festivities in other Mexican American communities also tended to resemble San Antonio's, just as did those of the *Diez y Seis*.[31]

Among the less important anniversaries gaining attention among nineteenth century Tejanos was June 24, when Hernando Cortéz reentered Tenochtitlán in 1520 with reinforcements. When commemorated in San Antonio in 1882, festive spectators crowded San Pedro Springs to observe the elaborate program prepared for the occasion. They were treated to renditions of some of the best selected musical pieces of Aztec days, and dancers portrayed the

Aztec Monarch, his magistrate, courtiers, and Cortéz' companion Malinche. Attired in gaudy costumes redolent of the times, the characters acted out Aztec roles of authority. Finally, they circled the national pyramid, a pole artistically decorated with ribbons of three colors, and performed a dance something akin to the May-day dance. The celebration lasted well into the night.[32]

The fiestas patrias celebrations in nineteenth century Texas reveal much about their celebrants. In holding them, Tejanos showed that, despite their adjustment to Anglo Texas, they were not being completely assimilated. Second, in affirming their common heritage, they made a contribution to the state's ethnic pluralism (the French-Texans commemorated July 14, the day of the fall of the Bastille) even if white society in general did not wish it. Third, they expressed a collective pride that identified them with the historical, for the elements and symbols of the ritual included Mexican music, dances, food, costumes, heroes, and other familiar things.[33] Fourth, the affairs themselves pointed to the kind of spirit of cooperation that self-help organizations like mutualistas could muster in the barrio and the leverage they exerted in raising funds for the fiestas. Also, the celebrations bore witness to the power Tejanos could wield amid an oppressive regime. It was no easy task, after all, to prod cities into letting them have certain areas exclusively for "Mexican" celebrations, to persuade politicians to join the festivities, or—what was even more formidable—to get military cooperation and participation when plainly that force was often used to put down Mexican rebellions and wars. And, finally, Tejanos displayed their ethnicity openly, virtually telling white society that, despite its attitudes, they were not about to relinquish their pride in themselves.

In addition to special occasions, to the fandangos, bailes, fiestas, and patriotic holidays, theatrical companies also regaled members of the Tejano community with concerts and stage presentations. Acting groups performed for the better class of Tejanos as well as the mass of ordinary people, and their material was subjects and themes common to Texas-Mexican tradition. Performances became common in the decades after the Civil War as the Tejano population increased, and were staged wherever communities demanded them. In San Diego, a Mexican theatre company imported to that city by Salvador J. de la Vega in April 1884 gave a performance for the benefit of the proposed San Diego College.[34] In 1888, Professor Manuel de Llano of Monterrey and his troupe delighted San Diego with a concert of good instrumental and vocal music, and de Llano thrilling his audience with some classical music on a fine piano.[35] In 1892, Monclovia and Rosa Tovar performed a Mexican comedy for a church benefit;[36] and, in 1893, San Diego actors put on a play dramatizing a pre-Columbian theme at the *teatro*.[37] In September 1893, the Santos Treviño theatrical troupe performed the play "Hasta el Cielo" and a comedy farce entitled "Lo Que Le Falta a Mi Mujer."[38] In Corpus Christi, the Maldonado Company and the Monterrey band (probably from Mexico) entertained at Corpus Christi's Market Hall in 1884 before an American and Tejano audience.[39] In 1893, the Mexican orchestra en route to the World's Fair gave a splendid performance in the city and apparently another at Laredo later in the year as it made its return to Mexico.[40]

Theatrics, both local and imported, seemed to have been especially common in San Antonio where they could touch the tastes of Béxar's heterogeneous population, both Mexicano and American. In July 1869, a Mexican Concertant, Operatic and Glasseology Company gave a series of performances under the direction of Gregorio Partida; in 1871, the Mexican Dramatic Troupe pleased the Tejano segment of the city with such presentations as "La Vuelta al Mundo, o La Bandera Mexicana," and "La Derrota del Convoy, o Entrada de los Libres a Monterrey"; and in January 1873, Don Eusebio Delgado and his troupe (apparently from Mexico) presented a musical concert before traveling to Austin for another performance.[41] In the late 1870s, Señor C. Mendoza, considered a gentleman of fine dramatic abilities, directed weekend Spanish theatrical performances at Krish's Hall. He discriminated almost totally in favor of Spanish masterpieces such as "El Patriarca del Furia, o la Boda de Felipe III," in catering to the wishes of the "more intelligent of the Spanish citizens."[42] Benefit performances in the city in 1878 included such poetical dramas as "La Trenza de Sus Cabellos," and the laughable farce "El Solterón y La Niña."[43] When the city hosted the San Antonio Fair and International Exposition in 1889, among the strongest features of the exposition was the performance of the Mexican band from Mexico.[44] In April 1890, the highly reputed Spanish Orchestra Company named the "Typic Mexicano" gave a series of musical exhibitions at Turner Hall.[45] Similar diversion continued as part of San Antonio's entertainment life in the 1890s.

Traveling shows also attracted their share of Tejano audiences. In their leisure time, tired workers and their families made their way toward open-air or canvas pavilions to catch the performance of the *maromeros, payasos,* and trapeze artists whenever the circus came to town. In 1870, the Gongora Circus performed to crowded houses in Brownsville;[46] in Corpus Christi a troupe of Mexican showmen that traveled all over the United States performed in 1886 and challenged anyone in leaping, jumping, walking the tight-rope, or performing on the trapeze,[47] while other shows journeyed to densely populated Tejano areas on their itinerant schedule.[48] San Antonio being larger always seemed to be hosting some sort of performance, and Bexareños enjoyed strolling circus grounds to buy cakes, sweetmeats, and *tamales* from vendors while delighting in the exhibition of tightrope dancing, slackrope performances, the tumbling of the *maromeros,* and the antics of payasos who rocked them with tirades.[49] The Great Havana and Mexican Circus Company came to town in the summer and winter of 1869,[50] and in November 1877 the famous Ortiz family of acrobats set up canvas west of San Pedro. The entourage thrilled spectators with evolutions in mid-air, rope performances, aerial flights across the rings, trapeze acts, feats with knives and balls, tumbling and other acrobatic excercises that left audiences amazed at their agility.[51] Other circuses found their way into San Antonio in search of eager crowds in the years that followed.

Cockfights also drew enthusiasts from the Tejano population until whites made attempts to outlaw the allegedly un-American activity; whites of course, then as now, figured in the game both as cockfighters and spectators. Notwithstanding its savage nature, the game in San Antonio attracted its body of fans every Sunday and lured them into specially built or makeshift enclosures. Once inside, the spectators—Tejanos as well as whites and according to the area, some blacks—sat on tiers of narrow benches arranged around the pit, and conversed or waged bets on upcoming matches. Others visited the food stands where tamales, chile con carne, stewed chicken, cabrito, fruits, and candy were available. At another section of the fighting house, judges matched roosters according to weight, and handlers fitted three-inch-long, slightly curved slashers over their rooster's blunted spurs. Meeting at the cockpit, a fighting arena about twenty feet in diameter, the principals got their birds in fighting condition by harassing them with side roosters or pulling feathers from the cock's shields. Then, each held his fowl forward for a preliminary peck at its opponent, placed it on the ground a few feet from the antagonist, and released the same birds. The roosters ferociously slashed away at each other until one toppled over and died. Spectators who had urged on their choice in the bout, now honored their bets and awaited the next duel.[52] All areas of the state passed laws after the Mexican War to put an end to the practice but the game continued as popular as before for Mexicanos now turned to holding cockfights surreptitiously.[53]

In their entertainment forms, Tejanos demonstrated much of themselves as a community. The fandangos, the bailes, and the fiestas patrias exemplified the notion that some had of good times. Fandangos and bailes, especially, were held away from the suspicious mind of white society, so that there, Tejanos could carry out their own ideal of a party time—singing in Spanish, drinking Mexican beverages, conversing and exchanging gossip, and, as oppressed groups are prone to do, ridiculing and criticizing their oppressors. At patriotic celebrations, they might have moderated those practices because fiestas patrias were held in public where Anglos, especially government officials, invariably attended and were quick to judge any deviance from their own standards of conduct as Mexican behavior. But that public deportment involved little deference. To the contrary, Tejanos remained defiant to the concepts of American idealism, for they proclaimed their Mexicanness proudly, showing the confidence they had in themselves and their way of life in a state that regarded them as un-American.

Entertainment also reflected the social divisions that existed within the community. The better classes chose modes of diversion supposedly more proper to people of class and more in keeping with so-called civilized society. Tejanos of means had their social clubs, private dances, and appreciated the literary works of Spain. They recognized their difference to the majority of the community and probably felt more comfortable interacting with other members of their ranking. Such identification with different scales of entertainment has persisted, as witnessed in the propensity of so-called cultured Chicanos today to prefer *orquesta* (orchestra) music and then associate the lower class Tejanos with what they consider a less-cultured *conjunto* (accordion-led combo) sound. Still, such divisions within the Tejano community have seldom proved uncompromising. Historically, that which classes identify with has been a case of preference and members of each group have generally managed to fit into whatever an occasion calls for.

Even while Tejanos retained these dimensions of Mexican culture they found preferable to the Anglo counterparts, they participated comfortably in events such as the Fourth of July and Columbus Day celebrations. Thus could they express their allegiance to Mexico on certain cases and to the United States on others without one interfering with the other. They showed allegiance to a Mexican-American world that they made and lived in on their own terms in Texas.

9

Culture and Community

Illiteracy plagued nineteenth century Tejanos (see Tables 19 and 20), but it had more to do with their status as a dependent people than lack of ambition. Parents in that epoch hurried their children off to school as circumstances permitted, and wherever growing cities established learning institutions, whenever religious proselytizers founded mission schools, and wherever Tejanos themselves set up educational facilities, Mexican American children made themselves visible. When the opportunity presented itself, Tejano scholars learned and excelled, and their success indicated the prospects that could have accrued to an entire people had circumstances been more favorable.

Poverty, isolation, and even the disorder of the emerging Texas educational system placed obvious barriers before Tejanitos, but school attendance testified to their thirst for knowledge where situations otherwise permitted enrollment. For the most part, the pattern of school enrollment corresponded to the spread of educational conveniences, either secular or religious, into those areas of dense Tejano concentration. Thus, when the Reverend John McCullough brought his Presbyterian Day School to San Antonio in the 1840s, Tejanitos comprised a sizeable portion of the student body.[1] In 1850, at least three teachers, Prudencio Guerrero, Pedro Florez, and Juan F. Barrera (all born in Mexico) taught in the Mission San Juan area in Béxar County.[2] No doubt Mexican Americans constituted part of San Antonio's 125 pupils as the city com-

187

_9. Estimates of the Educational Characteristics of the Mexican-American Anglo-American Populations of South, Central, and West Texas, 1850 (1860) 1900[a]

	Mexican-Americans		Anglo-Americans	
	1850 (1860)	1900	1850 (1860)	1900
Percent of Population	69.7%	51.5%	19.9%	40.4%
Number in the Population	13,907	74,005	3,975	58,039
Percent Children	46.3%	51.9%	24.1%	43.5%
Percent of Children Attending School	16.7%	17.3%	33.9%	38.9%
Percent Literate Population over 20 Years of Age	25.1%	12.4%	97.0%	92.8%

[a]This table combines sample data from Béxar County and the Lower Rio Grande Valley in 1850 with data from El Paso County in 1860. The 1900 estimates are based on combined data from Béxar, Cameron, El Paso, Starr, and Webb counties.

menced its free school system in the late 1860s.[3] By the 1880s and 1890s, such a system included Juan Rodríguez, Ada de la Torre, Florence de Zavala, Ramón Guerrero, Alberto F. Martínez, M. G. Treviño, and others among its Spanish-surnamed faculty.[4] Others listed as teachers in the census were Salistona Crail (married to an Italian) in 1860 and Dorotea Coy, Armanda Andrada, and Antonio Sánchez in 1880.[5]

The same patterns of school enrollment marked the Nueces and Duval county areas. Corpus Christi had 110 Tejano children enrolled in its schools in 1896.[6] In Duval, Manuel Fernández Blasco, Domingo Garza, Espiridion Martínez, Bernava López, and Francisco López attended to the county's teaching duties in 1880.[7] In San Diego proper in the mid-1880s, a significant Tejano student body made up the city's schools where Profesor Luis Puebla, a Mexican immigrant educated in Washington D. C., and former professor of ancient and modern languages and mathematics at Lagarto College, directed the public educational system as well as a private academy.[8] As part of their activities, students offered school concerts regularly. One in October 1887 featured piano performances and songs such as "El Barbero" and "La Jota,"[9] and in another in December 1887 the young scholars of Puebla's academy staged a Spanish drama called "La Flor de un Día."[10] In the 1890s, Miss Prejedes G. García and Guadalupe García assisted in a public school system of 200 scholars.[11] People like Domingo Garza,

Table 20. Estimates of the Educational Characteristics of the Mexican-American and Anglo-American Populations of Texas by Region, 1850(1860) and 1900[a]

	Béxar County		Lower Rio Grande Valley Cameron, Starr, Webb Counties		El Paso County	
	1850	1900	1850	1900	1860	1900
Percent of Mexican-American Population	46.7%	21.5%	79.8%	92.4%	74.7%	55.5%
Percent of Anglo-American Population	47.5%	65.3%	10.3%	6.1%	8.3%	38.1%
Number of Mexican-Americans in Population	2,225	15,104	7,916	45,563	3,466	13,338
Number of Anglo-Americans in Population	2,568	45,874	1,022	3,008	385	9,157
Percent of Mexican-American Children in Population	47.9%	50.4%	50.9%	52.4%	35.7%	49.3%
Percent of Anglo-American Children in Population	25.2%	46.7%	27.5%	43.1%	6.5%	38.0%
Percent Mexican-American Children Attending School	8.3%	30.7%	17.4%	16.3%	23.7%	17.8%
Percent Anglo-American Children Attending School	26.7%	38.3%	53.1%	34.9%	50.0%	42.7%
Percent Literate Mexican-American Populations over 20 Years of Age	24.3%	37.5%	27.3%	9.6%	21.9%	17.8%
Percent Literate Anglo-American Populations over 20 Years of Age	96.7%	94.6%	98.1%	79.9%	96.3%	96.8%

[a]Estimates for Lower Rio Grande Valley are based on sample data from the 1900 census returns for Webb, Cameron, and Starr counties.

Luz Sancho, Sixto Navarro, José Angel Navarro, Bernardo Fernández, and Elvira Garza held classes in various precinct areas.[12]

In adjacent areas, Tejanitos duplicated the performance of their counterparts in San Diego. When Professor Puebla moved from San Diego in the early 1890s, he resumed his teaching at Palito Blanco and conducted a prosperous school there with the help of his daughter, who aided in the instruction of music.[13] In an exhibition marking the end of Palito Blanco's school term in 1893, Alejandro Gonzales, Agapito Gonzales, Daniel Vela, Jesús Vela, and Pedro Martínez delivered speeches in English, while Alejandro Gonzales won the spelling bee and displayed a commendable grasp of math, while Alfonso Vela solved problems on the board.[14] In Benavides, Professor Francisco Carrillo, a refugee who had fled Porfirian Mexico and found employment in the United States as an interpreter (he spoke six languages) and public school teacher, was principal of the Spanish academy.[15] In the Benavides public schools, Tejano students won distinction in the recitation of English and Spanish and performed well in math.[16] In neighboring towns like Realitos and Hinojoseña, Tejano students studied dutifully as they did at Guajillo where Frank Aurelio carried out the teaching.[17] Education in the period marched routinely in this chaparral country between the Nueces and the Rio Grande border as the Texas-Mexican Railroad brought with it inhabitants and progress.

Children of rancheros and other more privileged families attended the better schools of South Texas and other parts of the country. Such men as Isidro Benavides and Pedro Eznal of San Diego sent their girls to Incarnate Word Convent in Corpus Christi, and some of the students like Miss J. Barrera, who performed on the piano during closing exercises there in 1888, participated in school activities proudly. In 1884, Duval County had sixty students attending schools outside the area, fourteen of them at the college in Rolla, Missouri.[18] Other Mexican Americans went to Goliad College and distinguished themselves; for instance, A. de la Garza of Duval who received a gold medal for declamation during examination and commencement exercises in 1884.[19] Some attended Lagarto College where in the first anniversary celebration of the College in 1885, Manuel García and Nicholas Hinojosa gave declamations.[20] Albert Vela, son of Don Macedonio Vela of the Rio Grande Valley, attended St. Joseph's College in Victoria, Texas, in 1893,[21] and Ignacio de la Garza of Randado Ranch in Zapata County attended the college at Rolla, Missouri, in 1885.[22] Their example revealed how Tejanos, when determining their own destiny, achieved at a level equal to anyone else in the state and pointed to the fact that accomplishments had more to do with good fortune than regressive cultural values as postulated by whites.

Ranchos like Randado in Zapata County and Los Ojuelos in Encinal County established schools within the settlements for the benefit of the vaqueros' children. Instruction compared favorably with that of the urban areas, and, in Randado, indeed, school children faced exams in a number of fields at the end of the school term. In December 1884, the program there consisted of reading proficiency in both languages and Eligio de la Garza, among others, distinguished himself in the translation of Spanish and English. The ninety-three children at Los Ojuelos in the 1890s studied under a like philosophy.[23]

Tejanitos enrolled optimistically in the Presbyterian school when Melinda Rankin, a Yankee missionary, established it in Brownsville in the 1850s.[24] Among Spanish-surnamed teachers in the city in 1860 were Joaquín Pérez and Matías Ramírez;[25] in 1870, Lucio Villareal and Pancho Rodríguez;[26] in 1880, Serapis Garza and Petra Lamasquita;[27] and in 1900, Esther Sada, Manuel Treviño, Genoveva Villareal, Rita Treviño, Virginia Cavazos, Luz Garza, María Guzmán, Manuela Valdez, Ignacio Lerma, and Antonio Tamayo.[28] In the city's public school system, students made English-speaking teachers responsive to them, as some teachers taught in Spanish to retain the interest of their Mexican American pupils.[29] Spanish texts came from Monterrey as English gradually came to be taught as a special subject and very much as a foreign language.

A coterie of individuals turned to teaching as a profession in other border regions. In Laredo, Plutarco Garza was a nineteen-year-old school teacher in 1860,[30] in 1870 Julián Garza and Jesús M. Garza attended to some of the teaching chores,[31] and in 1879, the city featured an integrated Spanish-English high school of some seventy-five students with Miss Alta G. Garza assisting in the instruction.[32] The pool of teachers in this historic city included Felipa Saenz, Reynaldo Rodríguez, Valentín Alcalá, Josefa Contreras, Luis García, Refugio Sánchez, Rosa Sevallis, Adela Montemayor, and María Villareal in 1900.[33] In the ranch sections of Hidalgo county in 1870 the yearning for knowledge was administered to by Manuel Gonzales and Peón Villanueva,[34] in 1880 by Mucio Codina (El Rucio

Ranch), Epifancio R. León (Villa Nueva Ranch), Jesús Hinojosa (Ojo de Agua Ranch), and José María Casada (La Noria Cardeneña Ranch),[35] and in 1900 by Alfredo Chapa and Refugia Cavazos.[36] In San Ygnacio (Zapata county), Antonio Barrera and Rosa Barrera attended to the schooling of local Tejanitos in the 1880s,[37] and among those listing their occupation as teachers in the Zapata County's 1900 census were E. Navarro, Josefa Navarro, Gertrudis Ramírez, Sofia Peña, Servando Ramírez, Leonardo Navarro, Refugio Campos, Edmundo Acosta, Lucinda Domínguez, Mercurio Martínez, José García, Francisco Martínez, Santos Zapata, María Torres, and José Sánchez.[38] In Starr County, Ygnacio Alanis was school master at Rancho de los Saens in 1860,[39] and in 1880, Fortunato Recio taught in Rio Grande City while Francisco Cortés taught in a rural area.[40] A man named Casimiro Pérez taught Spanish at his large school in the county seat.[41] Among those listed as educators in the 1900 census were Arturo Sains and Ernestine Vela (Rio Grande City), Jesús García, Gabriela Saenz, Pablo Guerra, and Eva Ramírez, in Precinct No. 2, and Jacobo Gonzales in Precinct No. 4.[42]

Judging from the census, Mexicanos in the extreme West Texas areas attempted to help themselves educationally long before Yankee progress moved to that section. Listed as "community school teachers" for El Paso County in 1860 were Carlota Valles and Josefa Valles (in Molina), Eugenia Onofa (in Ysleta), Pedro Cisneros (in San Elizario), Francisco Rodallijas (in Las Limpias), and Trancita Márques and Pablo Padilla (in Socorro).[43] For 1880, those included were Manuel E. Flores and Eduardo Elías in Ysleta, Pabla Luján in Socorro, and Octaviano Larrazolo in San Elizario.[44] And when Anglo American educators began moving into the area around the 1880s, Tejanos accepted them.[45] San Elizario in 1887 featured a private school under the direction of the Catholics and a public free school with more than thirty pupils taught by Daniel C. Hendricks, a Harvard man. In Ysleta, school directors often included Spanish-surnamed incumbents.[46] As the El Paso school system blossomed into maturity in the late 1880s and in the 1890s, Tejanitos joined its progress enthusiastically. In 1887, they came under the tutelage of a Spanish gentlemen named O. V. (Olivas Villanueva) Aoy. Most attended his Mexican Preparatory School for the first four years in preparation for promotion into the higher grades. Professor W. H. T. López served as principal of the Preparatory School and as a third grade teacher after Aoy's death in 1895. In addition, he taught two of three hours as day in the city's high school. Meanwhile, men like Felix Escontrias took an interest in Tejano education by running for election to the school board.[47]

El Paso's Mexican Preparatory School, also called the O. V. Aoy School, experienced such tremendous growth in the 1890s that in the fall of 1897 the school board overhauled the old custom house on South Oregon Street and outfitted its three large, airy rooms with nice furniture and new closets and constructed blackboards around the walls. Located near a large Mexican settlement, it accommodated 180 pupils but that proved inadequate to provide for the 294 students registering for school in 1898.[48] The school board in early 1899, responding to the affirmative Tejano vote on a school bond issue, strongly recommended that a six-room building to house 300 Tejanitos be erected at a cost of $6,000. The Mexican community further considered the idea of staging a dramatic entertainment for the benefit of the school. According to the El Paso *Times*, Tejano residents had chosen the drama "Mancha Que Limpia" and planned to give it either at the opera house or Chopin Hall, with proceeds going to the benefit of the Aoy school.[49] Still at the start of the 1899–1900 school year, officials turned away many eager Tejanitos from the school because of space limitations.[50] This enthusiasm was reflected in the El Paso school system's attendance honor roll where Spanish-surnames appeared repeatedly.[51]

While the majority of Tejanitos did not attend school because opportunity to do so was limited in nineteenth century Texas, those parents in more auspicious circumstances dispatched their offspring to school when feasible. School attendance in the nineteenth century resulted from a coalescing of various factors: resolve on the part of Mexican American parents to educate their children; interest on the part of communities in establishing schools, as in the cases of ranchos like Los Ojuelos and Randado; determination on the part of Spanish-speaking teachers to instruct the little ones; and application on the part of Tejanitos to perform well.

Faith in education also brings to light much about Tejano cultural values. If their education as a group was minimal, that deficiency rested on the fact that communities as a whole were unable to establish sound education systems. The state did not address the matter of instruction until the final decades of the century and the results still left much room for improvement—especially in Tejano neighborhoods where "separate but equal" was the philosophy of many Anglo boards. Yet, Tejanos refused to stand pat; in some cases, even turning to Lancastrian-type methods as an alternative. Attendance not only shows a quest for scholarship, but also a desire to pick up a different language, to familiarize themselves with Anglo-American institutions, and to change with the times. Only a static community would have acted otherwise.

Furthermore, an abiding faith in schooling ran abreast of a number of other effects of social change within the community. For one thing, it paralleled occupational and status mobility, for school attendance corresponded to Tejano presence in every economic stratum. A desire to get ahead in the schools matched their attempts to attain something in the agricultural and business spheres. It reflected the same kind of progressive attitudes. If the well-to-do achieved more on the educational front, as they did in economics, it only confirmed the cold reality that having the vital resources to do something for themselves got results.

The same could be said about political involvement. People who wished a better life politically wanted the same domestically—something education might make possible. How could a community wishing to help itself by involvement in local issues, protesting indignities, and attempting to make governments responsive to its needs fail to realize the importance of education?

Finally, their thirst for knowledge dispels the notion of a community beset with the blight of ignorance, superstition, and backwardness. Catholicism, for one, hardly retarded progressivism. Indeed, the insight they fashioned from that religion provided the same type of encouragement with regard to education as it did about other aspects of their life—a fact reflected by their attendance at schools established by several Protestant sects. And their folklore hardly obstructed those desires; to the contrary, it stimulated their dreams, schemes, and aspirations. In the end, the educational attainments of nineteenth century Tejanos buttress the argument that, as a people, they subscribed to the values of advancement and enterprise.

Considering the oppressive conditions that kept the Tejano community from calling upon white society for succor or intervention in its behalf, Tejanos turned to autonomous benevolent associations as an organized means of improving their circumstances. As self-aid organizations that understood the culture and experience of Tejanos, these *mutualistas* came to the aid of their members or to the assistance of residents of the barrio in time of dire need.

While a product of both the Mexican and immigrant experience in the United States (they had counterparts in the European immigrant associations elsewhere in the country), *mutualistas* displayed simultaneously their adaptation to the Texas scene. Newspaper editors, merchants, physicians, lawyers, and others who retained their *mexicanidad* despite their interaction with the power structure, usually figured in the guiding hand of the *mutualistas*. In San Antonio, for example, men who held public office belonged to the city's benevolent societies.[52] As such, benevolent associations conducted their affairs in Spanish, took their name from Mexican national heroes, and extolled their members' Mexican past. But they also sought to make life tolerable for Tejanos in the state and took the lead in mustering up enthusiasm for celebrations of American holidays while accepting tenets of Americanisms into their structure.

Making their appearance in Texas in the 1870s, mutualistas proliferated thereafter. Organizations like the Sociedad Benevolencia, Sociedad Mutualista, Sociedad Benito Juárez, Sociedad de la Unión, Círculo de Obreros, Unión Occidental, and Sociedad México-Texana sprang up one after the other in San Antonio.[53] In Brownsville, mutualistas like the Concordia, Miguel Hidalgo, Sociedad Obreros, and Sociedad Juárez flourished.[54] In Eagle Pass, the Sociedad Mutualista Mexicana emerged as an important association in the 1880s displaying a design of a five pointed star with a monogram of the society on its flag (the motto "Unión, Progreso, Fraternidad" surrounded the emblem).[55] La Sociedad Mutualista and the Mutually United Mexican Workingmen Society appeared in Laredo in the later decades of the century.[56]

Similar associations were active in Nueces and Duval counties. Tejanos in Corpus Christi founded the city's first mutualista, the Club Recíproco, in 1873.[57] In July 1879, a society of mechanics organized the Sociedad Mutualista Benito Juárez,[58] while Tejanas founded the Sociedad Beneficencia in 1890 for Mexican American women.[59] Other mutualistas in Corpus Christi included the Sociedad Ignacio Allende and Sociedad Ignacio Zaragoza.[60] In San Diego, the Duval County seat, the elite of the city organized the Sociedad

Juárez in 1884,[61] while the Club Sociedad Mutualista Hijos de Hidalgo, organized in 1898, included seventy members by 1899 and worked enthusiastically among the Tejano community.[62]

In El Paso, Víctor L. Ochoa and others organized La Unión Occidental Mexicana in the early 1890s for the purpose of assisting and defending its members and protecting their morality, working for the retention of the Spanish language, and spreading the spirit of fraternalism to Mexican nationals in the United States. About the same time, other Paseños seeing in the mutualistas a solution for the lack of unity that accompanied their poverty, established Los Caballeros del Progreso. El Paso's oldest mutual aid society (1888), the Sociedad Mutualista Mexicana 'La Protectora,' dedicated itself to the perpetuation of ethnic unity as well as the goals of other mutualistas: namely, helping members with hospitalization and funeral expenses.[63]

Organized for purposes of self- and community-help, mutualistas performed a number of functions. Initiation fees and monthly membership dues usually assisted sick members with a small weekly allowance and fees for medical attention and necessary medicines. In addition, mutualistas offered low-cost funeral privileges, low-interest loans, and other forms of financial help.[64] Moreover, mutualistas involved themselves in worthy causes—especially in providing protection for the poor. In 1892, for example, the Sociedad Unión of San Antonio planned a dance to raise money for Mexican border residents suffering from the effects of that year's great drought.[65]

Aside from these functions mutualistas provided a convenient forum for discussion of political and other matters and served as a fulcrum for organizing the social life of the community. In a familiar setting, poor people exchanged problems with members of the mutualistas, and, as the associations' officers frequently came from the ranks of the moderately-established and the politically-minded who understood the American system best, organizers frequently pressed for the amelioration of the Tejano community. At the same time the mutualistas acted as organizations that extolled the virtues of Mexican culture before a white society that insisted Mexicans were degenerate. As such, mutualistas operated as institutions committed to the preservation of those things Tejanos held dear and those other qualities Tejanos thought vital to their existence.

Texas cities accommodating Tejano enclaves seldom lacked Spanish-language newspapers. Under the editorial guidance of competent men, some of them educated in Mexico, Spanish-language news publications reported to Tejanos on matters of local interest, kept them in touch with current events in Mexico and the United States, presented their point of view on local controversies, encouraged their political awareness, and furnished them with a continuous identity as Mexicanos. Newspapers acted as media of expression for people who could relate to the news in Spanish and served as mechanisms that added to the dimension of familiarity that permitted Tejanos to survive in a white man's state. Their stands on affairs of interest to Tejanos, their assertiveness in insisting on printing the news in ways at times offensive to white society, and their mastheads bespeak an autonomous mode of expression uncowed by injustices.

Spanish-language newspapers appeared whenever Tejano communities demanded news, opinions, advertisements, and other items of general interest. The rise of these newspapers in San Antonio, for example, corresponded to the historical evolution of the city, and, as such, Béxar claimed Spanish-language editions earlier than any other town except for the border cities; it was virtually the only town in Central Texas with a large Spanish-speaking public and not until after Reconstruction did other cities in the interior with dense Tejano concentrations appear. Aside from reporting news, the antebellum publications of the city assumed the role (like other Tejano newspapers in that decade and afterwards) of adopting positions on issues of common concern to readers. As an example, in February 1855, *El Bexareño*, the first Spanish-language newspaper in the city since the 1820s, called for public education where Tejano school children might learn English but retain Spanish. The next month, it inveighed against the attacks upon Mexican cartmen by white teamsters who sought to supplant the carreteros in this thriving business.[66] Further, in 1856 it clashed with *El Ranchero* in a skirmish of sharp political exchanges, the former espousing Know-Nothing politics and the *Ranchero* the Democratic philosophy. In July of 1856, J. A. Quintero, a Cuban, translated and published an editorial in *El Ranchero* accusing the Know-Nothings of seeking to rob Mexicanos of their rights and guarantees and of advancing

anti-Catholicism and nativism. The article created great excitement
between the two factions and a bloody row ensued. Quintero, for
his part, placed the blame for the disorder upon Anglo Democrats
responsible for the original draft.[67]

Similar activism and reporting (dealing with issues in Mexico
and the United States) pertinent to the Tejano community continued in San Antonio's postbellum period. During Reconstruction,
Epistacio Mondragón, Juan Cárdenas, and their fellow radical Republicans used *El Mexicano de Texas* to propagate their views as
they waged a campaign against the blatant white supremacist views
of the Tejano conservative faction in the city.[68] In the late 1870s,
exiled supporters of ousted Mexican President Sebastian Lerdo de
Tejada established *El Tiempo* in San Antonio to agitate against the
usurper Don Profirio Díaz.[69] During the Catarino Garza anti-
Porfirian movement of 1891–92, Paulino Martínez editorialized
through the weekly *El Chinaco* in support of Garza and lashed out
at Díaz with vitriolic opinions.[70] And, while the United States and
Spain fought the war of 1898, the city's Spanish-language presses
split along patriotic lines: *El Regidor* and *El Correo Mexicano*
supporting the United States while *El Cronista* and *La Fe Católica*
sympathizing with Spain.[71]

Other city newspapers in the final decades of the century included *El Atalaya de Texas*, printed in the late 1860s;[72] the semiweekly *El Observador* edited by Narcisco Leal to "represent and
protect the rights of the Mexican people and the Latin-speaking
races in general";[73] *El Centinela; El Hogar;*[74] *El Heraldo; El
Mexicano-Texano;*[75] and, the biweekly *El Monitor*,[76] all published
in the 1880s. *El Látigo*,[77] *El Cronista, Don Pascasio* (a Mexican
humor piece), *El Regidor*, and *El Heraldo* reported in the 1890s—
the last three under the editorial hand of men like Abraham C.
Valdez, Pablo Cruz, and Victor Cruz.[78] The English-language San
Antonio *Express* carried a Spanish translation of its news between
January and May 1892 in a section designated as the "Departamento
Español" (later changed to "Edición en Castellano"). Despite its
dependency on the *Express*, this section often carried untranslated
Spanish items of specific interest to Tejanos. Among these were
biographies of Catarino Garza, an interview with Garza's father-in-
law that presented a description of the Garzista movement, letters

received such as those headlined "Opinión de un Ranchero Texano," and "Un Residente de Texas," excerpts from Spanish-language newspapers, and literary works such as extracts from *Doña Perfecta* by the great nineteenth century Spanish novelist Benito Pérez Galdos.[79]

In the Rio Grande Valley area, which had been settled generations before the American-Mexican War, the establishment of Spanish-language presses coincided with emergence of border cities and improvement of frontier conditions there. In Brownsville, early newspapers included the weekly *La Bandera* (1848–63?) and *Río Bravo* (1851–?).[80] As Anglos made their way into the section after the War, Spanish-language news sheets vied successfully with English-language editions in attracting Spanish-speaking and bilingual readers. During the 1860s, papers that rose and fell included the *Boletín Estraordinario* (1865–?), the weekly *El Zaragosa* (1865–?), the daily *Correo del Río Grande* (1866–?), and the semiweekly *El Republicano* (1865–67?). Journalistic activity increased in the 1880s and 1890s as demand heightened and the Tejano community evolved. *El Horizonte* (1879–80?), the semiweekly *El Mundo* (1885–87?),[81] and the *Látigo*, an anti-establishment and pro-raza organ,[82] promulgated news in the 1880s. By the 1890s, Brownsville boasted of three prosperous prensas: the semiweekly *El Demócrata* owned by the family of Cameron County Sheriff Santiago A. Brito; *El Porvenir*, also a semiweekly, and the *Two Republics*, which surfaced to "win recognition as a praiseworthy medium of daily intelligence for its Spanish patrons."[83]

The important city of Laredo similarly attended to the interests of the Tejano community with newspapers of diverse orientations and political philosophy. *El Tiempo*[84] and the semiweekly *La Colonia Mexicana* kept Spanish-language readers abreast of United States and Mexican news in the 1880s[85] and editor José López Montalbo and his brother, Fernando Montalbo, stayed up with events through *El Horizonte* and *El Disputado* until their assassination in 1885.[86] Similar to papers elsewhere in the state, *El Mundo* (published by a Mexican refugee) agitated against Porfirio Díaz and supported the Catarino Garza movement against the Mexican president in 1891–92. *El Guarda del Bravo* meantime responded to English-language papers attacking Mexico's inability to stop the border troubles of 1892–93.[87] *El Demócrata Fronterizo* provided further reading in the decade and continued its reporting well into the next century.[88] Meantime, the Laredo *Times* (1880-continued to the present) translated its news for Spanish-reading patrons.

Small Rio Grande City kept pace with these larger cities in bringing news to Starr County and neighboring municipalities. In the 1880s, it included *La Voz del Pueblo*,[89] the weekly *El Alacrán*, edited by David Leza,[90] and in the 1890s, *El Cromo* edited by A. G. del Tornel.[91]

Corpus Christi, where the Spanish-language *El Ranchero* had appeared in 1859,[92] served as headquarters for *El Comercio Mexicano*, which Catarino Garza used in the 1880s to agitate against Porfirian rule.[93] In the early 1890s, Juan B. Tijerina operated *La Libertad* to "upbuild Corpus Christi and Southwest Texas."[94]

Mexican American residents of Duval County seldom experienced long periods without news, for Spanish-language journals informed them of historic events on a regular basis. In 1882, F. P. de Gonzales launched *El Eco Liberal*, believed to be the first newspaper ever published in Duval County, and then in 1885 changed its name to *La Libertad*.[95] Also in 1882, Juan López Montalbo edited *El Navizante*, and in 1888, *El Clarín* published politically-oriented items.[96] Salvador J. de la Vega, a Mexican immigrant, edited the *Progreso* and, with the assistance of Professor Luis Pueblo, started a bilingual paper called *El Pueblo* in 1886. Through another newspaper named *El Licensioso* he attacked the politics of Mexican president Díaz.[97]

Newspapers served Mexican American communities in virtually every other center where Tejanos resided. In Eagle Pass, Catarino Garza continued his vociferous anti-Díaz diatribes in the 1880s through *El Libre Pensador*[98] before moving it to Palito Blanco in the early 1890s.[99] From Palito Blanco proper, the makeshift *El Internacional* published editorials in defense and support of Garza as he outmaneuvered Texas Rangers and other law officials in Starr and Duval counties.[100] *La Javelina* reported from Carrizo Springs in the 1890s,[101] while prensas like *El Ciudadano*, *El Defensor*, *Las Dos Américas*, *El Eco Fronterizo*, *El Hispano Americano*, *El Independiente*, *La Justícia*, *El Latino Americano*, *El Monitor*, *El Observador Fronterizo*, *La Opinión Pública*, *El Zurriago*, and other papers served a growing El Paso in the last two decades of the nineteenth century.[102]

For the most part, the publication of nineteenth century Spanish-language newspapers was integral to the process of change in the several Tejano communities. Their appearance often coincided with the growth and development of Tejano townsites (either in population or importance) and as such in many cases predated English-language papers, which hurriedly emerged thereafter to satisfy the demands of English-speakers coming into those cities. Growing neighborhoods demanded them as part of their existence and, where more than one paper existed in the same locality, editors often found their success to be at the mercy of readers. Newspapers faded for several reasons, not the least being their failure to live up to the expectations of their readers.

Besides their primary function of newsgathering and reporting, Spanish-language newspapers played vital roles in those communities: they informed people as to occurrences and events outside the community and thus reduced provincialism; provided enlightenment; politicized readers; gave the community an aura of the familiar; and, no less important, helped maintain a standard of literacy. Additionally, they served as vital vehicles that furthered the process of biculturation for Tejanos took an interest in Mexican affairs as much as in relevant United States items. Moreover, their existence testified to the autonomous spirit of the Tejano community which, despite its economic, social, and political dependence on white society, still maintained enough vitality to demand things on its own terms. The names of the papers, their content, and their involvement in controversial issues, attest to that assertiveness.

10

Epilogue

The thousands of immigrants coming to Texas in the early decades of the twentieth century did not arrive to find a defeated, demoralized, and ahistoric population of Tejanos. Indeed, in the decade immediately before the Mexican Revolution of 1910, the Tejano community repeatedly asserted itself. In 1901, for example, 200 Tejano construction workers employed by the El Paso Electric Street Car Company struck for an increase in pay and an end to the management's practice of hiring Mexicans from Juárez to replace them on the street car lines; while they lost on the issue of a salary raise, they won the latter demand.[1] In 1903, Tejano members of the United Mine Workers in Thurber challenged the Texas and Pacific Coal Company asking for a pay increase, an eight-hour day, the elimination of company fences around town, and the removal of armed guards; they won concessions for a pay hike and the eight-hour day.[2] In 1906, members of the socialist oriented Federal Labor Union No. 11,953 in Laredo successfully struck against the Mexican Railroad for a wage increase.[3] In 1909, politically oriented groups in many Texas-Mexican neighborhoods actively worked in support of Ricardo Flores Magón's *Partido Liberal Mexicano* (PLM) movement against Mexican President Díaz.[4] In 1910 and continuing for the next few years, the Hispanic community of San Angelo boycotted the city's public schools in protest of inadequate educational facilities and the policy of segregation, albeit unsuccessfully.[5] And in 1911, close to 150 delegates attended *El Primer Congreso*

Mexicanista in Laredo to act upon a number of social grievances.[6]
It should be obvious that a dynamic Tejano community thrived in
Anglo Texas all along and that Tejano history neither starts with the
mass migrations of the twentieth century when Mexicans suddenly
appeared in the Texas fields nor in the 1960s with Chicano activ-
ists, as Anglo American social scientists insist.

Actually, the history of nineteenth century Tejanos, and the
experience of Mexican Americans at other times, is not solely a
story of people victimized by oppression. It is much more the
history of actors who have sought to take measures in their own
behalf for the sake of a decent living. The argument of contemporary Anglo and Chicano political scientists that Mexican Americans
in the nineteenth century were apolitical, for example, is simply
not tenable.[7] Judged in the context of their times, what Tejanos did
for themselves in the nineteenth century was as assertive as twentieth century political movements. Resistance in the form of the
Juan Cortina episode of 1859, the El Paso Salt War of 1877, the
Catarino Garza movement of 1891–92, plus several other incidents
of remonstrance against the Anglo establishment—including, for
example, the Rio Grande City Riot of 1888[8]—were all instances in
which Tejanos attempted to prod things their way.

Yet, doing something for themselves goes beyond the realm of
politics. It entailed relying on old ranching skills and using them to
earn a living in agrarian Texas, turning to cotton picking, the grubbing of land, and railroad building as new ways of making a living
became available. It included the ability to hold on to old lands or
buy new ones. It meant anticipating the needs of the emerging
urban areas and serving those towns as artisans and craftsmen. It
meant accepting public works and bureaucratic openings and establishing businesses, both small and large, that offered goods and
services in ways familiar to Mexicanos. It involved carrying on
traditional methods of house construction, depending on foods
that sustained them even if they were dietarily deficient, and exploiting nature's yields—its foods, curative herbs, and other usables.
It involved keeping perfunctory religious beliefs that corresponded
to the needs of their existential circumstances and maintaining a
folklore that explained the supernatural, that stressed the benevolence of God, and functioned as a vehicle for expressing attitudes
toward love, acceptable behavior, and survival. It was accepting
new entertainment forms or holding on to old ones that perpetu-

ated tradition, using those occasions as a respite from a harsh life, and playing upon those occasions to defy white society's scorn of un-Americanisms. It required the wherewithal to establish Spanish-language presses and organize *mutualistas*. At the very private level, helping themselves included encouraging the young to do better and sending them off to school. It meant putting food on the table or keeping families together. The ability of Tejanos to continue striking out for social betterment after 1900 does not lie in any one of the factors, but in all of them.

In the light of this, can it be argued that Mexican Americans resigned themselves to a "que será, será" view because disabling cultural values prohibited them from improvement? Quite obviously not, and what has been presented herewith supports the Chicano social scientists' attack upon the advocates of the "assimilation/accommodation model," which posits that Mexican Americans have lived an ahistoric experience of passivity, resignation, complacency, irrationality, irresponsibility, and docility.[9] The people who lived in nineteenth century Texas had goals, were energetic and enterprising, success-oriented, and progressive; they had an interest in education, and their understanding of nature did not bewilder them. They were hardly priest-ridden. In short, they resembled nothing like what many Anglo social scientists have imagined.

These findings, then, provide a crucial insight into the meaning of Chicano culture. At the very least, Tejanos were no different in aspirations than black or white men. To argue that they were ambitious, aggressive, future-oriented, and postponed gratification means not that they were becoming like Anglos, but rather that they wanted what other human beings in other places and other times have wanted—nothing more, nothing less. If they did not achieve what Anglos did, it was because of their status as an oppressed minority. Years of oppression certainly defeated the spirit of many individual Mexican American workers, fathers, mothers, husbands, wives, children and families. But it was just that—the oppression that led to their defeat, and the defeat of an individual or a family's spirit, even on a scale of hundreds of thousands, is not to frustrate the spirit of a people, their legacy, and their culture. History plainly demonstrates that Tejanos with opportunity usually achieved what their Anglo counterparts did, their Mexicanness notwithstanding.

To be sure, though, some cultural and ethnic traits distinguished

Tejanos from other Texans. Spanish prevailed as their primary language. They ate a variety of Mexican foods, drank tequila made from maguey, and wore sombreros, serapes, and rebozos. Few households lacked the presence of metates, molcajetes, or santitos. Entertainment consisted of fandangos, bailes, and fiestas where Mexican music blared and Mexican games predominated. Mexican holidays were acknowledged, especially the *Diez y Seis* and the *Cinco de Mayo*. Homes were built in the forms of jacales and adobes. Businesses included vendedores who sold dulces mexicanos, chile con carne, and Mexican curios and tiendas de barata that often offered a pilón. Tilling the soil at times entailed the use of Mexican farming and irrigation methods. The language of the range came from Mexico and the manner of sheep tending from Spain. The names of ranchos included "Santa Cruz," and "Como se Llama," those of lakes "Espantosa," and those of people, José María, Nepomuceno, Santa Juanita, and so on. Religion included worshipping la Virgen de Guadalupe and other patron saints, celebrating holy days, believing in curanderos, and commemorating the Christmas season with the play "Los Pastores" and posadas. Such aspects of their culture remained intact.

At the same time, however, to be Tejano was not to be a Chihuahuense or a Tamaulipeco. For the adjustment to the Texas setting made them Mexican American in more than legal terms. At the very outset, Tejanos as citizens identified with Texas, not Mexico. Unlike their kindred south of the Rio Grande, many Tejanos had at least a rudimentary grasp of English—they had to if they were to survive. They were familiar with a different political and economic system and how to get along within that structure. They attended American schools. They were familiar with certain American heroes (some they admired, others they despised). Some went over to Protestantism. Rancheros and *comerciantes* used American business methods. American holidays such as George Washington's birthday and the Fourth of July attracted their share of revelers. The list goes on.

To have been Mexican American in Texas in the nineteenth century was to have been bicultural. Thus political campaigning and court trials in South Texas were often conducted in Spanish. Rancheros worked the range according to the Mexican method, then traded their stock to out-of-state buyers. Children attended Anglo schools while retaining their customs. Entire communities celebrated patriotic holidays of both countries. Such dexterity explains why at times Tejanos divided along ideologies or economic lines. It clarifies why in some instances they demonstrated against oppression and at others joined in support of the same system that oppressed them. Even if only a few could actually function in a bicultural setting, the community in general looked at itself as Mexican American. The titles of mutualistas (names like *Sociedad México-Texana*), the names of newspapers *(El Mexicano de Texas* and *Las Dos Américas)*, the designations of political clubs *(Club Republicano México Texano)* reveal the sentiments.

Admittedly not every Tejano fits into the above related profiles. The very fact that two social classes existed within the Tejano community precludes any sort of stereotyping. Moreover, people in general conform differently to similar situations, and no exceptions may be made for Tejanos. Some became *agringados*, some bicultural; others stayed Mexican. Some became conformers and others rebels. Indeed, the variety of work they performed, the diversity of positions they occupied, the difference in achievement, the degree that set apart the literate from the illiterate, the politicized from the uninterested ones, the pious and the nominal Catholics, the believers in curanderos and the skeptics, and other contrasts argue well for an image of a heterogeneous community. But, whatever future students of the Mexican in Texas may add to our knowledge of these complicated people, the old arguments of an ahistoric folk who did little for themselves because of degenerate cultural values no longer holds.

Appendix

Kenneth L. Stewart

Provided in this book are quantitative profiles of the Mexican and Anglo American populations in selected areas of South, Central, and West Texas between 1850 and 1900 to supplement discussions of Tejano politics, labor, and social life. The profiles are based upon sample data drawn from the federal census schedules for the following specific areas and years:

Lower Rio Gande Valley (South Texas), 1850
Béxar County (Central Texas), 1850 and 1900
El Paso County (West Texas), 1860 and 1900
Cameron County (South Texas), 1900
Starr County (South Texas), 1900
Webb County (South Texas), 1900

The size of the sample is 20,631. Of that, 4,943 come from the populations of Béxar County and the Lower Rio Grande Valley in 1850, plus El Paso County in 1860. The other 15,688 are from the populations of Béxar, Cameron, El Paso, Starr, and Webb counties in 1900.

The findings represent only part of a larger and more ambitious demographic study of Tejanos currently being conducted by Professors Arnoldo De León (History) and Kenneth L. Stewart (Sociology) at Angelo State University. In its finished form, the project will include a complete interpretation of trends relating to Tejano life in the last half of the nineteenth century. Since a comprehensive analysis falls beyond the purview of this monograph, the statistical profiles presented herein examine only those areas that were most representative of the overall Mexican American community in nineteenth century Texas. The analysis focuses on the three major geographical sections with the heaviest concentrations of Tejanos. It thus allows for careful, though not exhaustive, portraits of population characteristics in those areas at two historical moments, 1850–60 and 1900.

The data derive from a systematic sampling procedure. In those instances where the total census enumeration of a county or area was 12,000 or less, a 25 percent sample was drawn. A maximum of 3,000 cases were selected from those counties when the original census enumeration exceeded 12,000. Thus, the proportions of county-wide populations represented in the sample range from 25 percent (for counties of 12,000 or less in total population) to as little as 2 percent or 3 percent (for counties over 12,000 in population). However, the small proportions for those counties of over 12,000 population are not particularly damaging to the analysis since the general relationship between population size and the repesentativeness of a sample is inverse—that is, the larger the population the smaller the percentage needed to represent it.[1]

The importance of the federal census schedules is obvious. Their value may be seen in the writings of a new generation of Chicano quantifiers whose seminal works are based on scrupulous analyses of the schedules. But despite their relevence, census returns do pose problems, especially if the data are partial as is the case in this monograph. The limitations scholars must cope with when working with this type of primary document are explained below for the benefit of those wanting further insight into the intricacies of census research.

First, the reliability of any data set depends upon the accuracy of the original source. Underenumeration is always a problem. The historian Oscar J. Martínez, for example, estimates that Mexican Americans were underenumerated at a rate of 10 to 15 percent in the censuses for the last half of the nineteenth century.[2] Indeed, this problem appeared explicitly in our analysis of the 1850 census returns. At mid-century, the far western areas of Texas, such as El Paso County, were apparently so isolated that the census takers did not penetrate them. The substantial majority of inhabitants in those areas, undoubtedly Mexican Americans, were thus left out. To compensate for the absence of census reports from that area in 1850, we have combined a sample of the 1860 returns in El Paso County with data drawn from the 1850 census reports for Béxar County and the Lower Rio Grande Valley. This combination serves the purpose of developing comprehensive "estimates" of population characteristics, but readers should recognize it as a source of imprecision in those estimates.

Error resulting from reporting techniques and the biases of individual census takers is an additional obstacle in analyzing census returns. Quite likely, inaccuracies stemming from these sources introduced inexactness into a number of specific estimates reported in the text. For example, Tables 5 through 13 in the two chapters on obreros profile the Mexican and Anglo American working populations for the areas and years represented in the sample data. Specifically, Tables 8 and 11 suggest that the level of employment among Mexicanos was significantly lower than among whites in 1850–60, but more or less equal to that of Anglos by 1900. However, the appearance of this trend may lie on a number of factors other than the actual presence of a large discrepancy between the two people's employment levels at mid-century. Instead, racial biases among census takers or communication barriers between English-speaking observers and Spanish-speaking respondents may explain the disparity indicated by the tables. Such possibilities may have led to significant under-reporting of Tejano employments, and thus, an inaccurate image of the Mexican American employment rate. Similarly, biased and inadequate reporting may have distorted the estimates of wealth holdings, literacy rates, and other specific variables reported in the text.

A third important limitation in any analysis of census materials involves changes in reporting techniques across time. In some cases, such alterations entirely prohibit highly desirable types of comparisons. For example, Table 14 in the chapter on urban workers describes the distribution of personal wealth among Anglo and Mexican Americans in 1850–60. A similar description based on the 1900 census does not complement this table because the returns for that year did not include information on personal property holdings. The change in the specific types of observations made and reported in the two years eliminated the possibility of any meaningful comparison of personal property holdings and property over time.

In other cases, changes in reporting techniques allow for comparisons, but of undetermined validity. To illustrate, nearly all of the demographic profiles presented in this manuscript include data drawn from the Lower Rio Grande Valley in 1850 and 1900. However, the exact comparability of the data representing the area for the two census years is undetermined because the 1850 census enumerated residents of the entire area without distinguishing the population of one county from another. The 1900 census, on the other hand, enumerated on a county by county basis. The change in the enumeration process thus produced a slight variation in the geographical area represented by the data from the Lower Rio Grande Valley area in the two census years. Comparisons for this region across time are imprecise to an unknown extent.

Finally, serious error can occur through misinterpretation of sample data used in compiling profiles of given populations. In the case of this monograph, the objective is to estimate only the general similarities and differences between the Tejano and Anglo American populations of South, Central, and West Texas over the last fifty years of the nineteenth century. Thus, the estimate in Table 12, indicating the presence of 23,830 Mexican American workers and 20,546 Anglo American workers in the three areas covered should not be taken to mean that there were exactly 3,284 fewer Anglo workers than Tejano obreros. Instead, it should be interpreted to mean that Tejano workers slightly outnumbered their Anglo couterparts in the combined areas of South, Central, and West Texas. In other words, while readers should recognize the relevance of the quantitative evidence presented, it ought to be understood in a manner consistent with the presentation; as estimates rather than precise measures of similarities, differences, and trends among a designated portion of the population of Texas.

Appendix Notes

1. For a complete discussion of this relationship see H. F. Weisberg and B. D. Bowen, *An Introduction to Survey Research and Data Analysis* (San Francisco: W. H. Freeman and Co., 1977), pp. 17–42.
2. Oscar J. Martínez, "On the Size of the Chicano Population, 1850–1900," *Aztlan* VI (1975):43–67.

Notes

Preface

1. For a cursory review of this debate, see Ellwyn Stoddard, *Mexican Americans* (New York: Random House, 1973), pp. 38–49. See also Ray Padilla, "A Critique of Pittian History." *El Grito: A Journal of Contemporary Mexican American Thought* VI (Fall 1972). See in particular Juan Gómez Quiñones, "On Culture," *Revista Chicano-Riqueña* 5, no. 2 (*primavera* 1977): 29–47.

2. Charles A. Valentine, "Deficit, Difference, and Bicultural Models of Afro-American Behavior," *Harvard Educational Review* 41 (May 1971); 137–157; and Herbert G. Gutman, *The Black Family in Slavery and Freedom, 1750–1925* (New York: Pantheon Books, 1976), p. 261.

3. José María Sánchez, "A Trip to Texas in 1828," trans. by Carlos Eduardo Castañeda, *Southwestern Historical Quarterly* XXIX (April 1926): 283.

Chapter 1

1. Rupert N. Richardson, et al., *Texas: The Lone Star State* (Englewood Cliffs: Prentice-Hall, Inc., 1970), pp. 19–20.

2. Andrew Anthony Tijerina, "Tejanos and Texas: The Native Mexicans of Texas, 1820–1850"(Ph.D. diss., University of Texas at Austin, 1977), pp. 10–16, 32–33, and 44; T. R. Fehrenbach, *Lone Star: A History of Texas and the Texans* (New York: Macmillan, 1968), p. 56; Alicia V. Tjarks, "Comparative Demographic Analysis of Texas, 1777–1793," *Southwestern Historical Quarterly* 77 (January 1974); 322–34.

3. Tjark, "Comparative Demographic Analysis," p. 294.

4. Ibid., pp. 302–03.

5. Odie Faulk, *A Successful Failure* (Austin: Steck-Vaughn Co., 1965), pp. 176–78; Odie Faulk, *The Last Years of Spanish Texas, 1778–1821* (The Hague: Mounton & Co., 1964), pp. 50, 109–12; Tijerina, "Tejanos and Texas," pp. 142–43.

6. Tijerina, "Tejanos and Texas," pp. 106–12.

7. Faulk, *A Successful Failure*, pp. 176–78; *The Last Years of Spanish Texas*, pp. 50, 109–12.

8. Tijerina, "Tejanos and Texas," pp. 18, 35, 49, or, Tables 1, 8, 10.

9. Fane Downs, "The History of Mexicans in Texas, 1821–1845" (Ph.D diss., Texas Tech University, 1970), p. 30.

10. Tijerina, "Tejanos and Texas," pp. 215–58.

11. Ibid., pp. 67, 98–100; Downs, "History of Mexicans in Texas," pp. 70–71.

12. Tijerina, "Tejanos and Texas," p. 30.

13. Ibid., pp. 147–48.

14. J. C. Clopper, "Journal of J. C. Clopper," *Quarterly of the Texas State Historical Association* XIII (July 1909), 72; Mary S. Helm, *Scraps of Early Texas History* (Austin: Printed for the author at the office of B. R. Warner and Co., 1884), pp. 184–85. See also J. Frank Dobie, *A Vaquero of the Brush Country: Partly the Reminiscences of John Young* (Dallas: The Southwest Press, 1929), p. 19.

15. Neal John O'Neill, *The Guide to Texas* (Dublin: Joseph Blundell, 1834), p. 92; *Arkansas State Gazette*, October 10, 1826, p. 3; but also see Mary Austin Holley, *Texas* (Austin: The Steck Company, 1935), p. 134.

16. Tijerina, "Tejanos and Texas," pp. 157–58.

17. Downs, "History of Mexicans in Texas," pp. 55–62; Tijerina, "Tejanos and Texas," pp. 159–60.

18. Tijerina, "Tejanos and Texas," pp. 97–103.

19. Clopper, "Journal of J. C. Clopper," p. 73; Downs, "History of Mexicans in Texas," pp. 86–87.

20. Mrs. T. C. Allan, "Reminiscences of Mrs. Annie Fagan Teal," *By the Way*, I (July 1897), 5.

21. Downs, "History of Mexicans in Texas," p. 75; Albert Curtis, *Fabulous San Antonio* (San Antonio: The Naylor Company, 1955), p. 7; Adel Speiser, "The Story of the Theatre in San Antonio" (M.A. thesis, St. Mary's University, 1948), pp. 4–11.

22. Tijerina "Tejanos and Texas," pp. 77–78; Downs, "History of Mexicans in Texas," pp. 78–83.

23. Clopper, "Journal of J. C. Clopper," p. 76.

24. Andrew Forest Muir (ed.), *Texas in 1837: An Anonymous Contemporary Narrative* (Austin: University of Texas Press, 1958), p. 103.

25. Pearl Couser Wright, "Religious Fiestas in San Antonio" (M.A. thesis, St. Mary's University, 1946), pp. 36–42, as cited in Downs, "History of Mexicans in Texas," pp. 124–25. On September 8, 1833, San Antonio commemorated the anniversary of the birth of the Virgin Mary with clamoring church bells, rockets, and high mass. Benjamin Lundy, *Life, Travels, and Opinions of Benjamin Lundy, Including his Journey to Texas and Mexico* (New York: Negro University Press, 1969), p. 52.

26. E. G. Littlejohn, "The Holy Spring of Father Margil at Nacogdoches," in *Legends of Texas*, ed. J. Frank Dobie, pp. 204–5; Charles Merritt Barnes, *Combats and Conquests of Immortal Heroes* (San Antonio: Guessaz and Ferlet Co., 1910), pp. 77–79; S. J. Wright, *San Antonio de Béxar: Historical, Traditional, Legendary* (Austin: Morgan Printing Co., 1916), pp. 121–22.

27. Adina de Zavala, *History and Legends of the Alamo and other Missions in and Around San Antonio* (San Antonio: privately printed, 1917), pp. 116–17.

28. Ibid., 117.

29. Ibid., pp. 143–45.

30. Cited in Downs, "History of Mexicans in Texas," pp. 131–32.

31. Raymund Paredes, "The Origins of Anti-Mexican Sentiment in the United States," in Ricardo Romo and Raymund Paredes, eds., *New Directions in Chicano Scholarship* (La Jolla: University of California at San Diego, 1978), pp. 139–65.

32. Arnoldo De León, "White Racial Attitudes Toward Mexicanos in Texas, 1821–1900" (Ph.D. diss., Texas Christian University, 1974), pp. 29–30.

33. Lundy, *Life, Travels, and Opinions*, p. 48.

34. William F. Gray, *From Virginia to Texas . . .* (Houston: Fletcher Young Publishing Co., 1965), p. 6.

35. Quoted in James Ernest Crisp, "Anglo-Texan Attitudes Toward the Mexican, 1821–1845" (Ph.D diss., Yale University, 1976), p. 96.

36. Eugene C. Barker, ed., *The Austin Papers* (Austin: University of Texas Press, 1926), III, 345.

37. "Compendium of the Early History of Texas (Continued from the *Texas Almanac*, for 1858)," in James M. Day, comp., *The Texas Almanac, 1857–1873* (Waco: Texian Press, 1967), p. 180.

38. Quoted in Crisp, "Anglo-Texan Attitudes," p. 22.

39. Gray, *From Virginia to Texas*, p. 92.

40. David Woodman, *Guide to Texas Emigrants* (Boston: M. Hawes, 1835), p. 35.

41. Ernest W. Winkler, ed., *Manuscript Letters and Documents of Early Texians, 1821–1845* (Austin: The Steck Co., 1937), p. 32.

42. Dr. John Beales' Journal, 1833, in William Kennedy, *Texas: The Rise, Progress, and Prospects of the Republic of Texas* (Fort Worth: The Molyneaux Craftsman, Inc., 1925), p. 396.

43. Joshua James and Alexander McCrae, *A Journal of a Tour in Texas: With Observations, &c., by the Agents of the Wilmington Emigrating Society* (Wilmington, North Carolina: Printed by T. Loring, 1835), p. 15.

44. *Arkansas State Gazette*, December 8, 1835, p. 1.

45. Winnie Allen (introd. note), "The Autobiography of George W. Smyth," *Southwestern Historical Quarterly* XXXVI (January 1933), 202.

46. The fullest treatment of this topic is De León, "White Racial Attitudes."

47. Tijerina, "Tejanos and Texas," pp. 317–320.

48. Quoted in Crisp, "Anglo-Texan Attitudes," p. 342.

49. Cited in ibid., p. 350.

50. Ibid.

51. Quoted in ibid., p. 383.

52. Ibid., p. 384.

53. Quoted in ibid., p. 384.

54. Tijerina, "Tejanos and Texas," pp. 325–26.

55. De León, "White Racial Attitudes," pp. 134–40.

56. Ibid., pp. 144–47.

57. D. W. Meinig, *Imperial Texas: An Interpretive Essay in Cultural Geography* (Austin: University of Texas, 1969), pp. 51, 55–58.

58. Tijerina, "Tejanos and Texas," pp. 39–43.

59. Ibid., pp. 39, 320–21.

60. Ibid., pp. 327–28.

61. J. B. Wilkinson, *Laredo and the Rio Grande Frontier* (Austin: Jenkins Publishing Co., 1975), pp. 227–33.

62. Paul S. Taylor, *An American Mexican Frontier: Nueces County, Texas* (Chapel Hill: University of North Carolina Press, 1934), p. 180.

63. Rodolfo Acuña, *Occupied America: The Chicanos' Struggle Toward Liberation* (first edition; San Francisco: Canfield Press, 1972), pp. 43–44.

64. Taylor, *An American Mexican Frontier*, p. 31.

65. Acuña, *Occupied America*, pp. 46–50; De León, "White Racial Attitudes," pp. 149–51.

66. Meinig, *Imperial Texas*, pp. 55–56.

67. Ibid., p. 65.

68. San Antonio *Herald*, March 16, 1870, p. 3.

69. A. J. Sowell, *Early Settlers and Indian Fighters of the Southwest* (First published, 1900; reprinted in 2 vols.; New York: Argosy-Antiquarian Ltd., 1964), II, 754; San Antonio *Herald*, September 20, 1868, p. 2; October 15, 1868, p. 2.

70. San Antonio *Express*, June 12, 1874, p. 2; June 13, 1874, p. 2; June 14, 1874, p. 2; June 16, 1874, p. 2.

71. U. S. House Report No. 343, 44 Cong., 1 Sess., (Ser. 1709), p. 122.

72. Ibid., p. 124.

73. U. S. House Misc. Doc., No. 64, 45 Cong., 2 Sess., (Ser. 1820), p. 285.

74. San Antonio *Express*, June 21, 1875, p. 2.

75. Napoleon A. Jennings, *A Texas Ranger* (New York: Charles Scribner's Sons, 1899), p. 130.

76. U. S. House Report No. 343, p. 57.

77. C. L. Sonnichsen, *Ten Texas Feuds* (Albuquerque: University of New Mexico Press, 1957), pp. 130–54.

78. San Antonio *Express*, April 29, 1886, p. 4.

79. Ibid., February 7, 1891, p. 1.

80. Ibid., July 26, 1897, p. 8.

81. Ibid., October 8, 1895, p. 5; October 13, 1895, p. 3.

82. Ibid., January 31, 1896, p. 8.

83. Frank C. Pierce, *A Brief History of the Lower Rio Grande Valley* (Menasha: George Banta Publishing Co., 1917), p. 118; Jesse Sumpter, *Life of Jesse Sumpter* (Typewritten copy in the Mary Couts Burnett Library, Texas Christian University, Fort Worth, Texas), pp. 52–54.

84. San Antonio *Express*, December 28, 1897, p. 1; April 28, 1898, p. 5.

85. Ibid., April 23, 1898, p. 8; April 27, 1898, p. 4; May 10, 1898, p. 3.

86. Cited in Victor B. Nelson Cisneros, "La Clase Trabajadora en Tejas, 1900–1920," *Aztlán: International Journal of Chicano Studies Research* VI (Summer 1975), 240.

Chapter 2

1. For a discussion of the political mechanisms used by Anglo American society against Mexican Americans, see F. Chris García and Rudolph O. de la Garza, *The Chicano Political Experience: Three Perspectives* (North Scituate, Mass.: Duxbury Press, 1977), 66–68, 96–97, 114–18; and, Mario Barrera, Carlos Muñoz, and Charles Ornelas, "The *Barrio* as an Internal Colony," in F. Chris García, ed., *La Causa Politica: A Chicano Politics Reader* (Notre Dame: University of Notre Dame Press, 1974), pp. 292–94.

2. El Paso *Times*, July 22, 1886, p. 3.

3. Fane Downs, "The History of Mexicans in Texas, 1821–1845" (Ph.D. diss., Texas Tech University, 1970), pp. 255, 257. See also Mooney and Morrison, *Directory of the City of San Antonio for 1877–1878* (Galveston: Galveston News, 1877), pp. 38–39, for a complete listing of city officeholders in this era.

4. James E. Crisp, "Anglo-Texan Attitudes Toward the Mexican, 1821–1845" (Ph.D. diss., Yale University, 1976), pp. 336, 350–51, 408.

5. Arnoldo De León, "White Racial Attitudes Toward Mexicanos in Texas, 1821–1900" (Ph. D. diss., Texas Christian University, 1974), pp. 134–40.

6. Virginia Noel, "The Know Nothing Party in Texas" (Eugene C. Barker Library, University of Texas Archives, Austin, Texas), pp. 12–13.

7. San Antonio *Herald*, August 14, 1855, p. 2.

8. Ibid., July 26, 1856, p. 2; August 2, 1856, p. 1; August 9, 1856, p. 2; October 4, 1856, p. 2.

9. Ibid, December 9, 1866, p. 2; February 28, 1868, p. 2; April 11, 1868, p. 2; July 13, 1868, p. 3; July 16, 1868, p. 3; August 11, 1868, p. 3; August 15, 1868, p. 3; February 11, 1869, p. 2; September 2, 1869, p. 3. Other members of the conservatives were Alejo Pérez, Vicente Martínez, José Peñaloza, José García, Angel Navarro, Augustin Barrera, Juan Franco, Pedro Cevallos, José Martínez, Rafael M. Pereida, Eugenio Ruiz, Ylario Ozuña, Santiago Mesa, Ponciano Fernández, Felix Gotarri, Antonio Pérez, José M. Valdez, Nestor Carrillo, Nicaso Montez, León Váldez, Rafael Martínez, Juan Cortina, Romulo Z. Vallo, Felipe Vargas, Clemente Bustillo, José M. Morales, and Eugenio Navarro.

10. Ibid., July 13, 1868, p. 3; July 28, 1868, p. 3; September 5, 1871, p. 3; September 12, 1871, p. 3; September 19, 1871, p. 3.

11. Ibid., January 24, 1868, p. 3; August 8, 1868, p. 2; August 16, 1868, p. 2; March 2, 1869, p. 3; July 20, 1869, p. 3.

12. Ibid., January 3, 1873, p. 3.

13. Ibid., July 16, 1872, p. 2; August 20, 1872, p. 3; September 24, 1872, p. 3; San Antonio *Express*, September 10, 1872, p. 3.

14. San Antonio *Express*, September 8, 1872, p. 2; San Antonio *Herald*, August 24, 1873, p. 3.

15. San Antonio *Herald*, December 29, 1875, p. 3.

16. San Antonio *Express*, January 25, 1876, p. 4; January 29, 1876, p. 4.

17. Ibid., October 28, 1886, p. 3. See also San Antonio *Herald*, October 27, 1873, p. 3.

18. San Antonio *Express*, September 20, 1878, p. 4; September 21, 1878, p. 2.

19. Ibid., September 6, 1888, p. 8; January 25, 1893, p. 6.

20. San Antonio *Express*, August 8, 1883, p. 2; August 9, 1883, p. 4; August 11, 1883, p. 2.

21. San Antonio *Express*, October 28, 1893, p. 3; October 29, 1893, p. 6.

22. Arnoldo De León, *In re Ricardo Rodríguez: An Attempt at Chicano Disfranchisement in San Antonio, 1896–1897* (San Antonio: Caravel Press, 1979).

23. *Directory of San Antonio, 1877–1878*, pp. 39–41. Also in that decade, J. A. G. Navarro was collector and A. Menchaca was ditch commissioner, ibid.

24. San Antonio *Herald*, August 19, 1857, p. 2.

25. *Directory of San Antonio, 1877–1878*, pp. 41–43.

26. San Antonio *Herald*, January 11, 1862, p. 2.

27. *Directory of San Antonio, 1877–1878*, p. 43.

28. San Antonio *Herald*, February 4, 1868, p. 1.

29. Ibid., January 6, 1872, p. 3; San Antonio *Express*, February 16, 1876, p. 4.

30. Morrison and Fourmy's *Directory of the City of San Antonio, 1889–1890* (Galveston: Morrison and Fourmy, 1889), p. 43.

31. Johnson and Chapman's *General Directory of the City of San Antonio for the year 1891* (Galveston: Johnson and Chapman, 1890), p. 26; Jules A. Appler's *General Directory of the City of San Antonio, 1897–1898* (San Antonio: Jules A. Appler, 1897), p. 566; Jules A. Appler's *General Directory of the City of San Antonio, 1899–1900* (San Antonio: Jules A. Appler, 1899), p. 550.

32. Morrison and Fourmy's *General Directory of the City of San Antonio, 1885–1886* (Galveston: Morrison and Fourmy, 1885), p. 43; Morrison and Fourmy's *Directory of the City of San Antonio for 1887–1888* (Galveston: Morrison and Fourmy, 1887), p. 39; *Directory of San Antonio, 1889–1890*, p. 43; and, *Directory of San Antonio, 1891*, p. 26.

33. San Antonio *Herald*, August 31, 1869, p. 3; June 4, 1873, p. 3; June 12, 1873, p. 3; San Antonio *Express*, September 1, 1869, p. 3; September 5, 1873, p. 3; December 9, 1885, p. 3.

34. San Antonio *Herald*, January 28, 1868, p. 2.

35. *Directory of San Antonio, 1877–1878*, p. 47; Morrison and Fourmy's *General Directory of the City of San Antonio, 1879–1880* (Galveston: Morrison and Fourmy, 1879), p. 67.

36. San Antonio *Express*, November 5, 1880, p. 4; December 3, 1884, p. 3; Austin *Stateman*, Austin, Texas, March 27, 1889, p. 1; U.S. Bureau of the Census, *Tenth Census of the United States*, 1880 (Washington D.C.), Roll #1291, Bexar County, p. 16; Morrison and Fourmy's *Directory of the City of San Antonio for 1881 and 1882* (Galveston: Morrison & Fourmy, 1881), p. 70; Morrison and Fourmy's *General Directory of the City of San Antonio, 1883–1884* (Galveston: Morrison and Fourmy, 1883), pp. 73–74; *Directory of San Antonio, 1885–1886*, p. 42; *Directory of San Antonio, 1887–1888*, p. 37; *Directory of San Antonio, 1889–1890, p. 41; Directory of San Antonio, 1891*, pp. 27–28; *Directory of San Antonio, 1897–1898*, p. 150.

37. In 1880, the Mexican American population of San Antonio was estimated at 3,470 in a city of 21,707 people. *Directory of San Antonio, 1879–1880*, pp. 53–54. In 1900, other estimates indicate that the Mexican population of the city was 13,722 in comparison to 32,000 Anglo Americans and 7,538 Afro-Americans. See Richard A. García, "Class, Consciousness, and Ideology—The Mexican Community of San Antonio, Texas, 1930–1940," *Aztlán: International Journal of Chicano Studies Research* IX (Spring Summer Fall 1978); 23–70.

38. *Directory of San Antonio, 1883–1884*, p. 16; Jules A. Appler's *General Directory of the City of San Antonio, 1895–1896* (San Antonio: Jules A. Appler, 1895), p. 118; *Directory of San Antonio, 1897–1898*, p. 118.

39. *Directory of San Antonio, 1881–1882*, p. 54.

40. J. B. Wilkinson, *Laredo and the Rio Grande Frontier* (Austin: Jenkins Publishing Co., 1975), p. 242; J. Lee Stambaugh and Lillian J. Stambaugh, *The Lower Rio Grande Valley of Texas* (San Antonio: The Naylor Co., 1954), pp. 89, 90, and 95.

41. Brownsville *Ranchero*, Brownsville, Texas, February 25, 1868, p. 1. But compare the results reported in ibid., February 3, 1870, p. 2.

42. Ibid., November 25, 1869, p. 2.

43. San Antonio *Express*, December 17, 1880, p. 1; December 14, 1881, p. 1; January 24, 1882, p. 2; March 27, 1884, p. 1; April 3, 1884, p. 1; April 16, 1884, p. 1; Corpus Christi *Weekly Caller*, April 6, 1884, p. 4. On the history of Laredo during this period, see Gilberto M. Hinojosa, "Settlers and Sojourners in the 'Chaparral': A Demographic Study of a Borderlands Town in Transition, Laredo, 1755–1870" (Ph.D. diss., University of Texas at Austin, 1979).

44. San Antonio *Express*, December 14, 1881, p. 1; April 3, 1884, p. 1; April 4, 1884, p. 1; April 8, 1884, p. 1.

45. San Antonio *Express*, November 13, 1893, p. 6.

46. Ibid., September 24, 1882, p. 1; January 23, 1883, p. 2.

47. *Directory of San Antonio, 1881–1882*, p. 55; *Directory of San Antonio,*

1883–1884, p. 16; *Directory of San Antonio, 1885–1886*, p. 18; *Directory of San Antonio, 1887–1888*, p. 18; *Directory of San Antonio, 1889–1890*, p. 22.

48. Corpus Christi *Weekly Caller*, October 12, 1884, p. 4.

49. *Directory of San Antonio, 1891*, p. 38; *Directory of San Antonio, 1892–1893*, p. 79; *Directory of San Antonio, 1895–1896*, p. 118; *Directory of San Antonio, 1897–1898*, p. 118; *Directory of San Antonio, 1899–1900*, p. 118.

50. San Antonio *Express*, November 13, 1893, p. 6; Corpus Christi *Weekly Caller*, October 21, 1898, p. 7.

51. Seb S. Wilcox, "The Laredo City Election Riot of April, 1886," *Southwestern Historical Quarterly* XLV (July 1941): 1–23.

52. Corpus Christi *Weekly Caller*, December 24, 1887, p. 4; San Antonio *Express*, May 31, 1884, p. 1; July 12, 1892, p. 6.

53. New York *Times*, August 28, 1880, p. 5; San Antonio *Express*, July 12, 1892, p. 6, and, November 13, 1893, p. 6.

54. Brownsville *Ranchero*, Brownsville, Texas, February 23, 1868, p. 1; February 26, 1869, p. 2.

55. Corpus Christi *Weekly Caller*, December 16, 1883, p. 2; February 17, 1899, p. 7; *Directory of San Antonio, 1883–1884, p. 12; Directory of San Antonio, 1885–1886*, p. 14; *Directory of San Antonio, 1887–1888*, p. 14; *Directory of San Antonio, 1889–1890*, p. 34; Jules A. Appler's *General Directory of the City of San Antonio, 1892–1893* (San Antonio: Jules A. Appler, 1893), p. 76; *Directory of San Antonio, 1895–1896*, p. 114; *Directory of San Antonio, 1897–1898, p. 114; and, Directory of San Antonio, 1899–1900*, p. 114.

56. Corpus Christi *Weekly Caller*, March 15, 1885, p. 8; U. S. Bureau of the Census, *Tenth Census of the United States, 1880* (Washington D.C.), Roll #1327, Starr County, p. 20 (Rio Grande City), pp. 4, 34 (Precinct # 3 and # 4).

57. *Directory of San Antonio, 1889–1890*, p. 22; *Directory of San Antonio, 1891*, p. 38; *Directory of San Antonio, 1892–1893*, p. 79; *Directory of San Antonio, 1895–1896*, p. 117; *Directory of San Antonio, 1897–1898*, p. 117.

58. Corpus Christi *Weekly Caller*, February 11, 1888, p. 1; May 5, 1888, p. 8; September 23, 1892, p. 1; San Antonio *Express*, November 21, 1880, p. 1.

59. San Antonio *Express*, June 17, 1896, p. 4.

60. Corpus Christi *Weekly Caller*, November 9, 1884, p. 5; November 16, 1884, p. 5; September 29, 1888, p. 4.

61. Corpus Christi *Weekly Caller*, April 14, 1899, p. 5.

62. Ibid., July 30, 1887, p. 5; January 28, 1888, p. 5; February 18, 1888, p. 4; July 28, 1888, p. 4; August 11, 1893, p. 6; May 13, 1898, p. 4; February 17, 1899, p. 7; March 31, 1899, p. 8.

63. Arnoldo De León, *A Social History of Mexican Americans in Nineteenth Century Duval County* (San Diego, Texas: County Commissioners' Court, 1978), pp. 1–4.

64. *Directory of San Antonio, 1889–1890*, p. 115; U. S. Bureau of the Census, *Twelfth Census of the United States, 1900* (Washington D. C.), Roll #1692, Duval County, pp. 27B and 30A.

65. Corpus Christi *Ranchero*, May 12, 1860, p. 4; January 8, 1863, p. 1.

66. *Directory of San Antonio, 1883–1884*, p. 16; *Directory of San Antonio, 1885–1886*, p. 18; *Directory of San Antonio, 1889–1890*, p. 22; *Directory of San Antonio, 1891*, p. 38; *Directory of San Antonio, 1892–1893*, p. 79; *Directory of San Antonio, 1895–1896*, p. 118; *Directory of San Antonio, 1899–1900*, p. 118; U. S. Bureau of the Census, *Tenth Census of the United States, 1880* (Washington D.C.), Roll #1334, Zapata County, p. 12.

67. *Directory of San Antonio, 1887–1888*, p. 16; *Directory of San Antonio, 1895–1896*, p. 116; *Directory of San Antonio, 1897–1898*, p. 115; *Directory of San Antonio, 1899–1900*, p. 115; U. S. Bureau of the Census, *Twelfth Census of the United States, 1900* (Washington D. C.), Roll #1644, Hidalgo County, pp. 237A and 280A.

68. San Antonio *Express*, June 26, 1887, p. 3.

69. *Directory of San Antonio, 1892–1893*, p. 78; *Directory of San Antonio, 1897–1898*, pp. 115–17; *Directory of San Antonio, 1899–1900*, p. 117.

70. For population figures for the years 1880, 1890, and 1900, see Mario T. García, "Obreros: The Mexican Workers of El Paso, 1900–1920" (Ph.D. diss., University of California at San Diego, 1975), p. 58.

71. In 1885, Felix Escontrias ran for school board as candidate for the first ward and Victor L. Ochoa ran for alderman as candidate from the second ward. El Paso *Times*, July 12, 1885, p. 2.

72. García, "Obreros," p. 264.

73. House Executive Document, No. 93, 45 Cong., 2 Sess. (Ser. 1809), pp. 13, 16, 142, 143; *Directory of San Antonio, 1881–1882*, p. 53; C. L. Sonnichsen, *Pass of the North: Four Centuries on the Rio Grande* (El Paso: Texas Western Press, 1968), p. 232; El Paso *Times*, November 20, 1885, p. 4; February 15, 1887, p. 4; February 18, 1887, p. 3; November 21, 1888, p. 4; October 23, 1889, p. 7; El Paso *Herald*, July 22, 1883, p. 2; April 16, 1890, p. 1; May 21, 1890, p. 1. In February, 1887, the county commission took Alderete to district court in an attempt to remove him on grounds of incompetency, arguing that he could not speak English and thus could not function in the English-speaking commission. But Alderete argued that he was a native of El Paso County, had served as deputy sheriff, hide inspector, and mayor of Ysleta before his election to the commission, that he had received instruction in English and subscribed to a number of English-language newspapers. The jury ultimately ruled in his favor. El Paso *Times*, February 18, 1887, p. 3.

74. El Paso *Herald*, July 22, 1883, p. 2.

75. El Paso *Times*, October 31, 1886, p. 4; May 18, 1888, p. 3; November 25, 1888, p. 4.

76. El Paso *Herald*, November 6, 1890, p. 1; March 26, 1891, p. 4; March 11, 1893, p. 4; El Paso *Times*, October 21, 1890, p. 7; October 5, 1892, p. 6; October 11, 1892, p. 6.

77. El Paso *Times*, November 6, 1894, p. 6.

78. Ibid., November 8, 1898, p. 4.

79. Ibid., January 11, 1899, p. 8.

80. El Paso *Herald*, April 22, 1883, p. 1; March 25, 1890, p. 1; October 23, 1890, p. 1; April 8, 1891, p. 4.

81. San Antonio *Herald*, August 2, 1872, p. 2.

82. El Paso *Times*, April 4, 1885, p. 4; U. S. Bureau of the Census, *Eighth Census of the United States, 1860* (Washington D. C.), Roll #1293, El Paso County, p. 96.

83. El Paso *Times*, August 7, 1891, p. 7.

84. Both the El Paso *Herald* and the El Paso *Times* carried the story between March and August of 1890.

85. El Paso *Times*, April 5, 1891, p. 7.

86. San Antonio *Express*, October 22, 1884, p. 2; Corpus Christi *Ranchero*, October 6, 1860, p. 2; The Beeville *Bee*, March 11, 1892, p. 2; and San Angelo *Standard*, September 21, 1889, p. 1. See also, García, "Obreros," p. 265 passim.

An older generation of historians argued doggedly that Tejanos were the dupes of Anglo politicans and were "voted" according to the whims of the Mexicanos' benefactors. See the works of Walter Prescott Webb, *The Texas Rangers: A Century of Frontier Defense* (New York: Houghton Mifflin Co., 1935); Edgar Greer Shelton, *Political Conditions Among Texas-Mexicans Along the Rio Grande* (San Francisco: R & E Research Associates, 1974); and Ozzie G. Simmons, *Anglo Americans and Mexican Americans in South Texas* (New York: Arno Press, 1974).

Yet, the reality was more complex than these historians perceived it. No doubt, Anglo politicians coerced and even bribed certain Mexicanos, a practice common to machine and ethnic politics elsewhere in the country during the era. But, ethnic politics in other parts of the country also included calls for reforms, organization for protest purposes, and demands for concessions from political bosses. On this, see A. Gerber, *Black Ohio and the Color Line* (Urbana: University of Illinois Press, 1976); Thomas Holt, *Black Over White: Negro Political Leadership in South Carolina During Reconstruction* (Urbana: University of Illinois Press, 1977).

87. Corpus Christi *Weekly Caller*, November 27, 1891, pp. 2, 7.

88. Beeville *Bee*, March 11, 1892, p. 2.

89. San Antonio *Express*, November 1, 1894, p. 1. And see also a similar denunciation in ibid., October 22, 1884, p. 2.

90. García, "Obreros," pp. 262, 267, and 269.

91. Arnoldo De León, "Accomodacionistas: Defensores del Barrio," *Caracol* III (December 1976): 16–17.

92. Shelton, *Political Conditions Among Texas Mexicans Along the Rio Grande*, pp. 29–32.

93. See note 86 above.

Chapter 3

1. Among those are the work of J. Frank Dobie on Texas. Studies that look into the way that fiction writers have treated the Mexican in the rural scene include Cecil Robinson, *With the Ears of Strangers: The Mexican in American Literature* (Tucson: University of Arizona Press, 1969), and Francisco Armando Ríos, "The Mexican in Fact, Fiction and Folklore," *El Grito: A Journal of Contemporary Mexican American Thought* II (Summer 1969); 14–28. For more positive portrayals of Mexicanos in the agrarian sector, see Carey McWilliams, *North From Mexico: The Spanish-Speaking People of the United States* (New York: Greenwood Press, 1968); Américo Paredes, *"With His Pistol in His Hand": A Border Ballad and Its Hero* (Austin: University of Texas Press, 1971). Also, Jo Mora, *Trail Dust and Saddle Leather* (New York: Charles Scribner's Sons, 1946).

2. Francis Moore, Jr., *Description of Texas* (New York: T. R. Tanner, 1844), pp. 33–34; Neal John O'Neill, *The Guide to Texas* (Dublin: Joseph Blundell, 1834), p. 92; but see also Mary Austin Holley, *Texas* (Lexington, Ky: J. Clarke & Co., 1836; reprinted Austin: The Steck Co., 1935), p. 134.

3. A. B. Lawrence, *Texas in 1840, or the Emigrant's Guide to the New Republic, Being the Observations, Enquiry and Travels in the Beautiful Country* (New York: William W. Allen, 1840), p. 135.

4. W. Eugene Hollon, *Beyond the Cross Timbers: The Travels of Randolph B. Marcy, 1812–1887* (Norman: University of Oklahoma Press, 1955), p. 35; George A. McCall, *Letters from the Frontier* (Philadelphia: J. B. Lippincott, 1868), p. 437; and Corpus Christi *Weekly Caller*, March 24, 1888, p. 1.

5. William Wright, *Recollections of Western Texas* (London: W. and F. G. Cash, 1857), pp. 21–22; G. C. Robinson, "Mustangs and Mustanging in Southwest Texas," in J. Frank Dobie, et al., eds., *Mustangs and Cow Ponies*, Vol. XVI

of Publications of Texas Folklore Society (Dallas: Southern Methodist University, 1965), pp. 5–11; David Woodman, *Guide to Texas Emigrants* (Boston: M. Hawes, 1835), 60–61; McCall, *Letters from the Frontier*, p. 437; Carl of Solms-Braunfels, *Texas, 1844–1845* (Houston: Anson Press, 1936), p. 27; Mary S. Helm, *Scraps of Early Texas History* (Austin: Printed for the Author at the Office of B. R. Warner and Co., 1884), pp. 184–85; and see also, J. W. Moses, "A Mustanger in 1850," in Dobie, et al., eds., *Mustangs and Cow Ponies*, pp. 22–43, and Thomas W. Dwyer, "From Mustangs to Mules," ibid., pp. 47–60.

6. Andrew Forest Muir, ed., *Texas in 1837: An Anonymous Contemporary Narrative* (Austin: University of Texas Press, 1958), p. 108.

7. M. Krueger, *Pioneer Life in Texas: An Autobiography* (n.p.,n.d.), pp. 72–73; Woodman, *Guide to Texas Emigrants*, pp. 60–61; McCall, *Letters from the Frontier*, p. 437; Robinson, "Mustangs and Mustanging in Southwest Texas," in Dobie, et al., eds., *Mustangs and Cow Ponies*, pp. 6–7; and Moses, "A Mustanger in 1850," in ibid., pp. 27–32.

8. Amos Andrew Parker, *Trip to the West and Texas* (New York: Arno Press, 1973), p. 138; Corpus Christi *Weekly Caller*, March 24, 1888, p. 1.

9. Frederick Page, *Prairiedom: Rambles and Scrambles in Texas or New Estremadura* (New York: Paine and Burgess, 1845), p. 98.

10. J. Marvin Hunter, *The Trail Drivers of Texas* (2 vols; New York: Argosy-Antiquarian Ltd., 1963), I: 453. A trail driver remarked: "They had a reputation for being the dearest help in a long run that a drover can employ, although they will work for considerable less wages than white boys. Many were good faithful hands, and true to the interest of their employers. But as a rule they are unprofitable as well as unrealistic help." See Joseph G. McCoy, *Cattle Trade of the West and Southwest* (Ann Arbor: University Microfilms, Inc., 1966), p. 86.

11. Lela Neal Pirtle, ed., *Life on the Range and on the Trail: As Told by R. J. (Bob) Lauderdale and John M. Doak* (San Antonio: The Naylor Co., 1936), pp. 72, 175, and 179.

12. "Reminiscences of C. C. Cox," *Quarterly of the Texas State Historical Association* VI (January 1903): 208–9.

13. W. S. Henry, *Campaign Sketches of the War with Mexico* (New York: Arno Press, 1973), p. 46.

14. David Montejano, *Race, Labor Repression, and Capitalist Agriculture: Notes From South Texas, 1920–1930* (Berkeley: Institute for the Study of Social Change, 1977), pp. 5–6.

15. John C. Reid, *Reid's Tramp or a Journal of the Incidents of Ten Months Travel Through Texas, New Mexico, Arizona, Sonora, California. . . .* (Selma, Alabama: John Hardt and Co., 1858), p. 36; and W. G. Kingsbury, *A Description of South-Western and Middle Texas* (London: Waterlow and Sons Limited, 1878), p. 24; San Antonio *Express*, April 17, 1879, p. 4.

16. San Antonio *Express*, March 12, 1879, p. 4.

17. San Angelo *Standard*, September 21, 1889, p. 1.

18. San Antonio *Express*, March 12, 1879, p. 4.

19. San Angelo *Standard*, September 21, 1889, p. 1.

20. Krueger, *Pioneer Life in Texas*, p. 187; and Reid, *Reid's Tramp*, pp. 36–37.

21. Winifred Kupper, ed., *Texas Sheepman: The Reminiscences of Robert Maudslay* (Freeport, New York: Books for Libraries Press, 1951), pp. 36–37, 47–48.

22. V. W. Lehmann, *Forgotten Legions: Sheep in the Rio Grande Plain of Texas* (El Paso: Texas Western Press, 1966), p. 37; Drueger, *Pioneer Life in Texas*, p. 187; San Angelo *Standard*, September 21, 1889, p. 1.

23. San Antonio *Express*, March 12, 1879, p. 4.

24. Krueger, *Pioneer Life in Texas*, p. 187.

25. San Antonio *Express*, March 12, 1879., p. 4; Kingsbury, *A Description of South-western and Middle Texas*, p. 24; Reid, *Reid's Tramp*, pp. 36–37; Lehmann, *Forgotten Legions*, pp. 37, 49–50, and 55; Mary A. Jaques, *Texan Ranch Life: With Three Months Through Mexico in a "Prairie Schooner"* (London: Horace Cox, 1894), p. 68; Paul S. Taylor, *An American Mexican Frontier: Nueces County, Texas* (Chapel Hill: University of North Carolina Press, 1934), p. 100; W. C. Sutherland, "Adams Brothers of Jim Wells County" (Eugene C. Barker Collection, University of Texas Archives), p. 11; San Antonio *Express*, July 27, 1887, p. 3; July 31, 1890, p. 6; and September 4, 1891, p. 3.

26. San Antonio *Express*, April 4, 1884, p. 1.

27. Lehmann, *Forgotten Legions*, pp. 55–57; Jaques, *Texan Ranch Life*, pp. 68–69; Kupper, ed., *Texas Sheepman*, pp. 118–19; Winifred Kupper, *The Golden Hoof: The Story of the Sheep of the Southwest* (New York: A. A. Knopf, 1945), pp. 152–58; Sutherland, "The Adams Brothers of Jim Wells County," p. 11; Fermina Guerra, "Mexican and Spanish Folklore and Incidents in Southwestern Texas" (M.A. thesis, University of Texas at Austin, 1941), p. 50; San Antonio *Express*, April 29, 1879, p. 4.

28. Arnoldo De León, "Los Tasinques and the Sheep Shearers' Union of North America: A Strike in West Texas," *West Texas Historical Association Yearbook* (1979): 3–16.

29. San Antonio *Express*, December 4, 1877, p. 2. Concerning ranch labor in west Texas, see the San Angelo *Standard*, June 2, 1888, p. 1; June 26, 1888, p. 1.

30. Corpus Christi *Weekly Caller*, March 15, 1885, pp. 2 and 4; San Antonio *Herald*, May 5, 1858, p. 1; Brownsville *Ranchero*, May 28, 1867, p. 2; San Angelo *Standard*, September 21, 1889, p. 1; June 2, 1888, p. 1; June 26, 1888, p. 1; Montejano, *Race, Labor Repression and Capitalist Agriculture*, p. 18; and Taylor, *An American Mexican Frontier*, p. 105.

31. Mario Barrera, *Race and Class in the Southwest: A Theory of Racial Inequality* (Notre Dame: Notre Dame Press, 1979) has a full discussion about segmented labor in the Southwest market.

32. San Antonio *Herald*, February 17, 1867, p. 3; March 12, 1867, p. 3; April 7, 1867, p. 3; July 2, 1871, p. 3; August 27, 1872, p. 3.

33. Jennie Parks Ringgold, *Frontier Days in the Southwest* (San Antonio: The Naylor Company, 1952), p. 8.

34. Brownsville *Ranchero*, June 2, 1867, p. 2.

35. Susan G. Miller, *Sixty Years in the Nueces Valley, 1870–1930* (San Antonio: Naylor Printing Co., 1930), pp. 104–9.

36. San Antonio *Herald*, August 16, 1868, p. 2, citing the Brownsville *Courier;* San Antonio *Express*, December 4, 1877, p. 2; October 4, 1888, p. 3.

37. Corpus Christi *Weekly Caller*, March 15, 1885, p. 2; August 5, 1892, p. 4; September 8, 1893, p. 6.

38. San Antonio *Express*, September 26, 1892, p. 2; October 4, 1892, p. 2.

39. Ibid., September 23, 1894, p. 4.

40. Beeville *Bee*, Beeville, Texas, October 26, 1894, p. 1.

41. Miller, *Sixty Years in the Nueces Valley*, p. 34.

42. Tom Lea, *The King Ranch* (2 vols; Boston: Little, Brown, and Company, 1957), II: 501.

43. Carlysle Graham Raht, *The Romance of Davis Mountains and Big Bend Country* (El Paso: The Raht Books Company, 1919), p. 217.

44. Emanuel H. D. Domenech, *Missionary Adventures in Texas and Mexico: A*

Personal Narrative of Six Years' Sojourn in Those Regions (London: Longman, Brown, Green, Longmans, and Roberts, 1858), pp. 254–55.

45. R. W. Johnson, *A Soldier's Reminiscences in Peace and War* (Philadelphia: J. B. Lippincott Co., 1886), p. 67.

46. San Antonio *Express*, September 12, 1882, p. 2.

47. Mary A. Sutherland, *The Story of Corpus Christi*, ed. by Frank B. Harrison (Houston: Rein & Sons Co., 1916), p. 83.

48. As reported in the San Angelo *Standard*, January 15, 1887, p. 4.

49. Lee C. Harby, "Texan Types and Contrasts," *Harper's New Monthly Magazine*, July, 1890, p. 229.

50. San Antonio *Express*, July 26, 1891, p. 3.

51. José María Rodríguez, *Rodríguez Memoirs of Early Texas* (San Antonio: Passing Show Printing Co., 1913), pp. 75–76.

52. See the insights advanced by Herbert Gutman, *Work, Culture, and Society in Industrializing America: Essays in American Working Class and Social History* (New York: Knopf, 1976); Eugene D. Genovese, *Roll, Jordan, Roll: The World the Slaves Made* (New York: Vintage Books, 1976), pp. 285–324; and Mario T. García, "Americanization and the Mexican Immigrant, 1880–1930," *Journal of Ethnic Studies* VI (Summer 1978): 19–34.

53. El Paso *Herald*, July 21, 1898, p. 4.

54. Fane Downs, "The History of Mexicans in Texas, 1821–1845" (Ph.D. diss., Texas Tech University, 1970), p. 18, citing *Dr. John Beales' Journal, 1833,* in William Kennedy, *Texas: The Rise, Progress, and Prospects of the Republic of Texas* (Fort Worth: The Molyneaux, Craftsmen, 1925), p. 404; and Frederick Chabot, *With the Makers of San Antonio* (San Antonio: privately printed, 1937), p. 120.

55. Downs, "The History of Mexicans in Texas," p. 19, citing Hobart Huson, *Refugio: A Comprehensive History of Refugio County. . . .* (2 vols; Woodsboro, Texas: The Rooke Foundation, Inc., 1953), I: 160–61, and J. W. Petty, Jr., ed., *Victor Rose's History of Victoria* (Victoria, Texas: Book Mart, 1961), p. 123.

56. Ferdinand Roemer, *Texas: With Particular Reference to German Immigration*, trans. by Oswald Mueller (Waco: Texian Press, 1967), p. 145.

57. Julia Nott Waugh, *Castroville and Henry Castro, Empresario* (San Antonio: Standard Printing Co., 1934), pp. 90–91; and Frederick Page, *Prairiedom: Rambles and Scrambles in Texas or New Estremadura* (New York: Paine and Burgess, 1845), p. 139.

58. Frederick Law Olmsted, *A Journey Through Texas* (New York: Burt Franklin, 1969), pp. 271–72.

59. Corpus Christi *Ranchero*, April 6, 1861, p. 2; Brownsville *Ranchero*, April 28, 1868, p. 2; November 8, 1868, p. 1; San Antonio *Express*, December 27, 1888, p. 1.

60. W. H. Chatfield, *The Twin Cities of the Border and the Country of the Lower Rio Grande* (New Orleans: E. P. Brandao, 1893), p. 42; Emilia Schunior Ramírez, *Ranch Life in Hidalgo County After 1850* (Edinburg: New Santander Press, 1971), not numbered; and Corpus Christi *Ranchero*, October 10, 1866, p. 2.

61. Chatfield, *Twin Cities*, p. 42; Corpus Christi *Weekly Caller*, September 24, 1887, p. 4; October 22, 1887, p. 8; December 31, 1887, p. 5; June 2, 1888, p. 1; September 1, 1893, p. 1.

62. J. Lee Stambaugh and Lillian J. Stambaugh, *The Lower Rio Grande Valley of Texas* (San Antonio: The Naylor Co., 1954), p. 143.

63. Corpus Christi *Weekly Caller*, September 24, 1887, p. 4; October 22, 1887, p. 8; December 31, 1887, p. 5; June 2, 1888, p. 1; September 1, 1893, p. 1.

64. Richard Harding Davis, *The West from a Car Window* (New York: Harper and Brothers, 1892), p. 132; Corpus Christi *Weekly Caller*, January 18, 1885, p. 4; December 22, 1888, p. 1.

65. Corpus Christi *Weekly Caller*, March 11, 1883, p. 2. The 1880 census listed the following *ranchitos* for Hidalgo County:

Relámpago Ranch	Piedras	Tabasco	Soledad
Agua Negra Ranch	Valle Hermoso	Havana	San Pedro
La Blanca Ranch	La Mónica	Los Ebanos	Alta Colorada
Santa Anna Ranch	Teniente	Las Cuevas	Loma Blanca
Sauz Ranch	La Jara	Americana	Los Caballos
Capote Ranch	El Rucio	Guadalupe	La Chepena
Hidalgo Ranch	El Tule	San José	Tipaguaje
Derramadero Ranch	Villa Nueva	San Ramón	La Mesa
Tampacuas Ranch	Granjeno	Las Palomas	Vargas Rancho
Retama	Nuevo Rancho	Laguna Blanca	Las Viejas
Las Burras	Ojo de Agua	Encino de Pasos	Concepción
Pititas	Peñitas	Tajos	Santa Anita
			La Noria Cardena

For Zapata County, the same census includes:

Precinct #1	*Precinct #4*	*Precinct #4* (cont'd)
San Bartolo	Ranch of José María Bustamente	Rancho Potrera
Uribeño Ranch	Ranch of José María Vela	Rancho Ballena
Ranchito	Ranch of Felipe Vela	Rancho Tiposan
Labores de Uribeño	Ranch of Las Animas	Rancho del la Refugia
	Ranch of Pedro Flores	Rancho del Sabinito
Precinct #2	Ranch of de los Venados	Rancho Soledad
San Ygnacio	Ranch of Patrocinio	Rancho Clareño
San José de Corralitos	Ranch of Las Escobas	Rancho Cheneño
Dolores Ranch	Ranch of Las Escobitas	Rancho Refugia
	Las Ovejas Ranch	Rancho Penena
Precinct #3	Jose María Martínez	Rancho Lapoena
Salamoneño	Julián Zapata	Rancho Tigra
Ramireño	Evaristo Gutiérrez	Rancho Serenena
Las Comitas	Estanislado Flores	Rancho Ramireña
	Gargeño	Rancho Abritas
	Candelario Vela's Ranch	Rancho Coronado
	Rancho Randado	Rancho Arredondo

Unfortunately, the census does not provide information concerning size, owner-ship, worth, and other vital data. See U.S. Bureau of the Census, *Tenth Census of the United States, 1880* (Washington D. C.), Roll #1310 and 1311, Hidalgo Coun-ty, and Roll #1334, Zapata County.

66. Lela Neale Pirtle, ed., *Life on the Range and on the Trail: As Told by R. J. (Bob) Lauderdale and John M. Doak* (San Antonio: The Naylor Company, 1936), pp. 145–47; 131–32; and 141.

67. Corpus Christi *Weekly Caller*, January 24, 1886, p. 5; November 24, 1893, p. 1; January 28, 1898, p. 1; San Antonio *Express*, April 16, 1891, p. 6.

68. Corpus Christi *Weekly Caller*, October 6, 1893, p. 8; October 27, 1893, p. 7; November 24, 1893, p. 1.

69. Taylor, *An American Mexican Frontier*, pp. 74–75, citing the *Nueces Valley Weekly*, Corpus Christi, Texas, January 2, 1858. In the 1860s, when the Corpus Christi *Ranchero* set aside space for ranchers to publish their brands, the following persons advertised: Jesús García Ramírez of Rancho del Palo Blanco, seventy miles southwest of Corpus Christi; Rafael Aldrete, residence and rancho on the Aransas River in Refugio County; Felis Cadena, Rancho Palo Blanco, eighty-five miles southwest of Corpus Christi; Antonio García Flores, Rancho San Diego, fifty-five miles west of Corpus Christi; Francisco Flores Gonzales, Rancho San Diego, fifty-five miles west of Corpus Christi; Felipe Guerra, Rancho Las Escobas, Starr County; Rafael Hinojosa García, Rancho Palo Blanco, eighty-five miles southwest of Corpus Christi; Rafael López, Rancho Los Preseños, forty miles southwest of Corpus Christi; Trinidad Peña, Rancho Jaboncillos, eighty-five miles southwest of Corpus Christi; Juan Peña, Rancho Haboncillos, also eighty-five miles southwest of Corpus Christi; Tiburcio Ramírez, Rancho Concepción, seventy-eight miles south southwest of Corpus Christi; Cristobal Ramírez, Rancho Santa Dominga, fifty-six miles north of Roma; Pedro Barrera, Rancho Santa Dominga, fifty-six miles north of Roma; Santos Flores Gonzales, Rancho San Diego, fifty miles west of Corpus Christi; Rolando Hinojosa García, Rancho Palo Blanco, eighty-five miles southwest of Corpus Christi; Juan Saens, Rancho San Diego, fifty-five miles west of Corpus Christi; Pablo Pérez, Rancho at San Diego, fifty-five miles west of Corpus Christi, Doña Andrea Montes, stock at F. W. Latham's Rancho Las Motas, near Nueces County line. See the *Ranchero*, May 12, 1860, p. 4; November 17, 1860, p. 1; December 15, 1860, p. 1; December 22, 1860, p. 1; January 19, 1861, p. 1; and June 25, 1863, p. 1.

70. Corpus Christi *Weekly Caller*, July 6, 1884, p. 5; November 1, 1885, p. 4; November 8, 1885, p. 4; March 7, 1886, p. 4; March 21, 1886, p. 4; May 9, 1886, p. 4; May 30, 1886, p. 1; October 3, 1891, p. 7; April 15, 1892, p. 1; February 24, 1899, p. 5.

71. San Antonio *Express*, August 18, 1887, p. 3.

72. Corpus Christi *Weekly Caller*, September 6, 1885, p. 5: September 19, 1886, p. 8; September 26, 1886, p. 4; October 3, 1886, p. 4; October 10, 1886, p. 4; October 17, 1886, p. 4; October 29, 1887, p. 4; July 28, 1888, p. 1; October 13, 1888, p. 1; October 20, 1888, p. 1; November 17, 1888, p. 5; April 25, 1891, p. 1; June 6, 1891, p. 8; February 24, 1893, p. 1; May 5, 1893, p. 1; July 21, 1893, p. 1; October 27, 1899, p. 1; November 17, 1899, p. 1; and San Antonio *Express*, February 6, 1887, p. 3.

73. Raht, *The Romance of Davis Mountains and Big Bend Country*, pp. 176, 329.

74. Lehmann, *Forgotten Legions*, pp. 30, 67.

75. San Antonio *Express*, September 18, 1880, p. 2.

76. Ibid., April 8, 1879, p. 4.

77. Teresa Vielé, *"Following the Drum": A Glimpse of Frontier Life* (New York: Rudd and Carleton, 1859), p. 127; Noah Smithwick, *The Evolution of a State, or Recollections of old Texas Days* (Austin: Gammel Book Company, 1900), p. 47; Stephen Powers, *Afoot and Alone: A Walk from Sea to Sea by the Southern Route: Adventures and Observations in Southern California, New Mexico, Arizona, Texas, etc* (Hartford: Columbian Book Company, 1886), p. 163; Olmsted, *A Journey Through Texas*, p. 272; San Antonio *Express*, June 17, 1886, p. 7; Corpus Christi *Weekly Caller*, September 15, 1888, p. 4; William M. Pierson to Second Assistant Secretary of State, Paso del Norte, México, March 11, 1873, in Despatches from

United States Consuls in Ciudad Juárez (Paso del Norte), 1850–1906: Roll 2 and despatches January 16, 1871 to December 31, 1884; George G. Smith, *The Life and Times of George Foster Pierce, D. D., LL.D. Bishop of the Methodist Episcopal Church, South, with His Sketch of Lovick Pierce, D. D., his Father* (Sparta, Georgia: Hancock Publishing Co., 1888), p. 395; Bickford Mackey to Assistant Secretary of State, Paso del Norte, México, March 22, 1889, in Despatches from United States Consuls in Ciudad Juárez (Paso del Norte), 1850–1906; Roll 4 and despatches January 16, 1889 to July 31, 1891; San Antonio *Express*, January 30, 1883, p. 3; *Texas State Gazette*, Austin, Texas, August 27, 1859, p. 2; Brownsville *Ranchero*, November 18, 1866, p. 2; January 6, 1870, p. 2; W. H. Chatfield, *The Twin Cities of the Border: Brownsville, Texas, and Matamoros, Mexico* (New Orleans: E. P. Brandao., 1893), p. 42.

78. John Ernest Gregg, "The History of Presidio County" (M.A. thesis, University of Texas at Austin, 1933), p. 132.

79. San Antonio *Express*, January 30, 1883, p. 2.

80. Gregg, "The History of Presidio County," pp. 129–30.

81. Corpus Christi *Weekly Caller*, March 21, 1886, p. 4; San Antonio *Express*, February 6, 1887, p. 3; March 9, 1887, p. 7.

82. Corpus Christi *Weekly Caller*, July 28, 1888, p. 1; September 8, 1888, p. 4; January 5, 1889, p. 4; December 30, 1892, p. 1; September 29, 1893, p. 7.

83. Corpus Christi *Weekly Caller*, March 21, 1886, p. 4.

84. Corpus Christi *Weekly Caller*, January 5, 1889, p. 8; San Antonio *Express*, October 4, 1888, p. 3.

85. Corpus Christi *Weekly Caller*, May 2, 1891, p. 8.

86. San Antonio *Express*, January 24, 1883, p. 2.

87. As Table 8 shows, the number of Mexican Americans employed in the rural areas of South, Central, and West Texas is estimated at 30.1 percent in 1900. This compares to an estimated 32.9 percent of the Anglo Americans. The census reports for 1850 (1860) did not show parity in employment levels between the two ethnic populations. However, this may well be due in large part to under reporting of Mexican American employment, and to the fact that much of the Anglo population in 1850 consisted of males involved in employment relating to military activities.

88. For a strike involving a Tejano named Juan A. Gómez, see Robert E. Zeigler, "The Cowboy Strike of 1883: Its Causes and Meanings," *West Texas Historical Association Yearbook* XLVII (1971): 32–46,

Chapter 4

1. The rise and growth of urban settlements corresponds to the particular patterns of population spreads in the nineteenth century. Of course the Central Texas cities of San Antonio, Goliad, and Victoria were a part of the Texas landscape before 1836 and, along with newer towns that emerged after the Civil War, continued having a perceptible Hispanic population. The South Texas cities, as already discussed, emerged after the Mexican War of 1846–48. Only Laredo could trace its beginnings to the colonial period. Thus Brownsville in December 1848 became the county seat of newly-organized Cameron County, and Rio Grande City in Starr County received population and permanence with the establishment of Fort Ringgold there in 1848. Corpus Christi became the Nueces County seat in 1846. San Diego in Duval County made its appearance in the 1850s but did not thrive until after the Texas Mexican Railroad reached there in 1879. Edinburg in Hidalgo County and Falfurrias in Brooks County came along late in the century.

Farther west along the Rio Grande border, only two sizable cities could be found: Eagle Pass in Maverick County, only an emerging town in the 1850s, and Del Rio in Valverde County, just coming along in the 1880s. In extreme West Texas were the small towns of Fort Stockton (Pecos County), more of a military base than anything else for about twenty years after the Civil War and a small town thereafter, and Fort Davis in Jeff Davis County, also a military post in the postbellum period about which grew the little town with the same name. Although El Paso was old, it experienced its most rapid expansion and made its transition into cityhood in the 1880s. In West Texas it was the only major urban area of any distinction, for its neighboring towns of San Elizario, Ysleta, and Socorro remained small. Other towns like San Angelo, Abilene, and Alpine were barely surfacing in the 1880s.

2. Olmsted, *Journey Through Texas*, p. 160; Nathaniel Taylor, *The Coming Empire: or, Two Thousand Miles in Texas on Horseback* (New York: A. S. Barnes and Co., 1877), p. 126; San Antonio *Herald*, March 13, 1858, p. 2; John Russell Bartlett, *Personal Narrative of Explorations and Incidents in Texas, New Mexico, California, Sonora, and Chihuahua* . . . (2 vols; New York: D. Appleton and Co., 1854), I, p. 40.

3. Benjamin Lundy, *The Life, Travels and Opinions of Benjamin Lundy Including his Journeys to Texas and Mexico* (New York: Negro Universities Press, 1969), p. 46; Albert D. Richardson, *Beyond the Mississippi: From the Great River to the Great Ocean* (Philadelphia: Bliss and Co., 1867), p. 227; Olmsted, *Journey Through Texas*, p. 162; August Santleben, *A Texas Pioneer* (New York: Neale Publishing Co., 1910), pp. 107, 112; Charles Merritt Barnes, *Combats and Conquests of Immortal Heroes* (San Antonio: Guessaz & Ferlet Co., 1910), p. 125; Raht, *Romance of the Davis Mountains and Big Bend Country*, pp. 230–45; Pirtle, ed., *Life on the Range and on the Trail*, pp. 98–99; Ophia D. Smith, "A Trip to Texas in 1855," *Southwestern Historical Quarterly* LVIX (July 1955): 36; Vielé, "*Following the Drum*," p. 127; Noah Smithwick, *Evolution of a State* (Austin: The Gammel Co., 1900), p. 47; William M. Pierson to Second Assistant Secretary of State, Paso del Norte, México, March 11, 1873, in Despatches from United States Consuls in Ciudad Juárez (Paso de Norte), 1850–1906: Roll 2 and despatches January 16, 1871–December 31, 1884; George Wilkins Kendall, *Narrative of the Texas-Santa Fe Expedition* (2 vols; Wiley and Putnam, 1844), II; 44–46.

4. Sutherland, *The Story of Corpus Christi*, p. 49.

5. George P. Hammond and Edward H. Howes, eds., *Overland to California on the Southwestern Trail, 1849: The Diary of Robert Eccleston* (Berkeley: University of California Press, 1950), pp. 32, 57; "To California Through Texas and Mexico: The Diary and Letters of Thomas B. Eastland and Joseph G. Eastland, His Son," (foreword by Douglas S. Watson, Notes by Dorothy H. Huggins), *California Historical Society Quarterly* XVIII (June 1939): 120; San Antonio *Herald*, May 8, 1872, p. 3.

6. Robert G. Carter, *On the Border with MacKenzie: or, Winning West Texas from the Comanches* (Washington D.C.: Eynon Printing Co., 1935), p. 50.

7. Pirtle, ed., *Life on the Range and on the Trail*, pp. 98–99; San Antonio *Herald*, August 31, 1872, p. 3; September 4, 1872, p. 3; San Antonio *Express*, January 3, 1872, p. 1.

8. J. B. Wilkinson, *Laredo and the Rio Grande Frontier* (Austin: Jenkins Publishing Co., 1975), pp. 325–26.

9. Santleben, *A Texas Pioneer*, pp. 112–17.

10. San Antonio *Herald*, March 26, 1870, p. 3; March 29, 1870, p. 3; San Antonio *Express*, December 16, 1888, p. 2.

11. San Antonio *Express*, July 8, 1881, p. 4.

12. García, "Obreros," p. 110.

13. San Antonio *Herald*, May 25, 1868, p. 2. But there were also skilled tailors and shoemakers, according to the same reports.

14. W. Eugene Hollon, *Beyond the Cross Timbers: The Travels of Randolph B. Marcy, 1812–1887* (Norman: University of Oklahoma Press, 1955), p. 198.

15. Sutherland, *Story of Corpus Christi*, p. 83.

16. San Antonio *Express*, February 5, 1884, p. 3.

17. Smith, "A Trip to Texas in 1855," p. 36n. See also Chatfield, *Twin Cities*, p. 30; Nannie M. Tilley, ed., *Federals on the Frontier: The Diary of Benjamin F. McIntyre* (Austin: University of Texas Press, 1963), p. 262.

18. Domenech, *Missionary Adventures in Texas and Mexico*, p. 225.

19. Tilley, ed., *Federals on the Frontier*, p. 262; Chatfield, *Twin Cities*, p. 30; San Antonio *Express*, April 5, 1883, p. 2.

20. *Directory of San Antonio, 1881–1882*, p. 223; *Directory of San Antonio, 1885–1886*, p. 65; *Directory of San Antonio, 1889–1890*, pp. 76, 296; *Directory of San Antonio, 1892–1893*, p. 506; *Directory of San Antonio, 1897–1898*, pp. 137, 460.

21. *Directory of San Antonio, 1881–1882*, p. 196; *Directory of San Antonio, 1885–1886*, pp. 112; 210, 212; *Directory of San Antonio, 1889–1890*, pp. 247, 249, 131; *Directory of San Antonio, 1892–1893*, p. 681; *Directory of San Antonio, 1897–1898*, p. 613.

22. San Antonio *Express*, October 20, 1891, p. 3.

23. Vielé, *"Following the Drum,"* p. 148.

24. Tilley, ed., *Federals on the Frontier*, p. 260.

25. Chatfield, *Twin Cities*, pp. 29–30.

26. Lee C. Harby, "Texan Types and Contrasts," *Harper's New Monthly Magazine*, July 1890, p. 243.

27. San Antonio *Express*, September 12, 1882, p. 2.

28. Harriet Spofford, "San Antonio de Béxar," *Harper's New Monthly Magazine*, November 1877, pp. 837–38.

29. Adel Speiser, "The Story of the Theatre in San Antonio" (M.A. thesis, St. Mary's University, 1948), pp. 44–46; Pearson Newcomb, *The Alamo City* (San Antonio: Standard Printing Co., 1926), pp. 100–2; Mrs. S. J. Wright, *San Antonio de Béxar: Historical, Traditional, Legendary* (Austin: Morgan Printing Co., 1916), pp. 107–8; and San Antonio *Express*, June 3, 1879, p. 4.

30. Edward King and J. Wells Champney, *Texas: 1874, An Eyewitness Account of Conditions in Post-Reconstruction Texas*, edited by Robert S. Gray (Houston: Cordovan Press, 1974), p. 109.

31. Corpus Christi *Weekly Caller*, June 18, 1887, p. 4; October 29, 1887, p. 4; San Antonio *Express*, October 28, 1887, p. 5.

32. San Antonio *Express*, November 13, 1893, p. 6.

33. Corpus Christi *Weekly Caller*, November 7, 1886, p. 4; March 28, 1891, p. 8; May 30, 1891, p. 8; June 6, 1891, p. 8; July 4, 1891, p. 8; July 28, 1893, p. 7; March 18, 1898, p. 5.

34. Corpus Christi *Weekly Caller*, April 5, 1885, p. 5; November 12, 1887, p. 8; June 30, 1893, p. 7.

35. Harby, "Texan Types and Contrasts," p. 235.

36. *Directory of San Antonio, 1879–1880*, p. 181; *Directory of San Antonio,*

1881–1882, p. 190; *Directory of San Antonio, 1883–1884*, p. 338; *Directory of San Antonio, 1885–1886*, p. 356; *Directory of San Antonio, 1887–1888*, p. 213; *Directory of San Antonio, 1891*, p. 252; *Directory of San Antonio, 1892–1893*, p. 414.

37. *Directory of San Antonio, 1889–1890*, p. 276; *Directory of San Antonio, 1891*, p. 287; *Directory of San Antonio, 1892–1893*, p. 471.

38. *Directory of San Antonio, 1879–1880*, p. 181; *Directory of San Antonio, 1881–1882*, p. 150; *Directory of San Antonio, 1883–1884*, p. 163; *Directory of San Antonio, 1887–1888*, p. 153; *Directory of San Antonio, 1889–1890*, p. 172; *Directory of San Antonio, 1891*, pp. 454–55; *Directory of San Antonio, 1892–1893*, p. 311; *Directory of San Antonio 1895–1896*, p. 285; *Directory of San Antonio, 1897–1898*, p. 279.

39. *Directory of San Antonio, 1889–1890*, p. 315; *Directory of San Antonio, 1892–1893*, p. 542; *Directory of San Antonio, 1895–1896*, pp. 495, 501; *Directory of San Antonio, 1897–1898*, pp. 487, 495; *Directory of San Antonio, 1899–1900*, pp. 278, 468, 476.

40. *Directory of San Antonio, 1877–1878*, p. 157; *Directory of San Antonio, 1881–1882*, p. 223; *Directory of San Antonio, 1887–1888*, p. 264; *Directory of San Antonio, 1891*, p. 443; *Directory of San Antonio, 1897–1898*, p. 623.

41. *Directory of San Antonio, 1892–1893*, p. 414; *Directory of San Antonio, 1897–1898*, p. 390; *Directory of of San Antonio, 1899–1900*, p. 375.

42. Corpus Christi *Weekly Caller*, August 12, 1883, p. 2; December 20, 1885, p. 4; September 5, 1886, p. 8; August 27, 1887, p. 4; September 26, 1891, p. 6; December 30, 1892, p. 1. See also the directories of San Antonio for the 1880s and 1890s.

43. Corpus Christi *Weekly Caller*, April 25, 1891, p. 1; June 13, 1891, p. 6. See also the directories of San Antonio for the 1880s and 1890s.

44. *Directory of San Antonio, 1879–1880*, p. 135.

45. García, "Obreros," p. 143. See also the directories of San Antonio for the 1880s and 1890s.

46. *Directory of San Antonio, 1891*, p. 452; *Directory of San Antonio, 1895–1896*, p. 660.

47. Corpus Christi *Weekly Caller*, July 19, 1885, p. 5; April 18, 1886, p. 5; San Antonio *Herald*, April 19, 1870, p. 3. See also the directories of San Antonio for the 1880s and 1890s.

48. Corpus Christi *Weekly Caller*, June 18, 1887, p. 4; September 1, 1893, p. 1; San Antonio *Express*, July 11, 1891, p. 3.

49. Arnoldo De León, *A Social History of Mexican Americans in Nineteenth Century Duval County* (San Diego, Texas: Commissioners' Court, 1977), pp. 6–8.

50. Corpus Christi *Weekly Caller*, July 12, 1885, p. 1; San Antonio *Express*, April 15, 1884, p. 2.

51. San Antonio *Express*, May 6, 1898, p. 5.

52. U. S. Bureau of the Census, *Eighth Census of the United States, 1860* (Washington D. C.), Roll #1289, Cameron County, p. 64.

53. U. S. Bureau of the Census, *Tenth Census of the United States, 1880* (Washington D.C.), Roll #1294, Cameron County, p. 44. Also, *Ninth Census of the United States, 1870* (Washington D. C.), Roll #1578, Cameron County, p. 34 and p. 36 (Ward #3).

54. U.S. Bureau of the Census, *Twelfth Census of the United States, 1900* (Washington D. C.), Roll #1617, Cameron County, p. 238B.

55. *Twelfth Census of the U.S., 1900*, Roll #1670, Starr County, p. 55B.

56. *Twelfth Census of the U.S., 1900*, Roll #1678, Webb County, pp. 124A, 162A, 168A, 176B, 198B, and 239B.

57. *Ninth Census of the U.S., 1870*, Roll #1591, Hidalgo County, p. 20.

58. *Tenth Census of the U.S., 1880*, Roll #1289, Atascosa County, p. 5 (Precinct #3).

59. *Tenth Census of the U.S., 1880*, Roll #1319, Maverick County, p. 4 (Precinct #1).

60. Corpus Christi *Weekly Caller*, June 21, 1885, p. 8. See also San Antonio *Express*, April 15, 1884, p. 2.

61. *Twelfth Census of the U.S., 1900*, Roll #1629, Duval County, p. 28A. See also Corpus Christi *Weekly Caller*, September 12, 1891, p. 7.

62. *Directory of San Antonio, 1885–1886*, pp. 120, 270, 359; *Directory of San Antonio, 1887–1888*, pp. 283, 335; *Directory of San Antonio, 1889–1890*, pp. 136, 291, 431; *Directory of San Antonio, 1891*, pp. 95, 147, 451; *Directory of San Antonio, 1892–1893*, pp. 175, 261, 311, 442, 496, 694; *Directory of San Antonio, 1895–1896*, pp. 157, 235, 285, 659; *Directory of San Antonio, 1897–1898*, pp. 275, 571; *Directory of San Antonio, 1899–1900*, pp. 151, 278, 612. The local paper also made mention of a Dr. Manuel Yglesias and his sister Matiana C. Yglesias who treated patients in the city in 1889 for intestinal worms. San Antonio *Express*, April 28, 1889, p. 7; May 6, 1889, p. 5; May 11, 1899, p. 5. See further, *Twelfth Census of the U.S., 1900*, Roll #1611 and #1612, (Volume 7), Bexar County, pp. 125A and 232A.

63. García, "Obreros," pp. 149–50.

64. *Eighth Census of the U.S., 1860*, Roll #1289, Cameron County, p. 28.

65. *Ninth Census of the U.S., 1870*, Roll #1578, Cameron County, p. 30.

66. *Twelfth Census of the U.S., 1900*, Roll #1617, Cameron County, p. 175A.

67. *Twelfth Census of the U.S., 1900*, Roll #1678, Webb County, pp. 165A and 178B.

68. *Tenth Census of the U.S., 1880*, Roll #1322, Nueces County, p. 22.

69. *Tenth Census of the U.S., 1880*, Roll #1300, Duval County, p. 18; *Twelfth Census of the U.S., 1900*, Roll #1629, Duval County, p. 26A.

70. *Twelfth Census of the U.S., 1900*, Roll #1670, Starr County, p. 39B.

71. *Directory of San Antonio, 1891*, p. 272; *Directory of San Antonio, 1892–1893*, p. 291; *Directory of San Antonio, 1897–1898*, pp. 232, 253, 263; *Directory of San Antonio, 1899–1900*, pp. 196, 226, 245, 254; *Twelfth Census of the U.S., 1900*, Roll #1611 and 1612 (Volume 7), Bexar County, pp. 46A, 125A, 152A.

72. *Tenth Census of the U.S., 1880*, Roll #1332, Webb County, p. 76; *Ninth Census of the U.S., 1870*, Roll #1578, Cameron County, p. 36 (Ward #1).

73. *Twelfth Census of the U.S., 1900*, Roll #1678, Webb County, pp. 129A and 163A.

74. *Directory of San Antonio, 1895–1896*, pp. 267, 284, 628; *Directory of San Antonio, 1897–1898*, pp. 262, 279; *Directory of San Antonio, 1899–1900*, p. 269.

75. *Directory of San Antonio, 1885–1886*, p. 42; *Directory of San Antonio, 1892–1893*, p. 70; *Directory of San Antonio, 1895–1896*, pp. 235, 267. See also *Twelfth Census of the U.S., 1900*, Roll #1670, Starr County, p. 130A.

76. Corpus Christi *Weekly Caller*, August 10, 1884, p. 4; February 8, 1885, p. 4; February 15, 1885, p. 5; March 7, 1886, p. 4; February 26, 1887, p. 8; September 16, 1892, p. 7; February 25, 1898, p. 7; May 20, 1898, p. 7.

77. Corpus Christi *Weekly Caller*, August 8, 1891, p. 8.

78. See for example, *Eighth Census of the U.S., 1860*, Roll #1289, Cameron County, pp. 27, 28, 30.

79. Corpus Christi *Weekly Caller*, August 20, 1887, p. 4.

80. San Antonio *Express*, July 11, 1891, p. 1.

81. García, "Obreros," pp. 126–27.

82. El Paso *Times*, September 3, 1885, p. 4; October 23, 1889, p. 7; May 14, 1891, p. 7; May 15, 1891, p. 7; July 16, 1892, p. 2; January 10, 1893, p. 6; January 11, 1893, p. 6; December 12, 1893, p. 6; August 13, 1895, p. 7; September 10, 1895, p. 7; September 22, 1895, p. 3; May 10, 1898, p. 3; January 10, 1899, p. 3; April 18, 1899, p. 8; *Directory of San Antonio, 1887–1888*, p. 101; *Directory of San Antonio, 1889–1890*, p. 44.

83. Chatfield, *Twin Cities*, p. 26; *Eighth Census of the U.S., 1860*, Roll #1289, Cameron County, p. 61; *Tenth Census of the U.S., 1880*, Cameron County, Roll #1294, pp. 31, 38, 54, 63, 66.

84. San Antonio *Express*, February 24, 1888, p. 4; February 25, 1888, p. 4; February 28, 1888, p. 1; April 5, 1888, p. 1; April 17, 1888, p. 4; September 26, 1888, p. 2; January 9, 1889, p. 4; March 31, 1889, p. 2; April 5, 1889, p. 4; June 5, 1889, p. 4; November 1, 1889, p. 1; November 2, 1889, p. 2; August 9, 1891, p. 9; and Corpus Christi *Weekly Caller*, August 26, 1892, p. 4, citing the Brownsville *Cosmopolitan*.

Among Brownsville policemen listed in the 1900 census were Andres Váldez, Juntino López, Vidal Rivas, Severiano Garza, Manuel Cuellar, Bonifacio Galindo, and Francisco Galván. *Twelfth Census of the U.S., 1900*, Roll #1617, Cameron County, pp. 148A, 150A, 157A, 163A, 165A, 175B and 187A.

85. *Eighth Census of the U.S., 1860*, Roll #1308, Webb County, p. 5; *Directory of San Antonio, 1881–1882*, p. 55; *Directory of San Antonio, 1883–1884*, p. 16.

86. Corpus Christi *Weekly Caller*, July 14, 1888, p. 4; San Antonio *Express*, June 11, 1886, p. 1; June 12, 1886, p. 4; June 15, 1886, p. 4; June 20, 1886, p. 4; June 24, 1886, p. 4; June 27, 1886, p. 8; June 30, 1886, p. 4; December 14, 1886, p. 2; February 12, 1888, p. 3; July 14, 1889, p. 4.

87. Corpus Christi *Weekly Caller*, April 15, 1898, p. 1; January 28, 1898, p. 1; San Antonio *Express*, December 1, 1888, p. 5; July 2, 1898, p. 3; November 13, 1893, p. 6; August 7, 1894, p. 2; March 21, 1899, p. 1; *Directory of San Antonio, 1897–1898*, p. 118; *Directory of San Antonio, 1899–1900*, p. 118. Among deputy sheriffs in 1900 were Francisco Fierros, Francisco Benavides, and Malacio Benavides. *Twelfth Census of the U.S., 1900*, Roll #1678, Webb County, pp. 102A, 124A, 188B.

88. Corpus Christi *Weekly Caller*, October 21, 1883, p. 2; January 27, 1884, p. 5; December 3, 1887, p. 8; October 31, 1891, p. 4; March 3, 1893, p. 1; March 10, 1899, p. 1; San Antonio *Express*, April 5, 1883, p. 2; February 7, 1888, p. 3; May 17, 1890, p. 2; May 25, 1891, p. 1; January 1, 1893, p. 1; June 4, 1893, p. 3; June 1, 1899, p. 1. Also see *Tenth Census of the U.S., 1880*, Roll #1332, Webb County, pp. 23, 37, 78, 81; *Twelfth Census of the U.S., 1900*, Roll #1678, Webb County, pp. 101A, 102A, 105A, 124A, 124B, 125B, 132A, 132B, and 133B.

89. *Tenth Census of the U.S., 1880*, Roll #1334, Zapata County, p. 9 (Precinct #1), *Directory of San Antonio, 1883–1884*, p. 16.

90. San Antonio *Express*, January 29, 1871, p. 2; *Ninth Census of the U.S., 1870*, Roll #1591, Hidalgo County, p. 20; *Twelfth Census of the U.S., 1900*, Roll #1644, Hidalgo County, p. 259A.

91. San Antonio *Express*, August 17, 1886, p. 3; March 25, 1891, p. 3; August 8, 1892, p. 2; Corpus Christi *Weekly Caller*, March 28, 1891, p. 8.

92. San Antonio *Express*, January 29, 1871, p. 2; El Paso *Herald*, June 11, 1882, p. 4; April 15, 1883, p. 4.

93. Corpus Christi *Weekly Caller*, June 18, 1887, p. 8; April 25, 1891, p. 1; March 25, 1892, p. 1; January 6, 1893, p. 1; November 3, 1893, p. 3; San Antonio *Express*, September 24, 1876, p. 4; March 24, 1892, p. 2.

94. Corpus Christi *Weekly Caller*, February 11, 1883, p. 5; February 22, 1885, p. 5; May 23, 1886, p. 4.

95. Corpus Christi *Weekly Caller*, November 25, 1883, p. 5; December 30, 1883, p. 5; December 15, 1888, p. 4; May 23, 1891, p. 1.

96. San Antonio *Herald*, February 14, 1872, p. 3; April 4, 1872, p. 3.

97. San Antonio *Express*, January 31, 1888, p. 7; May 31, 1896, p. 20; *Directory of San Antonio, 1899–1900*, p. 118.

98. San Antonio *Herald*, August 16, 1870, p. 3.

99. San Antonio *Herald*, March 15, 1856, p. 2; San Antonio *Express*, May 29, 1885, p. 3; April 17, 1888, p. 5; *Directory of San Antonio, 1885–1886*, p. 277; *Directory of San Antonio, 1891*, p. 212; *Directory of San Antonio, 1892–1893*, pp. 467, 522; *Directory of San Antonio, 1897–1898*, p. 232; *Directory of San Antonio, 1899–1900*, p. 455.

100. San Antonio *Herald*, January 23, 1875, p. 3; San Antonio *Express*, July 27, 1879, p. 4; February 7, 1887, p. 1; February 3, 1889, p. 2.

101. San Antonio *Herald*, January 11, 1872, p. 3; July 25, 1872, p. 2; San Antonio *Express*, September 29, 1881, p. 4; November 17, 1885, p. 3.

102. San Antonio *Express*, February 7, 1887, p. 1; *Directory of San Antonio, 1881–1882*, p. 73.

103. San Antonio *Express*, September 11, 1890, p. 6; February 18, 1891, p. 5; April 28, 1891, p. 6; November 25, 1891, p. 6; June 23, 1892, p. 5; February 25, 1895, p. 8; *Directory of San Antonio, 1885–1886*, p. 43; *Directory of San Antonio, 1887–1888*, p. 40, 135, 335; *Directory of San Antonio, 1889–1890*, p. 172. Jesús Tejeda was county Jailer in the 1880s.

104. *Directory of San Antonio, 1891*, p. 119; *Directory of San Antonio, 1892–1893*, pp. 261, 467, 508; *Directory of San Antonio, 1895–1896*, pp. 205, 293, 435; *Directory of San Antonio, 1897–1898*, p. 473; *Directory of San Antonio, 1899–1900*, pp. 184, 226.

105. O. C. Fisher, *King Fisher: His Life and Times* (Norman: University of Oklahoma, 1966), pp. 117–43; Eugene Cunningham, *Triggernometry: A Gallery of Gunfighters* (Caldwell, Idaho: The Caxton Printers, Ltd., 1962), pp. 66–89.

106. García, "Obreros," p. 122.

107. San Antonio *Herald*, May 5, 1858, p. 2.

108. A list of approximately 300 people in San Antonio who in 1887 paid taxes on property valued at $10,000 or more included the following Spanish surnamed citizens:

G. B. and María Boero	$15,700
Jesusa C. Cantú	10,225
M. Castañola and Son	23,725
José I. Flores	17,700
Juanita Montezda Flores	38,300
Flores, estate of Mrs. Melchoa viuda de	16,450
Nic Flora	13,455
Leonardo Garza	50,165
Concepción Navarro de Callaghan	10,600
Trinidad Pérez	16,800
Antonio Rivas	10,605
Juan F. Rodríguez	10,950

See the San Antonio *Express*, February 7, 1887, p. 1.

Of approximately fifty-five people in Starr County paying taxes in 1891 on property worth more than $10,000, the following were Mexican American:

Blas Peña	$13,898
Juan García Peña	90,624
Pablo Ramírez	18,190
Pablo Ramírez, agent	12,951
Gabriel Valle Recio	19,876
Antonio Peña Saens	21,376
Matías García Saldaña	48,896
Juan Barrera Salinas	10,292
Antoni Yzaguirre	13,952
Jesús Yzaguirre & Bros	51,045
Estate of C. G. Falcón	10,360
Eligio García	29,500
Octaviano Longoria	13,200
Antonio G. Ramírez & Co.	30,000
Bruno Martínez	10,200
Concepción G. Moreno	19,000
D. and L. P. Peña	32,500
Ygnacio Ramírez	18,500
Jose Ramírez	15,955
Ramón Salinas Flores	12,000
Casimero García	11,600
Donaciano G. García	15,400
Lorenzo García	13,600
Rafael García	10,200
Alejo de la García	34,500
Leandro Gonzales Garza	10,000
Jesús Guerra Gonzales	14,800
Francisco Peña y Peña Guerra	11,000
Manuel Guerra	50,537
Felipe Guerra Hinojosa	53,816
Julián Guerra Hinojosa	12,700
Juárez Francisco Peña	13,260
Lazaro López	27,700
Martínez & Bros	33,733
Luis Martínez	46,171
Julián G. de Montalbo	24,908
Eduardo Villarreal	50,800
José María García Villarreal	23,600
Enrique Vizcaya	44,000
Martina Yzaguirre	12,000

See the Corpus Christi *Weekly Caller*, November 27, 1891, p. 7, and October 7, 1883, p. 2. In 1883, Macedonio Vela of Hidalgo County paid taxes on property worth $19,069.

Of approximately 100 people in Nueces County paying taxes in 1891 on property worth over $10,000, the following had Spanish surnames:

José Acebo	$10,225
Luciano Bazán	15,301
Antonio Cadena	19,220
Andrés Canales	30,686

Albino Canales	44,428
Alejandro Gonzales	38,012
Zeferino de Leal Moreno	11,152
Ramón Moreno	13,217
Anacieto Moreno	10,087
Abrán Pérez	14,072
Francisco Ramírez	12,985
T. P. Rivera	14,250
Dimingo Rotge	16,290
José María Treviño	22,869
Crisanto Vela	21,187
Porfirio Zamora	14,145

Of about twenty-four nonresidents, the following were Mexicanos:

Anastacio Pérez	$18,322
Manuel Pérez	16,522
Jesús Yzaguirre & Bros	31,500
Manuel G. Canales	24,505

See the Corpus Christi *Weekly Caller*, August 22, 1891, p. 1; September 19, 1886, p. 4; March 15, 1885, p. 3.

Of approximately sixty names of people in Brownsville in 1894 whose property was assessed at $5,000 and upwards, the following were Tejanos:

Manuel Alonzo	$12,070
Manuel Barrera	5,755
Mrs. Julia P. de Beastero	11,020
estate María Josefa Cavazos	48,625
Simón Celaya	26,745
Andreas Cuero	7,230
Miguel Fernández	19,360
Juan H. Fernández	14,729
Gerónimo Fernández	6,400
Victoriano Fernández	5,625
Caledonia Garza	5,868
Augustus Miralles	11,000
Feliciano San Román	11,755
Manuel Treviño	11,000
Yndalencio Treviño	5,000
Antonio Ysnaga and wife	10,079
Francisco Yturri	16,578
Francisco Yturri and others	8,029

See the San Antonio *Express*, May 28, 1894, p. 6. For Cameron County, see also the Corpus Christi *Weekly Caller*, October 7, 1883, p.2.

The following Spanish surnames were listed among approximately 115 people in El Paso who paid taxes on property worth over $5,000 in 1883:

Guadalupe Alarcón	$6,500
Bacca Alarcón	7,500
Francisco Ochoa	8,500
Inocente Ochoa	18,580
A. Marquis	6,000

See the El Paso *Herald*, September 30, 1883, p. 4.

109. Albert Camarillo, *Chicanos in a Changing Society: From Mexican Pueblos to American Barrios in Santa Barbara and Southern California, 1848–1930* (Cambridge: Harvard University Press, 1979); Richard Griswold del Castillo, "Myth

and Reality: Chicano Economic Mobility in Los Angeles, 1850–1880," *Aztlán: International Journal of Chicano Studies Research* VI (Summer 1975): 151–73; Griswold del Castillo, "Tuconenses and Angeleños: A Socio-Economic Study of Two Mexican American Barrios, 1860–1880," *Journal of the West* XVIII (1979): 58–66; Ricardo Romo, "The Urbanization of Southwestern Chicanos in the Early Twentieth Century," *New Scholar* VI (1977): 183–208; and, Mario Barrera, *Race and Class in the Southwest: A Theory of Racial Inequality* (Notre Dame: University of Notre Dame Press, 1979).

110. Alwyn Barr, "Occupation and Geographic Mobility in San Antonio, 1870–1900," *Social Science Quarterly* LI (September 1970): 396–403; Griswold del Castillo, "Myth and Reality," pp. 151–72.

Chapter 5

1. For an excellent piece of literature of these types of edifices, see Willard B. Robinson, "Colonial Ranch Architecture in Spanish-Mexican Tradition," *Southwestern Historical Quarterly* LXXXIII (October 1979): 123–50.

2. Lundy, *Life, Travels, and Opinions of Benjamin Lundy*, p. 48; J. C. Clopper, "Journal of J. C. Clopper," *Quarterly of the Texas State Historical Association* XIII (July 1909): 70; Hobart Huson, ed., *Dr. J. H. Barnard's Journal, December 1835 to June 1836* (Goliad: n.p., 1950), pp. 9–10; Taylor, *The Coming Empire*, p. 124; Alexander Sweet and Armoy Knox, *Sketches from Texas Siftings* (New York: Texas Siftings Publishing Co., 1882), p. 57; Alexander Sweet and Armoy Knox, *On a Mexican Mustang* (New York: J. S. Ogilvie Publishing Co., 1883), p. 171; William Seaton Henry, *Campaign Sketches of the War with Mexico* (New York: Arno Press, 1973), p. 24; Julia Nott Waugh, *Castroville and Henry Castro, Empresario* (San Antonio: Standard Printing Co., 1934), p. 92; W. Eugene Hollon and Ruth Lapham Butler, eds., *William Bollaert's Texas* (Norman: University of Oklahoma Press, 1956), p. 217; Smith, *Life and Times of George Foster Pierce*, p. 376; Harby, "Texan Types and Contrasts," pp. 236, 244; William John Knox, "The Economic Status of the Mexican Immigrant in San Antonio, Texas" (M.A. thesis, University of Texas at Austin, 1927), pp. 3–4; San Antonio *Express*, February 21, 1886, p. 15; Diary of William Russell Story (Eugene C. Barker Texas History Center, University of Texas, Austin), pp. 25–26; Lydia Van Wyke to Margaret Van Dyke, January 30, 1874, Lydia Van Wyke Letter (Eugene C. Barker Texas History Center, University of Texas, Austin); and "W. Steinert's View of Texas in 1849," ed. and trans. by Gilbert J. Jordan, *Southwestern Historical Quarterly* LXXX (October 1976): 200.

3. Albert Curtis, *Fabulous San Antonio* (San Antonio: Naylor Press, 1955), p. 272; Page, *Prairiedom: Rambles and Scrambles in Texas or New Estremadura*, p. 127; Tilley, ed., *Federals on the Frontier*, p. 254.

4. Philip Graham, ed., *Sidney Lanier: Florida and Miscellaneous Prose*, VI of Collective Works (Baltimore: The Johns Hopkins Press, 1945), 240; Sweet and Knox, *Sketches from Texas Siftings*, p. 57; Lundy, *Life, Travels, and Opinions of Benjamin Lundy*, p. 48; Taylor *The Coming Empire*, p. 124; "Journal of J. C. Clopper," p. 70; "W. Steinert's View of Texas in 1849," ed. and trans. by Jordan, p. 200; Diary of William Russell Story, p. 25; and Knox, "Economic Status of the Mexican Immigrant," pp. 3–4.

5. Harby, "Texan Types and Contrasts," pp. 244, 235–36.

6. Sweet and Knox, *On a Mexican Mustang*, pp. 171–72; Lundy, *Life, Travels, and Opinions of Benjamin Lundy*, p. 48; Taylor, *The Coming Empire*, p. 124;

Olmsted, *Journey Through Texas*, p. 160; Spofford, "San Antonio de Béxar," p. 838; and Knox, "Economic Status of the Mexican Immigrant," pp. 3–4.

7. Sweet and Knox, *Sketches from Texas Siftings*, p. 57; Taylor, *The Coming Empire*, p. 124; Olmsted, *Journey Through Texas*, p. 160; Harby, "Texan Types and Contrasts," p. 236; and Emilia Schunior Ramírez, *Ranch Life in Hidalgo County after 1850* (Edinburg: New Santander Press, 1971), not numbered.

8. Mrs. William L. Cazneau (Cora Montgomery), *Eagle Pass: Or, Life on the Border* (Austin: Pemberton Press, 1966), pp. 56–57; "Journal of J. C. Clopper," p. 74; Olmsted, *Journey Through Texas*, p. 160; Taylor, *The Coming Empire*, p. 124; Sweet and Knox, *Sketches of Texas Siftings*, p. 57; Tilley, ed., *Federals on the Frontier*, p. 254; Harby, "Texan Types and Contrasts," p. 236. Homes of Anglos, built under the same circumstances, resembled these abodes in every fashion. See "W. Steinert's View of Texas in 1849," ed. and trans. by Jordan, p. 200.

9. Taylor, *The Coming Empire*, p. 124; Knox, "Economic Status of the Mexican Immigrant," pp. 3–4.

10. "Journal of J. C. Clopper," p. 73; Seth Eastman, *A Seth Eastman Sketchbook, 1848–1849* (Austin: University of Texas Press, 1961), p. xxii; Taylor, *The Coming Empire*, p. 124; Spofford, "San Antonio de Béxar," p. 838.

11. Olmsted, *Journey Through Texas*, p. 160; Sweet and Knox, *Sketches from Texas Siftings*, p. 57.

12. This observation is based on an informal count of advertisements of lithographs for sale in newspapers. See also, Corpus Christi *Weekly Caller*, December 28, 1884, p. 4.

13. Henry, *Campaign Sketches of the War with Mexico*, p. 65; Olmsted, *Journey Through Texas*, p. 160; Sweet and Knox, *Sketches from Texas Siftings*, p. 57; Harby, "Texan Types and Contrasts," p. 236.

14. Ferdinand Roemer, *Texas: With Particular Reference to German Immigration*, trans. by Oswald Mueller (Waco: Texian Press, 1967), p. 120; King and Champney, *Texas, 1874*, p. 111; Spofford, "San Antonio de Béxar," p. 838.

15. Carland Elaine Crook, "San Antonio, Texas, 1846–1861" (M.A. thesis, Rice University, 1964), p. 2.

16. Francis Latham, *Travels in the Republic of Texas* (Austin: Encino Press, 1971), p. 36; Eastman, *A Seth Eastman Sketchbook*, p. xxii; Spofford, "San Antonio de Bexar," p. 836.

17. Graham, ed., *Sidney Lanier*, VI of Collective Works, p. 241.

18. Jennie Parks Ringgold, *Frontier Days in the Southwest* (San Antonio: The Naylor Co., 1952), p. 9; "Adobe: Past and Present," *El Palacio* LXXVII, No. 4; and *Adobe Notes, or How to Keep the Weather Out With Just Plain Mud* (Taos: The Laughing Horse Press, 1930).

19. Herman Ehrenberg, *With Milam and Fannin* (Austin: The Pemberton Press, 1968), p. 73; and Latham, *Travels in the Republic of Texas*, p. 36.

20. Bartlett, *Personal Narrative of Exploration and Incidents in Texas, New Mexico, California, Sonora, and Chihuahua*, I, pp. 188–90; Henry B. Dielmann, "Emma Altgelt's Sketches of Life in Texas," *Southwestern Historical Quarterly* LXIII (January 1960): 368; and Vielé, *"Following the Drum,"* p. 104.

21. Hammond and Howes, eds., *Overland to California on the Southwestern Trail, 1849*, p. 132; and San Antonio *Express*, February 16, 1883, p. 2.

22. García, *"Obreros,"* pp. 223–24; Rudolf Eickemeyer, *Letters from the Southwest* (Astor Place, New York: J. J. Little and Co., 1894), p. 15.

23. Tom Lea, *The King Ranch* (2 vols; Boston: Little, Brown, and Co., 1957), I: 119.

24. R. W. Johnson, *A Soldier's Reminiscences in Peace and War* (Philadelphia: Lippincott, 1886), p. 68.

25. Raht, *The Romance of Davis Mountains and Big Bend Country*, p. 130; and Wright, *San Antonio de Béxar: Historical, Traditional, Legendary*, p. 106.

26. Raht, *Romance of Davis Mountains*, pp. 217, 256.

27. Cazneau, *Eagle Pass*, pp. 92–93. For cases of a similar nature in western Texas, see Ringgold, *Frontier Days*, pp. 10–11.

28. T. R. Fehrenbach, *Lone Star: A History of Texas and the Texans* (New York: The Macmillan Company, 1968), p. 633.

29. Eugene D. Genovese, *Roll, Jordan, Roll: The World the Slaves Made* (New York: Vintage Books, 1976), p. 526.

30. Graham, ed., *Sidney Lanier: Florida and Miscellaneous Prose*, p. 241; King and Champney, *Texas, 1874*, Gray, ed., p. 110.

31. Juan Almonte, "Statistical Report on Texas," trans. by Carlos E. Castañeda, *Southwestern Historical Quarterly* XXVIII (January 1925): 197.

32. Waugh, *Castroville and Henry Castro*, p. 91; and, Dielmann, "Emma Altgelt's Sketches of Life in Texas," p. 368.

33. Taylor, *The Coming Empire*, p. 125.

34. "To California Through Texas and Mexico: The Diary and Letters of Thomas B. Eastland and Joseph G. Eastland, His Son," (foreword by Douglas S. Watson, Notes by Dorothy H. Huggins), *California Historical Society Quarterly* XVIII (June 1939): 121; and Bartlett, *Personal Narrative*, pp. 190–91. According to William M. Pierson, the U. S. Vice Consul in El Paso del Norte (Ciudad Juárez), writing in 1873:

> "Each and every family [in this district] grows red pepper extensively and although spoken of as a relish, yet, it enters largely into every dish on their tables, except coffee, it is cooked, stewed, and eaten here in like manner as the Kirshaw in the North. And while this extraordinary and fiery dish, is by the Mexicans, eaten with great ease and extreme pleasure; it would transform the mouth of an American into a fiery furnace and his eyes into flowing springs of boiling hot water. This spicy dish attracts the careful attention, and curious inquiry of the tourist, and calls forth sharp raids of ink from the humorists. By the latter I have been informed that 'when this peculiar people journey across the desert plains, each cart has its two or three large bags of red pepper, and that when they camp and commence the fiery ordeal of preparing their favorite and frugal meals, that, the vicious tarantula scuds from its call, while the venemous rattle snake rushes from his hole, and both in unison flee at the very height of their speed in search of foreign domiciles. Also, that, were you to deprive one of these denisons of the Rio Grande of his favorite red pepper, that, he would consider his balance wheel wrecked, his rudder unshipped, and his crazy hulk in mid ocean beating about by force of adverse winds'."

William M. Pierson to Second Assistant Secretary of State, Paso del Norte, Mexico, March 11, 1873, in Despatches from United States Consuls in Ciudad Juárez (Paso del Norte), 1850–1906; Roll 2 and despatches January 16, 1871 to December 31, 1884.

35. Reverend P. F. Parisot, *The Reminiscences of a Texas Missionary* (San Antonio: Johnson Bros. Printing Co., 1899), p. 38.

36. Tilley, ed., *Federals on the Frontier*, p. 262.

37. George Wilkins Kendall, *Narrative of the Texas Santa Fe Expedition* (2 volumes; Austin: The Steck Co., 1935), II: 31; and Mary Jaques, *Texan Ranch Life, With Three Months Through Mexico in a "Prairie Schooner"* (London: Horace Cox, 1894), p. 40.

38. Roy Holt, "Frijoles," in *Texian Stomping Grounds*, ed. by J. Frank Dobie, Mody C. Boatright, and Harry H. Ransom (Dallas: Southern Methodist University Press, 1967), p. 52.

39. Jaques, *Texan Ranch Life*, pp. 41–42; "Journal of J. C. Clopper," p. 74; Parisot, *Reminiscences of a Texas Missionary*, p. 38; Ehrenberg, *With Milam and Fannin*, p. 192; and, Ruth Dodson, *"Tortilla* Making," in *In the Shadow of History*, ed. J. Frank Dobie, et al., Vol. XV of Publications of the Texas Folklore Society (Hatboro, Penn.: Folklore Associates, Inc., 1966), pp. 137–41.

40. George A. McCall, *Letters from the Frontier* (Philadelphia: J. B. Lippincott, 1868), p. 436.

41. Elena Zamora O'Shea, *El Mesquite: A Story of the Early Spanish Settlements Between the Nueces and the Rio Grande as Told by "La Posta del Palo Alto"* (Dallas: Mathis Publishing Co., 1935), pages not numbered.

42. San Antonio *Express*, October 30, 1881, p. 1.

43. O'Shea, *El Mesquite*, pages not numbered.

44. José María Sánchez, "A Trip to Texas, 1828," (trans. by Carlos E. Castañeda), *Southwestern Historical Quarterly* XXIX (April 1926): 251; Stephen Powers, *Afoot and Alone: A Walk from Sea to Sea by the Southern Route. . . .* (Hartford: Columbia Book Company, 1886), p. 165; "To California Through Texas and Mexico," p. 127; Smith, *Life of George F. Pierce*, p. 395; and, O'Shea, *El Mesquite*, pages not numbered.

45. Adeline Short Dinger, *Folk Life and Folklore of the Mexican Border* (Edinburg, Texas: Hidalgo County Historical Society, 1974), p. 33.

46. O'Shea, *El Mesquite*.

47. Lela Neale Pirtle, ed., *Life on the Range and on the Trail: As Told by R. J. (Bob) Lauderdale and John M. Doak* (San Antonio: The Naylor Company, 1936), pp. 51–52; Ramírez, *Ranch Life in Hidalgo County;* Harby, "Texan Types and Contrasts," p. 242; Del Weniger, *Cacti of the Southwest: Texas, New Mexico, Oklahoma, Arkansas, and Louisiana* (Austin: University of Texas Press, 1969), pp. 168–71; and, Donald Culross Peattie, *A Natural History of Western Trees* (Boston: Houghton Mifflin, 1953), pp. 643–50.

48. Ramírez, *Ranch Life in Hidalgo County;* "To California Through Texas and Mexico," p. 127; Smith, *Life of George F. Pierce*, p. 395; and, Powers, *Afoot and Alone*, p. 165.

49. Pirtle, ed., *Life on the Range and on the Trail*, pp. 50–52.

50. Hollon and Butler, eds., *William Bollaert's Texas*, p. 219.

51. Susan Miller, *Sixty Years in the Nueces Valley* (San Antonio: The Naylor Co., 1930), p. 15.

52. Jaques, *Texan Ranch Life*, pp. 40–42.

53. Ramírez, *Ranch Life in Hidalgo County*.

54. Jaques, *Texan Ranch Life*, pp. 40–42; Ramírez, *Ranch Life in Hidalgo County*. Reporting on the method Mexicanos employed to slaughter beef, a cowboy wrote in 1854:

> "It would astonish a regular bred butcher to see with what dispatch three Mexicans can rope, kill, and have a beef cut into ropes. The beef is first thrown down by means of rope then stuck, not struck on the head. The_

head is turned to one side which holds the beef in the proper position, one side is skinned, the skinned side is allowed to turn up—half of the beef is dissected, the entrails then taken out, the ribs are left whole and roasted before the fire, the other half and head is made into ropes and exposed on a line in the sun until jerked."

James G. Bell, "The Log of the Texas-California Cattle Drive, 1854," *Southwestern Historical Quarterly* XXXV (January 1932): 212.

Carne seca, also called *charqui*, or *tasajo*, provided Mexicanos with a convenient source of meat during migrations and hard times. Salting and slicing it into collops and hanging it up until thoroughly cured allowed for its preservation. Oxen that died or stock killed while traveling could be butchered, cut into small strips, attached to the outside of the vehicle, and exposed to the sun for curing. See Sweet and Knox, *On a Mexican Mustang*, p. 173; John C. Reid, *Reid's Tramp or a Journal of the Incidents of Ten Months Travel Through Texas, New Mexico, Arizona, Sonora, California. . . .* (Selma, Alabama: John Hardt and Co., 1858), p. 41; Robert G. Carter, *On the Border With MacKenzie: or, Winning West Texas from the Comanches* (Washington: Eynon Printing Co. Inc., 1935), p. 284; Vielé, "*Following the Drum*," p. 148; Rena Maverick Green, ed., *Memoirs of Mary A. Maverick* (San Antonio: Alamo Printing Co., 1921), p. 52; San Antonio *Express*, September 18, 1880, p. 2; Ramírez, *Ranch Life in Hidalgo County*; and Edward N. Wentworth, "Dried Meat: Early Man's Travel Ration," *Agricultural History* XXX (January 1956): 3–10.

55. Mary A. Sutherland, *The Story of Corpus Christi* (Corpus Christi: Corpus Christi Chapter of Daughters of the Confederacy, 1961), p. 84; Jaques, *Texan Ranch Life*, p. 42; Sweet and Knox, *On a Mexican Mustang*, pp. 173–74; Miller, *Sixty Years in the Nueces Valley*, p. 105.

56. Sutherland, *Story of Corpus Christi*, p. 84.

57. Parisot, *Reminiscences of a Texas Missionary*, p. 38; New Orleans *Bee*, November 5, 1834, p. 2; San Antonio *Express*, June 24, 1888, p. 3; Harby, "Texan Types and Contrasts," p. 238.

58. Ramírez, *Ranch Life in Hidalgo County*; and, O'Shea, *El Mesquite*. On this topic, see also W. D. Smithers, "Nature's Pharmacy and the *Curanderos*," *West Texas Historical and Scientific Society Publications* XVIII (1961): 15–39.

59. Pirtle, ed., *Life on the Range and on the Trail*, pp. 50–52.

60. Lundy, *Life, Travels, and Opinions of Benjamin Lundy*, p. 95; Pirtle, ed., *Life on the Range and on the Trail*, pp. 50–52; Albert D. Richardson, *Beyond the Mississippi: From the Great River to the Great Ocean . . . .1857–1867* (New York: American Publishing Co., 1867), pp. 231–32.

61. Ramírez, *Ranch Life in Hidalgo County*.

62. Olmsted, *Journey Through Texas*, p. 161.

63. Sutherland, *Story of Corpus Christi*, p. 84. For similar reports, see Vielé, "*Following the Drum*," p. 104; and Sweet and Knox, *On a Mexican Mustang*, p. 172.

64. Bernard Doyon, *Cavalry of Christ on the Rio Grande: 1849–1883* (Milwaukee: Bruce, 1956), pp. 132–33.

65. Spofford, "San Antonio de Béxar," pp. 836–37.

66. Sutherland, *Story of Corpus Christi*, p. 83.

67. Vielé, "*Following the Drum*," pp. 154–55.

68. Graham, ed., *Sidney Lanier*, VI of Collective Works, p. 240; San Antonio *Herald*, March 28, 1866, p. 2; Diary of William Russell Story, p. 26.

69. Smithwick, *The Evolution of a State*, pp. 47–48.

70. Hammond and Howes, eds., *Overland to California on the Southwestern Trail, 1849*, p. 137.

71. Taylor, *The Coming Empire*, p. 126.

72. Ramírez, *Ranch Life in Hidalgo County*.

73. W. H. Chatfield, *The Twin Cities of the Border: Brownsville, Texas, and Matamoros, Mexico* (New Orleans: E. P. Brandao, 1893), p. 30. The 1900 federal census for Cameron County shows that indeed many Tejanas made their living doing Mexican drawn work. *Twelfth Census of the U.S., 1900*, Roll #1617, Cameron County.

74. Ramírez, *Ranch Life in Hidalgo County*.

75. Nannie Emory Holding, *A Decade of Mission Life in Mexican Mission Homes* (Nashville: Publishing House Methodist Episcopal Church, 1895), p. 47.

76. For the current debate over the status of the Mexican American family, and especially an overview discrediting old views of that family, see Michael V. Miller, "Variations in Mexican American Family Life: A Review Synthesis of Empirical Research," *Aztlán: International Journal of Chicano Studies and the Arts* (Spring 1977): 209–31; see further, Maxine Baca Zinn, "Chicano Family Research: Conceptual Distortions and Alternative Directions," *The Journal of Ethnic Studies* VII (Fall 1979): 59–72.

77. Hammond and Howes, eds., *Overland to California on the Southwestern Trail, 1849*, pp. 132–33. For a general treatment of fashions that touches on the dress of Mexicanos, see Billie Mae Persons, "Clothing in Texas, 1821–1860" (M.A. thesis, University of Texas, 1956), pp. 126–37.

78. Bartlett, *Personal Narrative of Explorations and Incidents*, I, p. 192.

79. Tijerina, "Tejanos and Texas," p. *vi;* William Wright, *Recollections of Western Texas* (London: W. and F. G. Cash, 1857), p. 32; and, Miller, *Sixty Years in the Nueces Valley*, p. 15.

80. Wright, *Recollections of Western Texas*, p. 32; Olmsted, *Journey Through Texas*, p. 162; Hammond and Howes, eds., *Overland to California on the Southwestern Trail, 1849*, pp. 132–33; Miller, *Sixty Years in the Nueces Valley*, p. 15.

81. Bartlett, *Personal Narrative of Explorations and Incidents*, I, p. 192; Miller, *Sixty Years in the Nueces Valley*, p. 15; Letter of Lydia Van Wyke, January 30, 1874; Harby, "Texan Types and Contrasts," p. 242; Persons, "Clothing in Texas, 1821–1860," p. 128; Corpus Christi *Weekly Caller*, November 7, 1891, p. 8.

82. Wright, *Recollections of Western Texas*, p. 32.

83. Hammond and Howes, eds., *Overland to California on the Southwestern Trail, 1849*, pp. 132–33; Lydia Van Wyke letter, January 30, 1874.

84. Tilley, ed., *Federals on the Frontier*, p. 261.

85. Hollon and Butler, eds., *William Bollaert's Texas*, p. 218.

86. Taylor, *The Coming Empire*, p. 125.

87. Tijerina, "Tejanos and Texas," pp. 286–88.

88. Vielé, *"Following the Drum,"* p. 158; Chatfield, *The Twin Cities*, p. 29.

89. H. H. McConnell, *Five Years a Cavalryman, or Sketches of Regular Army Life on the Texas Frontier* (Jacksboro, Texas: J. N. Roberts Co., 1889), p. 34.

90. Andrew Forest Muir, ed., *Texas in 1837: An Anonymous Contemporary Narrative* (Austin: University of Texas Press, 1958), p. 102.

91. As to the vulgar side, Tejano vocabulary included those pornographic idioms found in languages elsewhere. The word *huevos,* as today, connoted sexuality—testicles. An itinerant warned visitors: "When buying eggs, use the word *blanchillos* [sic] instead of the Spanish *'huevos'* which would be considered as great a solecism as speaking of a cock to a Texan, instead of 'rooster'." Jaques, *Texan Ranch Life*, p. 262. In an episode printed in the San Antonio *Express* of April 17, 1888, a

drunken Alfredo Valdez resisted Deputy Sheriff's Stevan Sandoval's attempts at arrest by intimidating the policeman with a razor and bellowing defiantly, "Ningún cavrón hijo de un chingado me lleva."

92. The literature on nineteenth century Tejano language is practically nonexistent. The exhaustive bibliography *Spanish and English of United States Hispanos: A Critical Annotated, Linguistic Bibliography* (Arlington, Virginia: Center for Applied Linguistics, 1975), by Richard V. Teschner, et al., and its supplement "Current Research on the Language of United States Hispanos," *Hispania* XL (May 1977): 347–58, make virtually no mention of such studies. Instead, most work done by linguists concentrates on twentieth century language patterns and more specifically on bilingualism, particularly for the period beginning in the 1960s. The more recent and pertinent work by Professor Roberto A. Galván, *El Diccionario del Español Chicano* (Silver Springs, Md: Institute of Modern Languages, Inc., 1977), also does not study the Tejano language of the nineteenth century.

A couple of reasons explain this paucity. First, nineteenth century Tejanos did not leave a vast body of written material that might make itself available for scrutiny. And even an analysis of the Spanish language press, for example, would net the results of a formal Spanish and not the everyday vernacular of the common man. Second, the study of Mexican American language is a new field that has not yet turned its attention to the last century. As a result the extant literature on contemporary language does not match the sophistication that would allow the historian of the Mexican American people to write an essay comparable to Professor Eugene Genovese's "The Language of Class and Nation" in *Roll, Jordan, Roll: The World the Slaves Made* (New York: Pantheon Book; 1974), pp. 431–41. Until such a lacuna is filled, this aspect of the nineteenth century Tejano community cannot be capably treated.

Chapter 6

1. José Roberto Juárez, "La Iglesia Católica y el Chicano de Sud Texas, 1836–1911," *Aztlán: Chicano Journal of the Social Sciences and the Arts* IV (Fall 1973): 217–55.

2. Anita Brenner, *Idols Behind the Altars* (New York: Biblo and Tannen, 1967); Frank Tannenbaum, *Mexico: The Struggle for Peace and Bread* (New York: Alfred A. Knopf, 1964), pp. 123–24; and Robert E. Quirk, *The Mexican Revolution and the Catholic Church, 1910–1929* (Bloomington: Indiana University Press, 1973), pp. 3–8.

3. The religion herein analyzed is the nominal Catholicism discussed in Alwyn Stoddard's *Mexican Americans* (New York: Random House, 1973), pp. 89–90. According to recent studies cited by Stoddard, the religion of Mexicans in Mexico falls under the following typology: a) formal Catholicism—that which requires "an adequate knowledge of Church dogma, ritual, and proscriptions"; b) nominal Catholicism—that which demands "an identification with, and an allegiance to the Catholic Church but only perfunctorily"; c) cultural Catholicism—"a nonspiritual affiliation with the Church"; and, d) folk Catholicism—that "practiced outside the formal scope of the Catholic Church." According to Stoddard, Mexican Americans and Mexicans in Mexico today are nominal Catholics. See also Albert Carrillo, "The Sociological Failure of the Catholic Church Toward the Chicano," *Journal of Mexican American Studies* I (Winter 1971): 75–83.

No doubt, such beliefs are an extension of nineteenth century practices. In fact, a comparison between the religious views and traditions of Mexicans in Mexico and those in Texas at that time reveals many an affinity between the two beliefs.

Both people accepted the miracle of the Virgen de Guadalupe, worshipped the numerous saints and held *fiestas* in the saints' honor, respected Catholic tradition, yet slighted part of its dogma, ritual, and proscriptions. Indeed, Frederick A. Ober, who travelled in Mexico in the 1880s, portrayed the Mexican population as "nominally Catholic" and presented a description of a religion not much unlike that of the nineteenth century Tejanos. See Frederick A. Ober, *Travels in Mexico and Life Among the Mexicans* (Boston: Estes and Lauriat, 1883), pp. 291–304. Other observers at different times stated much the same thing. See, for example, Fanny Calderón de la Barca, *Life in Mexico During a Residence of Two Years in that Country* (New York: E. P. Dutton and Co., Inc., 1946), pp. 129–30; 132–39; 147–49; 255; 279; 288; 293–95; 353–55; 359–60; 361–66. Also see Robert A. Wilson, *Mexico: Its Peasants and Its Priests* (New York: Harper & Brothers, Publishers, 1856), pp. 192–95; and Mrs. Alec Tweedie, *Mexico As I Saw It* (New York: Thomas Nelson & Sons, 1911), pp. 116–27, 202–15.

Although parts of these accounts come close to describing the folk Catholicism mentioned by Stoddard, they are probably the products of the itinerant's jaundiced eye. Stoddard's own assessment that folk Catholicism is "probably one of the least common of the four types of religious practices" would apply to the nineteenth century. Otherwise, why would the Catholicism of Tejanos be different from that of the mother country? And why would it continue to be unaffected when Mexicans from Mexico supposedly brought that folk Catholicism with them to Texas during the decades under study?

4. John C. Duval, *Early Times in Texas, or Adventures of Jack Dobell* (Dallas: Tardy Publishing Co., 1936), p. 88; Cazneau, *Eagle Pass*, p. 91.

5. Bernard Doyon, *Cavalry of Christ on the Rio Grande: 1849–1883* (Milwaukee: Bruce, 1956), pp. 66, 63n, 133.

6. Juárez, "La Iglesia Católica y el Chicano de Sud Texas," p. 238.

7. Doyon, *Cavalry of Christ on the Rio Grande*, pp. 66, 63n, 113.

8. Juárez, "La Iglesia Católica y el Chicano de Sud Texas," pp. 234–35.

9. Ibid., p. 219.

10. Ibid., p. 248, n.6.

11. Chatfield, *The Twin Cities*, p. 8; Ramírez, *Ranch Life in Hidalgo County After 1850;* Jovita Gonzalez, "Social Life in Cameron, Starr, and Zapata Counties" (M.A. thesis, University of Texas at Austin, 1930), pp. 67–69; Doyon, *Cavalry of Christ on the Rio Grande*, pp. 119–41. See further Corpus Christi *Weekly Caller*, October 31, 1886, p. 4; April 14, 1888, p. 1; August 5, 1892, p. 1; June 31, 1891, p. 8; October 7, 1892, p. 1; September 22, 1893, p. 1; October 20, 1899, p. 4; October 14, 1892, p. 7; and San Antonio *Express*, September 22, 1893, p. 3; September 10, 1885, p. 1.

12. William E. Connelley, *Doniphan's Expedition and the Conquest of New Mexico and California* (Kansas City: Bryant and Douglas Book and Stationery Company, 1907), p. 96.

13. Juárez, "La Iglesia Católica y el Chicano de Sud Texas," p. 248, n.6.

14. Wright, *San Antonio de Béxar*, pp. 132–34. Crosses marking lonely roads where unfortunate victims had met their death symbolized another aspect of Tejano Catholic tradition. See Smith, *The Life and Times of George Foster Pierce*, p. 378.

15. Herman Ehrenberg, *With Milam and Fannin: Adventures of a German Boy in Texas' Revolution* (Austin: The Pemberton Press, 1968), p. 101.

16. Taylor, *The Coming Empire*, p. 126.

17. Harry Hansen, ed., *Texas: A Guide to the Lone Star State* (revised edition; New York: Hastings House, 1969), p. 96.

18. Pearson Newcomb, *The Alamo City* (San Antonio: Standard Printing Co., 1926), p. 54.

19. Pearl Couser Wright, "Religious Fiestas in San Antonio" (M.A. thesis, St. Mary's University, 1946), pp. 36–42, as cited in Fane Downs, "History of Mexicans in Texas, 1821–1845," pp. 124–25; Corpus Christi *Ranchero*, April 23, 1863, p. 2.

20. Newcomb, *The Alamo City*, p. 54.

21. Hansen, ed., *Texas: Guide to the Lone Star State*, p. 96; Charles August Arnold, *The Folklore, Manners, and Customs of the Mexicans in San Antonio, Texas* (San Francisco: R & E Research Associates, 1971), p. 20; Gonzalez, "Social Life in Cameron, Starr, and Zapata Counties," pp. 54–55; Ramírez, *Ranch Life in Hidalgo County*.

22. San Antonio *Express*, July 1, 1895, p. 3; July 2, 1893, p. 3; Corpus Christi *Weekly Caller*, June 29, 1884, p. 1; July 2, 1887, p. 8; June 27, 1886, p. 4; June 25, 1887, p. 8; June 30, 1899, p. 1.

23. San Antonio *Express*, August 3, 1876, p. 4.

24. Ibid., May 6, 1888, p. 5; Barnes, *Combats and Conquests of Immortal Heroes*, p. 121; Gonzalez, "Social Life in Cameron, Starr, and Zapata Counties," pp. 54–55; Adeline Dinger, *Folk Life and Folklore of the Mexican Border* (Edinburg: Hidalgo County Historical Museum, 1972), pp. 33–34; J. Frank Dobie, *A Vaquero of the Brush Country* (Dallas: The Southwest Press, 1929), p. 19.

25. Corpus Christi *Weekly Caller*, August 8, 1886, p. 4; San Antonio *Express*, July 27, 1888, p. 3; July 28, 1888, p. 7.

26. "W. Steinert's View of Texas in 1849," trans. and ed. by Jordan, p. 401.

27. Corpus Christi *Weekly Caller*, September 12, 1886, p. 4.

28. Vielé, *"Following the Drum,"* p. 161.

29. Rena Maverick Green, ed., *Samuel Maverick, Texan: 1803–1870* (San Antonio: privately printed, 1952), p. 34; Chatfield, *Twin Cities*, p. 30; Arnold, *Folklore, Manners, and Customs of Mexicans in San Antonio, Texas*, p. 21; Dinger, *Folk Life and Folklore of the Mexican Border*, p. 44.

30. Newcomb, *The Alamo City*, p. 54.

31. Rena Maverick Green, ed., *Memoirs of Mary A. Maverick* (San Antonio: Alamo Printing Co., 1921), pp. 53–54; Wright, *San Antonio de Béxar*, p. 98; Arnold, *Folklore, Manners, and Customs of Mexicans in San Antonio*, p. 21.

32. El Paso *Times*, December 9, 1884, p. 4.

33. Chatfield, *Twin Cities*, p. 30; Mary A. Sutherland, *The Story of Corpus Christi*, ed. by Frank B. Harrison (Corpus Christi: Corpus Christi Chapter of the Daughters of the Confederacy, 1916), pp. 48–49; Hansen, ed., *Texas: A Guide to the Lone Star State*, pp. 94–95; Newcomb, *The Alamo City*, pp. 56–58; Arnold, *Folklore, Manners, and Customs of Mexicans in San Antonio*, pp. 22–24; Lota M. Spell, *Music in Texas: A Survey of one Aspect of Cultural Progress* (Austin: n. p., 1936), p. 20; San Antonio *Express*, December 25, 1890, p. 3; January 10, 1893, p. 6; Corpus Christi *Weekly Caller*, January 13, 1893, p. 6; and see especially San Antonio *Express*, January 7, 1894, p. 9, and January 10, 1888, p. 3. For an interpretation of the play, see Helen W. Barsun, "Los Pastores: A Remnant of Medieval Drama in San Antonio" (M.A. thesis, St. Mary's University, 1943).

34. Hansen, ed., *Texas: A Guide to the Lone Star State*, p. 94; Newcomb, *The Alamo City*, pp. 58–59; Arnold, *Folklore, Manners, and Customs of Mexicans in San Antonio, Texas*, pp. 22–24; Dinger, *Folk Life and Folklore of the Mexican Border*, p. 44; Spell, *Music in Texas*, pp. 17–20. See also, Barsun, "Los Pastores: A Remnant of Medieval Drama."

35. Hansen, ed., *Texas: Guide to the Lone Star State*, p. 95; Gonzalez, "Social Life in Cameron, Starr, and Zapata Counties," p. 55.

36. Hansen, ed., *Texas: A Guide to the Lone Star State*.

37. El Paso *Herald*, July 22, 1883, p.4.

38. San Antonio *Herald*, June 11, 1872, p. 4; October 17, 1872, pp. 2, 3; October 7, 1873, p. 3.

39. Corpus Christi *Weekly Caller*, October 21, 1892, p. 1; October 28, 1892, p. 7.

40. William F. Gray, *From Virginia to Texas. . . .* (Houston: Fletcher Young Publishing Co., 1965), pp. 97–98. Emphasis are Gray's. See also Cecil Robinson, *With the Ears of Stangers: The Mexican in American Literature* (Tucson: University of Arizona Press, 1963), pp. 94–99.

41. Sweet and Knox, *On a Mexican Mustang*, p. 181.

42. Harby, "Texas Types and Contrasts," p. 244.

43. Corpus Christi *Weekly Caller*, June 3, 1898, p. 1; June 17, 1888, p. 1.

44. H. C. Arbuckle III, "Don José and Don Pedrito," in Francis Edward Abernethy, ed., *The Folklore of Texan Cultures* (Austin: The Encino Press, 1974), p. 84; Corpus Christi *Weekly Caller*, April 4, 1886, p. 4. *Curanderos* have relied heavily on religious paraphernalia, dependence on prayer, and a sublime atmosphere as aids in their craft, and have demanded faith in their powers as prerequisites for treatment. See Ari Kiev, *Curanderismo: Mexican American Folk Psychiatry* (New York: Free Press, 1968); and W. D. Smithers, "Nature's Pharmacy and the *Curanderos*," *West Texas Historical and Scientific Society Publications*, Vol. XVIII: 15–39.

45. Corpus Christi *Ranchero*, January 12, 1861, p. 2; January 19, 1861, p. 2; February 9, 1861, p.2.

46. El Paso *Herald*, March 12, 1896, p. 1; June 17, 1896, p. 1; August 25, 1896, p. 1; August 27, 1896, p. 4; September 8, 1896, p. 1; September 23, 1896, p. 1; San Antonio *Express*, March 16, 1896, p. 4; August 14, 1896, p. 8; August 30, 1896, p. 15; September 4, 1896, p. 3; September 12, 1896, p. 14; January 13, 1897, p. 5; El Paso *Times*, June 14, 1896, p. 3; June 18, 1896, p. 3; June 20, 1896, p. 3; June 21, 1896, p. 3; June 23, 1896, p. 3; June 27, 1896, p. 3; July 11, 1896, p. 3; July 26, 1896, p. 3; August 14, 1896, p. 3; August 15, 1896, pp. 3, 4; August 16, 1896, p. 3.

The two most recent biographies of Teresita are William Curry Holden, *Teresita* (Owings Mill: Stemmer House Publishers, Inc., 1978), and Carlos Larralde, "Santa Teresa: A Chicana Mystic," *Grito del Norte* III (April-June, 1978). Although both provide good and interesting material on the life of this *curandera*, neither ventures an incisive explanation as to the workings of *curanderismo*, its meaning, and its significance vis-à-vis the culture of Mexicans and Mexican Americans.

47. Ruth Dodson, "Don Pedrito Jaramillo: The Curandero of Los Olmos," in *The Healer of Los Olmos and other Mexican Lore*, ed. Wilson M. Hudson, vol. XXIV of Publications of the Texas Folklore Society (Dallas: Southern Methodist University, 1951).

48. Corpus Christi *Ranchero*, March 3, 1860, p. 2.

49. William Wallace McCullough, Jr., *John McCullough: Pioneer Presbyterian Missionary and Teacher in the Republic of Texas* (Austin: The Pemberton Press, 1966), pp. 71–73, 81; Crook, "San Antonio, Texas, 1846–1861," pp. 103–4.

50. R. Douglas Breckenridge and Francisco O. García-Treto, *Iglesia Presbiteriana: A History of Presbyterians and Mexican Americans of the Southwest* (San Antonio: Trinity University Press, 1974), p. 11.

51. Warner P. Sutton to Second Assistant Secretary of State, Matamoros, Mexico, January 31, 1880, in Despatches from United States Consuls in Matamoros, 1826–1906: Roll 6 and despatches May 7, 1879 to July 15, 1881.

52. Chatfield, *Twin Cities*, p. 10; San Antonio *Express*, February 25, 1887, p. 2.

53. San Antonio *Herald*, November 3, 1871, p. 3.

54. Ibid., June 9, 1876, p. 3; October 25, 1875, p. 3. Among Methodist working there were the Reverend Crecencio A. Rodríguez, Reverend Manuel Treviño, Reverend Ignacio Sánchez Rivera, Reverend Santiago Tafolla, and Pablo G. Verduzco. The Baptist pastor in the early 1890s was the Reverend M. G. Treviño and in the latter nineties, Rodrigo Cruz and E. R. Robles attended to the Mexican Baptists. *Directory of San Antonio, 1883–1884*, p. 79; *Directory of San Antonio 1885–1886*, p. 45; *Directory of San Antonio, 1889–1890*, pp. 45–46; *Directory of San Antonio, 1891*, pp. 51, 54; *Directory of San Antonio, 1892–1893*, p. 57; *Directory of San Antonio, 1897–1898*, p. 491; *Directory of San Antonio, 1899–1900*, p. 214.

55. San Antonio *Express*, September 19, 1894, p. 6.

56. Corpus Christi *Weekly Caller*, April 27, 1884, p. 5; San Antonio *Herald*, October 25, 1875, p. 3; June 9, 1875, p. 3.

57. Corpus Christi *Weekly Caller*, August 17, 1884, p. 4; San Antonio *Herald*, October 25, 1875, p. 3; San Antonio *Express*, March 16, 1888, p. 3.

58. San Antonio *Express*, February 16, 1886, p. 7.

59. El Paso *Times*, January 27, 1899, p. 6.

60. El Paso *Herald*, August 30, 1892, p. 1.

61. El Paso *Times*, August 27, 1893, p. 7; August 31, 1893, p. 7; September 13, 1893, p. 7.

62. Juárez, "La Iglesia Católica y el Chicano de Sud Texas," p. 242.

63. Stoddard, *Mexican Americans*, pp. 89–90; Carrillo, "Sociological Failure of the Catholic Church Toward the Chicano," pp. 75–83; and Leo Grebler, Joan W. Moore, Ralph Guzmán, *The Mexican American People: The Nation's Second Largest Minority* (New York: The Free Press, 1970), pp. 364–66, 473–77.

Chapter 7

1. Studies concerning the kinship between history and folklore include Arthur L. Campa, "Folklore and History," *Western Folklore* XXIV (January 1965): 1–6; Américo Paredes, "Folklore and History," in *Singers and Storytellers*, ed. Mody C. Boatright, et al., Vol. XXX of Publications of the Texas Folklore Society (Dallas: Southern Methodist University, 1961), pp. 56–68; Richard M. Dorson, ed., *American Folklore and the Historian* (Chicago: The University of Chicago Press, 1971); Richard M. Dorson, ed., *Folklore and Folklife: An Introduction* (Chicago: University of Chicago Press, 1972). J. Mason Brewer in *Worser Days and Better Times* (Chicago: Quadrangle Books, 1965), p. 21, notes: "The folklore of any nation or race is the surest key to its thinking, for folk materials offer a true and unbiased picture of the ways in which a given people in a special locality think and act." For a more recent study of folklore and history, see Lawrence W. Levine, *Black Culture and Black Consciousness: Afro-American Folk Thought from Slavery to Freedom* (Oxford: Oxford University Press, 1977).

2. J. Frank Dobie, "An Inquiry into the Sources of Treasure Legends in Texas," in *Legends of Texas*, ed. J. Frank Dobie, Vol. III of Publications of the Texas Folklore Society (Hatboro, Penn: Folklore Associates, Inc., 1924), pp. 6–9; Dobie, "The Legends of the San Saba or Bowie Mine," ibid., pp. 12–19; Dobie, "Legendary Spanish Forts Down the Nueces," ibid., pp. 43–48; R. E. Sherrill, "Lost Copper Mines and Spanish Gold, Haskell County," ibid., pp. 74–75; J.

Leeper Gay, "The Accursed Gold in the Santa Anna Mountains," ibid., pp. 78–79; Louise von Blittersdorf, "Buried Treasure Legends of Milam County," ibid., pp. 100–101; Jovita Gonzalez, "Folklore of the Texas-Mexican Vaquero," in *Texas and Southwestern Lore*, ed. by J. Frank Dobie, Vol. VI of Publications of the Texas Folklore Society (Austin: Texas Folklore Society, 1927), pp. 14–18; Leon Denny Moses, "Five Legends of the Southwest," in *Tone the Bell Easy*, ed. J. Frank Dobie, Vol. X of the Publications of the Texas Folklore Society (Austin: Texas Folklore Society, 1932), pp. 71–72; Susan G. Miller, *Sixty Years in the Nueces Valley* (San Antonio: Naylor Printing Co., 1930), pp. 84–85; Charles Merritt Barnes, *Combats and Conquests of Immortal Heroes* (San Antonio: Guessaz and Ferlet Co., 1910), pp. 88–91.

Sources with related material include Cleve Hallenbeck and Juanita H. Williams, *Legends of the Southwest* (Glendale: The Arthur H. Clark Company, 1938); Adeline Short Dinger, *Folk Life and Folklore of the Mexican Border* (Edinburg, Texas: Hidalgo County Historical Society, 1974); Miriam Webb Hiester, "Los Paisanos: Folklore of the Texas Mexican of the Lower Rio Grande Valley" (M.A. thesis, University of Texas at Austin, 1954); Juanita Stroud Phillips, "The Spanish Folklore of Texas, No. 1, Cameron County" (M. A. thesis, University of Texas at Austin, 1950); and María del Refugio González, "The Spanish Folklore of Webb and Zapata Counties" (M.A. thesis, University of Texas at Austin, 1952).

3. Riley Aiken, "A Pack Load of Mexican Tales," in *Puro Mexicano*, ed. J. Frank Dobie, Vol. XXII of Publications of Texas Folklore Society (Austin: Texas Folklore Society, 1935), pp. 49–54. Although Aiken collected these tales in the 1920s, they were certainly very much a part of nineteenth century folklore. See in this respect the comments of Jovita González in "Tales and Songs of the Texas-Mexicans," in *Man, Bird, and Beast*, ed. J. Frank Dobie, Vol. VIII of the Publications of the Texas Folklore Society (Austin: Texas Folklore Society, 1930), p. 86.

4. Brownie McNeil, "Corridos of the Mexican Border," in *Mexican Border Ballads*, ed. Mody C. Boatright, Vol. XXI of the Publications of the Texas Folklore Society (Austin: Texas Folklore Society, 1946), p. 4; and Ben D. Wood, "A Mexican Border Ballad," in *Round the Levee*, ed. Stith Thompson, Vol. I of the Publications of the Texas Folklore Society (Austin: Texas Folklore Society, 1916), pp. 55–57.

5. González, "Folklore of the Texas-Mexican Vaquero," in *Texas and Southwestern Lore*, ed. Dobie, p. 22.

6. Dobie, "Treasure Legends of McMullen County," in *Legends of Texas*, ed. Dobie, pp. 33–43.

7. Américo Paredes, *A Texas-Mexican Cancionero: Songs of the Lower Border* (Urbana: University of Illinois Press, 1976), pp. 23–24; 48–49.

8. Paredes, "Folklore and History," in *Singers and Storytellers*, ed. Boatright, et al., pp. 63–68.

9. McNeill, "Corridos of the Mexican Border," in *Mexican Border Ballads*, ed. Boatright, pp. 15–22.

10. Dobie, "The Battlefields of Palo Alto and Resaca de la Palma," in *Legends of Texas*, ed. Dobie, pp. 51–52.

11. L. D. Bertillion, "Steinheimer's Millions," pp. 91–94 and Blittersdorf, "Buried Treasure legends of Milam County," in ibid., pp. 101–2.

12. Paredes, "Folklore and History," in *Singers and Storytellers*, ed. Boatright, et al., pp. 66–68.

13. McNeill, "Corridos of the Mexican Border," in *Mexican Border Ballads*, ed. Boatright, pp. 15–22.

14. Frank Goodwyn, "Folklore of the King Ranch Mexicans," in *Southwestern*

Lore, ed. J. Frank Dobie, Vol. IX of the Publications of the Texas Folklore Society (Hatboro, Penn: Folklore Associates, 1931), pp. 48–49.

15. The miracle explained the ever-presence of deer about the head of the San Antonio River and in the San Pedro Park. See Barnes, *Combats and Conquests of Immortal Heroes*, pp. 77–81; and Wright, *San Antonio de Béxar*, pp. 121–22.

16. Littlejohn, "The Holy Spring of Father Margil at Nacogdoches," in *Legends of Texas*, ed. Dobie, pp. 204–5.

17. González, "Folklore of the Texas-Mexican Vaquero," in *Texas and Southwestern Lore*, ed. Dobie, pp. 9–10, 13.

18. Fermina Guerra, "Mexican and Spanish Folklore and Incidents in Southwest Texas" (M.A. thesis, Univeristy of Texas at Austin, 1941), pp. 14–17,

19. Boatright, "The Devil's Grotto," in *Texas and Southwestern Lore*, ed. Dobie, pp. 102–6. Also, Elton R. Miles, "The Devil in the Big Bend," in *Folk Travelers: Ballads, Tales, and Talk*, ed. by Mody C. Boatright, et al., Vol. XXV of the Publications of the Texas Folklore Society (Dallas: Texas Folklore Society, 1953), pp. 205–16; and Elton R. Miles, "Christ in the Big Bend," in *Mesquite and Willow*, ed. Mody C. Boatright, et al., Vol. XXVII of the Publications of the Texas Folklore Society (Dallas: Texas Folklore Society, 1957), pp. 171–79.

20. Zavala, *History and Legends of the Alamo*, pp. 116–17.

21. El Paso *Herald* (supplement), September 17, 1898, p. 1.

22. Goodwyn, "Folklore of the King Ranch Mexicans," in *Southwestern Lore*, ed. Dobie, pp. 48–50.

23. González, "Tales and Songs of the Texas Mexican," in *Man, Bird, and Beast*, ed. Dobie, pp. 92–98; and Aiken, "A Pack Load of Mexican Tales," in *Puro Mexicano*, ed. Dobie, pp. 19–20.

24. Goodwyn, "Folklore of the King Ranch Mexican," in *Southwestern Lore*, ed. Dobie, pp. 53–54.

25. Dobie, "Legendary Spanish Forts Down the Nueces," in *Legends of Texas*, ed. Dobie, pp. 46–47. For a related legend about Fort Ramírez, see J. Frank Dobie, *Coronado's Children: Tales of Lost Mines and Buried Treasures of the Southwest* (New York: Grosset and Dunlap, 1930), pp. 99–108.

26. González, "Folklore of the Texas Mexican Vaquero," in *Texas and Southwestern Lore*, ed. Dobie, p. 19. Also see Miller, *Sixty Years in the Nueces Valley*, p. 78.

27. Barnes, *Combats and Conquests of Immortal Heroes*, pp. 88–91.

28. San Antonio *Express*, April 17, 1879, p. 4. For related legends about the Espantosa, see Dobie, *Coronado's Children*, pp. 68–70.

29. Josefina Escajeda, "Tales from San Elizario," in *Puro Mexicano*, ed. Dobie, pp. 115–17.

30. San Antonio *Express*, July 4, 1888, p. 3.

31. Zavala, *History and Legends of the Alamo*, pp. 116–17.

32. González, "Folklore of the Texas-Mexican Vaquero," in *Texas and Southwestern Lore*, ed. Dobie, p. 13.

33. Barnes, *Combats and Conquests of Immortal Heroes*, pp. 83–86.

34. Wood, "A Mexican Border Ballad," in *Round the Levee*, ed. Thompson, p. 55, and González, "Tales and Songs of the Texas-Mexican," in *Man, Bird, and Beast*, ed. Dobie, pp. 115–16.

35. Aiken, "A Pack Load of Mexican Tales," in *Puro Mexicano*, ed. Dobie, pp. 61–66.

36. Goodwyn, "The Folklore of the King Ranch Mexican," in *Southwestern Lore*, ed. Dobie, pp. 53–54.

37. González, "Tales and Songs of the Texas-Mexican," in *Man, Bird, and Beast*, ed. Dobie, p. 103.

38. Aiken, "A Pack Load of Mexican Tales," in *Puro Mexicano*, ed. Dobie, pp. 2–4, 7–10, 46–47.

39. Zavala, *History and Legends of the Alamo*, pp. 58–60.

40. Boatright, "The Devil's Grotto," in *Texas and Southwestern Lore*, ed. Dobie, pp. 102–6. Also Miles, "The Devil in the Big Bend," in *Folk Travelers*, ed. Boatright, et al., pp. 205–16; and Miles, "Christ in the Big Bend," in *Mesquite and Willow*, ed. Boatright, et al., pp. 171–79.

41. Escajeda, "Tales from San Elizario," in *Puro Mexicano*, ed. Dobie, pp. 118–19.

42. Hugh McGehee Taylor, "The Little White Dog," in ibid., pp. 201–10.

43. Aiken, "Pack Load of Mexican Tales," in ibid., pp. 36–41.

44. Escajeda, "Tales from San Elizario," in ibid., pp. 120–21.

45. Carlysle Graham Rhat, *The Romance of the Davis Mountains and Big Bend Country* (El Paso: The Raht Books Co., 1919), pp. 77–81.

46. Aiken, "Pack Load of Mexican Tales," in *Puro Mexicano*, ed. Dobie, pp. 27–29.

47. Escajeda, "Tales from San Elizario," in ibid., pp. 117–18.

48. González, "Tales and Songs of the Texas-Mexican," in *Man, Bird, and Beast*, ed. Dobie, p. 103.

49. Goodwyn, "Folklore of the King Ranch Mexican," in *Southwestern Lore*, ed. J. Frank Dobie, pp. 54–55. For another legend that alludes to the swift reprisals lawbreakers received, see "The Law of Mondragón," in Newcomb, *The Alamo City*, pp. 14–15.

50. González, "Tales and Songs of the Texas-Mexican," in *Man, Bird, and Beast*, ed. Dobie, pp. 92–98.

51. Paredes, "Folklore and History," in *Singers and Storytellers*, ed. Boatright, et al., pp. 65–66; Américo Paredes, *"With His Pistol in His Hand": A Border Ballad and Its Hero* (Austin: University of Texas, 1958), pp. 147–50; Paredes, *A Texas-Mexican Cancionero*, p. xviii; Paredes, "José Mosqueda and the Folklorization of Actual Events," *Aztlán: Chicano Journal of the Social Sciences and the Arts* IV (Spring 1973): 1–30; McNeill, "Corridos of the Mexican Border," in *Mexican Border Ballads*, ed. Boatright, p. 16–22.

52. González, "Tales and Songs of the Texas-Mexican," in *Man, Bird, and Beast*, ed. Dobie, pp. 106–9.

53. Aiken, "Pack Load of Mexican Tales," in *Puro Mexicano*, ed. Dobie, pp. 57–60.

54. Goodwyn, "Folklore of the King Ranch Mexican," in *Southwestern Lore*, ed. Dobie, p. 57.

55. González, "Tales and Songs of the Texas-Mexican," in *Man, Bird, and Beast*, ed. Dobie, pp. 113–14.

56. Aiken, "Pack Load of Mexican Tales," in *Puro Mexicano*, ed. Dobie, pp. 72–75 and 61–66.

57. Escajeda, "Tales from San Elizario," in ibid., pp. 119–20.

58. Aiken, "Pack Load of Mexican Tales," in ibid., pp. 4–7 and 36–44. See also González, "Tales and Songs of the Texas-Mexican," in *Man, Bird, and Beast*, ed. Dobie, pp. 106–8 for the story of Pedro de Urdemañas in which Pedro tricks the Devil into letting him out of Hell. Also, *corridos* show how Tejano figures outwitted strong and dominating forces.

59. See the discussion by the historian Herbert G. Gutman concerning the role

of folklore as a resistance behavior among dependent and exploited social classes: *The Black Family in Slavery and Freedom* (New York: Pantheon Books, 1976), pp. 603–4, 58n.

Chapter 8

1. Albert Curtis, *Fabulous San Antonio* (San Antonio: The Naylor Company, 1955), p. 7; Adel Speiser, "The Story of the Theatre in San Antonio" (M.A. thesis, St. Mary's University, 1948), pp. 4–11.

2. Brownsville *Ranchero*, July 29, 1868, p. 3; August 11, 1868, p. 3; Galveston *Weekly News*, Galveston, Texas, August 31, 1858, p. 1, citing correspondence to the Brownsville *Flag*.

3. Barnes, *Combats and Conquests of Immortal Heroes*, pp. 113–14; James Robert Crews, "Reconstruction in Brownsville, Texas" (M.A. thesis, Texas Tech University, 1969), p. 28; San Antonio *Herald*, November 26, 1872, p. 3.

4. Corpus Christi *Weekly Caller*, March 23, 1884, p. 4; San Antonio *Express*, May 31, 1879, p. 4; June 18, 1881, p. 2; August 20, 1881, p. 1; September 12, 1882, p. 2; September 26, 1892, p. 2; and October 4, 1892, p. 2.

5. González, "Social Life in Cameron, Starr, and Zapata Counties," pp. 53–54.

6. Miller, *Sixty Years in the Nueces Valley, 1870–1930*, pp. 105–6.

7. Rena Maverick Green, ed., *Memoirs of Mary A. Maverick* (San Antonio: Alamo Printing Co., 1921), p. 55; San Antonio *Herald*, December 25, 1866, p. 3.

8. San Antonio *Express*, September 22, 1883, p. 1.

9. Ibid., February 24, 1884, p. 4.

10. San Antonio *Express*, January 4, 1891, p. 3. For types of wedding receptions generally celebrated by the well-to-do, see the El Paso *Herald*, El Paso, Texas, September 16, 1898, p. 4, and the San Antonio *Express*, March 4, 1888, p. 6.

11. San Antonio *Express*, July 13, 1891, p. 8; January 3, 1892, p. 8.

12. Corpus Christi *Weekly Caller*, May 26, 1888, p. 1; June 9, 1888, p. 1; July 28, 1888, p. 1; September 22, 1888, p. 1.

13. Harby, "Texan Types and Contrasts," p. 239.

14. San Antonio *Express*, March 24, 1887, p. 3.

15. Corpus Christi *Weekly Caller*, March 24, 1888, p. 1; San Antonio *Express*, March 18, 1888, p. 3. See also Hortense Warner Ward, "It was Texas' First State Fair: Next Thursday Marks a Century Since Corpus Christi Show," *Houston Chronicle Magazine*, April 27, 1952.

16. San Antonio *Express*, November 10, 1880, p. 4; May 15, 1886, p. 4; November 26, 1886, p. 2.

17. Harby, "Texan Types and Contrasts," pp. 244–46; Corpus Christi *Weekly Caller*, May 27, 1883, p. 5; October 7, 1892, p. 1; July 7, 1889, p. 8.

18. John C. Rayburn and Virginia Kemp Rayburn, eds., *Century of Conflict, 1821–1913, Incidents in the Lives of William Neale and William A. Neale, Early Settlers of South Texas* (Waco: Texian Press, 1966), p. 16.

19. Adeline Short Dinger, *Folk Life and Folklore of the Mexican Border* (Edinburg, Texas: Hidalgo County Historical Museum, 1972), pp. 39–42.

20. San Antonio *Herald*, February 23, 1869, p. 3; February 17, 1870, p. 3; San Antonio *Express*, February 20, 1869, p. 3.

21. Corpus Christi *Weekly Caller*, February 28, 1886, p. 4.

22. San Antonio *Express*, March 6, 1889, p. 3.

23. El Paso *Herald*, February 23, 1899, p. 5.

24. Chatfield, *The Twin Cities of the Border*, pp. 13–14, 30.

25. Corpus Christi *Weekly Caller*, October 28, 1892, p. 7.

26. San Antonio *Herald*, July 14, 1869, p. 3; Corpus Christi *Weekly Caller*, July 9, 1887, p. 8; El Paso *Herald*, July 5, 1898, p. 2. Also, J. B. Wilkinson, *Laredo and the Rio Grande Frontier* (Austin: Jenkins Publishing Co., 1975), p. 314.

27. El Paso *Times*, El Paso, Texas, September 2, 1899, p. 8; September 5, 1899, p. 7.

28. Green, ed., *Memoirs of Mary A. Maverick*, p. 53.

29. San Antonio *Express*, September 16, 1869, p. 3; September 16, 1877, p. 4; September 18, 1877, p. 4; September 17, 1878, p. 4; September 18, 1878, p. 2; September 10, 1879, p. 4; September 16, 1879, p. 4; September 16, 1880, p. 4; September 17, 1880, p. 4; September 15, 1881, p. 4; September 16, 1881, p. 4; September 16, 1883, p. 4; September 16, 1884, p. 4; September 12, 1885, p. 3; September 16, 1885, p. 3; September 16, 1886, p. 8; September 16, 1887, p. 5; September 9, 1888, p. 4; September 16, 1888, p. 4; September 6, 1889, p. 8; September 16, 1889, p. 4; September 16, 1890, p. 2; September 17, 1890, p. 8; September 18, 1890, p. 5; September 16, 1891, p. 8; September 17, 1891, p. 8; September 17, 1892, p. 6; September 18, 1892, p. 3; September 16, 1893, p. 8; September 16, 1894, p. 3; September 17, 1894, p. 8; September 15, 1895, p. 5; September 18, 1895, p. 8; September 5, 1896, p. 8; September 15, 1896, p. 5; September 16, 1896, p. 5; September 16, 1897, p. 5; September 16, 1897, p. 5; September 16, 1898, p. 4; and, September 16, 1899, p. 5. For the same celebrations during the same time period in other central Texas towns, see Austin *Statesman*, Austin, Texas, September 17, 1892, p. 1; September 16, 1894, p. 10; and San Antonio *Express*, September 19, 1894. For the celebrations in the Corpus Christi area, see Corpus Christi *Weekly Caller*, September 20, 1885, p. 5; September 24, 1887, p. 5; September 8, 1888, p. 5; September 22, 1893, p. 6; September 22, 1899, p. 5; San Antonio *Express*, September 16, 1888, p. 3; September 18, 1897, p. 3. For the celebrations in Duval County, see San Antonio *Express*, September 21, 1886, p. 6; September 21, 1887, p. 6; September 23, 1894, p. 4; Corpus Christi *Weekly Caller*, September 23, 1883, p. 5; September 20, 1885, p. 4; September 19, 1886, p. 8; September 22, 1888, p. 1; September 26, 1891, p. 7; September 22, 1893, p. 1; September 22, 1899, p. 8; and see May 9, 1886, p. 4, for celebrations in neighboring areas of Nueces County. For celebrations in the border cities of South Texas, see Corpus Christi *Weekly Caller*, September 24, 1887, p. 4; September 22, 1888, p. 1; September 21, 1884, p. 8; San Antonio *Express*, September 17, 1886, p. 2; September 20, 1887, p. 6. And for the celebrations in El Paso, see El Paso *Herald*, September 17, 1890, p. 1; September 15, 1896, p. 1; September 16, 1896, p. 1; September 16, 1898, p. 4; September 15, 1898, p. 3; El Paso *Times*, September 12, 1897, p. 3.

30. San Antonio *Express*, May 4, 1891, p. 8; May 6, 1896, p. 5.

31. For the *Cinco de Mayo* celebrations in Corpus Christi, see Corpus Christi *Weekly Caller*, May 7, 1887, p. 5; May 9, 1891, p. 1; May 6, 1892, p. 5; May 12, 1893, p. 6; San Antonio *Express*, May 7, 1899, p. 5. For the celebrations in Duval County, see Corpus Christi *Weekly Caller*, May 12, 1888, p. 1; May 9, 1891, p. 1; San Antonio *Express*, May 8, 1888, p. 6.

32. San Antonio *Express*, June 25, 1882, p. 4. The *Express*, reports 1518 as the year in which Cortez entered Mexico City. That cannot possibly be correct. See Bernal Díaz del Castillo, *The Discovery and Conquest of Mexico, 1517–1521*, ed. by Genaro García, trans. by A. P. Maudslay, introd. by Irving Leonard (New York: Farrar, Straus, and Cudahy, 1956), p. 296. Why Bexareños decided upon this day in particular the *Express* does not state.

33. Margarita B. Melville, "The Mexican American and the Celebration of the Fiestas Patrias: An Ethnohistorical Analysis," *Grito del Sol* III (January-March, 1978): 107–16.

34. San Antonio *Express*, April 15, 1884, p. 2.

35. Ibid., March 14, 1888, p. 7.

36. Corpus Christi *Weekly Caller*, October 21, 1892, p. 1; October 28, 1892, p. 7.

37. Ibid., September 29, 1893, p. 1.

38. San Antonio *Express*, September 22, 1893, p. 3.

39. Corpus Christi *Weekly Caller*, July 27, 1884, p. 5.

40. Ibid., August 4, 1893, p. 5; November 10, 1893, p. 7.

41. San Antonio *Herald*, July 20, 1869, p. 3; April 25, 1871, p. 3; May 5, 1871, p. 3; January 7, 1873, p. 3; January 9, 1873, p. 3; January 14, 1873, p. 3; February 2, 1873, p. 3.

42. Ibid., February 19, 1878, p. 4; March 5, 1878, p. 4.

43. Ibid., April 28, 1878, p. 4.

44. San Antonio *Express*, November 15, 1889, p. 2.

45. Ibid., April 4, 1890, p. 5.

46. Brownsville *Ranchero*, June 4, 1879, p. 2; June 18, 1870, p. 2.

47. Corpus Christi *Weekly Caller*, April 4, 1886, p. 5. See also July 30, 1887, p. 5, and, San Antonio *Express*, February 9, 1882, p. 1.

48. San Antonio *Express*, September 11, 1887, p. 3; Corpus Christi *Weekly Caller*, August 4, 1888, p. 1.

49. Curtis, *Fabulous San Antonio*, pp. 6–7; Speiser, "The Story of the Theatre in San Antonio," p. 11; Carland Elaine Crook, "San Antonio, Texas, 1846–1861" (M.A. thesis, Rice University, 1964), p. 76.

50. San Antonio *Herald*, June 17, 1869, p. 3; June 22, 1869, p. 3; June 26, 1869, p. 3; July 1, 1869, p. 3; December 20, 1869, p. 3; December 22, 1869, p. 3.

51. San Antonio *Express*, November 4, 1877, p. 4.

52. San Antonio *Express*, December 23, 1875, p. 3; August 5, 1879, p. 4; January 9, 1885, p. 3; November 25, 1889, p. 4; January 2, 1893, p. 5; Beeville *Bee*, Beeville, Texas, May 2, 1889, p. 2; Curtis, *Fabulous San Antonio*, pp. 7–8; Barnes, *Combats and Conquests of Immortal Heroes*, p. 118, Crews, "Reconstruction in Brownsville, Texas," p. 29; Wilkinson, *Laredo and the Rio Grande Frontier*, p. 314.

53. Crews, "Reconstruction in Brownsville, Texas," p. 29; Curtis, *Fabulous San Antonio*, pp. 7–8; Barnes, *Combats and Conquests of Immortal Heroes*, p. 118.

Chapter 9

1. William Wallace McCullough, Jr., *John McCullough: Pioneer Presbyterian Missionary and Teacher in the Republic of Texas* (Austin: The Pemberton Press, 1966), p. 73.

2. Mrs. V. K. Carpenter, *The State of Texas Federal Population Schedules, Seventh Census of the United States, 1850* (4 vols; Huntsville, Arkansas: Century Enterprises, 1969), I: 178–79.

3. San Antonio *Express*, March 13, 1869, p. 2.

4. Ibid., July 6, 1887, p. 4; June 1, 1893, p. 6; May 6, 1898, p. 5. *Directory of San Antonio, 1881–1882*, p. 236; *Directory of San Antonio, 1887–1888*, p. 43; *Directory of San Antonio, 1889–1890*, p. 48; *Directory of San Antonio, 1891*, p. 60; *Directory of San Antonio, 1892–1893*, p. 65; *Directory of San Antonio, 1895–1896*, pp. 13, 134, 281; *Directory of San Antonio, 1897–1898*, p. 14; *Directory of San Antonio, 1899–1900*, pp. 13, 308. In addition, there existed some private

schools. Among those in the early 1890s were ones under the instruction of Miss María Ximénes, Miss Carrie Saenz, and Miss Antonia Morín. *Directory of San Antonio, 1889–1890*, p. 48; *Directory of San Antonio, 1891*, p. 60. Anna Guerra and Clara Chapa taught music in the nineties. *Directory of San Antonio, 1891*, p. 197; *Directory of San Antonio, 1897–1898*, p. 300; *Directory of San Antonio, 1899–1900*, pp. 196, 288, 332, 543. See also U. S. Bureau of the Census, *Twelfth Census of the U.S., 1900* (Washington D. C.), Roll #1611 and 1612 (Volume VII), Béxar County, pp. 183B and 236B.

5. U. S. Bureau of the Census, *Eighth Census of the U.S., 1860* (Washington D. C.), Roll #1288, Béxar County, p. 30; U. S. Bureau of the Census, *Tenth Census of the U. S., 1880* (Washington D. C.), Roll #1291, Béxar County, pp. 15, 25.

6. Paul S. Taylor, *An American Mexican Frontier: Nueces County, Texas* (Chapel Hill: University of North Carolina Press, 1934), p. 216. See also *Tenth Census of the U. S., 1880*, Roll #1322, Nueces County, p. 48.

7. *Tenth Census of the U. S., 1880*, Roll #1300, Duval County, pp. 18 (San Diego), 70, 75 (Precinct #2), and 13, 20 (Precincts #3 and #4).

8. Corpus Christi *Weekly Caller*, October 4, 1885, p. 4.

9. San Antonio *Express*, October 27, 1887, p. 3.

10. Ibid., September 21, 1887, p. 6; December 28, 1887, p. 3.

11. Corpus Christi *Weekly Caller*, September 16, 1892, p. 1; September 1, 1893, p. 1; October 14, 1898, p. 1.

12. *Twelfth Census of the U.S., 1900*, Duval County, Roll #1629, pp. 58B, 68A, 68B, 108A.

13. Corpus Christi *Weekly Caller*, April 15, 1892, p. 1.

14. Ibid., July 7, 1893, p. 4.

15. Ibid., December 29, 1888, p. 1; January 14, 1898, p. 6.

16. Ibid., December 22, 1888, p. 1.

17. Ibid., March 3, 1893, p. 6; May 13, 1898, p. 1.

18. Ibid., February 17, 1884, p. 4; June 30, 1888, p. 5; July 4, 1891, p. 6; June 23, 1893, p. 5; June 30, 1899, p. 4.

19. Ibid., June 29, 1884, p. 4.

20. Ibid., October 4, 1885, p. 4.

21. Ibid., September 15, 1893, p. 8.

22. Ibid., January 18, 1885, p. 4.

23. Ibid., January 18, 1885, p. 4; October 6, 1893, p. 8.

24. Melinda Rankin, *Twenty Years Among the Mexicans: A Narrative of Missionary Adventure* (Cincinnati: Central Book Co., 1881), pp. 84–85.

25. *Eighth Census of the U.S., 1860*, Roll #1289, Cameron County, pp. 26 and 55.

26. U. S. Bureau of the Census, *Ninth Census of the U. S., 1870* (Washington D. C.), Roll #1578, Cameron County, p. 25 (Ward #2), and p. 22 (Ward #3).

27. *Tenth Census of the U. S., 1880*, Roll #1294, Cameron County, pp. 10 and 66. In 1880, Juan Váldez and Fernando Rodríguez taught in Precinct #1 in Cameron County. Ibid., p. 32 (Precinct #1).

28. *Twelfth Census of the U. S., 1900*, Cameron County, Roll #1617, pp. 141A, 144A, 144B, 157A, 163A, 164B, 165B, 179B, 197A. Among instructors in Cameron county precincts in 1900 were P. Aribi, M. Delgado, Juan Treviño, Eugenio Villareal, Adela Treviño, and Guadalupe Valdez. Ibid., 96A, 97B, 104A, 112B, 117A, 208B, and 232B.

29. Arnuflo S. Martínez, "History of Education in Starr County" (Ph.D. diss., University of Texas, 1966).

30. *Eighth Census of the U. S.*, *1860*, Roll #1308, Webb County, p. 6.

31. *Ninth Census of the U.S.*, *1870*, Roll #1608, Webb County, p. 37.

32. San Antonio *Express*, September 24, 1879, p. 4; June 22, 1888, p. 3.

33. *Twelfth Census of the U.S.*, *1900*, Roll #1678, Webb County, pp. 101A, 123B, 130B, 136B, 164B, 168A, 195B, 220B. Ascención García, Julián García, Juan Gonzales, Teodora Vizcaya, and Amelia Carbajal taught in the precinct areas. Ibid., pp. 2A, 22B, 50A.

34. *Ninth Census of the U.S.*, *1870*, Roll #1591, Hidalgo County, p. 1 (Precinct #2) and p. 5(Precinct #5).

35. *Tenth Census of the U.S.*, *1880*, Roll #1310 and 1311, Hidalgo County, pp. 47–49 (Precinct #2) and pp. 12 and 52 (Precinct #3).

36. *Twelfth Census of the U.S.*, *1900*, Hidalgo County, Roll #1644, pp. 253B and 268A.

37. *Tenth Census of the U.S.*, *1880*, Roll #1334, Zapata County, p. 24 (Precinct #2); San Antonio *Express*, September 1, 1893, p. 3.

38. *Twelfth Census of the U.S.*, *1900*, Roll #1681, Zapata County, pp. 291A, 291B, 309A, 312A, 313A, 315A, 318B, 326B, 327B, 329A, 335B, 339A.

39. *Eighth Census of the U.S.*, *1860*, Roll #1305, Starr County, p. 39.

40. *Tenth Census of the U.S.*, *1880*, Roll #1327, Starr County, p. 15, p. 16 (Precinct #3 and #4).

41. San Antonio *Express*, October 20, 1891, p. 3.

42. *Twelfth Census of the U.S.*, *1900*, Roll #1670, Starr County, p. 38B, 54B, 93A, 126A, 127B, and 141A.

43. *Eighth Census of the U.S.*, *1860*, Roll #1293, El Paso County, pp. 6, 34, 113, 66, 57, 52.

44. *Tenth Census of the U.S.*, *1880*, Roll #1301, El Paso County, pp. 1, 10 (Precinct #1), p. 13 (Precinct #3), and p. 1 (Precinct #4).

45. In 1883, Fort Davis children enrolled in Mrs. Mattie Belle Anderson's new public school when it opened for instruction, and others attended another facility where Spanish was taught and spoken. Reminiscences of Mrs. Mattie Belle Anderson (Eugene C. Barker Texas History Center, University of Texas, Austin, Texas), pp. 2, 9.

46. El Paso *Times*, February 9, 1887, p. 2; October 28, 1893, p. 6.

47. El Paso *Herald*, June 2, 1896, p. 1; September 5, 1898, p. 4; August 28, 1899, p. 8; El Paso *Times*, January 5, 1888, p. 5; July 12, 1885, p. 2. See also C. L. Sonnichsen, *Pass of the North: Four Centuries on the Rio Grande* (El Paso: Texas Western Press, 1968), pp. 233–34.

48. El Paso *Herald*, September 14, 1898, p. 4; September 29, 1898, p. 2; October 4, 1898, p. 2; El Paso *Times*, September 1, 1897, p. 3.

49. El Paso *Herald*, January 17, 1899, p. 7; El Paso *Times*, April 9, 1899, p. 7.

50. El Paso *Herald*, October 28, 1899, p. 1; November 11, 1899, p. 3; El Paso *Times*, January 22, 1899, p. 8.

51. El Paso *Herald*, April 26, 1890, p. 4; May 6, 1890, p. 4; October 3, 1890, p. 1; November 22, 1890, p. 1; November 11, 1899, p. 3.

52. *Directory of San Antonio, 1887–1888* (addenda); *Directory of San Antonio, 1889–1890*, p. 61; and *Directory of San Antonio, 1891*, p. 50.

53. Charles August Arnold, *The Folklore, Manners, and Customs of the Mexicans in San Antonio, Texas* (San Francisco: R & E Research Associates, 1971), p. 7. Also, *Directory of San Antonio, 1881–1882*, p. 84; *Directory of San Antonio, 1887–1888*, p. 56; *Directory of San Antonio, 1889–1890*, p. 61; *Directory of San Antonio, 1891*, p. 50; *Directory of San Antonio, 1892–1893*, pp. 62–63; and *Direc-*

tory of San Antonio, 1899–1900, p. 10. For a study of *mutualistas* in San Antonio in the early part of the twentieth century, see Julie Leininger Pycior, "La Raza Organizes: Mexican American Life in San Antonio, 1915–1930 As Reflected in Mutualista Activities" (Ph.D. diss. University of Notre Dame, 1979).

54. W. H. Chatfield, *The Twin Cities of the Border (Brownsville and Matamoros) and the Country of the Lower Rio Grande* (New Orleans: E.P. Brandao, 1893), p. 30; Corpus Christi *Weekly Caller*, April 22, 1892, p. 1; San Antonio *Express*, January 31, 1888, p. 4.

55. San Antonio *Express*, September 20, 1887, p. 6; March 16, 1888, p. 3; March 23, 1888, p. 3.

56. San Antonio *Express*, May 27, 1884, p. 1; Corpus Christi *Weekly Caller*, July 20, 1884, p. 5.

57. Corpus Christi *Gazette*, March 22, 1873, in Corpus Christi *Caller*, February 27, 1921, as cited in Taylor, *An American Mexican Frontier*, p. 173.

58. Taylor, *An American Mexican Frontier*, p. 173, citing the Corpus Christi *Free Press*, September 24, 1879, as included in the Corpus Christi *Caller*, of February 4, 1923.

59. Taylor, *An American Mexican Frontier*, p. 174.

60. Corpus Christi *Weekly Caller*, April 14, 1899, p. 5.

61. San Antonio *Express*, April 15, 1884, p. 2.

62. Corpus Christi *Weekly Caller*, May 26, 1899, p. 1; September 22, 1899, p. 8; San Antonio *Express*, September 21, 1886, p. 6.

63. García, "Obreros," pp. 312–14; and El Paso *Times*, January 8, 1899, p. 6.

64. Miguel David Tirado, "Mexican American Community Political Organization: The Key to Chicano Political Power," *Aztlán: Chicano Journal of the Social Sciences and the Arts* I (Spring 1970): 55. See further, Camarillo, *Chicanos in a Changing Society*, pp. 147–54, for a discussion of mutualistas in the Santa Barbara, California, area in the early twentieth century.

65. San Antonio *Express*, May 4, 1892, p. 2.

66. Cited in Felix Gutiérrez, "Spanish-language Media in America: Background, Resources, History," *Journalism History* IV (Summer 1977): 41.

67. San Antonio *Herald*, July 26, 1856, p. 2; August 2, 1856, p. 1; August 9, 1856, p. 2; August 16, 1856, p. 2; October 4, 1856, p. 2.

68. San Antonio *Herald*, June 27, 1868, p. 3; August 8, 1868, p. 2; August 16, 1868, p. 2.

69. San Antonio *Express*, October 3, 1877, p. 2. According to a city directory, Rafael Pereida, Sixto F. Barrera, and Alfred R. Dubois were the publishers of *El Tiempo*. *Directory of San Antonio, 1877*, pp. 62, 85, 157.

70. San Antonio *Express*, September 23, 1891, p. 3.

71. Ibid., May 5, 1898, p. 6; May 6, 1898, p. 5; May I9, 1898, p. 5. *Directory of San Antonio, 1892–1893*, p. 227. Alberto F. Martínez, a public school teacher in the city and the editor of *El Cronista*, was fired for his pro-Spanish sentiments. The mayor dismissed Martínez upon learning of his ideas with the statement: "This is an American government and only Americans should be allowed to hold public offices." The editor was also harassed by white juveniles for harboring Spanish sympathies.

72. San Antonio *Herald*, January 27, 1869, p. 3; San Antonio *Express*, December 24, 1868, p. 3.

73. San Antonio *Express*, July 24, 1886, p. 2.

74. *Directory of San Antonio, 1881–1882*, pp. 88, 136; *Directory of San Antonio, 1883–1884*, p. 89.

75. San Antonio *Express*, September 4, 1887, p. 2; *Directory of San Antonio, 1887–1888*, p. 54; *Directory of San Antonio, 1889–1890*, p. 67.

76. Herminio Rios and Lupe Castillo, "Toward a True Chicano Bibliography: Mexican American Newspapers,1848–1942," *El Grito: A Journal of Contemporary Mexican American Thought* III (Summer 1970): 24.

77. Rios and Castillo, "Toward a True Chicano Bibliography—Part II," *El Grito* VI (Summer 1972): 47. *Directory of San Antonio, 1892–1893*, p. 277, 310, 321.

78. San Antonio *Express*, July 21, 1891, p. 5. *Directory of San Antonio, 1891*, pp. 140, 449; *Directory of San Antonio, 1892–1893*, p. 695; *Directory of San Antonio, 1895–1896*, p. 660; and *Directory of San Antonio, 1897–1898*, p. 628.

79. San Antonio *Express*, January 7, 1892, p. 3; February 2, 1892, p. 3; March 2, 1897, p. 3; January 25, 1892, p. 2. All citations are from the Spanish edition of the paper.

80. Richard G. Santos, *A Chronicle of Events Concerning the Spanish Language and the Spanish North American Frontier* (San Antonio: Intercultural Development Research Association, 1977), p. 12; Rios and Castillo, "Toward a True Chicano Bibliography," *El Grito*, III, p. 22. The question mark indicates that the termination date of the newspaper is unknown.

81. Rios and Castillo, "Toward a True Chicano Bibliography," p. 22.

82. San Antonio *Express*, February 27, 1884, p. 1.

83. Chatfield, *Twin Cities*, p. 25.

84. San Antonio *Express*, December 22, 1882, p. 2.

85. Rios and Castillo, "Towards a True Chicano Bibliography," p. 23.

86. Corpus Christi *Weekly Caller*, October 21, 1883, p. 2; July 20, 1884, p. 4; July 12, 1885, p. 1; August 31, 1884, p. 4.

87. San Antonio *Express*, February 1, 1892, p. 8; January 30, 1893, p. 6.

88. Rios and Castillo, "Toward a True Chicano Bibliography," p. 23.

89. Corpus Christi *Weekly Caller*, June 18, 1887, p. 4; January 28, 1888, p. 1.

90. Ibid., June 9, 1888, p. 1.

91. San Antonio *Express*, August 22, 1891, p. 2; October 30, 1891, p. 3; November 6, 1891, p. 2.

92. Santos, *A Chronicle of Events Concerning the Spanish Language and the Spanish North American Frontier*, p. 13.

93. San Antonio *Express*, September 22, 1888, p. 4.

94. Corpus Christi *Weekly Caller*, February 19, 1892, p. 2.

95. Ellis Arthur Davis, ed., *The Historical Encyclopedia of Texas* (2 vols; Austin: The Texas Historical Society, n.d.), II: 866.

96. Corpus Christi *Weekly Caller*, October 20, 1888, p. 1; San Antonio *Express*, August 11, 1882, p. 4; August 20, 1891, p. 3; October 24, 1888, p. 2.

97. Corpus Christi *Weekly Caller*, October 26, 1884, p. 1; San Antonio *Express*, June 6, 1884, p. 2; January 30, 1886, p. 7; April 15, 1884, p. 2.

98. San Antonio *Express*, March 31, 1887, p. 3; September 29, 1887, p. 4; August 18, 1891, p. 3.

99. Ibid., September 25, 1891, p. 5.

100. Ibid., January 16, 1892, p. 3; January 25, 1892, p. 2.

101. Rios and Castillo, "Toward a True Chicano Bibliography," p. 22.

102. Ibid., p. 23; El Paso *Times*, November 20, 1887, p. 5; Louis M. Buford to Assistant Secretary of State, Paso del Norte, Mexico, September 9, 1896, in Despatches from United States Consuls in Cuidad Juárez (El Paso del Norte), 1850–1906; Roll 5 and despatches August 10, 1891 to October 13, 1897.

Chapter 10

1. Mario T. García, *"Obreros*: The Mexican Workers of El Paso, 1900–1920" (Ph.D. diss., University of California at San Diego, 1975), p. 205.

2. Juan Gómez-Quiñones, "The First Steps: Chicano Labor Conflict and Organizing, 1900–1920," *Aztlán: Chicano Journal of the Social Sciences and Arts* IV (Spring 1972): 27.

3. Emilio Zamora, Jr., "Chicano Socialist Labor Activity in Texas, 1900–1920," *Aztlán: International Journal of Chicano Studies Reseach* VI (Summer 1975): 223–25.

4. Juan Gómez-Quiñones, *Sembradores, Ricardo Flores Magon y El Partido Liberal Mexicano: A Eulogy and a Critique* (Los Angeles: Chicano Studies Center, 1976), pp. 35–36.

5. Arnoldo De León, "Blowout 1910 Style: A Chicano School Boycott in West Texas," *Texana*, XII (1974): 124–40.

6. José Limón, *"El Primer Congreso Mexicanista de 1911*: A Precursor to Contemporary Chicanismo," *Aztlán: Chicano Journal of the Social Sciences and the Arts* V (Spring and Fall 1974): 85–142.

7. This argument is advanced in Alfredo Cuellar, "Perspectives on Politics," in Joan W. Moore, *Mexican Americans* (Englewood Cliffs: Prentice Hall, 1970), pp. 137–56, and repeated in F. Chris García and Rudolph O. de la Garza, *The Chicano Political Experience: Three Perspectives* (North Scituate, Mass.: Duxbury Press, 1977), pp. 24–27, and in Maurilio Vigil, *Chicano Politics* (Washington, D.C.: University Press of America, 1978), pp. 59–61. Armando Navarro in "The Evolution of Chicano Politics," *Aztlán* V (Spring and Fall 1974): 59–60, notes that the predominant type of politics was the "politics of insurrection." He barely touches on any other type of participation.

8. Arnoldo De León, "White Racial Attitudes Toward Mexicanos in Texas, 1821–1900" (Ph.D. diss., Texas Christian University, 1974), pp. 234–37.

9. For the seminal studies taking the "assimilation/accommodation" school to task, see Octavio I. Romano-V, "The Anthropology and Sociology of the Mexican American," Romano, ed., *Voices* (Berkeley: Quinto Sol Publications, Inc., 1973), 43–56; Nick C. Vaca, "The Mexican American in the Social Sciences, 1912–1970, Part I: 1912–1935," *El Grito: A Journal of Contemporary Mexican American Thought* III (Spring 1970): 3–24; Vaca, "The Mexican American in the Social Sciences, Part II: 1936–1970," *El Grito* IV (Fall 1970): 17–51; and Mario Barrera, Carlos Muñoz, and Charles Ornelas, "The *Barrio* as an Internal Colony," in F. Chris García, ed., *La Causa Política: A Chicano Politics Reader* (Notre Dame: Notre Dame Press, 1974), pp. 283–86.

Bibliography

PRIMARY SOURCES

Government Documents

House Report No. 343, 44 Cong., 1 Sess., (Ser. 1709).
House Exec. Doc., No. 93, 45 Cong., 2 Sess., (Ser. 1809).
House Misc. Doc., No. 64, 45 Cong., 2 Sess., (Ser. 1820).

MANUSCRIPTS

Anderson, Mrs. Mattie Belle. Reminiscences of Mrs. Mattie Belle Anderson. Eugene C. Barker Texas History Center, University of Texas Archives, Austin, Texas.
Noel, Virginia. "The Know Nothing Party in Texas." Typescript in Eugene C. Barker Library, University of Texas Archives, Austin, Texas.
Story, William Russell. Diary of William Russell Story. Eugene C. Barker Texas History Center, University of Texas Archives, Austin, Texas.
Sutherland, W. C. "The Adams Brothers of Jim Wells County." Typescript in Eugene C. Barker Texas History Center, University of Texas Archives, Austin, Texas.
Van Wyke, Lydia. Lydia Van Wyke Letters. Eugene C. Barker Texas History Center, University of Texas Archives, Austin, Texas.

Consular Dispatches

Despatches from United States Consuls in Ciudad Juárez (Paso del Norte), 1850–1906: January 16, 1871–December 31, 1884. General Records of the Department of State, Record Group 59, National Archives.

Despatches from United States Consuls in Ciudad Juárez (Paso del Norte), 1850–1906: January 16, 1889–July 31, 1891. General Records of the Department of State, Record Group 59, National Archives.

Despatches from United States Consuls in Ciudad Juárez (El Paso del Norte), 1850–1906: August 10, 1891–October 13, 1897. General Records of the Department of State, Record Group 59, National Archives.

Despatches from United States Consuls in Matamoros, 1826–1906: May 7, 1879–July 15, 1881. General Records of the Department of State, Record Group 59, National Archives.

Census Schedules

Carpenter, Mrs. V. K. *The State of Texas Federal Population Schedules, Seventh Census of the United States, 1850. 4 vols; Huntsville, Arkansas: Century Enterprises, 1969.*

Population Schedules of the Eighth Census of the U.S., 1860 (Washington D.C.), Roll 1288, Bexar County.

————. *Eighth Census of the U.S., 1860.* Roll 1289, Cameron County.

————. *Eighth Census of the U.S., 1860,* Roll. 1293, El Paso County.

————. *Eighth Census of the U.S., 1860,* Roll 1305, Starr County.

————. *Eighth Census of the U.S., 1860,* Roll 1308, Webb County.

————. *Ninth Census of the U.S., 1870,* Roll 1578, Cameron County.

————. *Ninth Census of the U.S., 1870,* Roll 1608, Webb County.

————. *Tenth Census of the U.S., 1880,* Roll 1289, Atascosa County.

————. *Tenth Census of the U.S., 1880,* Roll 1291, Bexar County.

————. *Tenth Census of the U.S., 1880,* Roll 1294, Cameron County.

————. *Tenth Census of the U.S., 1880,* Roll 1300, Duval County.

————. *Tenth Census of the U.S., 1880,* Roll 1301, El Paso County.

————. *Tenth Census of the U.S., 1880,* Roll 1310, Hidalgo County.

————. *Tenth Census of the U.S., 1880,* Roll 1311, Hidalgo County.

————. *Tenth Census of the U.S., 1880,* Roll 1319, Maverick County.

————. *Tenth Census of the U.S., 1880,* Roll 1322, Nueces County.

————. *Tenth Census of the U.S., 1880,* Roll 1327, Starr County.

————. *Tenth Census of the U.S., 1880,* Roll 1332, Webb County.

————. *Tenth Census of the U.S., 1880,* Roll 1334, Zapata County.

————. *Twelfth Census of the U.S., 1900,* Rolls 1611 and 1612, Bexar County.

————. *Twelfth Census of the U.S., 1900,* Roll 1617, Cameron County.

————. *Twelfth Census of the U.S., 1900,* Roll 1629, Duval County.

————. *Twelfth Census of the U.S., 1900,* Rolls 1630 and 1631, El Paso County.

————. *Twelfth Census of the U.S., 1900,* Roll 1644, Hidalgo County.

————. *Twelfth Census of the U.S., 1900,* Roll 1670, Starr County.

————. *Twelfth Census of the U.S., 1900,* Roll 1678, Webb County.

————. *Twelfth Census of the U.S., 1900,* Roll 1681, Zapata County.

City Directories

Appler, Jules A. *General Directory of the City of San Antonio, 1892–1893.* San Antonio: Jules A. Appler, 1893.

————. *General Directory of the City of San Antonio, 1895–1896.* San Antonio: Jules A. Appler, 1895.

————. *General Directory of the City of San Antonio, 1897–1898*. San Antonio: Jules A. Appler, 1897.

————. *General Directory of the City of San Antonio, 1899–1900*. San Antonio: Jules A. Appler, 1899.

Johnson and Chapman. *General Directory of the City of San Antonio for the Year 1891*. Galveston: Johnson and Chapman, 1890.

Mooney and Morrison. *Directory of the City of San Antonio, 1877–1878*. Galveston: Galveston News, 1877.

Morrison and Fourmy. *General Directory of the City of San Antonio, 1879–1880*. Galveston: Morrison and Fourmy, 1879.

————. *Directory of the City of San Antonio for 1881 and 1882*. Galveston: Morrison & Fourmy, 1881.

————. *General Directory of the City of San Antonio, 1883–1884*. Galveston: Morrison and Fourmy, 1883.

————. *General Directory of the City of San Antonio, 1885–1886*. Galveston: Morrison and Fourmy, 1885.

————. *Directory of the City of San Antonio, for 1887–1888*. Galveston: Morrison and Fourmy, 1887.

————. *Directory of the City of San Antonio, 1889–1890*. Galveston: Morrison and Fourmy, 1889.

Newspapers

Austin Statesman. Austin, Texas, 1871–1899.
Corpus Christi Weekly Caller. Corpus Christi, Texas, 1883–1899.
El Paso Daily Herald. El Paso, Texas, 1881–1899.
El Paso Times. El Paso, Texas, 1883–1899.
San Angelo Standard. San Angelo, Texas, 1884–1899.
San Antonio Express. San Antonio, Texas, 1869–1899.
San Antonio Herald. San Antonio, Texas, 1855–1878.
The Beeville Bee. Beeville, Texas, 1892.
The Ranchero. Corpus Christi (Matamoros and Brownsville), 1859–1870.

Books

Barker, Eugene C., ed. *The Austin Papers*. 2 vols. Austin: University of Texas Press, 1926.

Bartlett, John Russell. *Personal Narrative of Explorations and Incidents in Texas, New Mexico, California, Sonora, and Chihuahua*. 2 vols. New York: D. Appleton and Co., 1854.

Calderón de la Barca, Fanny. *Life in Mexico During a Residence of Two Years in that Country*. New York: E. P. Dutton and Co., Inc., 1946.

Carter, Robert G. *On the Border with MacKenzie: or, Winning West Texas from the Comanches*. Washington, D.C.: Eynon Printing Co., 1935.

Cazneau, Mrs. William L. (Cora Montgomery). *Eagle Pass: or, Life on the Border*. Austin: Pemberton Press, 1966.

Chatfield W. H. *The Twin Cities of the Border and the Country of the Lower Rio Grande*. New Orleans: E. P. Brandao, 1893.

Connelley, William E. *Doniphan's Expedition and the Conquest of New Mexico and California*. Kansas City: Bryant and Douglas Book and Stationery Company, 1907.

Davis, Richard Harding. *The West From a Car Window*. New York: Harper and Brothers, 1892.

Day, James M., compiler. "Compendium of the Early History of Texas (continued from the *Texas Almanac* for 1858)." *The Texas Almanac, 1857–1873*. Waco: Texian Press.

Domenech, Emanuel H. D. *Missionary Adventures in Texas and Mexico: A Personal Narrative of Six Years' Sojourn in Those Regions*. London: Longman, Brown, Green, Longmans and Roberts, 1858.

Duval, John C. *Early Times in Texas, or Adventures of Jack Dobell*. Dallas: Tardy Publishing Co., 1936.

Eastman, Seth. *A Seth Eastman Sketchbook, 1848–1849*. Austin: University of Texas Press, 1961.

Ehrenberg, Herman. *With Milam and Fannin*. Austin: The Pemberton Press, 1968.

Eickemeyer, Rudolf. *Letters from the Southwest*. Astor Place, New York: J. J. Little and Co., 1894.

Graham, Philip, ed. *Sidney Lanier: Florida and Miscellaneous Prose*, VI of Collective Works. Baltimore: The Johns Hopkins Press, 1945.

Gray, William F. *From Virginia to Texas*. Houston: Fletcher Young Publishing Co., 1965.

Green, Rena Maverick, ed. *Memoirs of Mary A. Maverick*. San Antonio: Alamo Printing Co., 1921.

———. *Samuel Maverick, Texan: 1803–1870*. San Antonio: privately printed, 1952.

Hammond, George P. and Edward H. Howes, eds. *Overland to California on the Southwestern Trail, 1849: The Diary of Robert Eccleston*. Berkeley: University of California Press, 1950.

Helm, Mary S. *Scraps of Early Texas History*. Austin: Printed for the author at the office of B. R. Warner and Co., 1884.

Henry, W. S. *Campaign Sketches of the War with Mexico*. New York: Arno Press, 1973.

Holding, Nannie Emory. *A Decade of Mission Life in Mexican Mission Homes*. Nashville: Publishing House Methodist Episcopal Church, 1895.

Holley, Mary Austin. *Texas*. Austin: The Steck Company, 1935.

Hollon, W. Eugene. *Beyond the Cross Timbers: The Travels of Randolph B. Marcy, 1812–1887*. Norman: University of Oklahoma Press, 1955.

Hollon, W. Eugene and Ruth Lapham Butler, eds. *William Bollaert's Texas*. Norman: University of Oklahoma Press, 1956.

James, Joshua and Alexander McCrae. *A Journal of a Tour in Texas: With Observations, & c., by the Agents of the Wilmington Emigrating Society*. Wilmington, North Carolina: Printed by T. Loring, 1835.

Jaques, Mary A. *Texan Ranch Life: With Three Months Through Mexico in a "Prairie Schooner."* London: Horace Cox, 1894.

Jennings, Napolean A. *A Texas Ranger*. New York: Charles Scribner's Sons, 1899.

Johnson, R. W. *A Soldier's Reminiscences in Peace and War*. Philadelphia: J. B. Lippincott Co., 1886.

Kendall, George Wilkins. *Narrative of the Texas-Santa Fe Expedition*. 2 vols. Wiley and Putnam, 1844.

King, Edward and J. Wells Champney. *Texas, 1874: An Eyewitness Account of Post-Reconstruction Texas*. Edited by Robert S. Gray. Houston: Cordovan Press, 1974.

Kingsbury, W. G. *A Description of South Western and Middle Texas.* London: Waterlow and Sons Limited, 1878.

Krueger, M. *Pioneer Life in Texas: An Autobiography.* n.p., n.d.

Kupper, Winifred, ed. *Texas Sheepman: The Reminiscences of Robert Maudslay.* Freeport, New York: Books for Libraries Press, 1951.

Latham, Francis. *Travels in the Republic of Texas.* Edited by Gerald S. Pierce. Austin: Encino Press, 1971.

Lawrence, A. B. *Texas in 1840, or the Emigrant's Guide to the New Republic, Being the Observations, Enquiry and Travels in the Beautiful Country.* New York: William W. Allen, 1840.

Lundy, Benjamin. *Life, Travels, Opinions of Benjamin Lundy, Including his Journey to Texas and Mexico.* New York: Negro University Press, 1969.

McCall, George A. *Letters from the Frontier.* Philadelphia: J. B. Lippincott, 1868.

McConnell, H. H. *Five Years a Cavalryman, or Sketches of Regular Army Life on the Texas Frontier.* Jacksboro, Texas: J. N. Roberts Co., 1889.

McIntyre, Benjamin F. *Federals on the Frontier: The Diary of Benjamin F. McIntyre.* Edited by Nannie M. Tilley. Austin: University of Texas Press, 1963.

Miller, Susan G. *Sixty Years in the Nueces Valley, 1870–1930.* San Antonio: Naylor Printing Co., 1930.

Moore, Francis Jr. *Description of Texas.* New York: T. R. Tanner, 1844.

Muir, Andrew Forest, ed. *Texas in 1837: An Anonymous Contemporary Narrative.* Austin: University of Texas Press, 1958.

Ober, Frederick A. *Travels in Mexico and Life Among the Mexicans.* Boston: Estes and Lauriat, 1883.

Olmsted, Frederick Law. *A Journey Through Texas.* New York: Burt Franklin, 1969.

O'Neill, John Neal. *The Guide to Texas.* Dublin: Joseph Blundell, 1934.

Parisot, Reverend P. F. *The Reminiscences of a Texas Missionary.* San Antonio: Johnson Bros. Printing Co., 1899.

Page, Frederick. *Prairiedom: Rambles and Scrambles in Texas or New Estremadura.* New York: Paine and Burgess, 1845.

Parker, Amos Andrew. *Trip to the West and Texas.* New York: Arno Press, 1973.

Petty, J. W. Jr., ed. *Victor Rose's History of Victoria.* Victoria, Texas: Book Mart, 1961.

Pirtle, Lela Neal, ed. *Life on the Range and on the Trail: As Told by R. J. (Bob) Lauderdale and John M. Doak.* San Antonio: The Naylor Co., 1936.

Powers, Stephen. *Afoot and Alone: A Walk from Sea to Sea by the Southern Route: Adventures and Observations in Southern California, New Mexico, Arizona, Texas, etc.* Hartford: Columbian Book Company, 1886.

Rankin, Melinda. *Twenty Years Among the Mexicans: A Narrative of Missionary Adventure.* Cincinnati: Central Book Co., 1881.

Reid, John C. *Reid's Tramp or a Journal of the Incidents of Ten Months Travel Through Texas, New Mexico, Arizona, Sonora, California . . . .* Selma, Alabama: John Hardt and Co., 1858.

Richardson, Albert D. *Beyond the Mississippi: From the Great River to the Great Ocean . . . 1857–1867.* New York: American Publishing Co., 1867.

Rodríguez, José María. *Rodríguez Memoirs of Early Texas.* San Antonio: Passing Show Printing Co., 1913.

Roemer, Ferdinand. *Texas: With Particular Reference to German Immigration.* Translated by Oswald Mueller. Waco: Texian Press, 1967.

Ringgold, Jennie Parks. *Frontier Days in the Southwest.* San Antonio: The Naylor Company, 1952.

Santleben, August. *A Texas Pioneer.* New York: Neale Publishing Co., 1910.

Smith, George G. *The Life and Times of George Foster Pierce, D. D., LL.D. Bishop of the Methodist Episcopal Church, South, with His Sketch of Lovick Pierce, D. D., his Father.* Sparta, Georgia: Hancock Publishing Co., 1888.

Smithwick, Noah. *The Evolution of a State, or Recollections of old Texas Days.* Austin: Gammel Book Company, 1900.

Solms-Braunfels, Carl of. *Texas, 1844–1845.* Houston: Anson Press, 1936.

Sowell, A. J. *Early Settlers and Indian Fighters of the Southwest.* 2 vols. New York: Argosy-Antiquarian Ltd., 1964.

Sumpter, Jesse. *Life of Jesse Sumpter.* Typewritten copy in the Mary Couts Burnett Library, Texas Christian University, Fort Worth, Texas.

Sutherland, Mary A. *The Story of Corpus Christi.* Edited by Frank B. Harrison. Houston: Rein & Sons Co., 1916.

Sweet, Alexander and Armoy Knox. *On a Mexican Mustang.* New York: J. S. Ogilvie Publishing Co., 1883.

———. *Sketches from "Texas Siftings."* New York: Texas Siftings Publishing Co., 1882.

Taylor, Nathaniel. *The Coming Empire: Two Thousand Miles in Texas on Horseback.* New York: A. S. Barnes and Co., 1877.

Tweedie, Mrs. Alec. *Mexico As I Saw It.* New York: Thomas Nelson & Sons, 1911.

Viele, Teresa. *"Following the Drum": A Glimpse of Frontier Life.* New York: Rudd and Carleton, 1859.

Wilson, Robert A. *Mexico: Its Peasants and Its Priests.* New York: Harper and Brothers Publishers, 1856.

Winkler, Ernest W., ed. *Manuscript Letters and Documents of Early Texians, 1821–1845.* Austin: The Steck Co., 1937.

Woodman, David. *Guide to Texas Emigrants.* Boston: M. Hawes, 1835.

Wright, William. *Recollections of Western Texas.* London: W. and F. G. Cash, 1857.

Articles

Allan, Mrs. T. C. "Reminiscences of Mrs. Annie Fagan Teal," *By the Way,* I (July 1897): 1–7.

Almonte, Juan. "Statistical Report on Texas." Translated by Carlos E. Castañeda. *Southwestern Historical Quarterly,* XXVIII (January 1925): 177–222.

Altgelt, Emma. "Emma Altgelt's Sketches of Life in Texas." Edited by Henry B. Dielman. *Southwestern Historical Quarterly,* LXIII (January 1960): 364–84.

Bell, James G. "A Log of the Texas-California Cattle Trail, 1854." Edited by J. Evetts Haley. *Southwestern Historical Quarterly,* XXXV (January 1932): 208–37.

Clopper, J. C. "Journal of J. C. Clopper." *Quarterly of the Texas State Historical Association,* XIII (July 1909): 44–80.

Cox, C. C. "Reminiscences of C. C. Cox." *Quarterly of the Texas State Historical Association,* VI (January 1903): 204–35.

Harby, Lee C. "Texan Types and Contrasts." *Harper's New Monthly Magazine* (July 1890): 229–46.

Sánchez, José María. "A Trip to Texas in 1828." Translated by Carlos E. Castañeda. *Southwestern Historical Quarterly,* XXIX (April 1926): 249–88.

Smith, Ophia D. "A Trip to Texas in 1855." *Southwestern Historical Quarterly,* LVIX (July 1955): 24–39.

Spofford, Harriet. "San Antonio de Bexar." *Harper's New Monthly Magazine* (July 1890): 831–50.

Steinert, W. "W. Steinert's View of Texas in 1849." Edited and translated by Gilbert J. Jordan. *Southwestern Historical Quarterly,* LXXX (October 1976): 177–200.

"The Autobiography of George W. Smyth." Introductory notes by Winnie Allen. *Southwestern Historical Quararerly,* XXXVI (January 1933): 200–214.

"To California Through Texas and Mexico: The Diary and Letters of Thomas B. Eastland and Joseph G. Eastland, His Son." Foreword by Douglas S. Watson. Notes by Dorothy H. Huggins. *California Historical Society Quarterly,* XVIII (June 1939): 99–135; 217–50.

SECONDARY SOURCES

Books

Abernathy, Francis Edward, ed. *The Folklore of Texan Cultures.* Austin: The Encino Press, 1974.

Acuña, Rodolfo. *Occupied America: The Chicano's Struggle Toward Liberation.* San Francisco: Canfield Press, 1972.

Adobe Notes, or How to Keep the Weather Out with Just Plain Mud. Taos: The Laughing Horse Press, 1930.

Arnold, Charles August. *The Folklore, Manners, and Customs of the Mexicans in San Antonio, Texas.* San Francisco: R & E Research Associates, 1971.

Barnes, Charles Merritt. *Combats and Conquests of Immortal Heroes.* San Antonio: Guessaz and Ferlet Co., 1910.

Barrera, Mario. *Race and Class in the Southwest: A Theory of Racial Inequality.* Notre Dame: Notre Dame Press, 1979.

Boatright, Mody C., et al., eds. *Folk Travelers: Ballads, Tales, and Talk.* Vol. XXV of the Publications of the Texas Folklore Society. Dallas: Texas Folklore Society, 1953.

———. *Mesquite and Willow.* Vol. XXVII of the Publications of the Texas Folklore Society. Dallas: Texas Folklore Society, 1957.

———. *Mexican Border Ballads.* Vol. XXI of the Publications of the Texas Folklore Society. Austin: Texas Folklore Society, 1946.

———. *Singers and Storytellers.* Vol. XXX of Publications of the Texas Folklore Society. Dallas: Southern Methodist University, 1961.

Breckenridge, R. Douglas and Francisco O. García-Treto. *Iglesia Presbiteriana: A History of Presbyterians and Mexican Americans of the Southwest.* San Antonio: Trinity University Press, 1974.

Brenner, Anita. *Idols Behind the Altars.* New York: Biblo and Tannen, 1967.

Brewer, J. Mason. *Worser Days and Better Times.* Chicago: Quadrangle Books, 1965.

Camarillo, Albert. *Chicanos in a Changing Society: From Mexican Pueblos to American Barrios in Santa Barbara and Southern California, 1848–1930.* Cambridge: Harvard University Press, 1979.

Chabot, Frederic. *With the Makers of San Antonio.* San Antonio: privately printed, 1937.

Curtis, Albert. *Fabulous San Antonio.* San Antonio: The Naylor Co., 1955.

Davis, Ellis Arthur, ed. *The Historical Encyclopedia of Texas.* 2 vols. Austin: The Texas Historical Society, n. d.

De León, Arnoldo. *A Social History of Mexican Americans in Nineteenth Century Duval County.* San Diego, Texas: County Commissioners' Court, 1978.

––––––. *In re Ricardo Rodríguez: An Attempt at Chicano Disfranchisement in San Antonio, 1896–1897.* San Antonio: Caravel Press, 1979.

Dinger, Adeline Short. *Folk Life and Folklore of the Mexican Border.* Edinburg, Texas: Hidalgo County Historical Society, 1974.

Dobie, J. Frank. *A Vaquero of the Brush Country: Partly the Reminiscences of John Young.* Dallas: The Southwest Press, 1929.

––––––. *Coronado's Children: Tales of Lost Mines and Buried Treasures of the Southwest.* New York: Grosset and Dunlap, 1930.

Dobie, J. Frank et al., eds. *In The Shadow of History.* Hatboro, Penn.: Folklore Associates, Inc., 1966.

––––––. *Legends of Texas.* Vol. III of Publications of the Texas Folklore Society. Hatboro, Penn.: Folklore Associates, Inc., 1924.

––––––. *Man, Bird, and Beast.* Vol. VII of the Texas Folklore Society. Austin: Texas Folklore Society, 1930.

––––––. *Mustangs and Cow Ponies.* Vol. XVI of Publications of the Texas Folklore Society, Dallas: Southern Methodist University, 1965.

––––––. *Puro Mexicano.* Vol. XXII of Publications of the Texas Folklore Society. Austin: Texas Folklore Society, 1935.

––––––. *Southwestern Lore.* Vol. IX of the Publications of the Texas Folklore Society. Hatboro, Penn.: Folklore Associates, 1931.

––––––. *Texian Stomping Grounds.* Dallas: Southern Methodist University, 1967.

––––––. *Texas and Southwestern Lore.* Vol. VI of Publications of the Texas Folklore Society. Austin: Texas Folklore Society, 1927.

––––––. *Tone the Bell Easy.* Vol. X of the Publications of the Texas Folklore Society. Austin: Texas Folkore Society, 1932.

Dorson, Richard M., ed. *American Folklore and the Historian.* Chicago: The University of Chicago Press, 1971.

––––––. *Folklore and Folklife: An Introduction.* Chicago: University of Chicago Press, 1971.

Doyon, Bernard. *Cavalry of Christ on the Rio Grande: 1849–1883.* Milwaukee: Bruce, 1956.

Faulk, Odie. *A Successful Failure.* Austin: Steck-Vaughn Co., 1965.

––––––. *The Last Years of Spanish Texas, 1778–1821.* The Hague: Mounton & Co., 1964.

Fehrenbach, T. R. *Lone Star: A History of Texas and Texans.* New York: Macmillan, 1968.

Fisher, O. C. *King Fisher: His Life and Times.* Norman: University of Oklahoma Press, 1966.

García, F. Chris and Rudolph O. de la Garza, *The Chicano Political Experience: Three Perspectives.* North Scituate, Mass.: Duxbury Press, 1977.

Galván, Roberto A. *El Diccionario del Español Chicano.* Silver Springs, Md: Institute of Modern Languages, Inc., 1977.

Genovese, Eugene D. *Roll, Jordan, Roll: The World the Slaves Made.* New York: Vintage Books, 1976.

Gerber, A. *Black Ohio and the Color Line.* Urbana: University of Illinois Press, 1976.

Gómez-Quiñones, Juan. *Sembradores, Ricardo Flores Magón Y El Partido Lib-*

eral Mexicano: A Eulogy and a Critique. Los Angeles: Chicano Studies Center, 1976.

Grebler, Leo, Joan W. Moore, and Ralph Guzmán. *The Mexican American People: The Nation's Second Largest Minority.* New York: The Free Press, 1970.

Gutman, Herbert G. *The Black Family in Slavery and Freedom.* New York: Pantheon Books, 1976.

Hallenbeck, Cleve and Juanita H. Williams. *Legends of the Southwest.* Glendale: The Arthur H. Clark Company, 1938.

Hansen, Harry, ed. *Texas: A Guide to the Lone Star State.* Revised edition. New York: Hastings House, 1969.

Holden, William Curry. *Teresita.* Owings Mill: Stemmer House Publishers, Inc., 1978.

Hudson, Wilson M., ed. *The Healer of Los Olmos and other Mexican Lore.* Vol. XXIV of Publications of the Texas Folklore Society. Dallas: Southern Methodist University, 1951.

Hunter, J. Marvin. *The Trail Drivers of Texas.* 2 vols. New York: Argosy-Antiquarian Ltd., 1963.

Kennedy, William. *Texas: The Rise, Progress, and Prospects of the Republic of Texas.* Fort Worth: The Molyneaux Craftsman, Inc., 1925.

Kiev, Ari. *Curanderismo: Mexican American Folk Psychiatry.* New York: Free Press, 1968.

Kupper, Winifred. *The Golden Hoof: The Story of the Sheep of the Southwest.* New York: A. A. Knopf, 1945.

Lea, Tom. *The King Ranch.* 2 vols. Boston: Little, Brown, and Company, 1957.

Lehmann, V. W. *Forgotten Legions: Sheep in the Rio Grande Plain of Texas.* El Paso: Texas Western Press, 1966.

Levine, Lawrence W. *Black Culture and Black Consciousness: Afro-American Folk Thought from Slavery to Freedom.* Oxford: Oxford University Press, 1977.

McCoy, Joseph G. *Cattle Trade of the West and Southwest.* Ann Arbor: University Microfilms, Inc., 1966.

McCullough, William Wallace Jr. *John McCullough: Pioneer Presbyterian Missionary and Teacher in the Republic of Texas.* Austin: The Pemberton Press, 1966.

McWilliams, Carey. *North from Mexico: The Spanish-Speaking People of the United States.* New York: Greenwood Press, 1968.

Meinig, D. W. *Imperial Texas: An Interpretive Essay in Cultural Geography.* Austin: University of Texas, 1969.

Montejano, David. *Race, Labor Repression, and Capitalist Agriculture: Notes from South Texas, 1920–30.* Berkeley: Institute for the Study of Social Change, 1977.

Moore, Joan W. *Mexican Americans.* Englewood Cliffs: Prentice Hall, 1970.

Mora, Jo. *Trail Dust and Saddle Leather.* New York: Charles Scribner's Sons, 1946.

Newcomb, Pearson. *The Alamo City.* San Antonio: Standard Printing Co., 1926.

O'Shea, Elena Zamora. *El Mesquite: A Story of the Early Spanish Settlements Between the Nueces and the Rio Grande as Told by "La Posta del Palo Alto."* Dallas: Mathis Publishing Co., 1935.

Paredes, Américo. *A Texas Mexican Cancionero: Songs of the Lower Border.* Urbana: University of Illinois Press, 1976.

———. *"With His Pistol in His Hand": A Border Ballad and Its Hero.* Austin: University of Texas Press, 1971.

Peattie, Donald Culross. *A Natural History of Western Trees*. Boston: Houghton Mifflin, 1953.

Pierce, Frank C. *A Brief History of the Lower Rio Grande Valley*. Menasha: George Banta Publishing Co., 1917.

Quirk, Robert E. *The Mexican Revolution and the Catholic Church, 1910–1929*. Bloomington: Indiana University Press, 1973.

Raht, Carlysle Graham. *The Romance of Davis Mountains and Big Bend Country*. El Paso: The Raht Books Company, 1919.

Ramírez, Emilia Schunior. *Ranch Life in Hildago County After 1850*. Edinburg: New Santander Press, 1971.

Rayburn, John C. and Virginia Kemp Rayburn, eds. *Century of Conflict, 1821–1913, Incidents in the Lives of William Neale and William A. Neale, Early Settlers of South Texas*. Waco: Texian Press, 1966.

Richardson, Rupert N., et al., *Texas: The Lone Star State*. Englewood Cliffs: Prentice-Hall, Inc., 1970.

Robinson, Cecil. *With the Ears of Strangers: The Mexican in American Literature*. Tucson: University of Arizona Press, 1969.

Romo, Ricardo and Raymund Paredes, eds. *New Directions in Chicano Scholarship*. La Jolla: University of California at San Diego, 1978.

Santos, Richard G. *A Chronicle of Events Concerning the Spanish Language and the Spanish North American Frontier*. San Antonio: Intercultural Development Research Association, 1977.

Shelton, Edgar Greer. *Political Conditions Among Texas-Mexicans Along the Rio Grande*. San Francisco: R & E Research Associates, 1974.

Simmons, Ozzie G. *Anglo Americans and Mexican Americans in South Texas*. New York: Arno Press, 1974.

Sonnichsen, C. L. *Pass of the North: Four Centuries on the Rio Grande*. El Paso: Texas Western Press, 1968.

————. *Ten Texas Feuds*. Albuquerque: University of New Mexico Press, 1957.

Spell, Lota M. *Music in Texas: A Survey of one Aspect of Cultural Progress*. Austin: n. p., 1936.

Stambaugh, J. Lee and Lillian J. Stambaugh. *The Lower Rio Grande Valley of Texas*. San Antonio: The Naylor Co., 1954.

Stoddard, Ellwyn. *Mexican Americans*. New York: Random House, 1973.

Tannenbaum, Frank. *Mexico: The Struggle for Peace and Bread*. New York: Alfred A. Knopf, 1964.

Taylor, Paul S. *An American Mexican Frontier: Nueces County, Texas*. Chapel Hill: University of North Carolina Press, 1934.

Teschner, Richard V., et al. *Spanish and English of United States Hispanos: A Critical Annotated, Linguistic Bibliography*. Arlington, Virginia: Center for Applied Linguistics, 1975.

Thompson, Stith, ed. *Round the Levee*. Vol. I of the Publications of the Texas Folklore Society. Austin: Texas Folklore Society, 1916.

Vigil, Maurilio. *Chicano Politics*. Washington D. C.: University Press of America, 1978.

Waugh, Julia Nott. *Castroville and Henry Castro, Empresario*. San Antonio: Standard Printing Co., 1934.

Webb, Walter Prescott. *The Texas Rangers: A Century of Frontier Defense*. New York: Houghton Mifflin Co., 1935.

Weninger, Del. *Cacti of the Southwest: Texas, New Mexico, Oklahoma, Arkansas, and Louisiana*. Austin: University of Texas Press, 1969.

Wilkinson, J. B. *Laredo and the Rio Grande Frontier.* Austin: Jenkins Publishing Co., 1975.

Wright, S. J. *San Antonio de Bexar: Historical, Traditional, Legendary.* Austin: Morgan Printing Co., 1916.

Zavala, Adina de. *History and Legends of the Alamo and other Missions in and Around San Antonio.* San Antonio: privately printed, 1917.

Articles

"Adobe: Past and Present." *El Palacio,* LXXVII, No. 4.

Barr, Alwyn. "Occupation and Geographic Mobility in San Antonio, 1870–1900." *Social Science Quarterly,* LI (September 1970): 396–403.

Barrera, Mario, Carlos Muñoz, and Charles Ornelas. "The Barrio as an Internal Colony." In *La Causa Politica: A Chicano Politics Reader.* Edited by F. Chris García. Notre Dame: University of Notre Dame Press, 1974, 281–301.

Campa, Arthur L. "Folklore and History," *Western Folklore,* XXIV (January 1965): 1–5.

Carrillo, Albert. "The Sociological Failure of the Catholic Church Toward the Chicano." *Journal of Mexican American Studies,* I (Winter 1971): 75–83.

Cisneros, Victor B. Nelson. "La Clase Trabajadora en Tejas, 1900–1920." *Aztlán: International Journal of Chicano Studies Research,* VI (Summer 1975): 239–268.

De León, Arnoldo. "Accomodacionistas: Defensores del Barrio." *Caracol,* III (December 1976): 16–17.

———. "Blowout 1910 Style: A Chicano School Boycott in West Texas." *Texana,* XII (1974): 124–40.

———. "Los Tasinques and the Sheep Shearers' Union of North America: A Strike in West Texas." *West Texas Historical Association Yearbook* (1979): 3–16.

García, Mario T. "Americanization and the Mexican Immigrant, 1880–1930." *Journal of Ethnic Studies,* VI (Summer 1978): 19–34.

García, Richard A. "Class, Consciousness, and Ideology—The Mexican Community of San Antonio, Texas, 1930–1940." *Aztlán: International Journal of Chicano Studies Research,* IX (Spring, Summer, Fall 1978): 23–70.

Gómez-Quiñones, Juan. "On Culture." *Revista Chicano-Riqueña,* V, No. 2 (primavera 1977): 29–47.

———. "The First Steps: Chicano Labor Conflict and Organizing, 1900–1920." *Aztlán: Chicano Journal of the Social Sciences and the Arts,* IV (Spring 1972): 13–50.

Griswold del Castillo, Richard. "Myth and Reality: Chicano Economic Mobility in Los Angeles, 1850–1880." *Aztlán: International Journal of Chicano Studies Research,* VI (Summer 1975): 151–72.

———. "Tucsonenses and Angeleños: A Socio-Economic Study of Two Mexican American Barrios, 1860–1880." *Journal of the West,* XVIII (1979): 58–66.

Gutiérrez, Felix. "Spanish Language Media in America: Background, Resources, History." *Journalism History,* IV (Summer 1977): 34–47.

Juárez, José Roberto. "La Iglesia Católica y el Chicano de Sud Texas, 1836–1911." *Aztlán: Chicano Journal of the Social Sciences and the Arts,* IV (Fall 1973): 217–56.

Larralde, Carlos. "Santa Teresa: A Chicana Mystic." *Grito del Norte,* III (April-June 1978): 9–114.

Limón, José. "El Primer Congreso Mexicanista de 1911: A Precursor to Contemporary Chicanismo." *Aztlán: Chicano Journal of the Social Sciences and the Arts,* V (Spring and Fall, 1974): 85–118.

Melville, Margarita B. "The Mexican American and the Celebration of the Fiestas Patrias: An Ethnohistorical Analysis." *Grito del Sol,* III (January-March 1978): 107–18.

Miller, Michael V. "Variations in Mexican American Life: A Review Synthesis of Empirical Research." *Aztlán: International Journal of Chicano Studies and the Arts* (Spring 1977): 209–31.

Navarro, Armando. "The Evolution of Chicano Politics." *Aztlán: Chicano Journal of the Social Sciences and the Arts,* V (Spring and Fall 1974): 57–84.

Paredes, Américo. "José Mosqueda and the Folklorization of Actual Events." *Aztlán: Chicano Journal of the Social Sciences and the Arts,* IV (Spring 1973): 1–30.

Padilla, Ray. "A Critique of Pittian History." *El Grito: A Journal of Contemporary Mexican American Thought,* VI (Fall 1972): 3–44.

Rios, Francisco Armando. "The Mexican in Fact, Fiction and Folklore." *El Grito: A Journal of Contemporary Mexican American Thought,* II (Summer 1969): 142–82.

Rios, Herminio and Lupe Castillo. "Towards a True Chicano Bibliography: Mexican American Newspapers, 1848–1942." *El Grito: A Journal of Contemporary Mexican American Thought,* III (Summer 1970): 17–24.

———. "Towards a True Chicano Bibliography—Part II." *El Grito: A Journal of Contemporary Mexican American Thought,* VI (Summer 1972): 38–47.

Robinson, Willard B. "Colonial Ranch Architecture in Spanish-Mexican Tradition." *Southwestern Historical Quarterly,* LXXXIII (October 1979): 123–50.

Romano-V, Octavio I. "The Anthropology and Sociology of the Mexican American." In *Voices.* Edited by Octavio Romano-V. Berkeley: Quinto Sol Publications, Inc., 1973, 43–56.

Smithers, W. D. "Nature's Pharmacy and the *Curanderos.*" *West Texas Historical and Scientifc Society Publications,* XVIII (1961): 15–39.

Tirado, Miguel David. "Mexican American Community Political Power." *Aztlán: Chicano Journal of the Social Sciences and the Arts,* I (Spring 1970): 53–78.

Tjarks, Alicia V. "Comparative Demographic Analysis of Texas, 1777–1793." *Southwestern Historical Quarterly,* LXXVII (January 1974): 291–338.

Vaca, Nick C. "The Mexican American in the Social Sciences, Part I: 1912–1935." *El Grito: A Journal of Contemporary Mexican American Thought,* III (Spring 1970): 3–24.

———. "The Mexican American in the Social Sciences, Part II: 1936–1970." *El Grito: A Journal of Contemporary Mexican American Thought,* IV (Fall 1970): 17–51.

Valentine, Charles A. "Deficit, Difference, and Bicultural Models of Afro-American Behavior." *Harvard Educational Review,* 41 (May 1971): 137–57.

Ward, Hortense Warner. "It was Texas' First State Fair: Next Thursday Marks a Century Since Corpus Christi Show." *Houston Chronicle Magazine,* April 27, 1952.

Wentworth, Edward N. "Dried Meat: Early Man's Travel Ration." *Agricultural History,* XXX (January 1956): 2–10.

Wilcox, Seb S. "The Laredo City Election Riot of April, 1886." *Southwestern Historical Quarterly,* LXV (July 1941): 1–23.

Zamora, Emilio Jr. "Chicano Socialist Labor Activity in Texas, 1900–1920." *Aztlán: International Journal of Chicano Studies Research,* VI (Summer 1975): 221–38.

Zeigler, Robert E. "The Cowboy Strike of 1883: Its Causes and Meanings." *West Texas Historical Association Yearbook*, XLVII (1971): 32–46.

Zinn, Maxine Baca. "Chicano Family Research: Conceptual Distortions and Alternative Directions." *The Journal of Ethnic Studies*, VII (Fall 1979): 59–72.

Theses and Dissertations

Barsun, Helen W. "Los Pastores: A Remnant of Medieval Drama in San Antonio." Master of Arts Thesis, St. Mary's University, 1943.

Crews, James Robert. "Reconstruction in Brownsville, Texas." Master of Arts Thesis, Texas Tech University, 1969.

Crisp, James Ernest. "Anglo-Texan Attitudes Toward the Mexican, 1821–1845." Ph.D. Dissertation, Yale University, 1976.

Crook, Carland Elaine. "San Antonio, Texas, 1846–1861." Master of Arts Thesis, Rice University, 1964.

De León, Arnoldo. "White Racial Attitudes Toward Mexicanos in Texas, 1821–1900." Ph.D. Dissertation, Texas Christian University, 1974.

Downs, Fane. "The History of Mexicans in Texas, 1821–1845." Ph.D. Dissertation, Texas Tech University, 1970.

García, Mario T. "Obreros: The Mexican Workers of El Paso, 1900–1920." Ph.D. Dissertation, University of California at San Diego, 1975.

González, Jovita. "Social Life in Cameron, Starr, and Zapata Counties." Master of Arts Thesis, University of Texas, 1930.

González, María del Refugio. "The Spanish Folklore of Webb and Zapata Counties." Master of Arts Thesis, University of Texas, 1952.

Guerra, Fermina. "Mexican and Spanish Folklore and Incidents in Southwestern Texas." Master of Arts Thesis, University of Texas, 1941.

Hiester, Miriam Webb. "Los Paisanos: Folklore of the Texas Mexican of the Lower Rio Grande Valley." Master of Arts Thesis, University of Texas, 1954.

Hinojosa, Gilberto M. "Settlers and Sojourners in the 'Chaparral': A Demographic Study of a Borderlands Town in Transition, Laredo, 1755–1870." Ph.D. Dissertation, University of Texas, 1979.

Knox, William John. "The Economic Status of the Mexican Immigrant in San Antonio, Texas." Master of Arts Thesis, University of Texas at Austin, 1927.

Persons, Billie Mae. "Clothing in Texas, 1821–1860." Master of Arts Thesis, University of Texas, 1956.

Phillips, Juanita Stroud. "The Spanish Folklore of Texas, No. 1, Cameron County." Master of Arts Thesis, University of Texas, 1950.

Pycior, Julie Leininger. "La Raza Organizes: Mexican American Life in San Antonio, 1915–1930, as Reflected in Mutualista Activities." Ph.D. Dissertation, University of Notre Dame, 1979.

Speiser, Adel. "The Story of the Theatre in San Antonio." Master of Arts Thesis, St. Mary's University, 1948.

Tijerina, Andrew Anthony. "Tejanos and Texas: The Native Mexicans of Texas, 1820–1850." Ph.D. Dissertation, University of Texas, 1977.

Wright, Pearl Couser. "Religious Fiestas in San Antonio." Master of Arts Thesis, St. Mary's University, 1946.

Index